FOOD PRODUCTION

OPERATION AND MANAGEMENT

About the Book

This book has been designed keeping in mind that there is no such text book on food production available as of now. The key note of this book is comprehensive details of each subject. "Food production is neither dull nor difficult if you study it intelligently. Indeed it might be argued in the hotels industry food production ranks higher among the arts." Food production is specially designed to meet the requirement of student's undergraduate, post graduate course in food production operation and management. This book will also be perfectly suited to those who are already in the industry. The inspiration to write this book came from the Hospitality industry where I have worked for seven years in a diligent manner. This book has all the necessary chapters relating to all different aspects of kitchen training in world cuisine.

The book is divide into seven unit's. The first unit of this book contains eight chapters which serve an introduction to hospitality and professional catering. Also provide details about raw materials, methods of cooking and basic preparation.

The second unit of this book contains four chapters which mainly emphasis on Commodities and farinaceous. This unit provides you detail about egg, rice, wheat, corn and dairy product with their composition and there structure, with some standard recipes.

The third unit of this book contain six chapters which mainly emphasis on meat and seafood cookery. This unit provide you details about their standard cuts with their used. With some standard recipes.

The fourth unit of this book contain four chapters which mainly emphasis on garde manager section. This unit provides you in details about the Hors d'oeuvres, salads and sandwich. With their composition and types. With some standard recipes.

The fifth unit of this book contain includes nine chapters which mainly emphasis on International cuisine which includes Chinese, Japanese, Indonesian, Philippines, European, Arabic, Mediterrian, Mexican, Spanish and India. In this unit you recognized there culinary regions with their common Ingredients and there method of cooking with their glossary and with the end of unit you find some regional recipes.

The sixth unit of this book contain six chapters which mainly emphasis on bakery. In this unit you know about the bakery, with their Ingredients, method of mixing and its preparation. With some standard recipes.

The seventh unit of this book contains four chapter which mainly emphasis on kitchen management. In this unit you learn about how to design a kitchen, how to plan a menu, detail about material management, how to control food cost, different law food regarding food and certain management standards of hygiene.

FOOD PRODUCTION

OPERATION AND MANAGEMENT

Volume II

GULSHAN SONI

Ph.D. in Hotel Management
and Tourism Studies (U.S.A.)
M. Phil. Tourism Management,
M.Sc. H.M. and C.T.,
Executive MBA,
Diploma in Training and Development,
G.H.O.T.P. (Jaypee Hotels Limited)

AMAN PUBLICATIONS
NEW DELHI

Published by
Rajiv Jain for Aman Publications
LG-4A, Ganpati Bhawan,
4675-B/21, Ansari Road,
Darya Ganj, Delhi - 110002
PH: 23255012, 23282127
E-mail: sshjbs@yahoo.com

First Published – 2010

ISBN-81-8204-056-4
ISBN-978-81-8204-056-4

SOLE DISTRIBUTOR
JINDAL BOOK SERVICES
LG-4A, Ganpati Bhawan,
4675-B/21, Ansari Road,
Darya Ganj, Delhi - 110002

Jacket Designed by :
S.M. Graphics

Printed by:
Abhinav Prints, Delhi - 110041

Preface

Food production operation and management has been developed with the vision of being one of the most sought after literature available. I have tried to capture all the details of cookery books which I think it has been developed in such a new pattern. The increasing competition and complexity of hospitality industry as well as high demand of travelers has meant an increase demands in terms of hospitality needs. Hospitality industry is the most diverse and specialized industry in the world. The emerging role of private sector in planning, organizing, managing and financing in the hospitality industry and the introduction of hotel management courses at senior secondary level by some of state boards shows the importance of hotel management in modern times.

This book was published to meet the need of the complete book on food production operation and management for the rapidly expanding educational institutes associated with Hotel management and Catering Technology, The Food Craft Institute and emerging requirements of the chef in the industry.

Food production is one of the major departments of the hotel. According to my experience, a student who enters in this field wants to be either a Chef or a Manager. Today the demand of chefs is on the rise around the world. All my efforts in this book are directed to arouse the interest of the student who will become future chefs of the industry.

The book is divide into seven unit's. The first unit of this book contains eight chapters which serve an introduction to hospitality and professional catering. Also provide details about raw materials, methods of cooking and basic preparation.

The second unit of this book contains four chapters which mainly emphasis on Commodities and farinaceous. This unit provides you detail about egg, rice, wheat, corn and dairy product with their composition and there structure, with some standard recipes.

The third unit of this book contain six chapters which mainly emphasis on meat and seafood cookery. This unit provide you details about their standard cuts with their used. With some standard recipes.

The fourth unit of this book contain four chapters which mainly emphasis on garde manager section. This unit provides you in details about the Hors d'oeuvres, salads and sandwich. With their composition and types. With some standard recipes.

The fifth unit of this book contain includes nine chapters which mainly emphasis on International cuisine which includes Chinese, Japanese, Indonesian, Philippines, European, Arabic, Mediterranean, Mexican, Spanish and India. In this unit you recognized there culinary regions with their common Ingredients and there method of cooking with their glossary and with the end of unit you find some regional recipes.

The sixth unit of this book contain six chapters which mainly emphasis on bakery. In this unit you know about the bakery, with their Ingredients, method of mixing and its preparation. With some standard recipes.

The seventh unit of this book contains four chapter which mainly emphasis on kitchen management. In this unit you learn about how to design a kitchen, how to plan a menu, detail about material management, how to control food cost, different law food regarding food and certain management standards of hygiene.

I am sure that this book will be a source of inspiration and each page will awaken a longing to pick up the phone and talk to me.

I express my gratitude to the management of Banarasi Das Chandiwala Institute of Hotel Management and Catering Technology, and Shri. Bhuwan Mohan ji, Secretary, Shri Banarsidas Chandiwala Sewa Smarak Trust Society for their motivation and encouragement to undertake this relatively less explored but highly poignant area of hospitality. I also extend my thanks to Principal Mr. R.K. Bhandri and Deputy Director (Administration) Mr. Pradeep Gupta, for their altruistic support.

I would like thanks to the Mr. Rajeev Jain and Mr. Pradeep Jain of Aman Publications, New Delhi for their persistence and support. Finally, I would like to thanks to all my friends and my well-wishers.

GULSHAN SONI

Authors Profile

Gulshan Soni is at present faculty in Banarasidas Chandiwala Institute of Hotel Management and Catering Technology, New Delhi. Earlier he had been associated with Hotel Jaypee Vasant Continental, New Delhi. After completing his graduation from Delhi University he joined Graduate Hotel Operation Traning Programme in Jaypee Group of Hotels (Hotel Jaypee Palace Agra). Simultaneously he completed his MSc in HM and CT and Executive MBA and has recently completed his M.Phil in Tourism Management .

He is presently working on his Fellowship Research in the area consumer protection

Contents

VOLUME II

UNIT 5: INTERNATIONAL CUISINE

UNIT 6: BAKERY

UNIT 7: KITCHEN MANAGEMENT

Weight, Volume and Liquid Measures

WEIGHT MEASURE

Oz	Gram	Oz	Gram
½ oz	14.17 grams	3 oz	85.05 gram
1 oz	28.35 grams	4 oz	113.4 grams
2 oz	56.7 grams	5 oz	141.75 gram

lb	oz	lb	oz
¼ lb	4 oz	1 lb	16 oz
½ lb	8 oz	1½ lb	24 oz
¾ lb	12 oz	2 lb	32 oz

lb	gram	lb	oz
¼ lb	114 gram	1 lb	454.45 gram
½ lb	228 gram	1½ lb	682.50 gram
¾ lb	340 gram	2 lb	908.80 gram

WEIGHT MEASURE

Gallon/British measurement	Litres	Gallon	Litres
1 gallon	4.5 litre	4 gallon	18.2 litre
2 gallon	9.1 litre	5 gallon	22.7 litre
3 gallon	13.6 litre	6 gallon	26.12 litre

VOLUME LIQUID

Cup	ml	Cup	ml
¼ cup	60 ml	1 cup	250 ml
½ cup	1255 ml	1½ cup	375 ml

DRY MEASURE EQUIPMNETS

3 teaspoon	1 tablespoon	½ Ounce	14.3 grams
2 tablespoon	⅛ cup	1 Ounce	28.3 grams
4 tablespoon	¼ cup	2 Ounce	56.7 grams
12 tablespoon	¾ cup	6 Ounce	375 pouns

OVEN TEMPERATURE GUIDE

Description of oven	Celsius (°)	Fahrenheit (°)
1 Cool	100	200
2 Very slow	120	250
3 Slow	150	300
4 Moderate	180	350
5 Hot	220	425
6 Very hot	230	450

Unit 4
GARDE MANGER

Chapter 20

Cold Preparation

After studying this chapter, the student must know

- Introduction and meaning of garde manager
- Aspic and its preparation method
- Chemiser
- Chaud froid and steps to used chaud froid
- Charcuterie and its types
- Salt cured and brined product
- Glazing cold meats
- Savoury cream and aspic garnish

GARDE MANGER

Garde manger, meaning "keeper of the food" or pantry supervisor, refers to the task of preparing and presenting cold foods. These typically include such food items as salads, hors d'œuvres, cold soups, aspics, and charcuterie. Larger restaurants and hotels may have the need for the garde manger to perform additional duties, such as creating decorative elements of buffet presentation like table arrangements and edible centerpieces made from materials such as ice, cheese, butter, salt dough or tallow.

The term "garde manger" originated in pre- revolution France. At that time, maintaining an ample supply of food was an outward symbol of power, wealth and prestige. Noble families had a household steward who would manage their cold store room. The steward was referred to as the "officer de bouche", a title that was eventually replaced with "garde manger". This position was tremendously important, because much of the food was butchered, pickled, salted, cured, or smoked during the fall season and stored for months, even into the spring months. It is because of this duty of supervising the preserving of food and managing its utilization that many interpret the term "garde manger" as "keeping to eat."

The food storage areas in these castles and manor houses were usually located in the lower levels, since the cool basement-like environment was ideal for storing food. These cold storage areas developed over time into the modern cold kitchen.

Charcuterie was the name of a guild that prepared and sold cooked items made from pigs. Through this organization, the preparation of hams, bacon, sausages, pates and terrines were preserved. When the guild system was abolished early in the French Revolution in 1791, garde mangers took on the responsibility for tasks that had formerly been performed by characutieres, who had difficulty competing with the versatile garde mangers due to the limited range of skills involved in charcuterie.

The position of "butcher" first developed as a specialty within the garde manger kitchen. As both the cost of and demand for animal proteins (in the form of pork, beef, etc.) increased, more space was required for the task of fabricating and portioning the raw proteins. This increased need for space was due not only to an upswing in the volume of protein sales, but also to the need for separating raw proteins from processed foods to avoid cross-contamination and the resulting possibility foodborne illness. Special "butcher shops" were created where portion sizes, product utilization, and temperature could be tightly controlled. Today butcher shops exist both as standalone establishments and alongside kitchens in large hotels, country clubs and high volume restaurants.

ASPIC

Is a jelly derived by boiling the meat and bones of most animals straining to get a clear stock and cooling to a gelatinous solid. This gelatinous solid is called aspic jelly. When the stock doesn't congeal sufficient it's become necessary to use commercial jelly in form of sheet and powder. Aspic or jelly place an important role in a preparation of innumerable garde manager delicacy by high lighting the ingredients been present, it also provide special protection for cold dishes enabling them to retain their original flavour and freshness for a longer period.

Aspic jelly must always be odor free crystal clear and of a light golden colour. Those easy to treat aspic required careful handling, foremost it's easily effected by temperature when the temperature is too high jelly is melt on other hand when temperature is too low it will become a rubber and not melt in the mouth. When set aspic should be neither to firm nor too soft the room temperature and length of time the dish must retain its shape have concerable varying in setting jelly. In summer month it's advisable to make a aspic little more stiff. To test in out ladle a couple of table spoon on a plate refrigerated for 10 to 15 minutes removes and checks the consistency and flavour.

Aspic is extremely is vulnerable to bacteria – it spoil within hour of it begin touch by hand should be tasted with a spoon and never touch by hand. If treated with care aspic can be stored in a cooler not freezer for more than 2 week, under no circumstance should it be allow to freeze the colour depend on the raw material uses. Aspic from meat is dark, from poultry medium, and from fish light in colour- The use of aspic correspond with the ingredients-meat aspic with meat delicase, chick aspic with chicken dish there is never any mixing with two however if the colour is to light add a few drops strained caramel colouring to correct.

Aspic can also be used for decorating dishes which are not molded for ex which can be used to garnished any cold roast. Infact it's the most on the cold buffet where it can easily enhance eye appeal.

How to prepare Aspic

In the past the base for aspic was prepared from the stock. Prepares from the head and feet of calf. Today this method is considered complicated and cumbersome. Instead meat broth and consommé are use the process is some as consommé except from the addition of gelatin. The gelatin must be stored constantly let lightly to prevent sticking and burning. Until it reaches boiling paint. There after summer over very low heat for an hours. For best result add all the ingredients. While the aspic been cooked. The addition of salt and wine at the latter stage lightly to make the aspic closely. It should be crystal clear. A Greece cloth or and improperly washed napkin can ruing your aspic.

CHEMISER

To process of lining mould with jelly to prepared cold buffet delicacy like chicken in the aspic, prawn in the aspic etc is called chemiser. To chemise a mould its important to first cool the mould to a temperature which will insure instant setting of aspic the best way to do it. Is to place a mould in a container with ice and water or it can be placed in a refrigerator. Then poured a little aspic in a mould roll it around to insure that the entire mould is coated with jelly decorated surface staring at the bottom. Cover with another layer of jelly than fill the mould with the food to the used pour jelly upto the rim and refrigerator till firmly set to demould dip the mould in hot water and gently turn it over in a serving dish.

CHAUDFROID

Literally hot-cold is the most extensively used cold sauce in garde manager its so called because its prepared hot and used cold there are four main types chaudfroid each with a different usage

1. Classical and basic
2. Cream sauce chaudfroid
3. Mayonnaise chaudfroid
4. Colour chaudfroid.

Chaudfroid is used to coat mean product to enhanced flavour and presentation.

How to use Chaudfroid

The application of this hot cold sauces place a signification role in the display in some cold foods. The consistency of the sauces is determined by the temperature When hot chaudfroid is light it becomes thick and cool however if its kept under refrigeration. It will congeal in which case it must be made to melt in a double boiler. It must be used only when its cold when not hot or congeal.

STEPS TO USE CHAUDFROID

1. Food to be coated should be kept refrigerates at least an hours and must have a smooth surface.
2. The item should be coated in a coiling rock with a tray underneath to collect a dripping sauce.
3. The chaudfroid should be ladle over the food only when its at the right temperature and consistency.
4. After coating its necessary to refrigerated the meat to enable the chaudfroid to congeal after the second an smoothing coating can be given
5. Two coating are usually enough if the surface is lumpy, you have a start a fresh and remaining the previous coating and put a fresh ones
6. The dripping sauces can be drop on the tray can be of reused.
7. Chaudfroid must devoid of bubbles.
8. Can be used to coat non edbile items like thermocol preparation.

CHARCUTERIE

Charcuterie are fancy pork and related products made by a charcutier, a fancy pork butcher. Originally, the art of charcuterie was used to preserve meat in the Middle Ages. The art continues in France as a hallmark of fine cuisine. While many charcuterie products contain only pork as their meat base, just as often the pork is combined with other meats, fowl or game. Modern charcuterie has expanded to include items with no pork at all—products made only of poultry, venison, vegetables or fish.

Charcuteri derived from the French words for flesh (*chair*) and cooked (*cuit*) is the branch of cooking devoted to prepared meat products such as bacon, ham, sausage, terrines, galantines, pâtés, and confit, primarily from pork. Charcuterie is part of the garde manger chef's Repertoire. Originally intended as a way to preserve meats before the advent of refrigeration, they are prepared today for their flavors derived from the preservation processesThe following products are common offerings of a charcutier:

- **Boudin**. The French word for pudding also doubles as the word for meat sausage, and, generically, any sausage-shaped mixture. Boudin blanc or white sausage, is a white sausage made of of veal, chicken, or pork. Boudin noir or red sausage, is pork blood sausage.
- **Fromage de Tête**. Not a cheese, but a terrine of meat from the head of a calf or pig (sometimes a sheep or cow) that would not otherwise be considered appealing. Originally it was made entirely from the meaty parts of the head, but now can include meat from the feet, tongue, and heart. It is usually eaten cold or at room temperature as a luncheon meat.

- **Galantine.** A preparation of boned meat or whole poultry that is stuffed or rolled, cooked, then glazed with gelatin and served cold. Unlike a pâté, the meat is not ground, and it is not spreadable. Galantines are most often served as a first course.
- **Pâté.** Pâté is the French word for *paste,* indicating elegant, well-seasoned ground meat, fish or vegetable preparations with a paste consistency. Pâtés are made in various spreadable textures and are served hot or cold as an *hors d'oeuvre* or a first course. They can be wrapped in fat or pastry. Technically, those wrapped in pastry should be called pâté, and those in pastry should be called *terrine* (see below). Pâtés are served cold, usually on toast. They are cooked one of two ways, either "pâté en croûte" (in crust) or "en terrine" (in a pork fat-lined container). Pâtés are probably the world's most adaptable culinary form and may be served as simply or as elegantly as suits the mood and the occasion.
- **Mousse.** A mousse is light, airy mixture usually containing eggs and cream, that can be sweet or savory. While savory mousses can have pudding-like consistencies just like chocolate mousse, a greater proportion of meat, fish or vegetable, creates a solid-form mousse. It is much lighter and spongier in texture than a pâté, and therefore more spreadable or malleable for hors d'oevres.
- **Poitrine**. Poitrine is a breast of meat or poultry, but when the word is modified, it refers to bacon. Poitrine demi-sel is an unsmoked slab bacon; poitrine fumée is smoked slab bacon; poitrine roulée is rolled bacon.
- **Rillettes.** A highly spiced spread of meat or poultry first cooked in seasoned fat and then minced or pounded into a paste, and served as an appetizer with crackers or bread. Classic French rillettes are pork or rillettes d'oie, goose; but the spread can also be made with duck, fish or rabbit. After the rillettes are made, they are commonly placed in a ramekin and sealed with a thin layer of fat.
- **Saucisse**. A small, fresh sausage. Variations include saucisse chaude, warm sausage; saucisse de Francfort, a hot dog; saucisse de Strasbourg, a redskinned hot dog; and saucisse de Toulouse, a mild country-style pork sausage.
- **Saucisson**. A large air-dried sausage, such as salami, eaten sliced as a cold cut. When eaten fresh and warm, it is called saucisson chaud, or hot sausage. Variations include saucisson à l'ail, garlic sausage, usually served warm; saucisson d'Arles, a dried salami-style sausage of pork, beef and seasonings from Arles, in Provence; saucisson de campagne, any country-style sausage; saucisson de Lyon, air-dried pork sausage, flavored with garlic and pepper and studded with chunks of pork fat; saucisson de Morteau, plump smoked pork sausage that takes its name from the town of Morteau in the Jura (it is distinctive because a wooden peg is tied in the sausage casing on one end and it is traditionally the sausage eaten at Christmas, hence it it also called Jésus de Morteau); saucisson en croûte, sausage cooked in a pastry crust; and saucisson sec, any dried sausage, or salami.
- **Terrine.** A terrine is an earthenware dish named after the French word *terre,* meaning "earth." It denotes that the dish has been baked in an dish. Traditionally, pâté baked in pastry were made in long, loaf-shaped earthenware terrines. Today, metal forms with releasable sides are often used for ease in removing the pate

PRODUCTS CREATED WITH FORCEMEATS

Forcemeat is a mixture of ground, lean meat emulsified with fat. The emulsification can be accomplished by grinding, sieving, or pureeing the ingredients. The emulsification may either be smooth or coarse in texture, depending on the desired consistency of the final product. Forcemeats are used in the production of numerous items found in charcuterie. Proteins commonly used in the production of forcemeats include pork, fish (pike, trout, or salmon), seafood, game meats (venison, boar, or rabbit), poultry, game birds, veal, and pork livers. Pork fatback is often used for the fat portion of forcemeat as it has a somewhat neutral flavour.

In American usage, there are four basic styles of forcemeat. Straight forcemeats are produced by progressively grinding equal parts pork and pork fat with a third dominant meat which can be pork or another meat. The proteins are cubed and then seasoned, cured, rested, ground and then placed into desired vessel. Country-style forcemeats are a combination of pork, pork fat, often with the addition of pork liver and garnish ingredients. The finished product has a coarse texture.[The third style is gratin which has a portion of the main protein browned; the French term *gratin* connotes a "grated" product that is browned. The final style is mousseline which are very light in texture utilizing lean cuts of meat usually from veal, poultry, fish, or shellfish. The resulting texture comes from the addition of eggs and cream to this forcemeat.

SAUSAGE

Sausage making

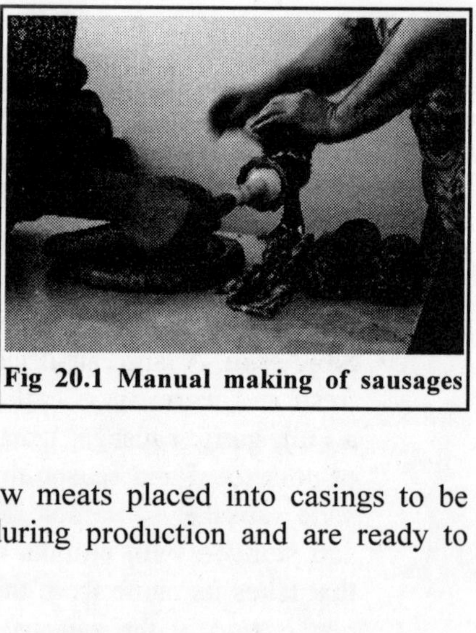
Fig 20.1 Manual making of sausages

Its name derived through French from the Latin *sal*, "salt", sausage-making is a technique that involves placing ground or chopped meats along with salt into a tube. The tubes can vary, but the more common animal-derived tubes include sheep, hog, or cattle intestinal linings. Additionally, animal stomachs and bladders, as well as inedible casings produced from collagen, plant cellulose or paper are used. Not all casings are edible; inedible ones are primarily used to shape, store, and age the sausage. There are two main variants of sausage, fresh and cooked. Fresh sausages involve the production of raw meats placed into casings to be cooked at a later time, whereas cooked sausages are heated during production and are ready to eat at the end of production.

EMULSIFIED SAUSAGE

Emulsified sausages are cooked sausages with a very fine texture, using the combination of pork, beef, or poultry with fat, salt, nitrate, flavorings, and water. These items are emulsified at high speed in a food processor or blender. During this process the salt dissolves the muscle proteins, which helps to suspend the fat molecules. Temperature is an important part of the process: if the temperature rises above 60 degrees for pork or 70 degrees for beef, the emulsification will not hold and fat will leak from the sausage during the cooking process.

SALT-CURED AND BRINED PRODUCT

Curing

Salt serves four main purposes in the preservation of food in the charcuterie kitchen. The first is inducing osmosis: this process involves the movement of water outside of the cell membranes of the proteins, which in turn reabsorb the salted water back into the cell; this process assists in the destruction of harmful pathogens. The second is dehydration, which means that the salt pulls excess water from the protein, which aids in the shelf-life of the protein as there is less moisture present for bacteria to thrive in. Fermentation is the third, in which salt assists in halting the fermentation process in meat which would otherwise completely break it down. Finally, salt assists in denaturing proteins, which in essence means that the structure of the proteins is effectively shifted, similar to the effects of cooking.

Before the discovery of nitrates and nitritezs by German chemists around 1900, curing was done with unrefined salt and saltpeter. As saltpeter gives inconsistent results, and has been outlawed in the United States for culinary uses since 1975, nitrate and nitrates (in the form of sodium nitrite and sodium nitrate)have increased in popularity for their consistent results. Nitrates take a considerably longer period of time to break down in cured foods than nitrites; because of this, nitrates are the preferred curing salts for lengthy curing and drying periods. Nitrites are often used in foods that require a shorter curing time and are used for any item that will be fully cooked. Eventually a portion of the nitrates will break down into nitrites.

Nitrite has multiple purposes in the curing process. One purpose is flavour, the nitrites giving a sharp, piquant flavour to the meat. Second, the nitrites react with substances in the meat to produce nitric oxide. Nitric oxide prevents iron from breaking down the fat in the meat, thus halting rancidity. The binding also creates the characteristic reddish colour found in most cured meats. Finally the nitrite inhibits the growth of botulism-causing organisms that would ordinarily thrive in the oxygen-deprived environment in the sausage casing. German scientists originally named botulism poisoning or "sausage poisoning". The term *botulism* derives its name from the Latin term for sausage.

Nitrates and nitrites have been noted to react with one another and form nitrosamines which are known to cause cancer. Recent research has proven this risk to be minimal, but regulations in the United States limit residual nitrates and nitrites to 200 parts per million (0.02%) as a precautionary measure.

CURING SALT BLENDS

There are two main types of curing salt mixture used by the charcutier. The first is known by multiple names, including "tinted cure mix", "pink cure", "prague powder", or "insta-cure ". The mixture is 94 percent sodium chloride and 6 percent sodium nitrate. When used, the recommended amount is a ratio of 4oz/113g for each 100lb/45.36kg of meat or 4 percent of the total weight of the meat. This blend is colored bright pink to keep the charcutier from confusing the mixture with regular salt.

The second curing salt blend is called "prague powder II" or "insta-cure". Also colored pink to differentiate it from table salt, this blend is produced from salt, sodium nitrite, and sodium nitrate. This mixture is used for dry sausages that require a longer drying period which requires the presence of nitrate.

Seasoning and flavoring agents

Sweeteners and other flavoring agents are necessary in the production of many cured products due to the harsh flavors of the curing salts. A number of sweeteners can be used in curing foods, including dextrose, sugar, corn syrup, honey, and maple syrup. Dextrose is seen often in cured meats as it not only mellows the harshness, but it also increases the moisture content of the cured product while not adding a sweet flavour to the cured meat. The sweeteners also assist in stabilizing the colors in meats and it also helps the fermentation process by giving a nutrient to the bacteria.

Numerous spices and herbs are used in the curing process to assist with the flavour of the final product. The sweet spices regularly used include cinnamon, allspice, nutmeg, mace, and cardamom. Other flavoring agents may include dried and fresh chilies, wine, fruit juice, or vinegar.

FERMENTED SAUSAGE

Salami

Fermented sausages are created by salting chopped or ground meat to remove moisture, while allowing beneficial bacteria to break down mild flavored proteins into highly aromatic and flavorful molecules. Bacteria, including Lactobacilli and Leuconostoc, break down these proteins and produce lactic acid which not only affects the flavour of the sausage, but also lowers the pH from 6 to 4.5-5, preventing the growth of bacteria that could spoil the sausage. These effects are magnified during the drying process, as the salt and acidity are concentrated as moisture is extracted.

Fig 20.2 Fermented sausages

The ingredients found in a fermented sausage include meat, fat, bacterial culture, salt, spices, sugar and nitrate. Nitrate must be added to fermented sausages to prevent the formation of botulism-causing bacteria. Sugar is added to aid the bacterial production of lactic acid during the 18-hour to three-day fermentation process; the fermentation time depends on the temperature at which the sausage is stored: the lower the temperature, the longer the required fermentation period. A white mold and yeast normally adheres to the outside of the sausage during the drying process. This mold adds to the flavour of the sausage and aids in preventing harmful bacteria from attaching to the sausage.

There are two main types of fermented sausage. The first is the dry, salted, spiced sausages found in the warmer climates of the Mediterranean, in countries such as Italy, Spain, and Portugal. Since these sausages contain 25-35% water and more than 4% salt, they may be stored at room temperature. The sausages of northern Europe usually contain less salt (around 3%) and 40-50% water, and as such do not dry well in the humid climate of countries like Germany.

TERRINE DE VIANDE

A cold meat minced preparation cooked blind without dough covering and fat coating) in a bread mould is called a meat loaf including the mould is cover with foil (to prevent the minced becoming dry or brown on top during cooking). Than placed in a double boiler. The double is then place in a pre cheated oven (373° F) and the meat cooked for 40 to 45 minutes there after the meat is cooled and refrigerates – Meat loaf can be prepared from chicken veal, part steak and mutton or combination of all or any or all.

Terrines :- The art of making terrines akin (is similar) to that of pates the only difference is that whenever pates is baked in a dough and terrines is baked with crust or in a fire proof, earthen or chinaware. The word terrines incorporates both paste as well as the dish.

Pates:- is a French used for paste and in a word of cooking it means a pie of fine and smooth meat fish or poultry. Paste its also the oldest among the garde manager delicacy there are innumerable reference in recipe books. The most common by use ingredients in a making of a pate are chicken liver (goose liver is the most sought after ingredients but its rarely and price necessities the use of the substitute and chicken liver soaped in milk for 24 hours as the usually substituted truffles and combination of fore meat accomplied by garnishes.

The art of pates involves four important and distinct procedure.

1. Preparation of dough
2. If preparation farce or filling
3. Baking
4. Preparation of jelly.

Ones a pates is ready it is important to allow it mature refrigerated or store in a cool place at least 2 to 3 days to allow fermentation which permits spices to enter the paste, improving taste and aroma never cut freshly baked pate.

Mousse

A versatile delicacy it can be served cold or hot and can be made with just about very thing—meats, vegetable fruits cheese and left over's. In garde manager term a mouse is a mixture of cook ingredients termed into a heavy puree bound with aspic gelatin mixed with cream and flavour. A mouse is used either has a filling of ham mousse for ham cornets or a topping (fish mouse on a poached fillet or on a canapé) mouse can be set in mould upon demoulding a mouse is decorated and napked with aspic to give it eye appeal.

Galentine:- The term is derived from galane old French name from chicken. In culinary term the words has came to mean a delicate filling in the centre of raw bone meat rolled and envelop in muslin tight and poached in fish stock.

The filing which must be seasoned carefully with a centre pieces and the preparation required great skill while deboning. Under no circumstance can the skin be allowed to leserat (not cut in skin) the cooking process is just as important it has to been done as perfection and never over cooked which would make galantine dry or hard, very often galantine are confused with balotines which too are prepared from similar basic ingredients. However balotines are bakes or braised shape into ballets and serve hot as entrees, galantines on the other hand are always served cold as a starter.

The best bases for galantine are larger capons fresh turkey and pheasant are two other commonly used poultry. Among meat veal (breast) and lamb (shoulder) are excellent bases for galantine as is fish.

A good garnish is as important canned mushroom pista. Pork fat liver filled of chicken cooked ham black olives stuff olives, hard boiled egg white, boiled carrot, truffle and foiegras are some of the garnished which can be used.

GLAZING COLD MEATS

Meat that is to be served cold is very much improved in appearance by being glazed. Remove all fate from a pint of meat stock—such as the liquor in which chicken or veal has been boiled. Put it in a stewpan with a sheet of gelatine and stir over gentle heat until the gelatine has dissolved; then boil quickly until the stock is reduced to a teacupful. Add a few drops of browning. Turn into a jar and keep in a cold place. When required for use, trim any very rough edges from the meat you wish to glaze. Stand the jar of glaze in a pan of boiling water, and as soon as it begins to melt sufficiently to brush over, take a pastry brush and brush a good boating of it over the meat; then leave to set. If broth, such as mutton, is used, two sheets of gelatine should be used, as the broth itself does not jelly alone.

SAVOURY CREAM AND ASPIC GARNISHES

For special occasions glazed meat can be decorated with savory cream. Whip three tablespoons of cream with a pinch of salt and a sprinkling of white pepper until it is quite stiff. Or butter may be used instead of cream, if more convenïent. Use the cream to fill an icing syringe, and pipe and pattern on the set glaze. A lattice pattern done with a small fluted pipe is very pretty on a glazed tongue or piece of beef. A diamond cut in aspic jelly may be placed in each square.

Aspic jelly, which can now be bought in packets, is very decorative finely chopped and placed in little mounds either on or around a glazed joint. Garnish cold beef with scraped horse-radish in little clusters; some springs of parsley may be added. The appearance of cold mutton is quite changed if nicely glazed and then decorated with copped aspic jelly. A pretty garnish for cold boiled beef is made by cutting boiled carrots and turnings in fancy shapes. Place them around the meat and add a fringe of tiny springs of parsley.

Garnish pork with sliced beetroot and tiny silver pickled onions. Glaze cold veal and garnish with sliced ham, forcemeat balls and parsley. White jellied sauce is the best decoration for cold mutton or lamb divided into cutlets. Give a coating of the sauce, them decorate with tomato or beetroot, cut in small fancy shapes.

Boiled chicken should also be garnished in this way. To make the sauce, take a pint of veal or chicken stock, add to it a slice of onion and carrot and a small piece of mace. Boil until reduced to half a pint. Strain and leave until cold. Remove any fat. Mix one teaspoon of arrow root smoothly with a little cold water. Heat the stock, put in the arrowroot, and stir while it boils for five minutes. Then add gradually a quarter pint of cream and two table-spoons of aspic jelly. Bring to the boil, then strain into a basin and use when it is cool and just beginning to thicken. Pour it gently over the chicken, smoothing with a brush. Trim off any edges when cold. Brush evenly over cutlets.etc., and leave until quite cold and set before adding any decoration

LEARNING OUTCOME

Garde manger, meaning "keeper of the food" or pantry supervisor, refers to the task of preparing and presenting cold foods. These typically include such food items as salads, hors d'œuvres, cold soups, aspics, and charcuterie. The food storage areas in these castles and manor houses were usually located in the lower levels, since the cool basement-like environment was ideal for storing food. These cold storage areas developed over time into the modern cold kitchen. Aspic is a jelly derived by boiling the meat and bones of most animals straining to get a clear stock and cooling to a gelatinous solid. This gelatinous solid is called aspic jelly.

Aspic jelly must always be odor free crystal clear and of a light golden colour. Those easy to treat aspic required careful handling , foremost its easily effected by temperature when the temperature is too high jelly is melt on other hand when temperature is too low it will become a rubber and not melt in the mouth. The process of lining mould with jelly to prepared cold buffet delicacy like chicken in the aspic, prawn in the aspic etc is called chemise. The application of this hot cold sauces place a signification role in the display in some cold foods. The consistency of the sauces is determined by the temperature When hot chaudfroid is light it becomes thick and cool however if its kept under refrigeration. Charcuterie are fancy pork and related products made by a charcutier, a fancy pork butcher. Originally, the art of charcuterie was used to preserve meat in the Middle Ages. The art continues in France as a hallmark of fine cuisine. Forcemeat is a mixture of ground, lean meat emulsified with fat. The emulsification can be accomplished by grinding, sieving, or pureeing the ingredients. Emulsified sausages are cooked sausages with a very fine texture, using the combination of pork, beef, or poultry with fat, salt, nitrate, flavorings, and water. Pâté and terrines are often cooked in a pastry crust or a earthenware container. Both the earthenware container and the dish itself are called a terrine. Pâté and terrine are very similar: the term *pâté* often suggests a finer-textured forcemeat utilizing liver, while terrines are more often made of a coarser forcemeat. There are two main types of curing salt mixture used by the charcutier. The first is known by multiple names, including "tinted cure mix", "pink cure", "prague powder", or "insta-cure. Fermented sausages are created by salting chopped or ground meat to remove moisture, while allowing beneficial bacteria to break down mild flavored proteins into highly aromatic and flavorful molecules. The art of making terrines akin (is similar) to that of pates the only difference is that whenever pates is baked in a dough and terrines is baked with crust or in a fire proof, earthen or chinaware. The word terrines incorporates both paste as well as the dish. For special occasions glazed meat can be decorated with savory cream. Whip three tablespoons of cream with a pinch of salt and a sprinkling of white pepper until it is quite stiff. Or butter may be used instead of cream, if more convenient

LESSON END ACTIVITY

- Go and collect the data on charcuterie items available near by your areas.
- Collect the information of types of sausages available in the market near by your areas.

QUESTIONS FOR DISCUSSION

1. Explain the term garde manager.
2. Explain the term aspic and how to prepare aspic.
3. Explain the term chemiser.
4. Explain the term chaud froid.
5. Explain the steps to use chaud froid.
6. Explain the term Charcuterie and its different varieties of products.
7. Explain those product which are created by force meat.
8. Explain the term emulsified sausages.
9. Explain the term pate and galantine.
10. Explain the difference between mousse and roulade.
11. Explain the term curing.
12. Explain the term fermented sausages.
13. Explain the term terrine di viande.
14. Explain the process of GLAZING COLD MEATS.
15. Difference between pate and terrine.

STATE TRUE AND FALSE

- Garde manger, meaning “keeper of the food

- The term "garde manger" originated in pre-Revolution France.
- "Charcuterie" was the name of a guild that prepared and sold cooked items made from pigs.
- Aspic jelly must always be odor free crystal clear and of a light golden colour.
- Aspic can also be used for decorating dishes.
- To process of lining mould with jelly to prepared cold buffet delicacy like chicken in the aspic, prawn in the aspic etc is called chemise.
- Literally hot- cold is the most extensively used cold sauce in garde manager.
- The chaudfroid should be ladle over the food only when it's at the right temperature and consistency.
- Charcuterie are fancy pork and related products made by a charcutier, a fancy pork butcher.
- Pâté is the French word for *paste.*
- A mousse is light, airy mixture usually containing eggs and cream, that can be sweet or savory.
- Forcemeats are used in the production of numerous items found in charcuterie.
- Emulsified sausages are cooked sausages with a very fine texture, using the combination of pork, beef, or poultry with fat, salt, nitrate, flavorings, and water.
- There are two main types of curing salt mixture used by the charcutier.
- Fermented sausages are created by salting chopped or ground meat to remove moisture

KEY TERMS

* Aspic	* Loaf
* Curing	* Salting
* Fermented	* Sausages
* Glaze	* Savoury

21

Hors d'oeuvre and Appetizers

After studying this chapter, the student must know

- Introduction to *hors d'oeuvre* and appetizers
- Types and definition of *hors d'oeuvre*
- Hot *hors d'oeuvre*
- Use of *hors d'oeuvre*
- Composition of *hors d'oeuvre* and appetizers
- Types of canapés
- Barquettes and tartlets
- Some common *hors d'oeuvre*
- Standard recepies of *hors d'oeuvre* and appetizers

HORS D'OEUVRES AND APPETIZERS

Hors d'oeuvres is a French term used to describe small portions of very flavourful food items serve either before the main meal lunch or dinner or as the first course of the meal. It is to be very small portion, two bites. It should be fairly light and delicate but very flavourful and attractive. A *Hors d'oeuvres* is served to stimulate the appetite for the meal to come.

Hors d'oeuvres are a very useful to start a meal. They can be prepared beforehand and form an extra course without any trouble. They are economical too, as so many of them can be made from small portions of food that have been left over. Simple *hors d'oeuvres* are served cold on small glass dishes and handed round or passed from guest to guest. The newest *hors d'oeuvres* dishes provide several separate glass sections fitted together on a round or oblong wooden tray. If preferred, rather more elaborate dishes can be planned by putting a selection on each plate before the meal is served. Now-a-days fascinating empty cases can be obtained quite cheaply, ready to fill with any mixture desired. Always serve white or brown bread and butter, or rolls of bread and shells of butter, with this course.

Hors d'oeuvres are finger foods usually served prior to a meal, or in between mealtimes, and are also called appetizers, antipasti, or starters, and may range from the very simple to the very complex, depending on the occasion and the time devoted to making them. They're a common accompaniment to aperitifs, cocktails served prior to a meal. The origin of hors d'oeouvres has been traced back to Romans who enjoyed eating spicy foods before a big dinner. At dinners, banquets and the like, *Hors d'oeuvres* may be served prior to a meal. This is especially common at weddings, when it takes time for the wedding party and guests to get to a reception after the marriage has taken place. *Hors d'oeuvres* may be served at long parties that occur after a regular meal time. A mid-afternoon party where there is no intent to serve dinner, or an evening party that occurs after dinner may feature appetizers so that guests can have the opportunity to snack. It is an especially a good idea when guests are consuming alcohol, since they help to cut down on alcohol absorption. Additionally, many restaurants feature a range of appetizers that are ordered just prior to a meal as a first course.

Some common examples of *hors d'oeuvres* include crudites, cheese plates, fruit plates, toasted nuts, tartines with various toppings, small tarts, and stuffed vegetables. Many of these *hors d'oeuvres* are easy to make, while others require some more preparation. In most cases, the *hors d'oeuvres* are set on on large platters next to smaller dishes with tongs so that guests can take their own. Generally, *hors d'oeuvres* are eaten with the fingers, although guests who are seated to eat may use utensils. At a dinner party, finger bowls are offered before the meal and again after the *hors d'oeuvres* so that guests can cleanse their hands.

Thin slices of ham, tongue, sausages garnished with aspic or small salad. Celery cut in thin shreds and dressed with oil and vinegar or mayonnaise. Dishes of pickle, cucumber, radishes. Sardines garnished with thin flakes of butter, preferably scraped off with a butter scraper. Olives (French or Spanish) served without garnish of any description. Filleted anchovies garnished with two or three tiny heaps of finely chopped yolk of hardboiled egg. Eggs in mayonnaise: Boil the eggs hard for ten minutes. When cold cut them in quarters lengthways and dress with mayonnaise. Macedonia of vegetables: For this dish use a mixture of cold cooked vegetables; peas, carrots, French beans and potatoes all cut into small cubes. Dress lightly with mayonnaise. Beetroot or tomatoes: Cut thinly and arrange in a row with each slice slightly overlapping the last. Garnish with chopped parsley or chopped egg and serve with an oil and vinegar dressing. Shrimp toast: Small rounds of toast spread with shrimp butter. Prawns may be served in their shells or shelled and tossed in mayonnaise. Tuna fish should be cut in thin slices and dressed with oil and vinegar. Smoked salmon cut in very thin slices and garnished with cucumber.

Hot Hors d'oeuvre

Attereaux: :- Very classical consist of very small identical sizes slices of very food items. Placed on a bamboo skewers. The alteration are coated with a reduces sauces such as dexulles béchamel or veloute, after chilling allow the sauce to set they are breaded with a standard breeding of eggs or bread crumbs they are deep fry for immediate service.

Beignetes (Fritter) : A term describe an item or a mixture of ingredients dips in a batter or deep fry. This can be made by variety of solid food item or salpcions (finally dices mixture of one or more item these are then dipped in batter fry.)

Boucheé : Mean mouth or mouthful its is similar to minachers vol-au-vent which is a puff paste patty shell. It can be filled with limited varieties of fillings.

Brochette : Preparation of a brochette is like a attereaux however brochette is not coated with sauces or breaded. After that brochette is grilled or broiled instant or deep fry. Its is normally marinated meat or sea food inter sperse of askewer with colourfull vegetables. It is served with a compound butter and piquant sauces or other light sauces

Rissole : Semi circular pocket of puff and or un sweetened pastry dough filled with finally dice mixture of occasionally a force meat its is deep fry. The filling should be flavour to overcome the masking of fried over coating.

Appetizers

Similar meaning as *Hors d'oeuvres* However it is also used as the name of the first course like appetizer, soup, salad, entrée, desert, other terms is used in a similar manner are starter / first course or opener.

Cold Hors d'oeuvres

1. **Á la Francainse**:- Presented in a long oblong dish called Ravier. The dish is needed because the *Hors d'oeuvre* is served with the marinade sauce, relish or other accompaniment and require a fork or spoon for service and eating.
2. **Finger Food**: - Small portion of food prepared or portioned so that they can be picked-up with finger. They are most appropriate for pre-meal reception where plates and service gear are not practical or wanted.
3. **Crudités:** - Essential meals food eaten raw.
4. **Canapés:** - Refers to a toasted or fried rectangular slice of crust less bread. Also termed as croutons. As *Hors d'oeuvre* the term canapé refers to small open faced sandwich which can be topped with endless variety of savoury food items

Use of *Hors d'oeuvre* in

(I) **Pre-meal Reception:** - A reception is a convential and pleasant way to allow for the varied arrival of guest. Normally the guest is offered *hors d'oeuvre* and some type of beverage in a room other than a dining room while waiting for guest to gather. This type of reception is follows by a full meal. Some guidelines to be remembered are:

1. Keep food light guest should not feel full before dinner.
2. Limit the variety of ingredient.
3. Avoid repetition of ingredients that will be served in the main meal.
4. Avoid highly acidic and highly spiced food.
5. Limited number of *hors d'oeuvre* serve.
6. Provide for practical serve based on facility being used.

(ii) **For full Reception**:- A meal does not follow this type of reception. It is an event in and of itself and can lost on an average from 1½ to 3 hours. Some guidelines to be remembered are:

1. A wider variety of both cold and hot can be offered.
2. The range of flavour and textures used can be broader.
3. Finger food can be accompanied on the buffet by those type requiring a fork or spoon for serving and eating.

(iii) **With in the Meal**: - *Hors d'oeuvre* served within the frame work of the meal as appetizers and starters should be planned as overall balance of the meal. The Colors, texture and flavour of the total menu must be considered. As always portion should be small, simple and with no repeating of ingredients. Finger food is not served here because the atmosphere is formal. Some famous international *Hors d'oeuvre* are:

1. Russian – *Zakuska*
2. Italian – *Anti Pasta*
3. Spanish – *Tapas*
4. English – *Tea Sandwiches*
5. Swedish – *Smorgasbord*
6. Japanese – *Sushi.*

Composition of *hors d'oeuvres* and appetiziers

It is composed of a base, main body and garnish.

A) Base : Should be firm so that canapés can be handle with two fingers without it topping it should be firm.

B) Spread: Add flavour and moisture to the canapés. Act as glue helping to hold all components of the canapés together. Spread provide a fat barrier to prevent the base to become soggy and limp form juice firm the main body. Spread are mainly two types:

I) A basic spread made up of 50% of butter and 50% cream cheese.

II) Any suitable compound matching the topping.

C) Main Body: Any savories food items such as sliced cold meat or sliced vegetables, meat or sea food salad.

D) Garnished: It add eye appeal which should enhance the over shadow the main body can be small leave or herb or pieces of a food which is in keeping with a canapés as a whole.

Types of Canapés

(i) **A' la Carte:** - Premium ingredients, exquisite decoration and individually prepared and charged high.

(ii) Banquet: - Made from less expensive food, leftover food usually sells at a lower price.

Barquéttes and Tartlets

Miniature pie shells made form short pie dough. The shells are filled with variety of filling can range from hot finely diced mixture to cold mousses.

Tartlets are round like miniature tarts. Barquettes are elongated diamond cuts represents miniature boats. Filling are varied but basically are filled with fish or sea food filling.

Fig 21.1 Types of canapes

SOME COMMON *HORS D'OEUVRES*

Oysters

See that the shells are clean, open the oysters and serve three or six to each guest on the shells arranged on plates, with a garnish of lemon and parsley and rolls of brown bread and butter.

Grapefruit

Allow half a grapefruit for each person. Wipe the fruit with a damp cloth and cut in halves across the sections. With a sharp penknife or special grapefruit knife cut all round to loosen the pulp from the rind. In the same way loosen the pith in the centre then cut it out with scissors. Sprinkle the grapefruit with a good spoonful of sugar and let it soak in for at least a quarter of an hour before serving. Keep it in a cool place and serve as cold as possible. If liked, place a little cream on each before serving, and garnish with a glace cherry. Cocktails of fish and fruit are also very popular. For fruit cocktails.

SOME HORS D'OEUVRES RECIPES

Almond Salted

Ingredients	*Quantity*
Almond	200 gram
Sweet Almonds	20 gram
Olive Oil or Fresh Butter	50 gram
Salt	To taste

Method

1. First blanch the almonds, drying each one well as it is blanched.

2. Fry over gentle heat in oil or butter until they are a pale brown.
3. Drain well on kitchen paper. Toss them in some salt, then shake them on a sieve to remove any superfluous salt.
4. Serve at room temperature.

Bengal Eggs

Ingredients	*Quantity*
Hard boiled Eggs	4 no.
Curry Powder	5 garm
Butter	15 garm
Anchovy	10 garm
Parsley	10 garm

Method

1. Cut the hard boiled eggs into halves, the round way, remove the yolks and pound them.
2. Mix the pounded yolks with the other ingredients, which have been previously well blended and cooked for a few minutes in a stew pan.
3. Fill the egg whites with the mixture piled rather high and serve on a dish garnished with parsley.

Fish And Green Peas:

Ingredients	*Quantity*
Cold boiled Fish	350 garm
Boiled green Peas	150 garm
shelled Shrimps	20 garm
Mayonnaise Dressing	40 garm
yolk of a hardboiled Egg.	50 garm
Salt and pepper	To taste

Method

1 See that the boil fish is free from skin and bone and flake it finely.
2 Shrimps with it, also the peas.
3 Rub the egg yolk through a sieve and add that also with the mayonnaise.

4 Serve in ramekin cases or individual casseroles garnished with a few pea or served on tossed bread

Lobster Cocktail

Ingredients	*Quantity*
Fresh Lobster /canned	300 garm
Tomato sauce/ketchup	20 garm
Lemon Juice	10ml
Salt and pepper	To taste
Ice berg Lettuce	100 garm

Fig 21.2 Lobster cocktail

Method

1 See that the lobster is quite free from shell or bone.
2 Wash the lettuce heart and shake it dry.
3 Shred it finely and put a little in each glass.
4 Mix the ketchup, lemon juice and a sprinkling of salt with the lobster,
5 Divide the mixture between the glasses and serve very cold.
6 If fresh lobster is used, arrange the tip of a claw to stand upright in each glass.

Oyster Cocktail

Ingredients	*Quantity*
Oysters	12number
Lemon Juice	10 garm
Tomato sauce / Ketchup	30 garm
Worcester Sauce	10 garm
Salt and Pepper.	To taste

Method

1 Beard the oysters and put three in each glass with their liquor.
2 Mix together the lemon juice, Ketchup. sauce, and a sprinkling of salt and pepper.
3 When well mixed, divide the mixture between the glasses and serve individually.

Prawns In Tomato Cases

Ingredients	*Quantity*
Plum Tomatoes	8no.
Egg	2 no.
Prawns	12 no
Butter	10 garm
Salt and Pepper	To taste
Watercress for garnishing	50 garm

Method

1 Cut the tomatoes through the centre and take out the pulp.
2 Put this in a little pan with the butter, a sprinkling of salt and pepper and cook gently till soft. Rub through a sieve.
3 Pound the yolk of a hard boiled egg with the tomato puree and mix with it the prawns. Fill the tomato cases with the mixture.
4 Serve on a bed of watercress garnished with white of egg cut in shapes.

Savouries

If you are planning a full course dinner, the savoury comes right at the end followed only by dessert. Savoury dishes, though, are excellent for supper or high tea. Always serve them piping hot, unless otherwise directed, taking pains to season them well and garnish. Oddments of food can be made into tempting dishes.

Anchovy Savouries

Ingredients	*Quantity*
Grated Cheese	60 garm
Hard boiled Eggs (yolks only)—	8no
Cayenne pepper	10 garm
Anchovy Essence	20 garm
Butter	30 garm
Squares of Buttered Toast	16no

Method

1 Put the anchovy essence, grated cheese, egg yolks, and butter into a basin and pound all together.

2 Season with cayenne pepper, and then spread thickly on small squares of buttered toast.

3 Brown in a very hot oven, and serve.

CHEESE STRAWS

Ingredients	*Quantity*
Dry Cheese	60 garm
Fine Flour	60 gram
Salt	to taste
Fresh Butter	60 garm
Breadcrumbs	60 garm
Cayenne pepper	5 gram

Fig 21.3 Cheese straws

Method

1 Mix together the flour, salt and cayenne, rub in the butter, mix with the cheese finely grated and the breadcrumbs.

2 Add just enough water to form a stiff paste. Roll out thinly. Cut into strips and twist them.

3 Bake about five minutes in a quick oven.

4 Bend only or two of the straws into circles before baking.

Cheese Toasts (Hot)

Ingredients	*Quantity*
Bread slices	4 no.
Dripping	60 garm
(sausage or bacon dripping if possible)	
Mustard paste	5 garm
Mango chutney	10 garm
Cheese	60 garm

Method

1 Slices of a jumbo bread loaf are best for this purpose.

2 Cut off the crust, and fry the bread until well browned in the fat.
3 Drain and put them in a shallow baking tin or fireproof dish.
4 Chop the chutney or pickle finely and spread it on the toasts with the mustard.
5 Grate the cheese, sprinkle it on the top and put under the grill until nicely browned.

LOBSTER

Sometimes fresh lobster may be found to be indigestible. Providing shellfish agrees with you, the tinned variety may suit you better.

Lobster Boats

Ingredients	*Quantity*
Barquette shells	16no.
Small Lobster, or small tin Lobster	100 garm
Breadcrumbs	20 garm
Butter	10 garm
Mace	5 garm
White Sauce	30 garm
Mustard paste	2 garm
Cayenne pepper	5 garm
Salt and pepper	To taste

Method

1 Take all the meat from the lobster and mince it finely.
2 Pound it in a mortar with the crumbs, the liquid butter, mace, mustard and cayenne.
3 Put this mixture in a saucepan and mix in the white sauce made very hot.
4 Fill the hot pastry cases with the mixture, garnish with a little mound of pounded spawn if available and serve at once.

Note: The spawn is the little coral coloured eggs to be found on the under side of the hen lobster.

Lobster Eclairs

Ingredients	*Quantity*
Choux Pastry – small	150 garm
Lobster or a small tin of Lobster	100 garm

Flour	30 garm
Butter	50 garm
Milk	30ml
Salt and Pepper	To taste
Lemon Juice	10ml
Anchovy Essence	5 garm

Method

1. Chop the meat of the lobster.
2. Heat the butter, add the flour and stir while it cooks gently for three or four minutes, add the milk gradually and, when quite smooth, add the anchovy essence, salt and pepper.
3. Stir while it boils very gently for eight minutes.
4. Add the lobster, and the lemon juice.
5. Bake choux pastry in small sponge finger-tins, cut them through, fill with the mixture and serve hot.
6. The lobster mixture may be used to fill small patty cases if preferred.

Shrimps and Eggs On Toast

Ingredients	*Quantity*
Shrimps	150 garm
Butter	60 garm
Salt and Pepper	To taste
Eggs	6 no
Milk	10 garm
Buttered Toast	8 no

Method

1. Shell the shrimps.
2. Beat the eggs just enough to mix whites and yolks, add the pepper and the milk.
3. Melt the butter in a small stewpan and when it is quite hot put in the egg mixture.
4. Stir with a wooden spoon, and as soon as it begins to set, add the shrimps and stir over gentle heat until lightly set.
5. Serve piled on squares of buttered toast.

Smoked Salmon Toasts

Ingredients	*Quantity*
Smoked Salmon	100 garm
Watercress Butter	50 garm
Bread	8no
Butter.	30 garm

Method

1 Melt the butter in a small pan and fry the slices of bread until lightly browned and crisp. Spread them plentifully with watercress butter, then with thinly cut slices of salmon.
2 On this spread a little more butter and put them under a hot grill for a few minutes.
3 Serve hot

LEARNING OUTCOME

Hors D'oeuvres are a very useful start to a meal. They can be prepared beforehand and form an extra course without any trouble. They are economical too, as so many of them can be made from small portions of food that have been left over. Simple *hors d'oeuvres* are served cold on small glass dishes and handed round or passed from guest to guest. The origin of hors d'oeouvres has been traced back to Romans who enjoyed eating spicy foods before a big dinner. At dinners, banquets and the like, *Hors d'oeuvres* may be served prior to a meal. Thin slices of ham, tongue, sausages garnished with aspic or small salad. Celery cut in thin shreds and dressed with oil and vinegar or mayonnaise. Dishes of pickle, cucumber, radishes. Sardines garnished with thin flakes of butter, preferably scraped off with a butter scraper. Similar meaning as *Hors d'oeuvres* However it is also used as the name of the first course like appetizer, soup, salad, entrée, desert, other terms is used in a similar manner are starter / first course or opener.

LESSON END ACTIVITY

- Made canapés from the bread as much you can make.
- Collect the pictures and recipe of different canapés from the books.

QUESTIONS FOR DISCUSSION

1. Explain the term hors d' oeuvres and appetizers.
2. Mention some hot and cold hors d' oeuvres.

3. Explain the use of hors d' oeuvres.
4. Explain the composition of *hors d'oeuvres* and appetizers.
5. Explain the types of canapés.
6. Explain the difference between Barquettes and Tartlets.

STATE TRUE AND FALSE

- Hors D'oeuvres are a very useful start to a meal.
- *Hors d'oeuvres* are finger foods
- *Hors d'oeuvres* may be served prior to a meal.
- *Hors d'oeuvres* may be served at long parties that occur after a regular meal time.
- Brochette is preparation of a brochette is like a attereaux however brochette is not coated with sauces or breaded.
- Canapés is refers to a toasted or fried rectangular slice of crust less bread. Also termed as croutons

KEY TERMS

* Canapés
* Croutons
* Meal
* Slices
* Toasted

Chapter 22

Salads

After studying this chapter, the student must know

- Introduction
- Salads and salad dressing
- Kinds and classification of salads
- Certain rules for salads
- Parts and types of salads
- Different varieties of side salads
- Standard recipes of salads

SALADS

A salad can be well defined as a combination of cold ingredients serve with a dressing. They play an important part in most menus. In most cases the ingredient includes a salad green. All salads are extremely wholesome regardless of ingredients used and provide many essential vitamins.

SALADS AND SALAD DRESSINGS

The term "Salad" is an elastic one in these days, for it includes every kind of vegetable, raw and cooked, from the humble dandelion to the aristocratic asparagus, as well as fruit of every type. By the aid of a good salad surround, scraps of fish or meat can be changed from an uninteresting dish to one that is attractive both to the eye and the palate. In fact salads have much to recommend them. They take very little trouble to prepare and at the same time effect a saving in fuel. A dressing of olive oil provides a nourishing food, whilst vinegar or lemon juice softens the tissues of the plants and makes them digestible. Raw vegetable salads are particularly good as they contain all the vitamins intact.

Salads need dainty serving. It has been well said that to make a perfect salad we need a spendthrift to add the oil, a miser to put in the vinegar and a fury to stir. So be generous with the oil, sparing with the vinegar and energetic when mixing. Another great point with salads is to have all the green meat perfectly fresh, and to use only the best quality oil and vinegar. Wash all salad thoroughly, looking it over most carefully for grubs, for they have a truly wonderful way of protecting themselves by pretending to be a part of the vegetable. Put it in cold water without salt and the grubs will then come out. If you use salted water, although they may be killed, they will remain in the salad.

Salad to be enjoyable must be very cold, crisp and not flabby, therefore never press it dry. Drain thoroughly in a colander or on a sieve, then shake dry in a cloth, butter-muslin bag or salad basket, lettuce, endive, etc., should not be cut with a knife, but just pulled in pieces. Be careful and very sparing in the use of garlic and onion. For most tastes it is quite sufficient just to rub over the inside of the salad bowl with a slice of either; remember to:

They can be generally found complementing most meals. Its popularity is because-

(A) It's considered a good health food.

(B) Lends themselves particularly to cold buffet.

(C) They blend with and thus complement many types of hot dishes.

(D) Traditionally they are served with main courses such as grills of meat and poultry or with roast meat, poultry or game usually in the place of second vegetable.

(E) Many salads can also be served as an *hors d'oeuvres* or side salad.

(F) If a salad is serving as a side salad, the rule is light salad with heavy entrée or heavy with light entrée.

There are two kinds of salad:

1. Raw vegetable salad or single commodity like cucumber bound with an appropriate dressings.
2. Combination of salad made with several ingredients bound with dressing and served in a complete form.

Crudités: - Are also a form of salads as they are cuts of crisp salad items for dipping in various cold sauces while awaiting the arrival of the first course.

Most salads are classified as under: -

1. Fruits
2. Vegetables
3. Leafy Greens
4. Meats
5. Sea Foods

Certain Rules:

1. Use simple colorful combination.
2. Ingredients should always be crispy and fresh.

3. Balance, flavour, texture and colour.
4. Use artistic arrangement.
5. Use form in arranging or molding the salad.
6. Purchase quality ingredients.
7. It's a work of art and should be attractive.
8. Always present a well chilled salad.

Parts of salad:- Any successful salad contain four parts.

1. Base,
2. Body,
3. Dressing and
4. Garnish.

All the parts should be prepared well or one part may destroy the whole salad:-

1. **Base:** - Base gives definition to the placement for salad on the plate. An example will be green lettuce haves used as an underline for the salad.
2. **Body**: - The body is the main ingredient of the salad. This should be the focal point and sets on the top of the base. An example is the simple tossed salad or sea food salad place on the top of the under liner of a leaf lettuce.
3. **Dressing**: - Dressing is used to enhance and add flavour to the body of the salad. It makes the salad more palatable. The dressing may be tossed with the body of the salad such as simple salad or served as an accompaniment to be poured over the salad at the table.
4. **Garnish**: - The garnish adds from, colour and texture to the salad. It should complement not complete with the body of salad. It may be part of the salad or may be an additional item that will blend with a complement the body. It should be simple attract and not distract and help to stimulate the appetite.

TYPES OF SALAD

There are three primary types of preparation:

1. **Simple Salads**: - A simple salad is the variety of one or more greens. A mild dressing usually a light vinaigrette is used so that the delicate taste of the green is not masked. These types of salad is normally used as a salad coarse before or after the entrée. It both cleanses and stimulates the palate.
2. **Mixed salad**: - Mixed salads are composed of cooked or raw vegetables either marinated or served with a complementary dressing. A variety of marinades and dressings can be used, however stronger marinades and long period of marinating should be reserved for harder vegetables. These salads can be used as appetizers, accompaniments or garnish or as the salad course.

3. **Combination Salads:** - Ingredients are presented separately but on the same plate. They can be served with the variety of dressings and are usually served as an entrée.

Side Salad vegetable

1. **Italian:** - Carrot, Turnip, Potatoes, Asparagus tips and Peas mixed with mayonnaise garnished with fillet of achieves, tomato, olives and capers, chopped chervil and hard boil egg.
2. **Mimosa**: - Beetroot, celery, potatoes, asparagus, tips, sprinkle top with chopped asparagus mayonnaise dressing.
3. **Nicose:** - Potatoes, French beans, anchovy fillet and capers, olives with vinaigrette dressing.
4. **Marquis:** - Juliennes of tomato, celery served on lettuce sprinkle with shredded walnut, mayonnaise dressing.
5. **Oxford**: - Juliennes of celery, pears, potatoes, truffle with asparagus tips at base with vinaigrette dressing.
6. **Allemande**: - - Boil potatoes, eating apple, mayonnaise,trimmed salt herring and gherkins are the garnish.
7. **Bagatelle**: - Julienne of carrot, mushroom, French beans, asparagus tips and vinaigrette dressings.
8. **Beat rice**: - Jullienne of chicken, truffles, potatoes, asparagus tips in mayonnaise
9. **Flemish:** - Seasons chicory and potatoes, onions, fillet of hearings and vinaigrette
10. **Chatelaine**: - Potatoes with mayonnaise,oyster and truffle.

Leafy Green Special Salads

1. **Cesar salad**: - Romaine lettuce, Boastan head lettuce, anchovy fillets, croutons parmesan cheese, coddled eggs, garlic.
2. **Danicheff**: - Truffles, artichoke, hearts, celeriac, potato, mushroom and asparagus tips.

Side Salad Fruit

1. **Diplomat**: - Place on a leaf of lettuce, apple, pineapple, celery,smeared with lemon juice, salt, sugar and mayonnaise sprinkle with chopped nuts and maraschino cherries.
2. **Fruited Slaw**: - Orange, cabbage, rasins and pineapple bound with orange and pineapple juice in vinaigrette dressing. Serve on shredded lettuce sprinkle with chop parsley.
3. **Florida**: - Heart of coarse lettuce with sliced and pealed orange. Fresh cream is used for dressing.
4. **Banana pecan**: - Banana soaked in fresh juice and is then dipped in mayonnaise and wiped cream served on lettuce and sprinkled with chopped maraschino cherries.
5. **Dalila**: - Banana, Celery and Apple in mayonnaise dressing.

6. **Woldroff salads**: - Diced of apples,juliennes of celery,chopped walnut with mayonnaise.

Side Salad Rice

1. **Egyptiene**: - Rice pilaf, chicken liver cooked ham, mushroom tomato and pimento with vinaigrette dressing.
2. **Oriental**: - Rice seasoned with vinaigrette, paprika and chopped onion, pepper, tomato, black olives and chervil.
3. **Andalousina**: - Diced tomatoes,pimento, onion and rice with vinaigrette dressings.
4. **Maharaja**: - Rice, crab flesh, celeriac, tomatoes. Garnish with egg yolk and chives.

Side Salad Meat

1. **Russian**: - Add to normal Russian salad, tongue, sausage, mushroom, lobster garnished with anchovy, truffle, tongue, capper and gherkins.
2. **Ham:** - Julienne of ham,celery, lettuces, tomatoes,parsley with mayonnaise.

Side salad Chicken

1. **Beat rice**: - Discussed before in vegetables
2. **Bressaine**: - Lettuce tossed in vinaigrette, chicken in mayonnaise with tomato juice and paprika.Garnish with truffle,peel green and red pepper, asparagus and eggs.
3. **Tosca:** - Chicken tongue, globe artichokes with mayonnaise
4. **Fanchedde**: Chicken mushroom endives and truffles in vinaigrette dressing

Side salad sea Food

1. **Alibaba**: - Shrimps in mayonnaise, potatoes, zucchini, tomato, eggs and vinaigrette.
2. **Mikado**: - Shrimps and potatoes in mayonnaise flavoured with soya sauce garnished with Chrysanthemum mum pettles seasoned with vinaigrette tomatoes and pimentos.

STANDARD RECEIPE OF SALADS

Beet Root Salad

Ingredients	*Quantity*
Beetroot	200 gram
Salt	10 gram
Pepper	20 gram
Oregano	20 gram

Vinegar	20 gram
Oil	20 ml
Basil Leaf	10 gram
Bay Leaf	2 No.
Sesame Seeds	10 gram

Method

1. Once you have cooked your beetroots you can make the dressing.
2. Put a fairly heavy based non-stick pan on high heat.
3. Melt 100 gram of unsalted butter.
4. Add a bit of salt and pepper, one tablespoon of very finely chopped oregano and about 2 tablespoons of balsamic vinegar, stir and leave.
5. In a glass bowl put some fresh basil leaves, fresh thyme, fresh oregano leaves, spring onions/shallots, some Spanish onion and bay leaves.
6. Then add a little bit of live oil to glass the leaves and incorporate all the flavours, toss and add. The beetroot.
7. Put the salad on a plate, aiming from the centre of the plate and working upwards.
8. Take the dressing a spoon it around the plate, then over the salad.
9. Put a bit more olive oil on the plate to give the salad a two-tone effect which makes the salad jump out at you.
10. Serve the salad straight away as the dressing is hot.
11. If you want to make this dish as an entrée not as a side dish you can crumble some Australian feta over the top and serve with fresh bread.

Oriental Rice Salad

Ingredients	*Quantity*
Cooked rice	200 gram
Bean Sprouts	100 gram
Raisins	20 gram
Red Pepper, chopped	20 gram
Green Onion, chopped	20 gram
Celery, Chopped	20 gram
Mushrooms, sliced	20 gram

Cashews	10 gram
Soya Sauce	10 ml
Oil	10 ml
Cloves garlic, minced	20 gram
Lemon Juice	20 ml

Method

1. In a large bowl add rice, bean sprouts, raisins, red pepper, green onion, celery and mushrooms. Add spinach and cashews and toss gently.
2. In a small blend soya sauce, oil, garlic and lemon juice. Pour over salad and toss well.
3. This rice salad tastes even better if left to marinate for an hour or so before eating.

South Indian Cabbage Salad

Ingredients	*Quantity*
Oil	1 tsp
Lemon	20 ml
Salt	To taste
Green Chilli	20 gram
Coriander Leaves	20 gram
Ginger	20 gram
Black Pepper	10 gram
Mustard seeds	10 gram
Chana Daal (Roasted)	10 gram
Peanuts(coarsely ground)	20 gram

Method

1. Finely chop the cabbage. Keep it in a serving tray.
2. Heat oil in a kadahi.
3. Add mustard seeds to the oil. Fry the peanuts and chana daal for half a minute.
4. Add the chopped cabbage. Put green chili, ginger and coriander.
5. Mix properly and serve.

Tossed Cucumber Salad

Ingredients	*Quantity*
Cucumber	250 gram
Roasted peanut	50 gram
Salt and pepper	10 gram
Oregano	10 gram
Lemon juice	20 ml
Green Chilies	10 gram.

Method

1. Cut cucumber in a cube.
2. Take a bowl, add cucumber, salt pepper, Oregano, green chilies, roasted peanuts and lemon juice mixed well

Creamy Garden Potato Salad

Ingredients	*Quantity*
Baby Potatoes	500 gram
Chop celery	30 gram
Red Bell pepper	20 gram
Whipped cream	50 ml
Mayonnaise	50 ml
Mustard	20 gram
Mustard seeds	10 gram
Salt and pepper	10 gram

Method

1. Boil potatoes.
2. In a bowl mixed mayonnaise, mustard, whipped cream, salt and pepper.
3. Add potatoes, mix properly, garnish with chop celery and potatoes.

Mimosa Salad

Ingredients	*Quantity*
Iceberg	100 gram
Hard Boil Egg	3 Nos
Mushroom	50 gram
Parsley	10 gram
For Dressing	
Oil	20 ml
Vinegar	10 gram
Lemon Juice	20 gram
Dry mustard	10 gram
Cayenne pepper	10 gram
Paprika	10 garm
Saltand pepper	10 garm

Method

1. Arrange lettuce on a platter .
2. Lay the sliced of the eggs and sliced mushrooms decoratively on the lettuce.Sprinkle parsley through the salad.
3. In a blender mix all the dressing ingredients and blend well.
4. Pour dressing over the salad before serving.

Pasta Salad

Ingredients	*Quantity*
Macaroni	100 garm
Oil	50ml
Salt and pepper	20 garm
Basil leaves	20 garm
Red bellpepper	20 garm
Yellow bellpepper	20 garm
Balsamic vinegar	20 garm
Garlic	10 garm

Method

1. Boil macaroni and cool in refrigerator
2. In a bowl add oil, crushed garlic,salt pepper, balsamic vinegar,chop basil leaves mix together thoroughly.
3. Add macaroni to the dressing tossed and served in salad bowl.

Cerole salad

Ingredients	*Quantity*
Melon	100 garm
Cooked cool rice	150 garm
Sour cream	20 garm
Fresh ginger	10 garm
Lemon juice	20ml
Lettuce	100 garm
Salt and pepper	10 garm

Method

1. Cut the melon in quarters, remove all the flesh, cut into neat segment into a bowl.
2. Add the cooked rice, part of the grated ginger, cream, lemon juice, salt and pepper
3. Gently mix, leave to stand for 30min
4. Dress on leaves and garnish with grated ginger

Celery Salad

Ingredients	*Quantity*
Head celery	200 garm
Mayaonnaise dressing	50ml
Beetroot	50 garm
Salt and pepper	15 garm

Method

1. Remove the outer leaves of the celery, wash it thoroughly, and cut the white part into one-inch lengths.

2. Put them in a salad bowl and just before serving mix in the mayonnaise dressing.
3. Garnish with the beetroot cut in stars and the young green leaves of the celery.
4. One large well flavoured apple peeled, cored, cut in cubes and added to the above makes a good variation

Cold Meat And Lettuce Salad

Ingredients	*Quantity*
Slices of cold meat	150 garm
Lettuce	100 garm
Salad oil	20ml
Vinegar	15ml
Salt and pepper	15 garm
Garlic	10 garm

Method

1. Remove the outer leaves from the lettuces.
2. Tear the remainder in shreds and wash well.
3. Drain and shake dry in a cloth. Rub the inside of a deep dish or bowl with the garlic.
4. Sprinkle it with salt and pepper, add oil and the vinegar and mix thoroughly.
5. Put in the prepared lettuce and toss it about until the dressing is evenly distributed.
6. Arrange the lettuce round the bowl and the slices of meat in the centre. (If the meat is too " scrappy" to cut into slices, cut it into cubes). It can be sprinkle with tomato catsup if liked

Macedoine Salad

Ingredients	*Quantity*
Green peas	100 garm
Carrots	50 garm
Turnip	50 garm
Potatoes	100 garm
cream salad dressing	100ml

Method

1. This salad is an excellent way of using cold boiled vegetables; otherwise it is a little trouble as each vegetable must be boiled separately to retain its distinctive flavour.

2. When boiled and quite cold out the carrots, turnips and potatoes into balls or fancy shapes with vegetable cutters, or they may be cut in shape and then boiled if preferred.
3. Mix them with the peas, toss in the dressing and serve.
4. The kind of dressing used is just a matter of taste, some preferring mayonnaise, others just a simple oil and vinegar dressing

Mock Crab Salad

Ingredients	*Quantity*
Crab	100 garm
Gruyere cheese	30 garm
Anchoy fillet	10 garm
White wine	10 ml
Vinegar	10 ml
Mustard pepper	5 garm
lettuce	50 garm
Cucumber	50 garm
Shrimps	30 garm

Method

1. Steam the crab, leave until cold, then remove shell and take out the flesh.
2. Grate the cheese and add a good seasoning of made mustard, pepper, and the anchovy.
3. Beat together with a wooden spoon, adding the vinegar gradually until thoroughly blended.
4. Arrange the lettuce on a glass dish, then a row of cucumber slices overlapping.
5. In the centre put the crab flakes and spread the cheese paste on the top. Cover with mayonnaise mixed with the shelled shrimps.

LEARNING OUTCOME

The term "Salad" is an elastic one in these days, for it includes every kind of vegetable raw and cooked, from the humble dandelion to the aristocratic asparagus, as well as fruit of every type. Salads need dainty serving. It has been well said that to make a perfect salad we need a spendthrift to add the oil, a miser to put in the vinegar and a fury to stir. So be generous with the oil, sparing with the vinegar and energetic when mixing. Salad to be enjoyable must be very cold, crisp and not flabby, therefore never press it dry. Drain thoroughly in a colander or on a sieve, then shake dry in a cloth, butter-muslin bag or salad basket

LESSON END ACTIVITY

- Collect the information of 10 international salads name with there ingredients.

QUESTIONS FOR DISCUSSION

1. Explain the term salads.
2. Define the salads and salads dressing.
3. How many types of salads ?
4. Explain the parts of salads.
5. Name five side salad vegetable.
6. Name five leafy green salad vegetable.
7. Name five side rice salad.
8. Name five side salad chicken.
9. Name five side salad seafood.
10. Mention the standard recipe of cerole salad.

STATE TRUE AND FALSE

- A salad can be well defined as a combination of cold ingredients serve with a dressing.
- Salads need dainty serving.
- Salad to be enjoyable must be very cold, crisp and not flabby,
- Salad considered a good health food
- Base gives definition to the placement for salad on the plate
- The body is the main ingredient of the salad.
- dressing is used to enhance and add flavour to the body of the salad
- A simple salad is the variety of two or more greens.
- Mixed salads are composed of cooked or raw vegetables either marinated or served with a complementary dressing

KEY TERMS

* Base
* Crispy
* Dressing
* Combination
* Dainty
* Ingredients

Chapter 23

Sandwich

After studying this chapter, the student must know :

- Introduction and meaning
- Classification of sandwich
- Type of sandwich
- Spread and dips
- Caviar and types
- Some variation of cold closed sandwich
- Tools and equipment needed for sandwich products

SANDWICH

Most common finger food not all sandwich can be included, only tea sandwich, fancy sandwich. Sandwiches are popular in today's culture. They are easy to make and eat practically anywhere and can be as fancy or as simple as we like. A sandwich is the most innovative and versatile food,which are acceptable on every occasion. Open or closed, single or decked, flat or rolled, sweet or savoury, hot or cold there are sandwiches with fillings and toppings which will take a life time to describe.

The first recorded sandwich was made by the famous Rabbi, Hillel the Elder, who lived during the 1st century B.C. A poor man, but a great scholar, he began the passover custom of sandwiching a mixture of chopped nuts, apples, spices, and wine between two matzohs to eat with bitter herbs. This sandwich is the foundation of the Seder and is named after him. But matzoh, being unleavened bread, is not absorptive of sauces and juices as today's sandwich has become. John Motagu, 4th Earl of Sandwich, invented the "meal between the slices" that has retained his name. The Earl lived in England in the 18th Century. Human beings, being adventurous, have developed the sandwich into both a quick and easy meal, and an art form. Po-boy, muffuletta, clubhouse, reuben, grilled, meat, tuna or egg salad – these are just some of the many different types of sandwiches frequently eaten for lunches or light dinners.

The term sandwich come into use about 200 years ago close to the time of birth of United States. Their lived a notorious gambler in the court of King George III of England whose name was John Montagu (Germy Twitchier).The fourth earls of sandwich from 1718-1792, the earls gambling affliction was such that he would enter in 24 hours beting marathons during which he would not remove himself from the table for any reason. Any eating had to be quick and not disturbing. The earl asked his butter to serve bread and cheese. His chef know his master's intensity and so made it easy for him by placing the cheese between two slices of butter bread and the rest is sandwich. Actually it becomes named after him in 1762.

SANDWITCH MEANING

A sandwich is a food item typically made of two or more slices of leavened bread with one or more layers of meat, seafood, vegetables, cheese or jam and butter. The bread can be used as is, or it can be coated with butter, oil, or other optional or traditional condiments and sauces to enhance flavour and texture. The slices of bread are stacked neatly, resting on a crust of bread. They are then buttered (unless this has been done before each slice is cut) and the prepared fillings are added, so the complete loaf is made into long sandwiches. If they are to be kept for any length of time the crusts are replaced and the loaf wrapped in clean cloth, greaseproof paper or foil. When required for service the sandwiches are easily and quickly cut into any required size or shape, neatly dressed on a doily on a flat dish and sprinkled with washed and drained mustard cress.

A typical set of fillings for a loaf could be: ham, tongue, smoked salmon, tomato, cucumber, egg., etc. Sandwiches are commonly carried to work or school in lunchboxes or brown paper bags (in sandwich bags) to be eaten as the mid-day meal on picnics, hiking trips, or other outings. In some parts of the world, they are also served in restaurants as entrées, and are sometimes eaten at home, either as a quick meal or as part of a larger meal. When eaten as part of a full meal, sandwiches are traditionally accompanied with such side dishes as a serving of soup (soup-and-sandwich), a salad (salad-and-sandwich), french fries/ chips, potato chips/ crisps and a pickle or coleslaw.

What is a Basic Sandwich

A Sandwich is a very simple culinary item which relies on a perfect balance of the basic elements to succeed.

(i) It is a balance of temperature – hot or cold.

(i) **Texture**:- Crunchy chewy, smooth, wet dry.

(ii) **Flavour**:- Ingredients of the various components

(iii) **Appearance**:- Simple and Correct.

It is this balance of the basics that the wide variety of sandwiches all originates.

TYPES OF SANDWICHES

Sandwiches may be made from every kind of bread, fresh or toasted, in a variety of shapes and sizes and with an almost endless assortment of fillings. Few example of general types of popular sandwiches are explained in this section. Combinations of sandwiches and fillings are endless and the limitation in number is merely a matter of limitation in individual's imagination.

Fig 23.1 Double decker sandwich

Double Decker (Fig. 23.1)

These types of sandwiches use three slices of bread. The filling is placed on the top of the first slice. The next slice is buttered and placed on top, lettuce, tomato and cucumber or fillings of choice are placed on top of this slice. The final slice is placed in position.

Pressed, trimmed and held together with a plastic cocktail stick with stuffed olive or cherry.

Fig 23.2 Sandwich cake

Sandwich Cake (Fig. 23.2)

These types of sandwiches are made from round bread loaves and look like iced layer cakes. They are sliced into two or three round slices with different savoury spread in each layer and iced on top with soft icing containing butter, cheese, etc. It is cut into wedges like cakes. Finished product may look like a cylinder. Sometimes, the regular ice cream of choice flavour may also be used as a spread and stored in the fridge before serving. It may be stored after cutting into slices or stored as a whole and cut into slices prior to serving.

Fig 23.3 Loaf sandwich

Loaf Sandwich (Fig. 23.3)

These types of sandwiches are made from bread loafs. The loaf of bread is taken and sliced lengthwise, filled with filling of choice and iced. It is sliced across the bread and served.

Pinwheel Sandwich (Fig. 23.4)

Pinwheel sandwiches are generally prepared using the top crust of the loaf. The top crust is taken out of the sandwich loaf. It is then sliced lengthwise, and butter and soft filling are spread evenly. Each slice is rolled and wrapped firmly in a foil and chilled till it is set. It is cut into thin slices and served. Pinwheel sandwiches may be served with other sandwiches or served as cold canapés.

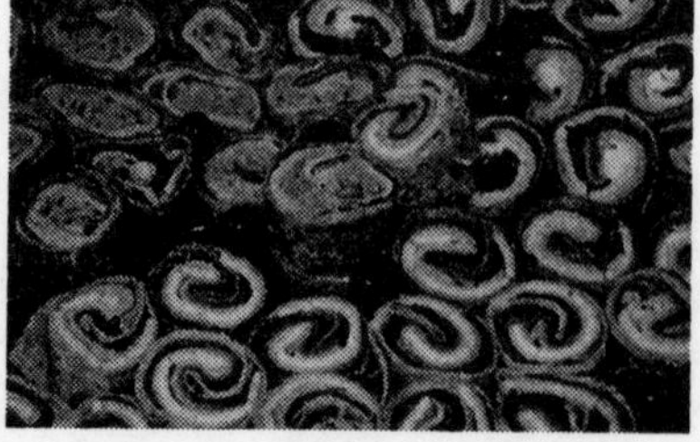

Fig. 23.4 Pinwheel Sandwich

Bookmaker Sandwich (Fig 23.5)

Bookmaker Sandwich has underdone (rare) minute steak between two slices of hot buttered toast

Fig 23.5 Book maker sandwich

Ribbon Sandwich (Fig 23.6)

Ribbon sandwiches are prepared using two coloured breads. Whole wheat loaf and white bread loaves are sliced lengthwise in ¼ inch strips. Whole wheat bread slice is tinted with chives and cheese. White bread slice is spreaded with deviled ham or minced tuna fish, salad mix. A five layered loaf is prepared by alternatively placing whole wheat bread slice and white bread slice on top of one another. They are then wrapped into waxed paper and chilled. They are then sliced into ½ inch bite sized strips

Fig 23.6 Ribbon sandwich

Club Sandwich (Fig 23.7)

A club sandwich, also called a clubhouse sandwich, is a type of sandwich sometimes served as a double-decker. The double-decker version is usually cut into quarters, and often held together by toothpicks. The traditional club ingredients are turkey, bacon, lettuce, and tomato. The sandwich is usually served on toasted bread, but untoasted bread can be used. Ham is sometimes substituted for bacon, and chicken sometimes for turkey

Fig 23.7 Club sandwich

Open Sandwich or Scandinavian Smorrebrod (Fig 23.8)

This is prepared from a buttered slice of any bread garnished with any type of meat, fish, eggs, vegetables, salads, etc. The varieties of open sandwiches can include some of the following spreads / fillings: smoked salmon, lettuce, potted shrimps, slice of lemon; s crambled egg, asparagus tips, chopped tomato; grilled bacon, cold fried egg, tomato sauce, mushrooms; cold sliced beef, sliced tomato, fans of gherkins (type of cucumber).

Fig 23.8 Open sandwich

Tea Sandwich (Fig 23.9)

Mostly closed made with of two pieces of bread.It is mainly eaten at tea time and are well suited as *hors d'oeuvre* being small and delicate. The filling in those are using very finally chopped and mixed with butter or cream or cheese ½ inch by 3 inch rectangular and ½ inch in thickness and option is to used paper thin vegetable slice or meat slice,ham, chicken,cucumber are common used.

Smorres Board : Means butter bread this is a Danish open face sandwich using substantial pieces of meat, fish or vegetables.these are art, fully arrange on the piece of bread its not unusual to serve an appropriate sauces with a smorresboard.

Fig 23.9 Tea sandwich

Spread and dips

Spread and dips are not themselves finger foods however when served sliced with baguette (types of breads) croutons,crackers, bread stick, vegetables sticks, or slice potatoes chips, corn chips or other similar item.The difference between spread and dips in there consistency . A 'Dip' is a mixture that loose or soft enough to cling to an item dip into it. A 'spread' are more solid mixture which needs to spread with a knife. Spread can be a thick mixture based on chop or pureed meats, fish or cheese.A high degree of fat is present, cream cheese spread is most common used spreads for *hors d'oeuvres*, soft cream cheese such as ricotta, brie etc.

Dips : Made either hot or cold,thin puree of fruit or vegetable based on whipped cream, type of cheese, sour cream, yoghurt, mayonnaise or a combination of these.

Fig 23.10 Beluga caviar

Cheese: Is a rich source of *hors d'oeuvre* as an ingredients, main body or themselves. If there is a meal to follow their used should to be limited, the higher the fat content of cheese the more filling in its

Caviar: The ultimate *hors d'oeuvre*. Caviar is a processed roe (egg of sturgeon fish) If the roe is from a fish other than a sturgeon. The finest caviar come from Caspian sea which is boader by Russian and Iran. The three spices of sturgeon harvested in this area are as

- **Belgua** (Fig 23.10)
- **Osetra** (Fig 23.11)
- **Sevruge** (Fig 23.12)

Fig 23.11 Osetra

Caviar is categorized not only the type of fish it come but also by the method of processing.

1. **Fresh caviar** : Most perishable to be kept refrigerated at all time.
2. **Pressed caviar** : Processed from the eggs of osetra and Sevruge sturgeon. when a high percentage of eggs are reputed or sunken. Pressed caviar is dried and spredable it has consistency like a jam, this caviar is highly priced.
3. **Pasteurized caviar** : Pasteurized and vacuum packed caviar longer shell life upto 3 months with cut refrigeration.It effect taste of the roe.

Fig 23.12 Sevruge caviar

4. **Frozen caviar** : Are roe from non sturgeon type fish like salmon, white fish, and lump fish. Roe berries are tougher and less expensive because of lower quality.

Types of caviar

1. **Belgua** : Largest most delicate berry which bust easily among the tongue.This is the most expensive and highest quality caviar. light to dark grey in colour (Fig. 23.10).
2. **Osetra :** Second largest berries delicates slightly fruity flavoured golden to dark brown or green. Second most expensive caviar (Fig. 23.11).
3. **Sevurga** : Smaller delicate berry of light to medium grey in colour.Very popular in Europe and less expensive (Fig. 23.12).

Caviar should be served accomplied by butter toast,point using salted butter, lemon wedges,presented in the original tim set on crushed ice.

CLASSIFICATION OF SANDWITCH

1. **Hot sandwich**:- There are three primary characteristics of hot sandwiches:
   (1) It must be hot.
   (2) They must remain hot throughout the services.
   (3) Hot sandwiches can have a hot sauce as an accompaniment.

Sandwiches are:

(A) **Closed**:- A closed hot sandwich is define as one which has a hot filling serve in bread, toast, roll or toasted roll. A closed hot sandwich can be subdivided into three grouping.

(i) **Simple closed Hot sandwich**: - A good example of this is French dip sandwich. The filling for this sandwich is roast beef which is thinly slice and dipped in aujus. It is then placed in soft or hard roll cut in half served with a cup of hot aujus. Some other variations are:

(1) **Steak Sandwich**: - Steak is cooked to guest's required order of doneness and serves with large roll with lettuce, tomato and onion as garnish. Horse radish or mustard sauce is the accompaniments.

(2) **Fish Sandwiches**:- Breaded deep fry boneless fillet of fish serve with a bun with a lettuce and tomato garnish. Normally serve with tartare sauce.

(3) **Barbeque Pork Sandwich**:- This is sliced smoked pork which is serve with 2 slice of bun or bread. It can be serve with or accompanied by barbeque sauce.

(4) **Hot Dog**:- This is a sausage serve on a special roll. It can be accompanied or topped with a hot topping such as chili or cheese sauce or with cold topping coleslaw, sauerkraut. It is often accompanied with relish, chopped onions and other condiments. Most specially ketchup and mustard.

(5) **Ham Burger**:- Most popular sandwich in the world. 2-6 oz paties of ground beef, broiled, fried or grilled to order served on a round bun with lettuce. Tomato and

onion garnish and the appropriate condiments. A basic variation of the burger is the meeting of a slice of American cheese on top called cheese burger.

(ii) **Grilled Closed Sandwiches**:- Two slices of bread encasing a filling. The casing is buttered on the outside top and bottom and then placed on a grilled or in a pan to brown on both sides. A grilled cheese sandwich is an excellent example. The browned outside is dry yet malted cheese inside is wet. The crunchy exterior of the sandwich is accentuated (enhanced) by the smooth interior. A light weight can be put on top of the sandwich during grilling to enhance the browning. Some variations are:

1. Grilled Tuna Salad and Cheese
2. Grilled Ham and Cheese

(iii) **Fried Closed sandwich**:- Are two pieces of some type of filling which has been dipped in an egg mixture and then deep or pan fried till golden. They are after finished in the oven to ensure that the interior is hot,. Common example is Monte Carlo, Mante Christo. Monte Christo is normally prepare with Swiss Cheese, ham, Dijon mustard or a light bread accompanied by red currant jelly.

(B) **Open Sandwich:-**

(i) **Grilled**:- Open hot sandwich are prepared with bread or toast laid side by side with the filling exposed on the surface. Sandwich is then heated throughout. It can be subdivide into grilled and meat combination. Examples are open faced grilled cheese, tuna melt and hot brown sliced turkey, bacon and tomato topped with cheese sauce and heated.

(ii) **Cold Sandwich**:- There are only two grouping closed and open.

Close Cold:- Slices of bread or 2 halves of a roll which have a spread applied an are filled with a cold fillings. This can again be subdivided into simple, combination and multi-decker.

(i) **Simple Closed Cold sandwich**: - have only one filling. Basic structure of this sandwich is consist of:-

1. **Bread**: - Should be selected to compliment the type of spread. Only the freshest bread is used because revival with heat is not possible.
2. **The spread / butter, mayonnaise,** mustard or other assist in protecting the bread from absorbing the moisture from the filling and becoming soggy. It also to the flavour of the sandwich so careful selection should be done so that it compliments the filling.
3. **The filling** may be cooked and sliced meat, shredded poultry cooked fish or shell fish shredded vegetables or vegetable spread.
4. **A secondary filling (Garnish)** may be used such as lettuce, tomato or pickle. Creativity of the secondary filling is vital to doing something out of the ordinary.

(ii) **Combination Closed Cold sandwich**:- They have more than one primary filling. Most common is BLT(bacon, lettuce,tomatoes) sandwich. The wetness of tomato and mayonnaise in combination with dry toast and become make an interesting contrast on the palate.

Some variations of cold closed sandwich are:

(A) **Ham and Cheese on rye bread:-** Normally accompanied by lettuce, tomato and pickle.

(B) **Turkey and pastrami on Pumpernickel**:- This is sliced or shaved turkey and Pastrami on pumpernickel bread garnished with Cole slow. Normally accompanied by mustard and pickle.

Note: Pastrami:- Mutton, beef or goat meat marinated with spices and garlic and then dry. It has a very strong taste, Turkish and Greek origin.

(C) **Submarine**:- This extremely popular sandwich is also called "Hero". It is a combination of cold cuts, vegetable or cheese on special bun. Mustard or mayonnaise is optional.

(D) **Peanut, butter and Jelly**:- Peanut, butter and grape jelly on white bread.

(iii) Multi Decker Cold Closed Sandwich:- More than two slices of bread or a roll split more than once. They also have several filling. Club sandwich is a classic example. It is composed of three pieces of toasted bread, bacon, lettuce, tomato and turkey filling. The toast is spread with mayonnaise and layered every with two levels of fillings. The sandwich is cut in quarters and normally toothpick with a fancy pick.

(iv) Open:- It is a single slice of bread with attractively arranged filling on top and garnish properly. They are larger version of canapés. Allows creative garnishing and dressing. There is also greater opportunity for flavour combination using layering affect.

(3) **Tea Sandwich**: - Do not fit exactly in other categories because they are fancy, light and delicate. They can be open, closed, rolled and cut and occasionally served hot use to impress guest with their beauty. Pastel green and pink coloured breads are often used and the sandwiches are always small. They arrange in assortment of trays and plates and passed on or serve buffet style.

TOOLS AND EQUIPMENTS NEEDED FOR SANDWICH PRODUCTION

- Refrigerators
- Reach in close by with all primary ingredients.
- Refrigerated tables with drawers – cold
- Version of Steam Table.
- Hand Tools
- Variety of Spatula
- Variety of spreader
- Knives
- Paring
- Ham Slicer
- French Knife
- Variety of Spoons

- Variety of Scoops
- Power Tools
- Meat Slicer
- Automatic Toaster
- Food Chopper and Grinder
- Mixing Bowls
- Measuring devices like scales, scoops etc.
- Cutting boars
- Holding container
- Plastic wrap
- Cooking equipment
- Grinder, Grill, Broiler
- Long table for assembly

LEARNING OUTCOME

Sandwiches are popular in today's culture. They are easy to make and eat practically anywhere and can be as fancy or as simple as we like. A sandwich is the most innovative and versatile food, which are acceptable on every occasion. Open or closed, single or decked, flat or rolled, sweet or savoury, hot or cold there are sandwiches with fillings and toppings. A sandwich is a food item typically made of two or more slices of leavened bread with one or more layers of meat, seafood, vegetables, cheese or jam or butter. The bread can be used as is, or it can be coated with butter, oil, or other optional or traditional condiments and sauces to enhance flavour and texture. The slices of bread are stacked neatly, resting on a crust of bread. The term sandwich come into use about 200 years ago close to the time of birth of United states. Their lived a notorious gambler in the court of King George III of England whose name was John Montagu (Germy Twitchier). Ribbon sandwiches are prepared using two coloured breads. Whole wheat loaf and white bread loaves are sliced lengthwise in ¼ inch strips. Whole wheat bread slice is tinted with chive cheese. White bread slice is spreaded with deviled ham or minced tuna fish salad mix. A club sandwich, also called a clubhouse sandwich, is a type of sandwich sometimes served as a double-decker. The double-decker version is usually cut into quarters, and often held together by toothpicks.

Spread and dips are not themselves finger foods however when served sliced with baguette (types of breads) croutons, crackers, bread stick, vegetables sticks, or slice potatoes chips, corn chips or other similar item.The difference between spread and dips in there consistency .Caviar should be served accomplied by butter toast,point using salted butter, lemon wedges,presented in the original tim set on crushed ice.

LESSON END ACTIVITY

- Try to make a different sandwitch according to the method given above.
- Collect the brand names of different types of bread available in the market.

QUESTIONS FOR DISCUSSION

1. Define sandwich and its types.
2. What is basic sandwich?
3. Explain in details the types of sandwich.
4. Explain the term spread and dips.
5. Explain caviar and in types.
6. Explain the categorization of caviar.
7. Explain the classification of sandwich.
8. Mention the some classification of cold sandwich.
9. Explain the term tea sandwich.
10. Mention the name of tools and equipment are required for sandwich production.

STATE TRUE AND FALSE

- A sandwich is a food item typically made of two or more slices of leavened.
- This sandwich is the foundation of the Seder and is named after him.
- Sandwiches may be made from every kind of bread.
- Loaf types of sandwiches are made from bread loafs.
- Pinwheel sandwiches are generally prepared using the top crust of the loaf.
- Ribbon sandwiches are prepared using two colored breads
- A club sandwich, also called a clubhouse sandwich.
- 'Dip' is a mixture that loose or soft enough to cling to an item dip into it.
- 'Spread' is more solid mixture which needs to spread with a knife.
- Caviar is the roe of bass fish

KEY TERMS

* Caviar	* Loaf
* Dips	* Pinwheel
* Leavened	* Spread

Unit 5
INTERNATIONAL CUISINE

Chapter 24

Asian Cuisine

After studying this chapter, the student must know

- Introduction of Asian cuisine
- Division Asian cuisine
- Common equipments
- Basic ingredients in Asian cuisine.

Asian cuisine styles can be broken down into several regional styles that have roots in the peoples and cultures of those regions. The major types can be roughly defined as East Asian with its origins in Imperial China and now encompassing modern Japan and the Korean peninsula; Southeast Asian which encompasses the areas once found in the Khmer Empire including Cambodia, Laos, Thailand and Vietnam as well as the countries of Brunei, Indonesia, Malaysia, Singapore, and the Philippines; South Asian derived the the states that once made up British India – Burma, India, Sri Lanka and Pakistan as well as several other countries in this region of the continent;Central Asian and Middle Eastern

DIVISIONS OF ASIAN CUISINE AREAS

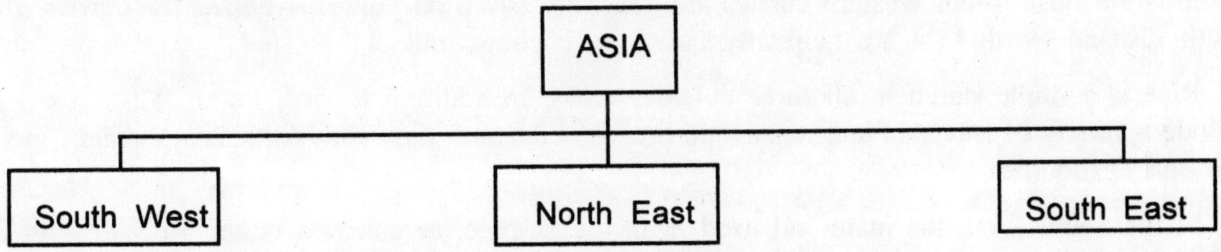

Fig 24.1 Divisions of Asian Cuisine

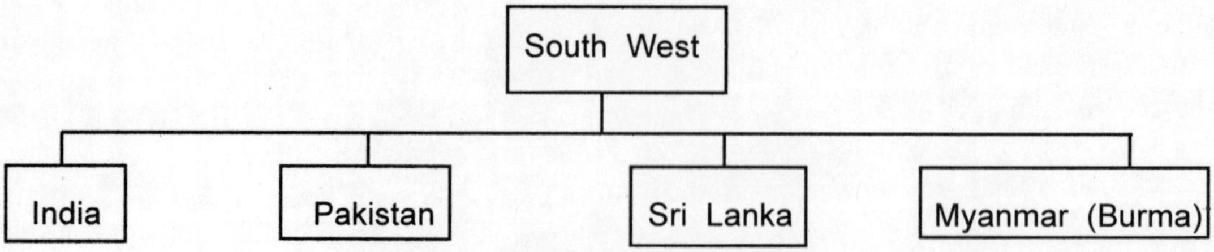

Fig 24.2 Divisions of South West Asian Cuisine

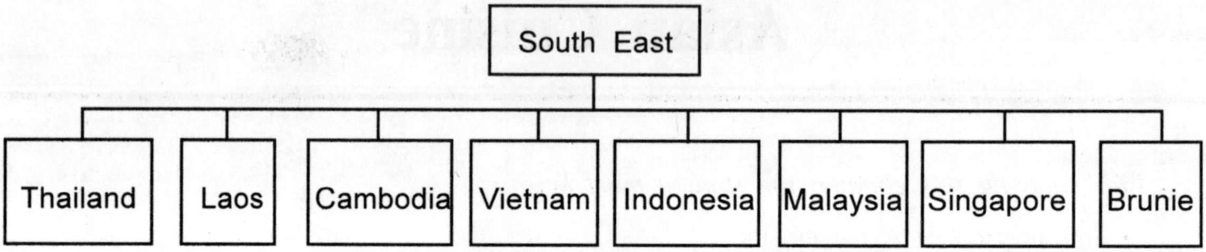

Fig 24.3 divisions of south east asian cuisine

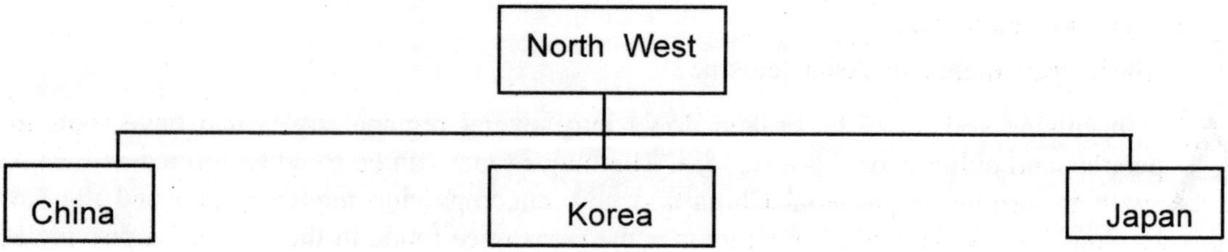

Fig 24.4 Divisions of north west asian cuisine

The South West - India, Pakistan, Sri Lanka, Burma (Myanmar).

The North East - China, Korea, Japan.

The South East - Thailand, Laos, Cambodia, Vietnam, Indonesia, Malaysia, Singapore, Brunei.

Curries are very important to the cuisines of the South East and SouthWest, less so in the cuisine of the North East. South Western curries are generally based on yogurt, whereas the curries of the South Eastand North East are generally based on coconut milk.

Rice is a staple starch in all three cuisines areas. In addition to rice, South Western cuisines include a variety of leavened and unleavend breads and South East and North East cuisines include rice and eggnoodles.

In the South West, the major oil used in frying is ghee, or clarified butter. In the South East and North East, the major oils are vegetable oils.

Garlic and ginger are used in all three cuisine areas, as are chilipeppers, although chilies are much more common in the South Westand South East. The North Eastern cuisines use soy sauce in nearly everything; the South East substitutes fish sauce; there is no equivalent in South Western cooking. In the South East, there are two additional flavourings that are not used in the other cuisines - galangal and lemon leaves

CUISINES OF THE SOUTH EAST

The original cuisine of the South East is probably the peasant cuisine of Thailand. Archaeology has recently discovered that the metal workingcultures of the central plain of Thailand date back to at least 3000 BC,easily in the same class as the ancient cultures of China and India. The peasant cuisine associated with these early metal workers spread east across the mountains into Laos, Cambodia and Vietnam, and south down the Malayan peninsula and the island arc of Indonesia.

This cuisine did not develop in isolation, of course. As it spread, it was influenced by ideas coming from the North East and South West, and influenced them in return. Most recently, of course, the cuisines of Europe have influenced the native ones. Vietnam, Laos and Cambodia were French colonies, Malaysia was a British Colony, Indonesia was a Dutch colony. Thailand was a rarity in that it successfully resisted European colonisation.

Rice is the staple grain of the North East and South East and is only slightly less important in the South West. It is the original crop that caused the conversion from hunter-gatherer to subsistence farmer inthis area; as such it spread across the region before regional cuisines began to evolve. Some Italians may object if you claim that Marco Polo brought spaghetti back from China, but there is little doubt tha tnoodles came to this region from China.

Curries are a very common across the region, but less common in Vietnam where the Chinese influence is strong. The concept probably came from India and spread east, but the people of the South East modified the original by substituting coconut milk for yogurt as the basis for the sauce.

The cooking utensil called the wok, and the stir fry technique using vegetable oils came to the area from the China.

Garlic and ginger are common all across Eurasia and probably arrived in the area at almost the same time as rice.

The arrival of chili peppers in the area can be placed with relative accuracy. Chili peppers, indeed all peppers, are native to the Americas and arrived in the region with European explorers/ exploiters. This means they could not have arrived before about 1520, and were widespread by 1600.

Fish sauce is probably a local invention, but the Romans had a similar concoction (liquamen), so it is possible the idea was imported. (Maybe that's where the lost legion ended up)

There are many spices used in the region; cinnamon comes from Sri Lanka, cardamom and cumin from India, coriander and star anise from China, cloves, nutmeg and mace are native.

Several herbs are common in the region, Thai basil, sweet basil and mint being the commonest. These herbs grow almost everywhere across tropical and subtropical Eurasia, so, while the idea of using them in cooking may have been imported, the actual herbs used are native varieties. This is especially true of Thai basil, with its purple stems and licorice flavour.

Citrus flavours are important to the region's cuisines, especially lime, which is native to the islands of Indonesia and Malaysia. Not just the juice and pulp are used, but also the zest and leaves.

Last, but certainly not least, are lemon grass and galangal. These two flavours are the flavours which make the cuisines of the region unique. They are undoubtedly of local origin, for they are used nowhere else in the world

EQUIPMENT

The Wok

The wok is the most important piece of cooking equipment in SouthEast Asia and China. If you plan to do much of this region's cooking you should invest in a good wok. A cast iron fry pan will serve in a pinch, but the rounded bottom of the wok provides a range of cooking temperatures in one pan, which can be important in stir frying.

There are many type of woks available - round- bottomed and flat-bottomed, on- handled and two-handled, mild steel, stainless steel, aluminum, and teflon coated. The most traditional is hand beaten of mild steel with a round bottom and two handles. Mild steel is preferred for its heat transfer properties; thin stamped stainless steel or aluminum just don't hold enough heat, and cast aluminum takes to long to heat upand cool down. The traditional round bottom is designed to sit in theround hole of a charcoal burner. In a modern kitchen equipped with agas stove, the round bottomed wok might fit the burners, depending onthe design of the stove. If the wok does not fit the burners, it may be placed on a wok ring. In an electic kitchen, a flat bottomed wok is best, both for stability and for heat transfer. A properly conditioned iron wok is at least as non-stick as any teflon coating ever made.

A new wok must be seasoned before use. Scrub it well with soap and water to remove any coating applied to protect it during shipping, rinse well, and dry. Place the wok over low heat, wipe lightly with vegetable oil and let stand on the heat for 10 minutes. Cool and wipe with paper towels to remove the dark film. Repeat the oiling, heating, cooling and wiping procedure until the paper towels come away clean. Once a wok has been seasoned, it should be cleaned with plain water only using a wok brush, never with soap or abrasive cleaners, then dried and oiled before storing. If the metal ever rusts, clean with steel wool or fine sand paper and re-season.

Wok Tools

The most important wok tool is the long handled shovel-shaved scoop used to stir fry. Other wok tools include; a ladle, used to transfer liquids to and from the wok; a strainer with a brass or steel basket to remove foods from hot oil; a strainer with a bamboo basket for removing foods from boiling water or stock; a bamboo whisk brush for cleaning; a rack which sits on the side of the wok for draining fried foods.

Steamers

Large dedicated steamers with multiple stacking are available instainless steel or aluminum, but more common are the stackable bamboo steamers. These are designed to be used in a wok over boiling water, and are often used as serving dishes.

Clay Pot

Clay pots - "hot pots", glazed on the inside but unglazed on the outside are used for baking or stewing. They are available in a range of sizes,and like woks, with either one handle or two.

Cleavers

The oriental cleaver is a very versatile instrument - it performs all the functions of the various knives of western kitchens. Light cleavers are used for general chopping, slicing and carving; heavier, thicker cleavers are used for chopping bones. A good set of kitchen knives can be substituted.

Rice Cooker

If you are cooking rice often, a rice cooker is worth the investment . Place rice and water in the cooker, plug it in and press the button. Perfect rice very time.

Hand Held Blender or Small Food Processor

Most South East Asian dishes require considerable fine chopping - a hand held blender with a mincer/chopper attachment or a small food processor will cut your preparation time in half.

BASIC INGREDIENTS IN ASIAN

Curry Pastes and Powders

Southeast Asian curries are normally based on curry pastes which are made from a variety of fresh and dried ingredients ground together in a mortar and pestle. This is the recommended process if you are cooking curries daily, but the pastes have a limited shelf life. If you are only cooking them from time to time it is more convenient to make up curry powders in advance and add the fresh ingredients at cooking time.

All the recipes given in thai menu are based on curry powders, recipes for which are given in the section on Sauces, Relishes and Spices for the appropriate country. I would recommend that you buy fresh whole spices and grind them yourself in a spice or coffee grinder rather than buy pre-ground spices. Stored in an air-tight container in a dry place, curry powders will keep for a couple of months before their flavours start to decline.

Chili Paste

The chili paste referred to in the recipes can be made at home by grinding fresh chilies in a mortar and pestle or food processor. A little salt and vinegar may be added to thin the mixture slightly. Alternately, you may buy a prepared chili paste, but be sure it contains only chilies (with a little salt and vinegar as above).

Obviously the colour of the paste will depend on the colour of the chilies used to make it. Use red chili paste in a red curry and green chili paste in a green curry if you can. If you can't, don't worries, the colour of the finished product may not live up to the name of the recipe, but the taste will be pretty much the same.

Coconut Milk

When coconut milk is specified in the recipe, use canned coconut milk with no dilution. When making curry, the first part of most recipes calls for you to put about 1/2 cup of coconut milk in a pan and heat it up. It is VERY important that you not shake the can first. Open the can and skim the top cream off and heat it until you see the oils starting to separate. Then add the curry paste/powder.

Tamarind Liquid

The Tamarind Liquid referred to in the recipes can be made as follows. Take 3 tablespoons of tamarind pulp, and soak in 1/2 cupwarm water for 10 minutes. Knead and rub with your fingers until the pulp dissolves. Strain the liquid to remove the seeds and fibers.

Tamarind liquid may also be made from concentrate by soaking 1tablespoon of concentrate in 1/2 cup warm water, but the concentrate tends to be very dark in colour, which can adversely affect the colour of the dish.

LEARNING OUTCOME

Asian cuisine styles can be broken down into several regional styles that have roots in the peoples and cultures of those regions. The major types can be roughly defined as East Asian with its origins in Imperial China and now encompassing modern Japan and the Korean peninsula; Southeast Asian which encompasses the areas once found in the Khmer Empire including Cambodia, Laos, Thailand and Viet Nam as well as the countries of Brunei, Indonesia, Malaysia, Singapore, and the Philippines; South Asian derived the states that once made up British India – Burma, India, Sri Lanka and Pakistan as well as several other countries in this region of the continent; Central Asian and Middle Eastern. The original cuisine of the South East is probably the peasant cuisine of Thailand. Archaeology has recently discovered that the metal working cultures of the central plain of Thailand date back to at least 3000 BC, easily in the same class as the ancient cultures of China and India. Curries are a very common across the region, but less common in Vietnam where the Chinese influence is strong. Garlic and ginger are common all across Eurasia and probably arrived in the area at almost the same time as rice. The wok is the most important piece of cooking equipment in SouthEast Asia and China. Large dedicated steamers with multiple stacking are available in stainless steel or aluminum, The oriental cleaver is a very versatile instrument - it performs all the functions of the various knives of western kitchens.

LESSON END ACTIVITY

- Collect the more information about asian cuisine .
- Collect as much as information regarding there ingredients .

QUESTIONS FOR DISCUSSION

1. Explain in detail about the Asian cuisine.
2. Explain in detail the classification of Asian cuisine.
3. Explain in detail about south west Asian cuisine.
4. Explain in detail about south east Asian cuisine.
5. Explain the common ingredients of Asian cuisine.

KEY TERMS

* Ingredients
* Cleavers
* Glazed
* Relishes
* Stackable
* Wok

Chapter 25
Chinese Cuisine

After studying this chapter, the student must know :

- Introduction
- Regional cooking
- Chinese cooking schools introduction and their specialty
- Chinese philosophy
- Chinese cooking method
- Chinese glossary

CHINESE CUISINE

Chinese Regional Cooking

In the mythology of ancient China, Han, the Chinese man, is distinguished from savages and barbarians by two features of his eating habit: he eats cereals and uses fire to process his food.

China is a vast country whose terrain, people, climate and natural resources vary greatly from region to region. Chinese cooking reflects this regionality with almost as many cooking styles as regions. Cooking methods vary, as does the use of spices, seasonings and sauces. The division of China by regional styles of cooking is based on historical evolution dating from the 12th Century. At that time the little town of Hangzhou, situated to the south of the mouth of the Yangtze River, was transformed into the capital after the court took refuge there as the result of pressure from the Mongols. It became a place for exchanges and intense mixing of peoples who had emigrated from the north, tradespeople from the west and the local inhabitants. Restaurants representing the tastes of the four horizons prospered and thus was born the concept of regional culinary style. Nowadays, the culinary division of China most often recognised distinguishes five great cooking styles. The northeastern style with Beijing and the Yellow River valley, stretching to the east up to the Shandong, the central style concentrating on Shanghai, western style, concentrated around

Szechuan but also including Ghuizou, Yunnan, Hunan and Hubei, the south eastern style from Canton and Guangdong (including TeCheow) and finally the Fujian (Fukien) style to the east.

In short, there are five predominate cooking schools:

- The Southeastern – Canton (Guangdong, TeCheow)
- Western – Szechuan (sometimes called Chungking)
- Northeastern – Peking (or Shantung)
- Central – Honan (and Shanghai) and
- East Coast – Fukien (Fujian)

Let's examine each of these regions a little closer:

South eastern – The Cantonese School

The seaport of Canton became the gateway to the West when Europe started trading with the Orient. The Cantonese readily absorbed these cosmopolitan influences, and being great travellers, soon emigrated to Europe and the Americas. They were the first to establish restaurants outside China and introduce the world to Chinese food. This is why the majority of restaurants in Australia, Europe and America are still Cantonese. Cantonese cooking is versatile and original, encouraged by the region's rich natural resources. When the Ming dynasty was overthrown in the 7th Century, many government officials migrated south from Peking to Kwangtung province, of which Canton is the capital. They also brought their chefs with them. These chefs, trained in classical Peking-style, assimilated other regional styles in their southward travels and once in Canton, took advantage of the area's rich produce to expand and enlarge their cuisine into what became known as Cantonese-style. This style is characterised by its ability to enhance the original taste of each ingredient and to blend natural flavours together. It uses very few seasonings (soy, ginger, wine) and specialises in the quick-cooking technique known as stir-frying, using chicken stock as a cooking medium. Cantonese cuisine is also noted for roast meats, poultry, steamed pork, lobster and fish dishes, fried rice and such delicacies as Bird's Nest Soup and Shark's Fin Soup.

North eastern – The Peking – Shantung School

Although the city of Peking and the province of Shantung are not geographically close, trade between them has always been active and back and forth migration continual. For centuries the two exchanged cultural ideas and chefs. Eventually their cooking styles became indistinguishable. Peking, however, being the site of the Imperial Palace and China's great intellectual and cultural centre, exerted a much stronger influence. Due to its wealth Peking attracted the country's best chefs who in turn brought cooking to its highest level. Peking was considered the gourmet capital of China until the 17th century and was well known for mammoth feasts and gargantuan banquets. (Some of the meals took three days to consume).

The Peking – Shantung school

The Peking – Shantung school is distinguished by light, elegant, mildly spiced rather than rich foods and the liberal use of garlic, green shallots, leeks and chives, soy sauce and vinegar. It is known also for the delicacy of Peking Duck and Chicken Velvet, soft-fried foods, the spring roll, delicious roasts, wine-cooked meats and a wonderful array of delicious dumplings. Most of Northern China, including the vast regions of Mongolia and Manchuria, are largely barren and sparsely populated. Its people are mainly nomadic, noted for their use of lamb and mutton with"balsamic" vinegar and for their chafing-dish cookery. The Mongolian Hot Pot is one of the more well-known dishes of this remote area.

Western – The School of Szechuan

The Szechuan Province is hot and humid, almost tropical. Consequently the food is highly spiced, peppery and somewhat oily. Szechuan's specialities include deep-fried chicken wrapped in paper, vegetables prepared in chicken fat, chicken and hot peppers and a variety of mushroom dishes. The use of dried chilli, Szechuan pepper, sesame seed oil and fermented bean curd paste produce the typical flavours for this school. It is interesting to note that although home cooking is hot and spicy, Szechuan banquet dishes are rather bland and quite light, due to a migration of Peking trained banquet chefs who brought such dishes with them for formal dining. The Northern influence is also obvious in Szechuan Duck, a variation on Peking Duck.

Central – The School of Honan

Honan province (the home of the Yellow River) is famous for its Yellow River carp and it is often referred to as the Kingdom of Fish and Rice. Tender vegetables, accompanied by freshwater fish and crustaceans are prepared with subtle flavours mainly using ginger and Shao Xing wine. It's noted also for its spiced concoctions, and rich seasonings. It is the only region where sweet and sour dishes are really appreciated.

East Coast – The School of Fukien

Fukien province on China's east coast is famous for seafood and for clear, light soups. These soups are noteworthy not only for their quality but also for their quantity. At most family meals at least two such soups are served. At banquets it is not unusual to encounter a quarter of all dishes as soups. Fukien is also noted for its subtle use of cooking wine, its soy sauce, egg rolls and suckling pig.

Chinese philosophy, yin and yang

In Chinese philosophy, yin and yang are the forces of nature, which should be balanced in order to attain harmony. They are seen as complementary rather than conflicting. Yin is seen as feminine, soft, dark and negative. Yin foods are said to nourish the body to help it conserve energy. Highly regarded *Yin* foods include Chinese yams, sweet potatoes and unpolished grains. *Yang* is masculine, hard, bright and positive. Yang foods stimulate the body to expand energy, and include ginger, garlic, chilli, tobacco and alcohol.

Chinese Cooking Methods

The art of Chinese cooking is not, contrary to popular belief, complicated and difficult. Most Chinese dishes do not require a complex processing and equipment in the kitchen as does one of China's most famous dishes, Peking duck. Simplicity is the key to Chinese cuisine as evidently shown in their various cooking methods. When you have the ingredients, seasonings and marinades ready, you can use one of the following methods to cook in Chinese.

Roasting - Roasting is not family cooking in China, since few Chinese kitchens have facilities for roasting. Only restaurants go much into roasts and Cantonese restaurants excel especially in these. In roasting, raw ingredients are marinated in seasonings before being roasted in an oven or barbecued over direct heat from charcoal fire, with the roast turning slowly round and round. Marinades is added inside and out from time to time so that the skin remains smooth and shiny, instead of rough and flaky, and the meat remains juicy instead of powdery. The Peking duck is one of China's most famous dishes cooked this way. Families can go to food shops to buy roast meat or poultry and eat it cold. But for the crisp juicy hot roast duck, one has to go to a restaurant.

Boiling - Strictly speaking, this means cooking food in boiling water (A liquid is boiling when the surface is continually agitated by large bubbles). Violent boiling should be avoided. It wastes fuel; it does not cook the food any faster, it tends to make the food break up and so spoils the appearance; the liquid is evaporated too quickly with the consequent danger of the food burning. There are one or two exceptions to this rule; for example, when one wants to drive off water quickly from syrup or a sauce to make it thicker, then violent boiling with the lid off hastens the process.

In Chinese cooking, there is very little big-fire boiling, as a complete process. Chinese would not consider eating boiled potatoes. After a thing is boiled, the natural question is - Now what of it? Quick plain boiling is often only a preparatory process for other ways of cooking - where the term parboil comes into place. There are some exceptions, such as plain boiled celery cabbage with salt and a little lard, or boiled yam, to eat with sugar. But celery cabbage and yam are such cook-proof things that they are good in any method prepared. It's not necessary to use continued big fire after water has started to boil, because water cannot be hotter than 100° C or 212°F.

Turn the fire to medium if you want but to make sure that it is at least hot in all parts, especially in a large tall boiling or steaming pot, the fire must be big enough for you to see the steam come out.

Shallow frying - shallow frying uses a small amount of oil in a frying pan or wok at a temperature lower than stir-frying. Ingredients are usually cut into slices or flat pieces, and are used as they are, slightly coated with batter or rubbed with seasonings. Fish is ideal for this cooking method. The presentation side of the food should be fried first as this side will have the better appearance because the oil is clean, then turned so that both sides are cooked and browned. Sauces, if called for, are then added. Food cooked this way is tender inside with some crispness outside. This method is quite similar to sautéing in the West.

Stewing is a time-honored moist cooking technique that transforms less tender cuts of meat unsuitable for quick-cooking methods into melt-in-your-mouth meats. Stewing allows the cook to assemble the dish, boil it and then let it simmer, with little or no attention for an hour or more. A stew usually has smaller pieces of food that may or may not be browned first, and calls for a large quantity of liquid (enough to cover the food). Many "crock-pot" dishes are essentially stewed. Stews can be frozen and their flavours mature as they stand, so they are even better a day or so after you cook them. Vary the flavour profile of the stew dish by experimenting with seasonings (wine, broth, beer and vegetable juices) and different herbs and spices. In the final step, the sauce is thickened either with cornstarch or reduced by simmering. Cuts ideal for stewing are shoulder and pork cubes. In China, stews are usually cooked in a clay pot over a charcoal fire. The stew is cooked for a very long time, producing meat almost jelly-like in tenderness.

Glossary

Abalone - A large marine snail and a delicacy in Chinese food called "Pao Yu" in Chinese, known as "awabi" in Japanese cuisine, as "loco" in South American, as "ormer" in the English Channel, as "muttonfish" in Australia and as "paua" in New Zealand. Abalone can be purchased fresh, canned, dried or salted. If purchased fresh, it should be alive and not fishy-smelling. Refrigerate fresh abalone as soon as possible and cook within a day of purchase (Fig. 25.1).

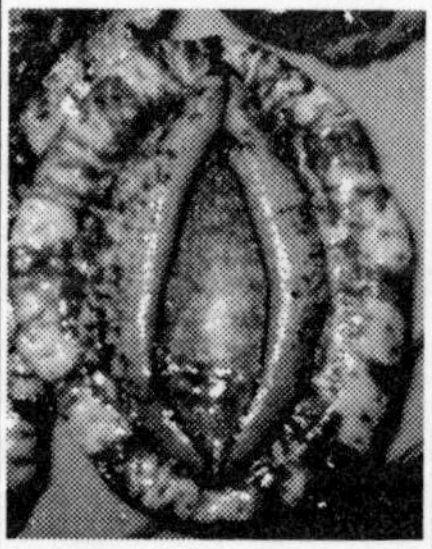

Fig 25.1 Abalone

Adzuki beans - A small reddish-brown bush bean cultivated in China and Japan. Extremely versatile, adzukis can be eaten fresh or dried, or ground into flour and used to make cakes. As the skin of the adzuki bean is quite thick, it requires long soaking and cooking time (Fig. 25.2).

Fig 25.2 Adzuki beans

Agaricus mushroom - Plump, dome-shaped mushrooms, ranging in size from small (button mushrooms) to big. The most widely cultivated and consumed mushroom, these common mushrooms have a mild and earthy flavour. Their colour can range from white to pale brown, and their caps should be firm and evenly colored (Fig. 25.3).

Fig 25.3 Agaricus mushroom

All purpose flour - Finely ground white wheat flour containing a moderate amount of protein; used for a wide variety of general baking and cooking.

Allspice - Named because it tastes like a blend of cinnamon, cloves and nutmeg. It is also known as Jamaican Pepper. Allspice is available whole or ground.

Almonds - Its varieties are classified as either sweet or bitter. Sweet varieties are edible and used in some Chinese stir fried dishes, though not very common. The bitter variety contains traces of toxic acid when raw and cannot be sold in the United States unless processed. Store them unopened in a cool, dry place. Raw unshelled almonds have a shelf life of six to

12 months, and shelled nuts will keep for three months. Once opened, put them in an airtight container and keep them in the refrigerator or freezer.

Asparagus -Succulent, thin stalks are popular throughout the world. Look for firm, bright-green (or pale-ivory) stalks with tight tips. Since asparagus starts losing flavour from the time it is cut, it's best cooked the same day it is purchased. Wash thoroughly and cut off all hard ends. Asparagus will keep, tightly wrapped in a plastic bag, up to four days in the refrigerator, or stored standing upright in a container with about an inch of water covered with a plastic bag. Asparagus is also available canned and frozen.

Cabbage -See Chinese Cabbage. Look for a cabbage with fresh, crisp leaves that are tightly packed and unblemished; the head should be heavy for its size. It may be refrigerated for up to a week. To dislodge insects from cabbage, soak it in salt water or vinegar water for about 15 minutes. Wash cabbage under running water after removal of the thicker and more fibrous outer leaves if it's free from worms. One pound cabbage yields 4 cups shredded or 2 cups cooked.

Capsicum - Family of peppers such as cherry, banana, bell, Tabasco, jalapeño, habañero, etc., which fall into two categories: chilies peppers and sweet/bell peppers.

Cashew - Sweet, buttery, kidney-shaped nuts that grow from the bottom of the tropical cashew apple. The shells are toxic and always removed before the nuts are marketed. They are sold blanched, plain or toasted and are eaten out of hand; a popular ingredient in many Chinese dishes. As with most nuts, cashews have a high fat content and should be refrigerated. Store them in a tightly sealed container to prevent them from absorbing food odors. They are cooked less frequently than other nuts because they become soft relatively quickly; it is thus important that they not be added to hot food until just before it is served.

Castor sugar -The standard sugar in Britain, equivalent to superfine sugar. It is more finely granulated and dissolves almost instantly. Granulated sugar can be substituted for castor sugar cup for cup.

Celery - Both the ribs and stalks of this vegetable are edible and can be used in many ways. The green Pascal variety is most often found in American markets. Look for thick, crisp stalks with vibrant, unwilted leaves. Wash celery thoroughly before using, and remove the coarse outer strings. Unused celery will keep in a tightly sealed plastic bag in the refrigerator for several weeks.

Cellophane Noodles (Fig. 25.4) - are thin, translucent threads made from mung beans. This Chinese noodle have little if any taste, but provide texture and a base for soup and stir fry dishes, absorbing the flavour of the foods they are cooked with and can also be deep fried. When deep-fried fried, they are crispy and used as a garnish. Before using, soak them briefly in hot water. Other names for cellophane

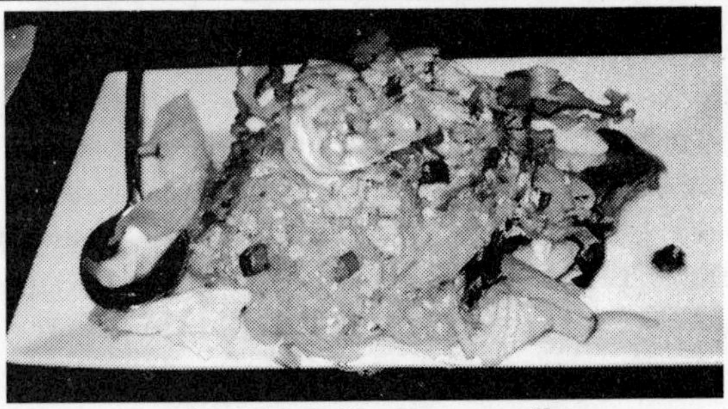

Fig 25.4 Cellephone noodles

noodles include bean threads, bean vermicelli/noodles, mung bean noodles, Chinese vermicelli, glass/transparent/slippery noodles.

Cheesecloth - Cotton gauze used in the kitchen for straining liquids and wrapping foods to make them easier to remove from vessels after cooking; available in fine o coarse weaves. Sometimes known as butter muslin in Britain.

Chicken Egg - Both brown and white eggs have the same nutritional value and it is a matter of personal taste which you choose to buy. These are the only eggs to be produced on a large commercial scale and are familiar standard by which other eggs are compared, the average weight being about 50g (2oz). For more about the roles of eggs in Chinese food.

Chicken stock - Is an important ingredient in most of the Chinese savory dishes. Alternatives are canned chicken consommé. Another to which we are more likely to resort, these days, is those very useful chicken cubes which are pretty generally available. A cube or part of one will make an acceptable stock. Another source of chicken stock is the giblets which can be bought at little cost.

Chow chow - A mustard-flavored mixed vegetable and pickle relish. The term was originally used to describe a condiment in Chinese cuisine made of orange peel and ginger in heavy syrup.

Chile bean paste/sauce - Sold in jars, this spicy paste is made from fermented soybeans, red chili peppers and garlic. Use this to add excitement to your favorite Chinese dish.

Chili Oil -Vegetable oil mixed with hot red chilies. The peppers are steeped in the oil to release their heat and flavour, while also giving the oil a reddish colour. This spicy oil is very popular in Chinese cooking, but should be used sparingly; best kept refrigerated.

Chili Pepper - or the hot pepper, is a fleshy berry containing numerous seeds in its inner cavity. Chile peppers are smaller and more pointed than sweet peppers and have a very sharp, almost fiery, flavour. Jalapeño, Serrano, poblano, cherry pepper, cayenne pepper, guero, habañero and japone are all in this family. Chili peppers are much more popular as a condiment than as a vegetable.

Chili powder - is a combination of various spices and dried hot peppers. It may contain black pepper, cumin, oregano, ,paprika, cloves, and garlic.

Chinese broccoli - Like Chinese cabbage and pak choy, Chinese broccoli or Gai lan (Cantonese) is one of the most sought after vegetables in Chinese market and said to be the best. Look nothing much like regular broccoli, it has long stems and big bluish green leaves. The stems and stalks should be blanched before stir frying as they are quite tough. Tips : Ask this in Cantonese (Gai lan) when ordering in the restaurant or you might be served with regular broccoli (Fig. 25.5).

Fig 25.5 Chinese broccoli

Chinese cabbage - As many as 33 varieties of Chinese cabbage have been identified in Asia, and the most common varieties in the West are celery cabbage or pe-tsai, pak-choi or "bok choy", and "choy sum" (Fig. 25.6).

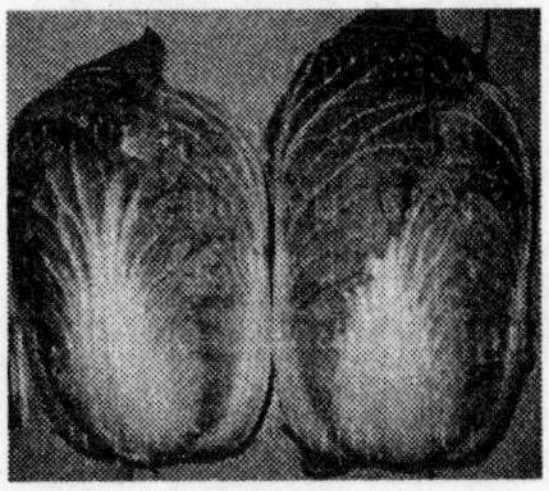

Fig 25.6 Chinese cabbage

Celery cabbage or "pe-tsai" - is native to China, where it has been consumed for thousands of years. Also known as Chinese celery cabbage or Napa Cabbage, it is eaten on a daily basis in northern China. Celery cabbage resembles a Romaine lettuce. The leaves are crisp and delicate with a faint cabbage taste. Use the crinkly inner leaves for salads and the outer leaves for stir-fry. Also called Chinese cabbage (Fig. 25.7).

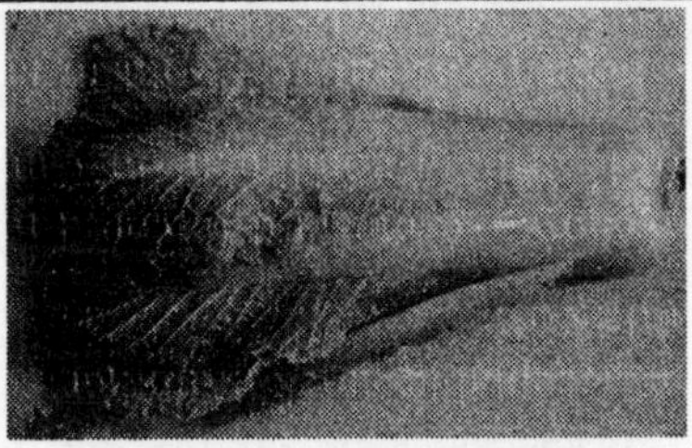

Fig 25.7 Celery cabbage

Pak-choi or bok choy also known as "Chinese white cabbage": Chinese chard, or Chinese mustard, it is a leafy vegetable similar to Swiss chard and celery. The leaves are dark green and its whitish ribs are crisp and thus frequently is used to give stir-fry dishes a crunchy texture. There are many varieties of pak-choi, some of which are short-ribbed while others have long ribs. A popular variety is baby pak choy or " siu pak choi ", a smaller version of pak choi. Pak-choi is available year-round in most supermarkets. Select bunches with firm, white stalks topped with crisp, green leaves and refrigerate in an airtight container for no more than three to four days.

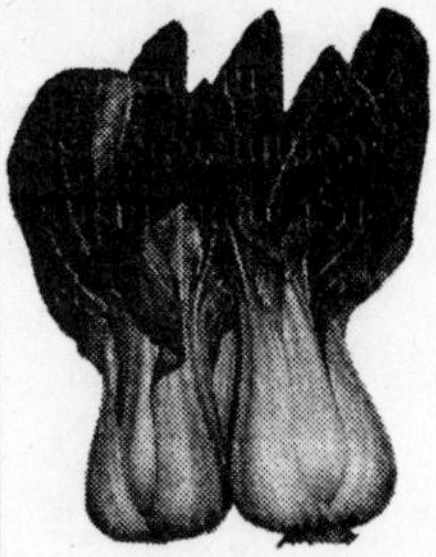

Fig 25.8 Bok choy

Another variety is called tsai shim, "choy sum", "bok choy sum" (Fig. 25.8) or "Chinese flowering cabbage". The light green leaves, pale green stems and clusters of tiny yellow flowers on the tips of the inner shoots are edible.

Chinese chives - Also known as garlic chives, the Chinese chive has been cultivated in China for over 2,000 years and is used extensively in Chinese cooking. Unlike regular chives, these have flat leaves and a distinct garlicky flavour. Chinese chives can be substituted by garlic shoots OR chives (not as pungent as Chinese chives) OR flower-ing chives (Fig 25.9).

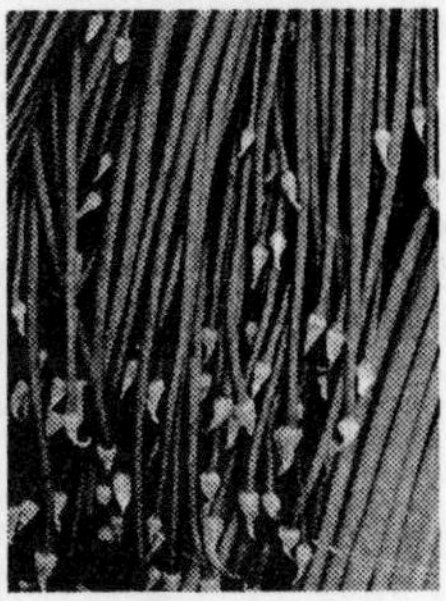

Fig 25.9 Chives

Chinese dried sausage - Made of pork, these sweet-salty tasting sausauge that look like pepperoni are obtainable in Chinese and other oriental supplies. Used in thin slices for cooking. No soaking is required. Called " lap cheong " in Cantonese (Fig. 25.10).

Fig 25.10 Chinese dry sausages

Chinese Egg Noodles - The most popular type of Asian noodle, also known as egg flour noodles made from wheat flour, water and eggs, these vary considerably, but typically they are 1/8in. (3 mm) wide and pale yellow in colour. There are endless delicious soup and stir fry recipes Chinese egg noodles i.e. Shrimp 'Chow Mein' is one particularly tasty variation where 'Chow' is fried and 'Mein' or 'Mien' is noodles in Chinese. Unlike in China, dried egg noodles are used instead of the soft fresh type in the preparation of chow mein in the west. After being cooked in boiling water, they are fried to give them their characteristic crispness. Egg noodles can be found fresh in some Asian supermarkets, and are readily available dried.

Fig 25.11 Chinese long bean

Chinese long bean (Fig. 25.11) - Also known as ward-long bean, long bean or asparagus bean. Usually half a yard long, the Chinese like to cut them into smaller pieces and add them to their stir-fried dishes.

Chinese Mushroom (Fig. 25.12) - Also called Shiitake mushroom, Chinese black mushroom and forest mushroom (not to be confused with European dried mush¬rooms), these are the most widely used mushrooms in Chinese cooking and are grown chiefly in China and Japan. Their fleshy caps are dense, and their stems are tough yet can be used for flavoring before being discarded. Shiitakes can easily replace other mushrooms in recipes. They have a pleasant flavour and absorb the taste of other ingredients. Chinese mushrooms are often sold dried and will keep for up to a year. Rinse well, then soak in hot water for at least 30 minutes. The soaking water can be strained and used to add flavour to a stock. Cut off the stem before using.

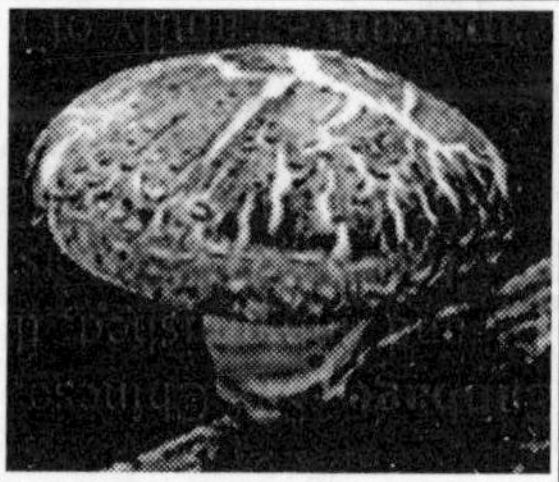

Fig 25.12 Chinese mushroom

Chinese mustard plant - can be obtained in cans from any emporium or supermarkets stocking Chinese and other oriental foods.

Chinese pickled cabbage - or mustard green is available in at least four different varieties, each having a special regional connection.

- Pickled mustard greens come from the north and have a sour flavour. After opening, remove from the can and store in a clean container in the refrigerator. Rinse before using. This cabbage will only keep for two weeks after opening.
- Red-in-snow, often called 'snow cabbage' or sometimes 'pickled cabbage' on the cans, is always salted. It is an Eastern specialty. Store after opening, in a clean container in the refrigerator, and always soak for five minutes in cold water before using to remove the salt.
- Tianjin pickled vegetables comes from the north of China and has a slightly sweet flavour, sometimes with garlic added. It is often cooked with a duck soup.

- Preserved mustard greens are a Hakka specialty with a smoky flavour and a very dark green colour. All these varieties of preserved greens can be stir fried with pork or finely chopped and mixed with minced pork, which is then shaped into balls and steamed.

Chinese spinach - Also known as Amarand, is a pseudo-cereal grain. This grain exceeds all common grains as a source of protein and, as such, is expected to experience wider availability. The leaves have a slightly sweet flavour and are often used like spinach. Amaranth is also called Chinese Spinach and "een choy".

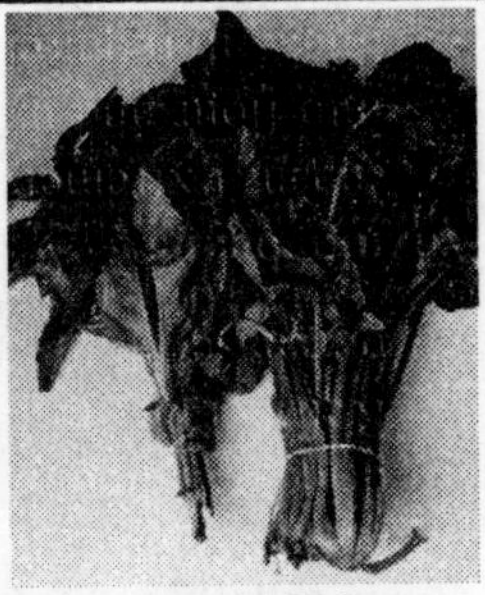

Fig 25.13 Chinese spinach

Chinese turnip – see Daikon

Chinese vermicelli - see Cellophane Noodles

Chives - Aromatic plants native to Asia, chives are related to the garlic, onion, and leek. Chives have slender, bright green, hollow stems with a very mild and delicate onion aroma. They serve to flavour and garnish everything from vegetables to soups, omelets, tofu, fish, seafood, meat and poultry. Fresh chives should be added near the end of cooking in retain flavour; however, it is best not to cook them at all and to add them just before serving. When buying chives, choose fresh, evenly green leaves that show no signs of yellowing, softness, or drying out. Chives may be kept in the refrigerator for a few days. When chopping chives, it is very easy to bruise them, which will release their flavour prematurely and give them a wilted appearance. To cut them without bruising, try slicing them with the tip of a very sharp knife. You can also try cutting them using a pair of kitchen shears.

Choy sum - see Chinese cabbage

Cilantro - See Coriander

Cinnamon - Cinnamon is the inner bark of a tropical evergreen tree. The bark is harvested during the rainy season when it is more pliable. When dried, the bark curls naturally and is sold as cinnamon sticks or is ground into powder.

Cloves - The dried, aromatic flower buds of an evergreen tree characterized by their pungent, long-lasting taste, as well as by their resemblance to small nails have been used in China for more than 2,000 years. Cloves are normally used whole, but the central "head" of the bud can also be ground into powder. They are used in sweet and savory dishes, spiced wines and liqueurs. Chinese courtiers sweetened their breath by sucking on cloves when addressing the emperor just like we use mints today. It is best to buy whole cloves, as ground cloves lose their flavour quickly and cannot be kept for as long. A good clove floats vertically in the water. It is stale if it sinks or floats horizontally. The famous Chinese five-spice has cloves in, besides anise-pepper, star anise, cassia, and fennel seed.

Coconut milk - A liquid made by combining grated fresh coconut meat and an equal amount of hot water. The mixture is simmered until foamy and then strained, extracting as much of the liquid as possible from the coconut meat..

Coriander - This aromatic herb from the parsley family is also called Chinese parsley or cilantro, is often used in Chinese dishes. It is tendered and and has richer flavour than American parsley. It has a distinctive, almost medicinal flavour and is used in fillings and as a garnish for soups and fish dishes. Some people, including Chinese, have to learn to like it but it's worth learning. Therefore, use it with discretion. A gracious host would ask if everybody like "coriander" before putting it in. When buying, choose fresh coriander that is firm, crisp, and green. Avoid yellow or wilted leaves. Briefly wash fresh coriander at the last minute, to preserve its flavour.

Corn flour - Corn flour is finely ground cornmeal obtained from kernels from which the germ has been removed in order to improve the storage life of the flour. Corn flour is used for breading and in combination with other flours in baked goods. Be aware that in British recipes the term "corn flour" means cornstarch, and the two cannot be substituted for each other.

Corn Oil (Fig. 25.14) - An odorless, almost tasteless oil derived from the endosperm of corn kernels; very good for deep-frying due to its high smoke point.

Fig 25.14 Corn oil

Cornstarch - fine white powder obtained by extracting the starch from the endosperm of the corn kernel. This fine white powder is added to a marinade, to give the ingredients a smooth texture and allows the seasonings to adhere to the ingredients. When used for thickening, cornstarch is first dissolved in cold liquid and then added to hot food during the last stages of cooking. It must be cooked and stirred until the sauce thickens. Cornstarch appears in most of the savory Chinese dishes. It is given in rather meager amounts because a thick sauce could spoil the dish. But if anyone prefers a thicker sauce, it is very easy to achieve. Simply increase the quantity of cornstarch given in the recipes.

Corn syrup (Fig. 25.15) - A thick, sweet syrup available in light or dark varieties. Corn syrup can be used as a less sweet replacement for table sugar.

Fig 25.15 Corn syrup

Crab - A marine crustacean that is highly prized throughout the world; its flavour and texture are considered by some to be the equal of lobster. Crabs should always be purchased alive. When buying whole crabs, whether alive or cooked, choose those that are heavy for their size and have a sweet fresh smell with no hint of ammonia. Crab meat may also be purchased canned.

Cucumber - A gourd and melon family, cucumbers are long and cylindrical in shape, and range in length from 3 inches to 2 feet. China is one of the largest producers of cucumbers in the world. Select cucumbers that are firm and evenly shaped. Medium-size cucumbers are preferable to overly large specimens, which tend to be bitter and bland tasting and contain numerous hard seeds. They are best when used immediately but will keep in the refrigerator for up to a week if wrapped tightly in plastic.

Cumin - An aromatic seed, either whole or powdered, used to flavour sausages, chutneys and a variety of Indian, Asian and Latin American dishes. This spice is used occasionally in northern Chinese cooking.

Curry Powder - A powder made by grinding and blending various herbs and spices, including cardamom, cinnamon, cumin, cloves, fenugreek, red peppers, nutmeg and mace.

Daikon (Fig. 25.16) - Also known as Chinese white radish or "lo bak". A large Asian radish with a sharp but somewhat sweet taste, daikon is a white-fleshed variety of radish that was brought to China around 500 B.C. Also known as Oriental radish, it is held in high esteem in Asia, where it is prepared in a wide variety of ways. Cooked daikon is used like the turnip; it is often added to soups and stews and is delicious in a stir-fry with other vegetables. The seeds, which are sprouted, have a hot flavour that is slightly reminiscent of watercress. The sprouts are often added to soups, or used to season tofu and fish. Add them at the last minute to ensure maximum crispness and flavour. The variety most commonly available in Western markets is shaped like a large carrot and is usually about 1 foot long. Look for daikons that are firm with smooth skin. They will keep for up to a week refrigerated in a plastic bag.

Fig 25.16 Daikon

Doufu - See Tofu

Dragon's eyes (Fig. 25.17) - see Longan

Fig 25.17 Dragons eyes

Dried chestnuts (Fig. 25.18) - Dried chestnuts look like small, wizened peeled chestnuts. Soak in cold water for 24 hours, then simmer in fresh water for 20 minutes.

Dried Hot Chili Peppers - Used in stir fry to flavour the oil for dishes like Kung Pao Chicken. Many varieties of dried hot chili peppers can be found in Asian groceries and supermarkets, and their size and degree of spiciness differ. You may have to experiment with the kind and amount to find what suits your taste. They are used mainly in Szechuan dishes.

Fig 25.18 Dried chestnuts

Dried mushrooms - see Chinese dried mushroom

Dried Shredded Seaweed - "Hai Dai Si" Before using, rinse and soak in water for 1 hour. Change water several times during soaking. When it has expanded and become soft, it is ready for use.

Dried shrimps - These small sun dried shellfish are used to give that concentrated shrimp flavour to dishes and also used in the filling of dumplings. Follow recipes' instruction, you might and might not need to soak them in hot water for 15 minutes before use. The water itself is also used as stock. When buying, choose the thick ones devoid of mold. Keep them in refrigerator..

Dried squid - Considered a delicacy to the Chinese, dried squid is produced after removal of the internal organs and sun dried. It has a strong smell and are used to add a very distinctive flavour to dishes and soups. For cooking, you need to soak the dried squid in fresh water over night to soften it. Some add 1/2 tsp bicarbonate of soda in the water so that the squid will expand more.

Dried Tangerine Peel - These sun dried peels are used to flavour master sauces and give orangey flavour to dishes. To dry your own, place tangerine peels on a flat baking pan in a slow oven (200° F) until dry.

Duck - Any of many species of wild or domestic web-footed birds that live in or near water. The Chinese are credited with being the first to raise ducks for food. Relative to chicken, duck is more commonly used in China tha n in the West, probably because of the greater variety of ways of preparing it. Ducks are slow-boiled, red-cooked, or roasted, but very rarely stir-fried

Duck Egg - These eggs are oilier-tasting than chickens' eggs and can acquire a harmful bacteria as they are usually laid in a dirty spot Great care should be taken with duck eggs. They must always be thoroughly cooked and should never be eaten uncooked nor should they be used for lightly cooked dishes such as poached eggs, scrambled egg, pancakes, etc. The Chinese usually eat salted duck as an accompaniment with congee.

Eel - A fish with a snakelike shape, eels generally have firm, fatty flesh and are gray, olive or black in colour. Recipes : Stewed Eel with Garlic and Stir Fried Eel with Celery

Egg Flour Noodles - See Chinese Egg Noodles

Eggplant - Also known as "aubergine" is a berry that is consumed like a vegetable and has been cultivated in China since around 500 B.C. The Chinese eggplant is whitish, both inside and outside. It is 6 to 8 inches long and shaped rather like a cucumber. You will find this vegetable all year round at Chinese grocery stores, but you can also substitute the common purple-skinned variety, for they are similar in taste and texture. There are several kinds of purple eggplants: the large American variety, and the very small ones native to the Mediterranean region and to Japan. These small ones are frequently more tasty and tender than the larger vegetable. Sometimes, eggplants, no matter what variety you are using, have a bit of harsh taste. Soaking them in water before using will remove this. The most common variety both in North America and in Europe is deep purple and pear-shaped. The skin is edible, although in certain varieties it can be bitter. The yellowish white flesh is spongy and contains small brownish edible seeds. Small and young specimens of eggplant contain fewer seeds and their skin is tenderer and less bitter so there is no need to peel them, but older ones should be peeled before preparing. When buying, look for firm, smooth skin with no blemishes. They can be kept in the refrigerator for a slightly longer period. Only cut the eggplant right before throwing into the wok as the flesh discolors quickly. One pound of eggplant equals 4 cups chopped eggplant. Recipes - Red-cooked Eggplant and Fried Eggplant

Egg roll wrappers - Eggroll wrappers or eggroll skins are made from wheat flour, egg yolk and salt. The popular appetiser deep fried eggrolls use these. Thicker than spring roll wrappers or rice paper.

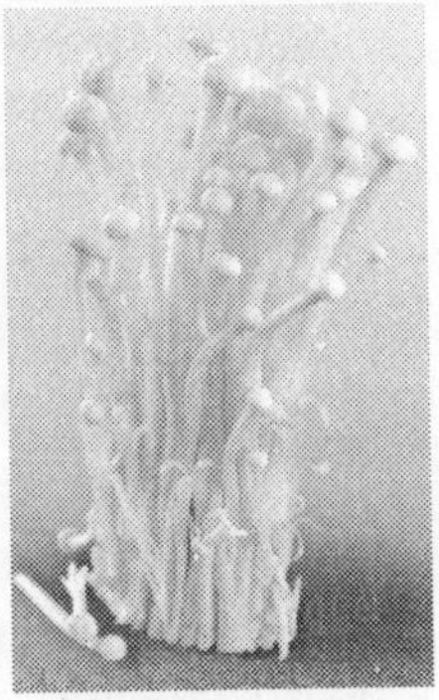

Fig 25.19 Enoki mushroom

Enoki mushrooms - Also called golden needles mushroom are small white mushrooms that grow in clumps with long, thin stems topped with a tiny white cap and a mild, almost fruity flavour. They have a crisp, crunchy texture when fresh, but tend to become tough when heated; also known as velvet stem/shank, snow puff and golden mushrooms. The enoki mushroom is highly esteemed in Asia and figures prominently in various Chinese dishes.

Fermented beancurd - Or beancurd cheese - made by fermenting bean curd cubes in rice wine, salt, sesame oil or chili. The taste is very unique, strong, salty and appetizing one have to learn to like it. Fermented beancurd is ideal as an accompaniment with congee and used in cooking some dishes. Usually comes in glass jars, keep in the refrigerator and it will last up to two years. Available in white and red (spicy) varieties.

Fermented black beans - see Black beans, fermented

Fresh rice noodles - Made from a thin dough of rice flour. These white noodles need only to be rinsed in hot water to loosen and separate and then drained. They come in thick or thin varieties but broad flat, or in a sheet that can be cut. Cantonese = "Hor fun"

Five-spice powder - A popular ancient spice used in Chinese cuisine for a variety of savory dishes e.g. stir fried meats or red-cooked dishes. It is a blend of spices consisting of ground star anise, cloves, cinnamon, fennel seeds and Szechuan peppercorns. Like curry powder, the combination of spices can vary according to the manufacturer, however star anise is usually the flavour that stands out. Store in an airtight container. If five-spice powder is not obtainable, substitute cloves or allspice.

Fish maw - Plays the role of a texture ingredient like the sea cucumber in Chinese food, fish maw is actually the air bladder of large fish, the function of which is to regulate water and oxygen flow so that the fish can ascend or descend in the water. The price of fish maw is far from cheap and it's one of the luxury ingredients in Chinese cuisine.

Gailan - see Chinese broccoli

Garlic - A member of the onion family, garlic's pungent flavour and aroma is an essential ingredient in Szechuan and northern-style cooking. When buying, look for plump, round heads that are free from sprouts. Once peeled, the cloves can be minced, chopped, crushed under the flat of a knife. The more finely the garlic is chopped or smashed, the stronger its flavour. Garlic can be found in powder, chopped, and paste form. While these preparations are practical, it is best to use fresh garlic for maximum flavour. Garlic should be stored in a dry and cool place and not refrigerated.

Ginger root - Knobbly and light brown, ginger root is u sed widely in Chinese food for its sharp, peppery, spicy, slightly sweet flavour and is especially good with fish as a "de-fisher". Ginger, when used in cooking is sliced into 1/16 inch slices. The slices are usually not eaten. When used for dipping together with vinegar, it is in fine shreds or fine dots and as much of it as will stick to the dipping piece will be eaten. Fresh ginger is peeled before using. The younger, less pungent ginger is best used in stir fried or steamed dishes while the harsher peppery mature ginger is good for braised dishes

Ginger sherry - This is made in the kitchen. Cut 1-2 oz. fresh ginger into thin strips. Turn them into a bottle and cover with a warm brown sherry. Leave to infuse, strain and use as directed. For 2 oz. fresh ginger, ½ bottle sherry will be the right amount to use.

Ginkgo - A nut from the center of the inedible fruit of the maidenhair tree. This nut turns bright green when cooked and has a delicately sweet flavour.

Fig 25.20 Ginkgo

Glass Noodles - see Cellophane Noodles

Golden Needle - see Tiger lily buds

Golden Needle Mushroom - see Enoki mushroom

Grass Mushroom - **see** Straw mushroom

Green onion - see Scallion

Ham - Ham is cured leg of pork. You can buy whole or half hams. Most hams offered in supermarkets are fully cooked but read the label to be sure

Hoi sin sauce - A sweet, smooth, brownish-red Chinese barbecue sauce (not to be confused with western or American barbecue sauce), and usually containing soya beans, garlic, chilies and other spices that are constantly used in Egg rolls, dumplings and barbecued pork (Cha Siu). It also makes a terrific barbecue sauce for chicken or beef. Best known as the sauce served with Peking Duck, also known as Peking sauce, it is sold in both cans and bottles (jar)-if you use it only rarely, it is better to buy a bottle, which will keep better. If you are using canned, remove any leftover sauce and store it in a screw-top container in the refrigerator. It will keep for up to six months. It can be obtained from Chinese or oriental provision stores and Asian markets.

Hair seaweed - Also known as black moss or black hair, these fine threads of black dried vegetable resemble hair and is tasteless. Slippery after being cooked, it is a traditional ingredient used in some vegetarian Buddhist dishes, soups and as garnish. Called "Fat Choy" in Cantonese, although of different Chinese character but sounds very much like "Good Fortune" and thus it is a must for Chinese homes to serve a dish that employs "Fat Choy" during Chinese New Year. Soak the hair seaweed briefly in warm water and rinse before use. Hair seaweed can be found in Asian supermarkets and Chinese markets.

Hot Bean Sauce - This sauce is a combination of hot chili sauce and brown bean sauce. It is used in spicy Szechuan and Hunan dishes.

Hot Chili Oil - Used abundantly in many regions in China, this is vegetable oil in which dried fiery hot chili peppers and other spices have been fried. When the oil becomes very spicy, the spices are removed and the oil transferred to an airtight jar. The hot oil is used as a condiment at the table or stirred into a dish during the final stages of cooking and is good in stir-fries, noodles and dumplings.

Hot Chili Sauce - This fiery sauce is made from crushed dried hot chilies, sweet red pepper. and soy sauce. If you like Szechuan or Hunan food, this sauce is essential. It is available in jars or you can make your own.

Hot Mustard Powder - Hot mustard powder is ground mustard seeds. It makes a very spicy condiment when combined with equal amounts of water and stirred until smooth. Serve it with egg rolls or dumplings or add it to salad dressing.

Hundred-year Egg - An egg that has been preserved with a coating of lime, ashes and salt before being buried for 100 days. The lime has a petrifying effect, making the egg look like it has been buried for at least a century. The black outer shell is removed to expose an amber-colored white and dark golden yolk. The egg has a pungent cheese-like flavour. Chicken eggs are most often used, though duck and goose eggs can be substituted. Hundred-year eggs can be found in Chinese markets and will keep at room temperature (under 70ºF) for up to two weeks or can be refrigerated up to a month; usually eaten uncooked, for breakfast or as an appetizer. Soy sauce or minced ginger makes a good accompaniment. Also called century egg, thousand-year egg and Ming Dynasty egg.

Fig 25.21 The 100 years eggs

Jellyfish - Jellyfish are salted and flaccid to the tough. Strictly speaking they are preserved, not dried. The best kind is amber in colour, large thick and firm pieces. It doesn't have any special taste of its own but its gelatinous texture is highly enjoyable. Usually used in salad and indispensable in assorted cold starters.

Kidney beans - The mature seeds of green beans; large, kidney-shaped beans with a robust, full-bodied flavour and soft texture. They come in dark reddish-brown, brown, black and white varieties and are usually only available dried or canned.

Kumquat - A very small Asian citrus fruit; oval to round in shape, with a soft bright orange rind and slightly tart orange flesh. The entire fruit can be eaten fresh or used for preserves. Select bright orange fruit with no greenish cast, and store in the refrigerator. Canned kumquats are also available, usually packed in sweet, heavy syrup.

Fig 25.22 Kumquat

Lard - For Chinese cooking, lard had better be made from leaf lard at the market. It is much better than ready lard in boxes. You cut it into two inch pieces and heat them in a dry pan. When all melted, press on the pieces gently to squeeze out the liquid. The 'leafing' then shrinks into fried pieces and becomes lard leavings. They are good to eat when hot and crisp, and usable to cook with stir fries dishes and particularly yummy with vegetables. When the leavings are brown, the lard is done. Pour into a heat-resisting container and let cool. Scoop as needed..

Leeks - Leeks have a subtle and delicate flavour that is milder and sweeter than that of onions. The white part grows underground and is formed of sheathed cylindrical leaves; it is the more tender part of this vegetable and that which is the most appreciated and most commonly used. The white adds a subtle touch to various dishes without masking other flavours. Select those with crisp, brightly colored leaves and an unblemished bulb. Avoid any with withered or discolored leaves. Leeks can be refrigerated in a plastic bag up to five days. Before using, trim roots and green tops and split the leeks from top to bottom and wash thoroughly to remove the earth and sand trapped between the leaf layers.

Lettuce - There are three common varieties of lettuce found in the supermarket : crisphead, which has a tight solid head ; cos or romaine, which has elongated, coarse leaves; and butteredheads or cabbage, which has loose, coarse leaves. Look for lettuce with a bright colour and no bruising or wilting. Leave those that are browning along the tips of the leaves or excessively pale. Rinse and thoroughly dry. Tear the leaves instead of cutting them to avoid bruising. Lettuce will keep in the refrigerator in plastic for two or three days, but is best when used immediately after purchase.

Linguine - Long, narrow, flat pasta noodles. The name means "little tongues."

Litchi, lychees - The litchi has been cultivated in China for thousands of years, where its sweet-tart flavour accents duck and pork dishes. This small fruit starts out rose colored, but develops a brown, rough, brittle skin as it matures. The translucent jelly-like flesh surrounds a single inedible seed. Fresh litchis are available in Asian markets and in some supermarkets during the summer months. Litchis are often called for in Chinese recipes, Chinese food recipe, especially for sauces.

Lobster - It is considered best to purchased lobsters while they are still alive; their large claws should be secured with strong rubber bands to allow safe handling. A live lobster should be fresh, heavy for its size, and still display much movement; the shell should be dark red to black. Live lobsters should be prepared immediately; however you can keep a live lobster in the refrigerator rolled loosely in damp newspaper and enclosed in a paper bag pierced with air holes in the vegetable compartment for no more than two days. Cooked lobsters are also available. You can test the freshness of cooked specimens by uncurling the tail; if it springs back into the curled position, the lobster was fresh when cooked. Avoid dead uncooked lobsters, as the meat spoils very quickly. Fresh cooked meat is sometimes available; canned and frozen meat is best used in seafood salads.

Longan - Also known as "Dragon's Eye", it is a small, round fruit native to southeast Asia; similar to the litchi with a subtler sweet flavour. Longans have a pink, red or yellow skin covering soft white pulp surrounding a large black seed. They can be peeled and eaten as a snack, or used in Asian dishes and desserts. Fresh longans are sometimes available in Asian markets in July and August and will keep refrigerated in a plastic bag for up to three weeks. Dried and canned longans are available throughout the year

Loquat - A small pear-shaped fruit native to China; has yellowish-orange skin and juicy flesh. Loquats are most often found in preserves and jellies since they quickly lose quality once picked

Lotus - A water lily, is the most versatile plant in China. The stem/root is sweet and can be eaten as fruit, sliced and stir fried, or stuffed with glutinous rice in its flue-shaped holes and steamed as dessert. Its leaf is a fine wrapper of food before steaming. When fresh, it is used to give a delicate scent to congee or steamed meat. Its flower is both majestic and fragrant. Its seeds, when young are juicy as fruit, whether eaten raw or boiled with sugar are commonly used in Chinese desserts and pastry fillings

Lotus leaves - Used to wrap around food (rice and fillings) and then steamed. These leaves of the water lily will impart a pleasant tea-like flavour to the food. Served bundled in the leaves and unwrapped only when to be eaten.

Lotus seeds or nuts - Lotus seeds or nuts are mainly available in shops specializing in Chinese foods. They can be bought loose as well as prepared, that is, shelled, halved and with the center germ removed. They are also available in sweet syrup or as paste. The lotus seed is popular made into sweet soups, rice desserts and snacks. Its use is traditionally associated with festivals. Cooked and mashed lotus seeds paste is used as mooncake filling. Require soaking for 24 hours, during which their size will double.

Master Sauce - This spicy concentrated sauce or marinade is known as Lu in Chinese. There are two types of master sauce: one is made with spices, rice wine, sugar and soy sauce and is called Brown Master Sauce; the other is made with the same ingredients except for the soy sauce, for which salt is substituted, and is called White Master Sauce. Different kinds of meats or fowl can be cooked simply by immersing in either a Brown or White Master Sauce and simmering until done. Food prepared this way is always to be cooked whole or in large chunks and is served cut up and at room temperature. Food cooked in a Brown Master Sauce is lighter in flavour than that which is red cooked (stewed in soy sauce).

Molasses - A thick, dark syrup that is a byproduct of refining sugar, with a distinctive, slightly bitter flavour; much less sweet than honey but more nutritious than sugar. Two types of molasses are available - light and dark. The darker the molasses, the less sugar it contains

Monosodium Glutamate (MSG) - A chemical food enhancer in the form of white granules derived from vegetable sources and that resembles coarse salt. The Chinese have used it for centuries to deepen and bring out the natural flavours of foods. Used in a very small amount, it can add a sparkle to the taste of a dish especially proteins. If top quality, fresh ingredients are used, MSG is not necessary. In another words, MSG is OPTIONAL in the recipes on this site. It is available under various proprietary names such as Accent, AjiNomoto, Mei Yen, Stress, Ve-Tsin.

Mung Beans - Also known as green gram or golden gram, it is small green beans used in Chinese cooking, it most frequently used sprouted; mung bean sprouts are one of the key ingredients in chop suey. Dried mung beans are ground into flour, which can be used to make noodles by the Chinese known as mung bean noodles. Mung beans can be used like any other legumes, either as a substitute or in combination.

Mung Bean Noodles - See cellophane noodles

Mung Bean Sheets - See Bean Sheets.

Mustard- Mustard seed has been widely used both as a condiment and as a medicine since biblical times. There are two main varieties of mustard plants: white mustard, which produces reddish-yellow seeds; and black mustard, which yields dark red or brown seeds. The Brown mustard seeds are used for pickling and as a seasoning, and are the main ingredient in European and Chinese mustards. The lighter yellow seeds are usually larger in size, have less spice, and are used as a primary ingredient in American mustards.

Napa Cabbage - See Chinese Cabbage

Nuts - The most important nuts for cooking purposes the Chinese way are chestnuts and walnuts, widely used both in salt dishes and as a part of sweet things. Almonds are less often used in Chinese dishes. Peanuts are important for giving cooking oil. As nuts, they are only served as snacks and do not often enter dishes.

Oil - Polyunsaturated oils are preferred for Chinese cooking. Chinese consider peanut oil as being the most flavorsome, but corn, safflower, and soya oils are used. Crisco is not suitable for cooking Chinese dishes as it tends to jelly when cold and spoil the texture of the food. In China, soya oil is more widely used because it is most available. In general, vegetable-oil-cooked things can be eaten cold or warmed over, while lard-cooked things are good only the first time Used oil can be saved, but strain it through several layers of cheesecloth and store it in the refrigerator. Discard frying oils that have darkened in colour, that flow more slowly than they did originally, or that foam to the top of the pot when you put the food in. Store unused oils in a cool place. See also smoking point.

Onion - Appreciated both as a vegetable and as a condiment in Chinese food, in addition to having many medicinal properties. With a characteristic of strong flavour and odor. The onion is made up of numerous concentric layers of fleshy, juicy whitish leaves, which are covered by several outer layers of paper-thin skin. Spanish onions are among the mildest, while white onions are mild and sweet, and red onions are the sweetest. Certain varieties known as scallions, green onions, or spring onions are often sold fresh in bunches.

Orange peel - In fact dried tangerine peel with a strong orange flavour. Soak in hot water for 20 minutes and use in stir fries. Thinly pared fresh orange or tangerine peel may be substituted.

Oyster sauce - A dark brown, delicate sauce made from oysters and soy sauce, is a staple condiment and seasoning in Chinese cooking that adds richess to dishes without dominating their natural flavours. Available in cans or bottles from Chinese or oriental provision stores. No substitute-omit from the recipe if unavailable.

Oyster mushrooms - A fan-shaped mushroom with white flesh and a gray to brown exterior. This soft, moist fungus has a peppery, robust flavour when raw, and is often used in salads. The flavour softens when cooked, and oyster mushrooms are a nice addition to casseroles, soups or stir-fried dishes. Available in some areas year-round, particularly in specialty produce and Asian markets; canned oyster mushrooms, which should be rinsed before using, are also available.

Fig 25.23 Oyster mushroom

Paprika - A powdered mixture of dried red-skinned chilies, ranging in flavour from slightly sweet and mild to acrid and hot. The colour can also range from bright reddish-orange to dark red. Used as a spice and garnish.

Fig 25.24 Paprika chillies

Parsnip - A long, white root vegetable with feathery green leaves. Its look and taste is similar to a carrot and it can be cooked in much the same way.

Peanut Oil -Clear oil pressed from peanuts; very useful in Chinese cooking. Peanut oil has a delicate flavour and high smoke point, making it perfect for deep-frying. American peanut oils tend to be mild-flavored, whereas Chinese peanut oils have a distinctive peanut flavour. Peanut oil will keep indefinitely if stored in a cool, dark place.

Pecans - The thin-shelled, richly flavored nut from a tree native to North America; high in fat, used to enrich cakes, pies and other confections. Pecans are widely available in supermarkets.

Fig 25.25 Pecans in different stages

Pepper -The berries of a climbing vine. The fruit grow green then red as the plant matures. To make black pepper, the berries are picked green and sun-dried, resulting in black peppercorns. To make white peppercorns, the dark husk is removed by soaking. Pepper should not be confused with the peppers more accurately known as capsicums or chilies.

Pickled bamboo shoots -Pickled bamboo shoots are similar in flavour to dried bamboo shoots. Put in boiling water and return to the boil. Drain and rinse in cold water. Repeat this process 2 to 3 times to remove the sour flavour. These keep for a long period in the refrigerator.

Pickled mustard green - See pickled Chinese cabbage.

Plum Sauce -Plums provide the sour flavour in Chinese dishes. It's a great combination with stir-fried pork and deep fried appetizers and dim sum.

Pomelo - The largest citrus fruit, the pomelo has a thick, coarse rind that ranges from greenish to yellow to pink, and pink or pale-yellow segmented flesh. The flavour can be either sweet or slightly tangy. Pomelos can be found in Asian or specialty produce markets in winter; also known as shaddock.

Fig 25.26 Pomelo

Potato flour - Potato flour gives a very smooth, transparent result when used for thickening soups or sauces.

Pot sticker wrapper - Very thin sheets of dough made from flour, eggs and salt; used for small meat and vegetable filled dumplings known as potstickers, as well as for won ton. These wrappers can vary in thickness, and are usually available prepackaged in square or round sheets in many supermarkets and Chinese markets; also known as won ton skins or wonton wrappers. Keep refrigerated or frozen and let them come to room temperature before using.

Pimento - The aromatic berry of a West Indian tree used to make allspice. Do not confuse with the Spanish sweet pepper "pimiento."

Fig 25.27 Pimento

Prawn Term commonly used for any large shrimp, although a true prawn has a thinner body and longer legs than a shrimp, and an average market length of 3 inches or 4 inches. Another distinction: Shrimp tend to live in saltwater, whereas prawns are generally thought to swim in freshwater, though they might migrate to saltwater to spawn. Prawns can be cooked and served in any way appropriate for shrimp.

Preserved Food - Food is preserved when it is salted, dried, frequently pickled or candied, and canned. Canned Chinese foods are rather looked down upon, except some specialties such as abalone. Almost anything may be preserved. Salted shrimps, shrimps eggs, salted fish, from the tiny one-inch fish to shark's fin, hundred-year-old eggs (which taste better when about 100 days old). Chinese ham are the commonest preserved animal foods. Dried lilies and golden needles, ears of wood, which is a fluffy kind of fungus, dried mushrooms, bamboo shoots, dried transparent pea-starch noodles) called in some Chinese food shops 'long bean rice') salted vegetables of various kinds, salted radishes and soy pickled cucumbers, sauce-pickled vegetables of various kinds-these are the commonest preserved vegetables. For preparing dried foods before cooking, the first step is to soak them in warm water or slightly boiling for several hours to several days.

Preserved mustard green - See pickled Chinese cabbage.

Preserved white radish or turnip - Are usually sun dried in strips, then salted or preserved in soy sauce. There are several different varieties. Care must be taken with the salted variety to add no more salt to any dish in which they are used. Wash well before cooking. Round turnips are sometimes preserved whole; they have a sweet, appetizing flavour and can be cut into thin batons and eaten as a relish

Fig 25.28 Quail egg

Quail Egg - Considered a delicacy, these small eggs are usually eaten hard-boiled or poached and in aspic.

Red beans - Dark red beans similar to red kidney beans, but smaller; popular in chili and as refried beans. They stay firm when cooked and are excellent when accompanying rice. They are available dried in most supermarkets; also known as Mexican Red Beans.

Red Dates - Red Dates are the dried fruit of the Chinese jujube tree, not a palm date, and have a bright red crinkly skin. Either soak for 3 hours or cook very slowly.

Red-in-snow - See pickled Chinese cabbage.

Rice-flour Noodles - Made with flour and water, they are available, from thin rice vermicelli to the thick broad flat noodles. They are a traditional ingredient in Chinese chicken salad, and are tasty in soups and stir-fries

Rice vermicelli - Thin translucent noodles, this rice-flour noodle is delicious when stir fried or used in soups. Rice vermicelli can be used to garnish several dishes when deep-fried. Soak in hot water until tender before using.

Rice Paper - Spring Roll wrapper - Made from rice flour and water, rice papers are available in either round or triangular form and are used for spring rolls. The unique patterning on each paper comes from their being dried on bamboo mats in the sun. Available only in dried form, usually in the size of 8.5 in. or 12 in. squares, they are firm and must be softened in hot water before use. Rice paper is very thin and so when deep fried, it is crispier than egg roll skin. Vegetarian use this as substitute for egg roll skins because it does not contain eggs.

If you don't have the time to make pancake wrappers for fresh lumpia, you can also use Vietnamese rice paper wrappers, which are sold in many Asian grocery stores. Look for round wrappers about 8 inches across. They're paper-thin, translucent, and brittle, with a delicate lattice pattern from the woven drying racks on which they're made. To soften them, dip them briefly in a bowl of warm water, shaking off the excess before you put the wrapper on your plate. In a few seconds, the wrapper will be soft enough to roll around the lettuce and the filling.

Rice Vinegar - There are three kinds of Chinese rice vinegars: white, black and red made from fermented rice. White vinegar is colorless, much milder than Western distilled vinegar and is used primarily in sweet-and-sour dishes. Black vinegar is milder than Western malt vinegar and is most often used as a table condiment (goes very well with shark's fin soup). Red vinegar or red vinegar sauce is a sweet, spicy flavored vinegar from Zhejiang. Unlike Western products, Chinese vinegars are more nutritious and feature more interesting flavours.

Rice wine - Called Shao Hsing in China, also known as Chinese cooking wine is a dry, strong, flavorful and clear wine made from fermented rice. If rice wine is not available, Japanese sake or dry sherry can be substituted. Rice wines are usually lower in alcohol and popular in Chinese stir fried and steamed dishes.

Rock Sugar - Rock sugar is crystallised raw sugar. Its flavour is more mellow and not as sweet as refined sugar. It is used in braised dishes and in the master sauce. It is available in Asian groceries.

Salt - A white granular compound (sodium chloride) used to season foods. One important thing in Chinese recipes is that salt in not freely exchangeable with soy sauce. When it is the white kind of cooking, of course salt should be used and the least bit of soy sauce will make it tastes wrong, though after the white cooking is done, soy sauce is used as the dipping.

Salted Jellyfish - See Jellyfish.

Salty or salted black beans - see Black beans, fermented

Scallion - Also known as green onion or bunching onion in the USA, spring onion in the UK and strangely enough, shallot in Australia, this aromatic plant has been cultivated in China for over 2,000 years. A scallion is an immature onion with long green stems and a small under developed white bulb at the root end, both of which are edible. Because of its crisp, sharp fresh taste and its bright green and white colour, it is used extensively in Chinese cooking. The scallion has a slightly hot flavour that is milder than the common onion but stronger than chives. See also leeks.

Scallops - Scallops is an edible marine mollusk. Since scallops are extremely perishable, they are often shelled and washed as soon as they are caught, then immediately covered with ice or frozen or dried. When buying shelled fresh scallops, ensure that the flesh is white, firm, and odorless. Dried scallops are widely used by the Chinese as a soup maker. When buying, avoid darkened or moldy ones. The best kind is amber in colour. To soften, wash under cold water, remove the tough parts and steam for 1 to 1 ½ hour. The water used to soften them serves as a stock

Fig 25.29 Scallops

Sea bass - This term commonly describes a number of saltwater fish on the market, many of which are not actually members of the bass family. Black sea bass is a true bass. It can vary from brown to dark gray, and has firm, moderately fatty flesh with a delicate flavour that is suitable for frying, steaming, broiling or roasting whole (the skin is also edible). White sea bass, which may be labeled in markets simply as "sea bass" is actually a member of the drum family.

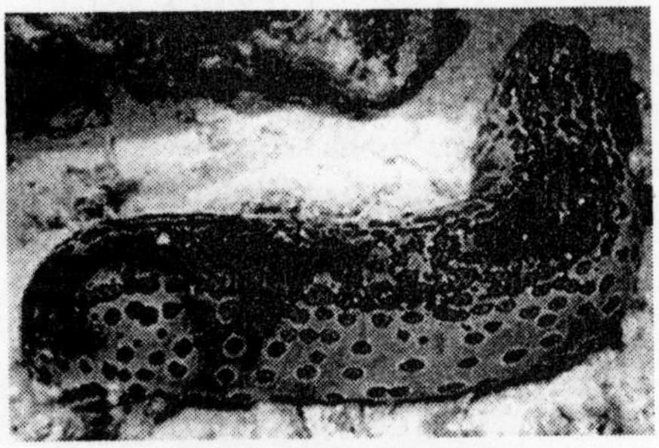

Fig 25.30 Seacumber

Sea Cucumber - Known as "bêcher-de-mer" in French or the not so appetizing name "sea rat" or "sea slug", the sea cucumber prized for its gelatinous texture has been a delicacy in Chinese cuisine since ancient times, often served in Chinese banquets, among other revered dishes such as the shark's fin soup. It's not a vegetable, but a marine animal that is soft and cylindrical, resembles a cucumber and hence the name.

Serrano - Fiery hot, but flavourful, green chili, available fresh or canned. Serrano chilies are about 1½ inches long and are slightly pointed.

Sesame Oil - Oriental sesame oil made from roasted sesame seeds has a dark orange hue and a pronounced, nutty, aromatic flavour. It is the most important flavoring oil in Chinese cuisine. Salads and stuffing need the magic touch of sesame oil to taste infinitely better. Use it sparingly as a flavoring, but never use it for long cooking, since it burns easily. Use it in the final stages of cooking instead. Recipes often call for a few drops of sesame oil to be drizzled on a dish just before serving. The best brand is Kadoya sesame oil from Japan. Non-roasted sesame oil is not a good substitute for the sesame oil used in Chinese cooking. Store in a cool place or in the refrigerator.

Sesame Paste - Roasted sesame seeds are ground into a paste. Peanut butter can be used as a substitute. Unroasted sesame paste (*tahini*) is runnier and not a good substitute as the taste is different. You can find sesame paste commonly sold in jars in supermarkets and Chinese groceries. Once opened, sesame paste should be placed in the refrigerator, where it will last for several months.

Sesame seeds - Sesame is believed to have been one of the first condiments as well as one of the first plants to be used for its edible oil. The tiny oval seeds are covered with a thin edible hull and have a nutty flavour, are used by the Chinese to flavour cakes, cookies, and popular desserts such as sesame seed balls and fried custard. Both black and white sesame seeds are used in Chinese cooking. Like sesame oil, white sesame seeds have a nutty flavour, while black sesame seeds taste more bitter. However, whether a recipe calls for white or black seeds often has more to do with the appearance of a dish rather than flavour. They can be found in stores other than those selling Chinese supplies, for instance, in places where Greek and Turkish foodstuff are sold. Sesame seeds can be kept in an airtight container at room temperature. They can last up to 3 months if stored in the refrigerator. Rancid smelling sesame seeds are bad.

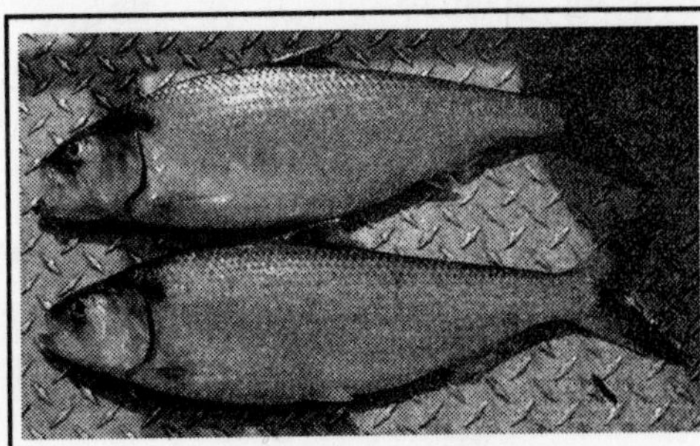

Fig 25.31 Shad

Shad - A member of the herring family, shad are extremely bony; even marketed fillets often have many bones that must be removed by the consumer. Shad are available whole (with or without roe) and in fillets. The roe of this fish is considered a true delicacy.

Shallots - A bulbous herb, it is more aromatic and subtle in flavour than the onion and less pungent than garlic. Unlike both of these herbs, shallots do not cause "bad breath". The size of a garlic bulb, the shallot has two or three cloves. It is often confused with leeks or scallions in recipes. Shallots are usually available year-round and can be identified by their small onion-like appearance and thin. Some parts in the Asia call it "small onion". Shallots can be kept for about 1 month when stored in a dark, cool, dry place with good air circulation. They will keep for only about 2 weeks in the refrigerator. Also known as potato onion and multiplier onion.

Shark's fin- This expensive delicacy has been revered in China for centuries. Mainly used in such exquisite dishes as shark's fin soup, shark's fin is prized for its slippery and glutinous texture that results in a thickened soup without the use of cornstarch, similarly to bird's nest, another Chinese top delicacies. Regarded as a tonic food and an aphrodisiac, the Chinese believe shark's fin strengthens the internal organs and retard aging.

Fig 25.32 Shark fin

Sherry - A fortified wine originating from an area of southwestern Spain. There are several types of sherries, ranging in colour, flavour and sweetness.

Shiitake mushroom - see Chinese mushroom

Shrimps - Shrimps is considered America's favorite shellfish. Select raw shrimp that have no hint of ammonia smell. When storing fresh, raw shrimp, rinse under cold running water and drain. Place in a tightly sealed container and refrigerate for up to two days. When the recipe says 'remove sand', it also means 'devein' where you slit the back of the shrimp (or take off the whole shell if the recipe calls for shelling), and take off the dark thread (intestinal vein) or line along the back, which would give an unpleasant gritty chew if left there. Learn more about Chinese seafood and recipes here. One pound of shrimp in shell equals about ½ pound peeled and cooked shrimp.

Slippery Noodles - see Cellophane Noodles

Snow Fungus - Also known as white tree ear fungus, silver fungus and silver ear is quite similar to wood ear but it is white in colour and almost transparent. Good-quality snow fungus has a pale and yellowish-white colour. It is often used in soups and desserts and believed to improve the complexion.

Snow peas - Also known as sweet peas, sugar peas and Chinese peas, it is a soft and flat pod, and entirely edible. Snow peas is ideal for stir frying.

Snow pickle - Also known as red-in-snow and salted cabbage, this is salted mustard greens that tastes somewhat sour.

Fig 25.33 Soy beans

Soya bean - Cultivated for over 3,000 years in China, it was one of the first foods to be domesticated by humans. To the Chinese, soybeans represented one of the five essential grains of life, along with rice, barley, wheat, and millet. They are more nourishing and tastier than mung bean sprouts, and can be used in the same way, either slightly cooked or raw. The most nutritious and easily digested of all beans, the soybean is better known for its products than for the bean itself: tofu (soybean curd), soybean oil, soy flour, soy milk and soy sauce. Dried soybeans, beans for sprouting and a huge variety of soybean products are available in supermarkets and health food stores.

Soy bean sauce - After soy sauce is brewed, the soybean pulp is removed from the vats and made into several types of condiments. The first is called Brown Bean Sauce/Paste, Yellow Bean Sauce/Paste or Soybean Condiment. Use this rich salty condiment to replace soy sauce where thicker gravy is desired. Especially good used as a marinade for roasted meats. Comes in jars or cans.

Soy sauce - A highly flavored brown liquid brewed from fermented soya beans and salt, soy sauce is the most important flavorer in Chinese cuisine. It is salty and tangy in flavour and is dark brown almost black in colour. With soy sauce, you can cook an untiring series of Chinese dishes with nothing but those foods you can get at a market. Chinese dishes are called red-cooked or white-cooked according as soy sauce is or is not used. But even in the white-cooked dishes, especially the slow cooking ones, the morsels, or rather the chopsticks of food are often dipped in soy sauce before eating. However, Chinese does not pour soy sauce on rice.

There are two main kinds of imported soy sauces available light (thin) or dark (black)

Both kinds are used for cooking; however, the light soy sauce is saltier than the black and is preferred for dipping. Kikkoman are the best brands. The best soy sauces are the ones imported from China (Pearl River Bridge is especially good) or Hong Kong. Always try to buy Chinese soy sauce when cooking Chinese food, Japanese for Japanese. They are quite different. Acceptable substitutes for soy sauce in the order of preference are as follows : Kikkoman (Japanese), 'Vesop' sauce (Italian), 'Maggi' (german) and 'Kub' (French). Soy sauce will keep for up to a year at room temperature.

Spinach - A plant with dark green spear-shaped leaves. Spinach, with its slightly bitter flavour, is high in nutritional content and can be eaten raw or cooked.

Spring onion - see Scallion

Spring roll wrapper - see Rice paper

Star anise -Also known as Chinese anise, it is a popular seasoning in Chinese cooking especially in red-cooking dishes, this spice resembles an eight-pointed star and is usually broken into "sections" or "pieces" before being used in cooking. It has a subtle licorice flavour and is used as an ingredient in Chinese five-spice. Remove the star anise from the dish before serving, since it is not to be eaten. Only available as a rule from Chinese or oriental provision stores, but try larger spice manufacturers too.

Fig 25.34 Star anise

Starch - The most important binder in Chinese cooking is starch. The starch commonly used for cooking in China is from water caltrops, pea flour or from the draining when the flour is washed for getting gluten. Corn flour is the recommended substitute. Pre-soaking sauces with starch protect the surface of the pieces and keep the juice in on frying. Wheat flour is a heavier binder. Fish is often rubbed with flour so that its skin will hold together better on frying

Fig 25.35 Straw mushroom

Straw Mushroom- This Asian mushroom gets its name from being cultivated on straw that has been used on a paddy. These grayish brown fungi are long with a conical cap over a bulbous stem, and have a mild flavour that makes a nice addition to Chinese dishes. They can sometimes be found fresh in specialty produce markets but are more readily available canned. Also known as paddy-straw mushrooms and grass mushrooms.

Sugar - Used in sweetish dishes. Adding some sugar can save your dish when you have put too much salt. In authentic Chinese cooking, in the order importance, granulated sugar, brown sugar, crystallized sugar are the sweeteners used.

Sweet Bean Sauce - Use this intriguing sauce along with or in place of Hoisin sauce for a similar but more subtle flavour. Mix it with Hot Bean Sauce in Szechuan dishes to cool things off a bit. Sweet Bean Sauce is also typically used in Peking style foods.

Sweet pepper - see Bell pepper

Fig 25.36 Szechuan pepper

Szechuan/Sichuan pepper/peppercorns - Very ingratiating spice which tastes only faintly hot but brings out the taste of many foods well. Even peanuts boiled with salt and Szechuan pepper become a revelation to those who have not had them this way. It is inexpensive and can be found at most asian grocery stores and markets. DO NOT substitute Szechuan peppercorns with red chili peppers. "hua jiao" in Chinese.

Szechuan pickle cabbage - Szechuan pickle cabbage - is a club-stalked vegetable with a peppery flavour of its own, enhanced by the preserving spices. Once open and removed from the can it will keep for 2 months in the refrigerator. It is often used in slices or shreds to add hot and salty flavour to a Chinese dish or soup. Rinse before use.

Taro - To choose a taro, it must be light and dry. The heavy ones are too moist inside and will be tough when cooked. Good taros will be floury (starchy) (Fig. 25.37).

Fig 25.37 Taro

Tapioca - Starchy substance available in several forms including granules, flakes, pellets and flour. Tapioca flour (also called cassava flour) is used as a thickening agent much like cornstarch. Tapioca of any type can be stored indefinitely in a cool, dark area (Fig. 25.38).

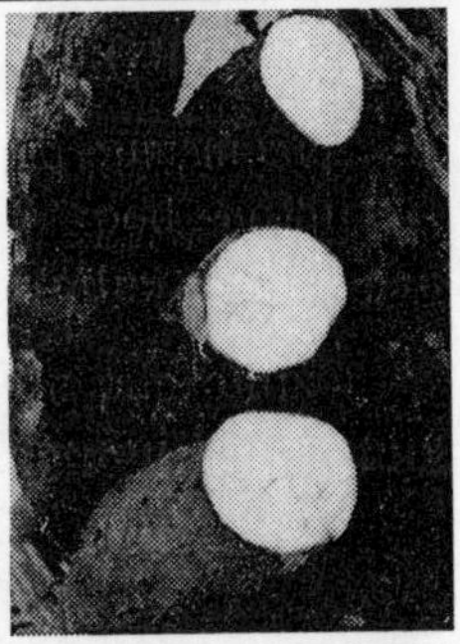

Fig 25.38 Tapioca

Tangerine peel - See orange peel

Tianjin pickled vegetables - See pickled Chinese cabbage.

Tiger lily buds - Also known as golden needles or lily flowers/bloom, they have a musky flavour and chewy. Usually tied into a knot for cooking to enhance texture. Soak for 30 minutes in hot water until soft before use. Remove the stem (hard end) before using (Fig. 25.39).

Tofu - Also known "dou fu", is obtained from the milky liquid extracted from soy beans. Usually sold fresh in cakes about 3 inches square. that look and feel rather like a soft, pale cheese. It can be kept for up to 10 days if drained and then stored, immersed in water, in a sealed container. Change the water daily. It is also available canned. With its high-protein, low-fat content, tofu is a popular meat substitute for vegetarians and health-conscious diners. Tofu has a bland flavour that absorbs other flavours, making it very versatile (Fig. 25.40).

Fig 25.39 Tiger lili buds

Tomato - Tomatoes are technically berries, though they are generally thought of as vegetables. Select firm, fragrant, richly colored tomatoes that are heavy for their size. Avoid any with blemishes. To peel a tomato, make a small x incision in the bottom of the tomato and place it in a pot of boiling water for about 15 seconds. Remove the tomato and shock it in ice water to stop the cooking and set the colour. The skin should now be easy to peel. Avoid cooking tomatoes in aluminum pots, as the corrosive effect of their acid makes them take on an unpleasant metal taste that can also be harmful. 2½ pounds tomatoes yields 3 cups chopped and drained tomatoes.

Fig 25.40 Tofu

Transparent noodles - see Cellophane Noodles

Turmeric - A relative of ginger, this spice has a bitter, somewhat harsh flavour and bright yellow colour that makes it useful as a dying agent. Turmeric is widely used in Indian cooking, especially in curries. Though its coloring properties are similar to saffron, the two are not interchangeable in taste.

Vegetables Oil - See Oil

Vinegar - See rice vinegar

Walnut - One of the most important nuts used in Chinese cooking beside chestnuts. It is widely used in salt dishes and as part of desserts.

Ward-long bean - Also known as Chinese long bean, long bean or asparagus bean, it is a very thin legume that resembles the green bean with a more pliable pod and less sweet flavour. Ward-long beans can be found year-round in most Asian markets and some supermarkets. Choose those that are small and very flexible. They can be refrigerated in a plastic bag for up to five days. Yard-long beans are most often cut into 2-inch lengths and stir-fried. Overcooking will make them mushy.

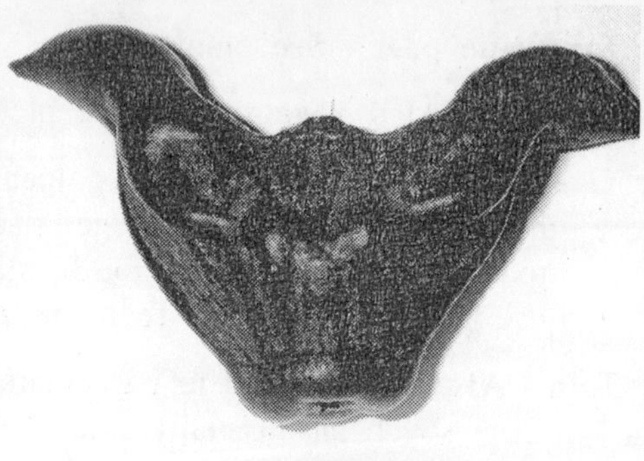

Fig 25.41 Water caltrop

Water Caltrop - This is the real name of "Ram Horn Nut". In Mandarin, it's called "Ling Jiao"; in Cantonese, it's called "Ling Gok". It also has a nickname "Peanut in Water". It's a plant grows in water. You can cook them in the shell or peel them first. Either way is fine but they'll need to be shelled before eating. They are not as sweet or crunchy as common water chestnuts, many find them tasteless on their own so they're good to chop and add to dishes much the same way as common water chestnuts are used. Many Asians boil or steam them in the shell as a snack. You can also roast them and they taste quite similar to chestnuts.

Fig 25.42 Chinese water chestnuts

Water chestnuts - Known as Chinese water chestnut or "ma tai" or "mah tai" in China, has a dark-brown skin, ivory flesh, crisp texture, and slightly sweet, nutty flavour. It has been consumed since ancient times and continues to play an important role in Chinese cooking especially in stir-fried dishes. Usually available canned though can be found fresh or dried from Chinese or oriental provision stores, or larger supermarkets. Store leftover canned chestnuts in a screw-top container, immersed in water, in the refrigerator. They will keep for up to one month, providing the water is changed daily. Fresh water chestnuts can be refrigerated, tightly wrapped in a plastic bag, for up to a week

Fig 25.43 Water cress

Watercress - Watercress has small, crisp, dark-green leaves and a strong, peppery, slightly bitter flavour; available year-round and customarily sold in small bunches. Look for crisp leaves with deep, vibrant colour. Avoid leaves that are yellowing or wilting. Refrigerate in a plastic bag or stems-down in a glass of water covered with a plastic bag for up to five days. Wash and shake dry just before using. Watercress may be used in Chinese stir fry dishes and soups.

Watermelon - They are called 'Xi Kua' by the Chinese; translated to 'west -melon' because they were introduced from the extreme west of China. Now they are grown almost everywhere in China. Besides eating melons as a special eating party, you can use the rind of watermelons for a stir fried dish.

Wheat Flour Noodles - Made with wheat flour, water and salt, and sometimes eggs, Chinese wheat noodles can be white or yellow, they are available fresh or dried, thin or thick. The thinner varieties are often used in light soups, while the thicker ones work well in thicker soups and stir-fries. Boil before using. Chinese egg noodles is one of the varieties.

White Pepper - Asians prefer ground white pepper because of its penetrating, potent flavour.

White rice - Rice stripped of its husk, bran and germ. White rice is a good source of starch and has a mild flavour and aroma; also known as polished rice. It is the main food of a meal in China.

White Tree Ear Fungus - See Snow Fungus

Winter pickle - Chinese cabbage preserved in salt and garlic, this vegetable is usually used to flavour a dish. Sold in earthenware jars and need a quick rinse before use.

Fig 25.44 Wolfberry

Wolfberry - Wolfberry is a wild bush found in the north west of China. Because of its nutrient value and pleasant taste, Chinese people have been growing this magic herb for hundreds of years. The Chinese use wolfberry fruit to make tea, soup, stew and wine or chewed them like raisins.

Wonton - A small Chinese dumpling made from egg-noodle dough dusted with cornstarch and filled with a mixture of seafood, meat or vegetables. Wontons may be boiled, deep-fried or steamed, and eaten in soups or as appetizers.

Wonton wrappers or wonton skins - see Potsticker wrapper

Fig 25.45 Wood ear fungi

Wood ear fungi - A popular ingredient in Szechuan cooking, wood ear, is also known as the tree ear, Jew's ear or cloud ear mushroom. It owes that name to its flat earlike shape. Its translucent brownish beige flesh is gelatinous but firm, crunchy and relatively tasteless. They absorb the liquid in which they are cooked and take on the taste of the other ingredients. Wood ears are often sold fresh in Asian specialty food stores. They are also available dried. Store fresh wood ears unwashed in the refrigerator. Although they keep for up to a month, it is best to use them within a week. To prepare for use in recipes, wash the fresh mushrooms quickly in cold water and remove the sticky parts. As for dried wood ears, soak them in warm water for ten minutes. Drain them, change the water, and let them soak for a further 10 to 15 minutes or until soft. They will expand to up to five times their initial dry size. Then rinse off any dirt carefully.

XO Sauce - XO sauce, originally created by Lee Kum Kee, a famous brand of Chinese sauces is an all purpose gourmet condiment made from ingredients such as dried shrimp, dried scallop, red chili pepper and spices. It is called so because it contains high-quality ingredients, and it is so delicate and special. It doesn't contain any XO, but it is believed that XO sauce is the finest sauce, just like people think that XO is the finest liquor. It is a delicious appetizer by itself, as well as an excellent addition to all dishes, Chinese dim sum, noodles, porridge and Japanese sushi. XO Sauce is also ideal for cooking meats, vegetables, seafood, tofu, fried rice and even pasta. XO Sauce is a little bit hot and spicy; on the other hand, there is Extra-Hot XO Sauce too.

Yellow bean paste/sauce - see Soy bean sauce

Yellow Chinese chives - Also known as yellow garlic chives and yellow chives. These are Chinese chives that have been shielded from the sun in order to stifle the production of chlorophyll. Use them just like ordinary Chinese chives.

Zhenjiang vinegar (labelled Chinkiang) - Is made from millet and has a sharp spicy flavour somewhat similar to Worcestershire sauce.

Zucchini- A long, cylindrical summer squash with skin colour ranging from dark to light green, sometimes with yellow markings that give it a mottled or striped look. The flesh is creamy white-green and has a mild, delicate

LEARNING OUTCOME

Chinese cooking reflects this regionality with almost as many cooking styles as regions. Cooking methods vary, as does the use of spices, seasonings and sauces. The division of China by regional styles of cooking is based on historical evolution dating from the 12th Century. There are five predominate cooking schools in china. **South eastern – The Cantonese School** Cantonese cooking is versatile and original, encouraged by the region's rich natural resources. When the Ming dynasty was overthrown in the 7th Century, many government officials migrated south from Peking to Kwangtung province, of which Canton is the capital. **North eastern – The Peking – Shantung School The Peking – Shantung** school is distinguished by light, elegant, mildly spiced rather than rich foods and the liberal use of garlic, green shallots, leeks and chives, soy sauce and vinegar. It is known also for the delicacy of Peking Duck and Chicken Velvet, soft-fried foods, the spring roll, delicious roasts, wine-cooked meats and a wonderful array of delicious dumplings. **Western – The School of Szechuan.** Szechuan's specialties include deep-fried chicken wrapped in paper, vegetables prepared in chicken fat, chicken and hot peppers and a variety of mushroom dishes. The use of dried chilli, Szechuan pepper, sesame seed oil and fermented bean curd paste produce the typical flavours for this school. **Central – The School of Honan** Tender vegetables, accompanied by freshwater fish and crustaceans are prepared with subtle flavours mainly using ginger and Shao Xing wine. **East Coast – The School of Fukien** Fukien province on China's east coast is famous for seafood and for clear, light soups. The art of Chinese cooking is not, contrary to popular belief, complicated and difficult. Most Chinese dishes do not require a complex processing and equipment

LESSON END ACTIVITY

- Collect the data on Chinese restaurants which are famous in India.
- Collect the data on Chinese food festivals in your near metro city.

QUESTIONS FOR DISCUSSION

1. Explain the term Chinese cuisine.
2. Explain in detail about south eastern – The Cantonese School with their specialty.
3. Explain in detail about north eastern – The peking School with their specialty.
4. Explain in detail about western school with their specialty.
5. Explain in detail about east coast school with their specialty.
6. Explain the Chinese philosophy of ying and yang.
7. Explain the different Chinese cooking method.
8. Explain the following term abalone and adzuki beans.

STATE TRUE AND FALSE

- Sea cucumber is resemble to the cucumber.
- Abalone is type of mushroom.
- Szechuan's specialties include deep-fried chicken wrapped in paper.
- Chinese cooking region also called Chinese cooking school.
- Watercress is also known as water melon.
- Water caltrop and water chestnut are same thing.
- Snow fungus is resemble to snow peas.

- The Szechuan Province is hot and humid, almost tropical
- Cantonese cuisine is also noted for roast meats

KEY TERMS

- * Beans
- * Cuisine
- * Fungus
- * Humid
- * Roast
- * Szechaun
- * Tender

Chapter 26

Indonesian Cuisine and Philippines Cuisine

After studying this chapter, the student must know :

- Indonesian cuisine introduction and their specialty
- Glossary of Indonesian cuisine
- Philippines cuisine introduction and their specialty
- Philippines cooking terms
- Philippines common vegetables.

INDONESIAN CUISINE

Indonesia consists of some 13,000 islands which stretch from west to east along the equator, from the island of Sumatra, directly south of Thailand, to Irian Jaya, just north of Australia. These islands support the fourth-most populous nation in the world, a population that is 90% Muslim, with hundreds of tribes, subcultures, and languages - and many long and varied histories. For centuries, these islands have been the center of international trade. Rich, volcanic soil produces an amazing number of fruits and vegetables, the seas yield vast numbers of fish. Spices, however, have been the main source of Indonesia's fame. Nutmeg, clove, and pepper drew traders from India, China, Africa, and the Arab world, and later, European explorers and colonists from the Netherlands, Portugal, and England. From the 8th through the 16th centuries, powerful polities on Java and Sumatra controlled much of what is today the Indonesian Archipelago. But, by the end of the 16th century, steady European colonial expansion left the nation a collection of weak, disconnected fiefdoms, all of which came under direct Dutch control within two centuries. The Republic of Indonesia was declared at the end of the Japanese occupation of Indonesia during World War II. Indonesian cuisine reflects this complex cultural history. Cooking varies greatly by region and combines many different influences. However, most Indonesian food shares the nearly universal food trinity of fish, coconut and chile.

The main meal in Indonesia is usually served at midday. Food which was cooked in the morning is set out all at once. Family members help themselves, serving with a spoon and eating with right hands. There is less family gathering or ceremony of communal eating than in other cultures, but there is communal cooking and a strict hierarchy that determines one's role and comportment at the table. Most meals are built around a cone-shaped pile of the long-grain, highly polished rice that Indonesians prefer. A meal may include a soup, salad, and another main dish. Whatever the meal, it is accompanied by at least one, and often several sambals, spice relishes that are mixed with the food. A light meal might consist of rice, some dried fish and a chile sambal.

Indonesian cooking is rich with coconut milk. Beverages, sauces, soups, and even rice are prepared with it. Traditional spicing builds on a base of coriander, pepper, and garlic. Added to those are turmeric, cassia (the local bark that is quite close in flavour to cinnamon), bay leaf, star anise, ginger, tamarind, galangal, cardamom, lemon grass, scallion, shallots, peanuts, dried anchovies, and prawns. Even ghee finds its way into many recipes.

GLOSSARY

Candlenut (tingkih/kemiri): A round, cream-colored nut with an oily consistency used to add texture and a faint flavour to many dishes. Substitute macadamia nuts or raw cashews.

Cardamom (kapulaga): About 8-12 intensely fragrant black seeds are enclosed in strawcolored, fibrous pod. Try to buy the whole pod instead of cardamom seeds or powder for maximum flavour, and bruise lightly with the back cleaver to break the pod before adding to seasonings.

Celery (seledri): The celery used in Indonesia is somewhat different form the celery used in the Western world. It has a very slender stems and particularly pungent leaves. It is often referred to as "Chinese celery" abroad and is used as a herb rather than a vegetable.

Chilies (cabai, also called cabe or lombok): There are several types of chili pepper used in Indonesia. One thing that is important about chili pepper, the amount of heat increases as the size of the chili pepper diminishes. Green chilies are the unripe fruit, and have a flovor different from red chilies. Fresh, finger-length red chilies are the most commonly used. Dried chilies also used in some dishes and they should be torn into pieces and soaked in hot water to soften before grinding or blending. Hottest of all chilies are the tiny fiery bird's-eye chilies (cabe rawit). To reduce the heat of the dish while retaining the flavour, remove some or ll the chili's seeds.

Cup Leaves (daun mangkok): The shape of the leaf is like a cup. It's also known as tapak leman and it usually used to cook stew dishes. A good substitute is curly kale

Kencur: It is sometimes known as lesser galangal. This ginger-like root has a unique, champor flavour and should be used sparingly. Wash it and scrape off the skin before using. Dried sliced kencur or kencur powder can be used as a substitute. Soak dried slices in boiling water for approximatley 30 minutes; use ½-1 tsp. of powder for 1-inch fresh root

Laos (lengkuas): Sometimes is called galangal, this is a member of the ginger family and it has a very tough but elusively scented root that must be peeled before use. Substitute slices of dried laos (soaked in boiling water for 30 minutes) or powdered laos (1 tsp = 1 inch).

Turmeric (kunyit): An essential root in Indonesian cooking, It imparts its yellow colour and pungent taste to many dishes. If you can buy fresh turmeric, pick roots that are dark in colour.

PHILLIPINES CUISINE

Philippine Considering that there are 16 regions in the Philippines, it is not surprising to taste "regional diversities" in their food. Although Filipino food consists of simple and tropical cuisine, yet various styles have mushroomed in major regions. The variations in regional taste buds are traceable based on factors like natural resources - the produce of different lands and seas, animals and plants as well as to the regional character of locals of different islandscooking is surprisingly simple; no special utensils are needed. Even a wok, which is commonly used in the Philippines and is almost essential for Chinese cooking, can be done without for most Philippines dishes. No special skills are needed, either.

Two styles of preparing food in the Philippines are part of the cuisine not only because of their delicious taste but also because they keep well without refrigeration. Dishes cooked adobo or sinigang style are preserved because of the effect of vinegar or souring ingredient. In rural tropical areas, this makes storing leftovers possible. Dishes prepared in both these manners seem to improve when stored, so it is a good idea to prepare large amounts to ensure having leftovers

COOKING TERMS

adobo - cooked in vinegar, soy sauce and garlic

guisado - sauteed

sinigang - boiled with a sour fruit or vegetable

paksiw - cooked in vinegar and garlic

estofado - prepared with a burnt-sugar sauce

ginataan - cooked in coconut milk

rellanado - stuffed

sarciado - a sauce

Vegetables

- Alogbati - Malabar spinach
- Ampalaya - bitter melon
- Dahon ng sili - chili pepper leaves

Fig 26.1 Alogbati leaves

- Gabi - taro
- Kabute - fungus
- Kamote - sweet potatoes
- Kamoteng Kahoy - cassava
- Kangkong - swamp cabbage
- Labanos - white radish
- Labong - bamboo shoots
- Malunggay - horseradish tree
- Munggo - mung beans
- Pechay - bok choi
- Puso ng Saging - Banana blossoms (Fig. 26.3)
- Sigarilyas - winged bean (Fig. 26.4)
- Singkamas - Jicama
- Sitaw - string beans
- Talong - egg plant
- Toge - bean sprouts
- Ube - purple yam (Fig. 26.5)
- Upo - winter melon fruits
- Atis - Sweetsop (sugar apple?) (Fig 26.6)
- Bayabas - Guava
- Balimbing - Carambola
- Cacao (Fig 26.8)

Fig 26.2 Chilli pepper leaves

Fig 26.3 Banana blossom

Fig 26.4 Winged bean

Fig 26.5 Purple yam

Fig 26.6 Atis

Fig 26.7 Balimbing leaves and its fruits

Chico

- Mangga - Mango
- Papaya
- Saging (kind of banana) (Fig 26.9)
- Sampalok - Tamarind
- Tubo - Sugar Cane

Spices

- Atsuete - Annatto
- Kinchay - Asian celerey
- Luya - fresh ginger

Fig 26.8 Cacao

Fig 26.9 Saging

Fig 26.10 Atsuete

- Murang sibuyas - spring onions
- Sili - chili peppers
- Tanglad - lemon grass

Fig 26.11 Dilis dry fish

Here are some ingredients or types of foods that only Filipinos could love

- Gulaman - agar-agar
- Bagoong - fermented small shrimps or anchovies
- Dilis
- Lumpia WrapperItlog na Maalat - salted eggs
- Pancit - Philippine pastas
- Patis - condiment made from fish drippings
- Balut - embryonated duck eggs (Fig. 26-12)
- Goto - tripe
- Tainga ng Baboy - pig ears
- Pata - pig hocks and pig feet

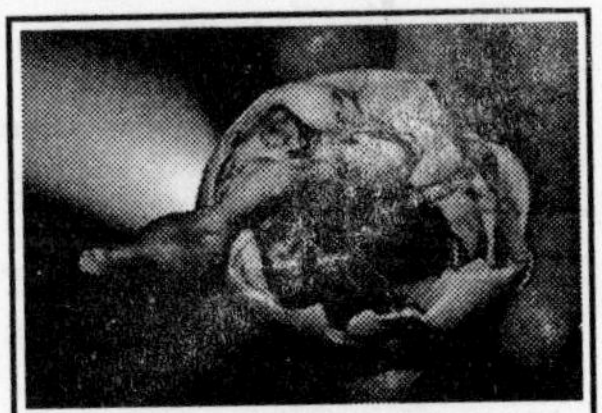

Fig 26.12 Balut

LEARNING OUTCOME

Indonesia consists of some 13,000 islands which stretch from west to east along the equator, from the island of Sumatra, directly south of Thailand, to Irian Jaya, just north of Australia. The main meal in Indonesia is usually served at midday. Food which was cooked in the morning is set out all at once. Indonesian cooking is rich with coconut milk. Beverages, sauces, soups, and even rice are prepared with it. Traditional spicing builds on a base of coriander, pepper, and garlic. Philippine Considering that there are 16 regions in the Philippines, it is not surprising to taste "regional diversities" in their food. Two styles of preparing food in the Philippines are part of the cuisine not only because of their delicious taste but also because they keep well without refrigeration. Dishes prepared in both these manners seem to improve when stored, so it is a good idea to prepare large amounts to ensure having leftovers

LESSON END ACTIVITY

- Collect the information on Indonesian cuisine receipe .
- Collect the information on Philippines cuisne receipe.

QUESTIONS FOR DISCUSSION

1. Explain in detail about the Indonesian cuisine ?

2. Explain in detail about the Philippines cuisine ?
3. Explain the different cooking terms of Philippines cuisine ?
4. Mention the name of Indonesian ingredients ?

KEY TERMS

* Adobo
* Anchovies
* Bark
* Pata
* Pile

Chapter 27

Japanese Cuisine

After studying this chapter, the student must know:

- Introduction of Japanese cuisine
- Glossary of Japanese food
- Method of cooking Japanese rice
- Culinary terms of Japanese cuisine
- Japanese menu guide and ingredients.

JAPANESE CUISINE

History of Japanese Cuisine

Japanese cuisine has developed over the past 2,000 years with strong influences from both China and Korea. But it is only in the past 300-400 years that all the influences have come together to form what nowadays can be described as Japanese cuisine.

One of the major influences was the introduction of rice from Korea around 400 B.C. and within a hundred years it had become the staple food of Japan. Korea's rice growing techniques were passed on to the Japanese during the Yayoi period, as migrating tribes settled in Japan. Rice later came to be used not only for eating, but also to make paper, wine, fuel, building materials and so on. Soy beans and wheat were introduced from China soon after rice and these two ingredients are now an integral part of Japanese cooking. During Japan's development tea, chopsticks and a number of other important food related items were also introduced from China.

Religion has also played a major part in Japan's culinary development. During the 6th century, Buddhism became the official religion of the country and the eating of meat and fish were prohibited. The first recorded decree prohibiting the eating of cattle, horses, dogs, monkeys, and chickens was issued by Emperor Temmu in A.D. 675. Similar decrees, based on the Buddhist prohibition of killing, were issued repeatedly by emperors during the eighth and ninth centuries. The number of regulated meats increased to the point that all mammals were included except whales, which were categorized as fish.

The taboo against the consumption of meat developed further when the Japanese indigenous religion, Shinto, also adopted a philosophy similar to that of the Buddhists. This did not mean, however, that meat eating was totally banned in Japan. Professional hunters in mountain regions ate game (especially deer and wild boar), and it was not uncommon for hunted bird meat to be consumed. However, a lack of animal breeding for meat kept its consumption very low. Indeed, it was only during the fifteenth century and its aftermath that the tradition of eating both the meat and eggs of domestic fowl was revived. Fowls, until then, had been regarded in Shinto as God's sacred messengers and were reared to announce the dawn rather than as a mere food resource.

Milk and other dairy products have failed to enjoy the same popularity in Europe as they do in Japan. The only Japanese dairy product known to history was produced between the eighth and fourteenth centuries. Cattle were often raised only for drawing carts or plowing fields. To utilize them for meat or even for milk was, until relatively recently, a long-forgotten practice.

The lack of meat products also minimized spice utilization. Pepper and cloves were known from the eighth century and were imported either via China or directly from Southeast Asia, and garlic was also grown on a small scale. But these spices were used mainly to make medicines and cosmetics.

In the absence of meat, fish was a significant substitute and as an island nation, this source of food was abundant and has influenced many of todays most famous dishes. However, before the introduction of modern delivery systems, the difficulty of preserving and transporting fresh marine fish minimized consumption in inland areas where freshwater fish were commonly eaten instead.

Preserving fish also became popular and sushi originated as a means of preserving fish by fermenting it in boiled rice. Fish that are salted and placed in rice are preserved by lactic acid fermentation, which prevents proliferation of the bacteria that bring about putrefaction. This older type of sushi is still produced in the areas surrounding Lake Biwa in western Japan, and similar types are also known in Korea, southwestern China, and Southeast Asia. In fact, the technique first originated in a preservation process developed for freshwater fish caught in the Mekong River and is thought to have diffused to Japan along with the rice cultivation.

A unique fifteenth-century development shortened the fermentation period of sushi to one or two weeks and made both the fish and the rice edible. As a result, sushi became a popular snack food, combining fish with the traditional staple food, rice. Sushi without fermentation appeared during the Edo period (1600-1867), and Sushi was finally united with Sashimi at the end of the eighteenth century, when the hand-rolled type, nigiri-sushi, was devised.

In the sixteenth century the Portuguese, followed by the Dutch, began to introduce foods that were adopted by the Japanese and later became cultural symbols. Fried foods such as tempura might seem to be very un-Japanese as a lack of meat and dairy products in the Japanese diet meant that oil was not commonly used for cooking. However, tempura was enjoyed by many people and has evolved into what it is today. Tobacco, sugar and corn were also brought by the traders.

In 1854 trade was renewed with West and soon a new Japanese ruling order took power. The new Emperor Meiji even went as far as staging a New Year's feast in 1872 designed to embrace the Western world. It had a European emphasis and for the first time in over a thousand years, the people publicly ate meat. The general population started to eat meat again after the Meiji Restoration which occurred in 1867.

CURRENT DAY CUISINE

Today, Japanese cuisine is still heavily influenced by the four seasons and geography. Seafood and vegetables are most commonly eaten. Whilst to some westerners, the food may seem almost bland, freshness, presentation and balance of flavours is of paramount importance

What makes Japanese Dishes Japanese?/ Enviroment, Climate and the Diet/ The Relationship with Rice/ The Sense of Season/ Even the colour of the chopstick counts

We think of Japan as a single island, but it actually is four large islands and thousands of smaller ones. The volcanic and mountainous terrain boasts lush forests and heavy rainfall, much of it from monsoons, and the scarce farm land is used predominantly for rice. As one would expect, fish plays a major dietary role, both fresh and preserved.

In the third century BC, Korea's already developed rice growing techniques were passed to the Japanese by the Yayoi, a migrating tribe that settled in Japan. Rice came to be used for more than eating, including paper, fuel, wine, building materials and animal feed.

During the development of Japan, the Chinese contributed soy sauce, tea, chopsticks and imperial rule. Other influences arrived in Japan via Korea, including Buddhism, which, despite the pre-existing Shinto and Confucian religions, became the official religion in the sixth century. For the next 1200 years, meat was officially forbidden to the Japanese people,

Then in the sixteenth century the Portuguese, followed by the Dutch, came looking to corner the trade market with Japan. The westerners introduced fried foods, which is why the breaded, fried tempura seem so very un-Japanese; while the Japanese enjoyed this type of cooking, it was not something that evolved naturally. Tobacco, sugar and corn were also brought by the traders.

Around 1600 (and lasting until 1868), Japan's shogun Tokugawa Ieyasu (of James Clavell's famous novel, "Shogun") feared the Europeans would spark great wars; so he closed the ports and expunged the foreigners. During this period of isolationism, Japan's culture became even more deeply rooted. The main religions of Buddhism and Shinto emphasize the seasons and this came to be reflected in the foods served. In fact, it is because of Buddhism that meals feature five flavors and colors, respectively being: sweet, spicy, salty, bitter and sour; and yellow, black, white, green, and red.

US Commodore Perry forced the Japanese to renew trade with the West in 1854, and soon a new Japanese ruling order took power. Interestingly, the new Emperor Meiji staged a New Year's feast in 1872 designed to embrace the Western world; it was completely European in detail and for the first time in over a thousand years, the people publicly ate meat.

"What makes Japanese dishes Japanese?"

If I asked you to think of one Japanese food, what comes to your mind?

Sushi, raw fish, tempura, tofu? Good.

With Japanese restaurants and Sushi bars popping all over the world these days,

Japanese food is no longer considered as one of the world's unsolved mysteries it once was,In fact, more number of people are recognizing Japanese food as one of the world's healthiest cuisines.

With rice and abundant marine products at it's mainstream, the traditional Japanese diet is impressingly low in cholestrol, fat, and calories, and high in fiber.No wonder Japanese people have the highest longetivity rate.

Anyway, like all other cuisines, Japanese food is a product of the culture that produced it.

JAPANESE FOOD GLOSSARY

Soy sauce (shoyu) - I'll slap you if I have to tell you what this is. Soy sauce replaces salt in Asian recipes. You can buy it in dark, light, reduced-salt (what's the point?), and flavored varieties, but for most recipes, the plain stuff is just dandy. Buy it anywhere; even Winn-Dixies in East Jesus carry

Kikkoman soy sauce. Any brand is good.

Rice vinegar - Sweeter than wine vinegar, which is what Westerners generally use. Buy it anywhere; chances are good that any large supermarket will have twelve-ounce bottles of Marukan rice vinegar shelved with the other vinegars, or with the Asian foods, or both. Any brand is good.

Mirin - Also called aji-mirin. A sweet, syrupy wine made from sake, used the way honey is used in Western cooking. (Mirin is runnier than honey and has its own distinctive taste, though, so honey is a poor substitute.) (Fig. 27-1).

Fig 27.1 Bottle of mirin

Dashi - Soup stock made from bonito flakes. Dashi is the foundation for hundreds of Japanese soups and sauces, including miso. You can be authentic and make your own from bonito flakes, or you can buy powdered dashi concentrate. Dashi comes in primary and secondary forms, depending on how often the bonito flakes have been used; if you're using powdered stock, read the back of the package to find out how much powder to use to make the right type of stock for the recipe. Buy it at an Asian store, where it will probably be shelved somewhere near the rice and soup flavorings. Occasionally supermarkets carry powdered dashi. I don't know how the brands stack up, but I use Shimaya Bonito Flavored Soup Stock and have no complaints.

Japanese rice (kome if it's uncooked, gohan if it's cooked) – Very short-grained, very sticky white or brown rice. (Most Japanese eat white rice; brown rice is considered health food.) The VERY short-grained, inhumanly sticky sweet Asian rice called "mochi" is sometimes sold as Japanese rice, but it's too sticky to eat for dinner; Asians pound it into a paste and make sweets with it. Buy it at a large supermarket, where it will probably be called "sushi rice" and be sold in small bags, or at an Asian store, where it will lie in huge piles of 10- and 20-pound bags and be much cheaper. All brands are good, but a discriminating palate can detect slight differences. Experiment until you find a brand you like (Fig. 27.2).

Fig 27.2 Japanese rice

Miso - The fermented soybean paste which gives miso soup its flavour, and which pops up in Japanese cooking in everything from roasts to salads to dips. Miso shades from chocolate-brown to pale yellow; the darker the miso, the higher the sodium content. (And miso is very salty.) Lighter misos are called shiro-miso, or white miso; darker types are aka-miso, red miso. Like beer, the exact taste of a type of miso depends on the bacteria involved in the fermentation, so each region has its own specialty miso. Unfortunately, most of these misos don't make it across the pond. The average Asian grocery has maybe two types of miso, three if you're lucky. Fortunately, you don't need anything fancy. If you're just starting out in Asian cooking, buy the smallest container of a middling-red—orange, really—miso; you'll probably end up with about a pound of miso for about $4. It looks small, but it will last you for over a year.

Nori – Thin sheets of nori seaweed used to wrap sushi, onigiri, crackers, and many other things. Nori comes both toasted and untoasted; if you buy the untoasted and the recipe calls for toasted, turn on the stove and hold the sheet of nori over the flame for a second. (It takes almost no time to toast.) Buy it just about anywhere; the trendiness of sushi means that any supermarket with even the poorest excuse for an Asian section will stock at least one brand of nori (Fig. 27.3).

Fig 27.3 Nori sheets

Kombu/Konbu - A kind of kelp which is used to flavour broths and sauces. It starts off looking like a grungy dried banana leaf, and turns into a massive, pulsating tentacle which hangs out both sides of the pot, writhing and thinking dirty thoughts about your Rei figurines. Japanese porn is instantly comprehensible when you use kombu for the first time and see what every Japanese child grows up seeing in Kaachan's kitchen. If you're still willing to use kombu after that introduction, wipe both sides of the dry kombu gently with a damp cloth, taking care not to wipe all of the white powder off—it's the powder which provides much of the flavour. (The kombu is safe to go near at this point, since it has no power in its dry state.) Place the kombu in the cooking water or broth to soak, and witness its mighty expansion. Two minutes before the recipe tells you to remove the kombu from the water, pick up your weapons and psyche yourself for battle. You will need both minutes. At the appointed time, enter the melee. When you have wrestled the kombu from the water and it hangs, limp and flopping, from your knife, nail it above the kitchen lintel and mock it while you bandage your wounds. Buy it at a Japanese grocery. Groceries of other nationalities are sometimes foolhardy enough to stock this menace to life and virtue, and American supermarkets occasionally indulge in fatal innocence concerning this ravage, but you'll have the best luck at a Japanese store. Kombu is usually near the nori and wakame, where it terrifies the delicate and sensitive wakame into fits. And that's it. The rest of these ingredients are common but not essential.

Daikon - Also called "Japanese radish." It's generally sold in chunks as big around as your arm, and if you get the whole daikon, you can brain kombu with it. Daikon is essential to Japanese cooking and is eaten both raw and cooked, but I have no expereince with it. This bit gets filled in later. Hey, I warned you that the site wasn't done, didn't I?

Fish sauce - A strongly-flavored brown liquid used heavily in Southeast Asian cooking. Japanese food doesn't call for it much, but it's worthwhile to try out. Put a few drops in your ramen.

Gyoza – Japanese pot stickers, smaller and thinner-skinned than the Chinese kind. They're traditionally filled with pork and vegetables, but you can get them in any flavour, including kimchee and vegetarian. I buy Day-Lee Pride brand gyoza, which come 48-50 to a $7 bag. Other kinds of dumplings can be substituted for gyoza—there are dozens of kinds of Korean dumplings on the market.

Fig 27.4 Gyoza

Inari-no-moto - Little pita pouches of fried tofu canned in mirin syrup or soy sauce. Essential for making Inari-zushi.

MSG (aji-no-moto) - Japanese food is full of MSG. A lot of foods, like powdered dashi, come preseasoned with MSG; other recipes call for a spoonful or two. In Japanese, MSG is called "aji no moto," which means "the origin of taste." MSG is a grainy white powder which is sold in bags and shaker

Oden - Japanese fried fish-paste cakes; they come in shapes ranging from flat sheets to round tubes to little nuggets, and are usually varying shades of tan. Very yummy once you get past the Western taboo against fried fish paste. Don't confuse oden with udon.

Pickles (tsukemono) - Not American pickles, Japanese pickles. The Japanese pickle everything which doesn't fall apart in vinegar, which makes for an amazing variety of pickles. Pickles are central to the Japanese diet, to the point that monks traditionally eat little but rice and pickles. Unfortunately, Japanese pickles haven't made it across the pond. Why this should be, I don't know, but perhaps it's because a lifetime of nothing but salty waffle-cut cucumbers spread limply over hamburgers doesn't prepare the mind for a true pickle experience. The Japanese word for "pickle" is "tsukemono." Pronounce it carefully. I learned "tsukemono".

Raw fish (sashimi) - *DO NOT BUY JUST ANY RAW FISH AND SLAP IT ON RICE*! Sushi-grade raw fish is very fresh and has been inspected to ensure that it is parasite-free. Some kinds of fish, like catfish, are never parasite-free, so they are never eaten raw. If you want to make sashimi, buy sushi-grade fish from a Japanese grocery or from an American supermarket which knows what it's doing, and eat the fish right away. If you can't get sushi-grade fish where you live, substitute smoked fish. It's not perfect, but it's close enough, and it's better than a parasitic infection.

Seafood balls - Balls of cooked seafood paste about an inch across. They come in fish, cuttlefish, and shrimp varieties. Delicious, even eaten cold straight from the package. Buy Venus brand; the other brands often have bits of bone or shell in them. (These might be Southeast Asian rather than Japanese. The Japanese version, oden, isn't quite the same.)

Sesame oil - A strongly-flavored oil used as a seasoning. Don't use it for frying! Everything you put in the pan will taste like sesame.

Somen - Fine noodles made of wheat flour. Somen is a summer dish, and is usually eaten cold.

Tofu - Blocks of white soybean goosh, and the reason that a land-hungry society managed to stay well-nourished despite an almost total lack of beef, pork, and chicken. Tofu soaks up the flavors of the food around it. Tofu comes in several consistencies, from hard tofus which can be fried to soft and silky tofus which are best blended into a paste and used in sauces.

Fig 27.5 Wakame

Udon - Thick noodles made of buckwheat. Udon is sold dried in packages, or moist and tightly-sealed as a ramen-like instant meal. Don't confuse udon with oden.

Wakame – A thin, frilled kind of seaweed which is used in soups and salads. It's hard to find outside of Japanese groceries, where it's stocked near the nori and kombu. Buy the bag nearest the kombu, since that bag will have the curliest wakame.

Fig 27.6 Fresh wasabi

Wasabi – Because every otaku worth his or her salt eats massive gloppy mounds of wasabi on their sushi. If you've never eaten wasabi before, don't be put off by the rumors; it's actually a sort of sweet paste. That's why it's that bright, candylike green. Wasabi is sold both premixed and powdered.

METHOD OF COOKING JAPANESE RICE

One of the first questions non-initiates ask is, "How does it stick together like that?" The answer: It just does. The shorter the grain of rice, the higher the starch content, and the higher the starch content, the stickier the rice. The kinds of rice favored in Japan are all very short-grained—the shortest and stickiest, mochi, looks like tiny pebbles—and as a result, the only way to get cooked Japanese rice off your fingers is surgical removal. (So be careful.) Wetting down the rice does cause it to lose cohesion, but you tend to end up with rice slime. (So be careful.)

Real rice cooking involves several steps:

1. Washing the rice.
2. Soaking the rice.
3. Cooking the rice.
4. Aftersteaming the rice.

We'll go through these step by step.

1. **Washing the rice**. The Japanese traditionally wash their rice to purify the flavour and to remove any impurities remaining in the dry rice. Modern mass-produced rice rarely has impurities, and manufacturers sometimes add a light dusting of nutrients to replace what was removed during production. Washing takes off this coating. If you don't want to bother washing your rice, skip to the next step. If you do want to wash your rice, place it in a pot and run water over it, then swirl the rice with your hands to stir it up. Pour out the milky water carefully and cover the rice with more water; repeat. Do this until the water runs clear.
2. **Soaking the rice.** Put the rice in the pot and add the cooking water (about 1¼ cups of water to each cup of dry rice if you didn't wash the rice, slightly less water if you did wash the rice; experiment to find out how much water you need to get the right texture). Let the rice soak until it has puffed up and is slightly softer. I find that this generally takes 10-15 minutes, less if I've washed the rice.
3. **Cooking the rice**. Plug the rice cooker in—this will automatically put the cooker on "warm"—then close the lid and hit the "cook" butto
4. **Aftersteaming the rice.** The cooker will go "click" or "ding" when it's done. Don't open the lid! Right now, the rice is half-cooked and runny. Let the cooker steam the rice on low heat for 10-15 minutes.

CULINARY TERMS JAPANESE CUISINE

A

abura	oil.
abura-age	fried tofu slices.
aemono	foods in vinegar dressing or sauces.
age	fried.
amiyaki	cooked over a wire grill.
an	sweet adzuki bean jam.
anmitsu	dessert made from (agar-agar), an, and sugar.
asa gohan	breakfast.
awabi	abalone.
azuki	a small red bean, adzuki.

B

bata	butter.
battera-zushi	Osaka-style pressed and molded mackerel sushi.
bento	traditional boxed lunch.
biru	beer.
burokkori	broccoli.

C

o-cha	green tea (the -o is an honorific).
chanko-nabe	seafood and vegetable stew eaten by sumo wrestlers.
chawan	rice bowl.
chawan mushi	egg custard with diced vegetables.
chazuke	rice and various toppings, over which green tea is poured.
chikuwa	tube shaped, hollow fish cake.
chirashi-zushi	assorted raw fish on a bed of vinegared rice.
chiizu	cheese.

D

daikon	a large white, carrot shaped Japanese radish.
daizu	soybeans.
dango	small, round, dumplings, usually served on a stick.
dashi	a soup stock made from kelp and fish (basic to Japanese cooking).
dengaku	tofu or konnyaku broiled with a sweet miso topping.

E

ebi	shrimp.
enoki	long, thin, white mushrooms.

F

fugu	blowfish, a highly prized sashimi delicacy.
furutsu	fruit.

G

gari	sliced pickled ginger (served in sushi restaurants).
genmai	brown rice.
gobo	burdock root.

gohan	formal word for rice, also meaning "meal" (the informal word "meshi" can also be used).
goma	sesame seeds.
gyoza	Chinese style dumplings of meat or vegetables.

H

hashi	the commonly used word for chopsticks.
hijiki	a variety of seaweed.
hiru-gohan	lunch.
hiyashi	cold.
hiyashi-bachi	served chilled in a bowl with ice and cold water.
hiya yakko	blocks of cold tofu.
horenso	spinach

I

iidako	small octopus
ika	squid
ikura	salmon roe.
inari-zushi	sushi rice in fried tofu pockets.

K

kabayaki	grilled eel on skewers without rice.
kabu	a small, round, white Japanese turnip.
kai	a generic term for shellfish.
kaiseki ryori	elaborate Kyoto style cuisine.
kanpyo	strips of dried gourd, used for tying foods placed in stews.
kanten	gelatin derived from seaweed, used mostly in making desserts.
kappa-maki	rolled sushi with a filling of rice and Japanese cucumbers.
katsuo-bushi	dried bonito (used to make dashi).
kinoko	generic term for mushrooms.
kissaten	coffee shop.
kohi	coffee.
konbu	kelp - used in making dashi (soup stock).
konnyaku	a gelatinous substance made from the "devils-tongue" tuber.
kyuri	long and thin, Japanese cucumber.

M

maguro	tuna.
maki	rolled.
meshi	informal word for cooked rice (can also mean "meal.")
mirin	sweetened cooking sake.
miso	fermented soybean paste.
mizu	water.
momo	peach.
mori-soba	cold buckwheat noodles served on a bamboo screen.
myoga	variety of ginger, highly prized and quite expensive.

N

nabemono	quick cooked stew.
nasu	Japanese eggplant.
natto	sticky fermented soybeans.
nigiri-zushi	raw fish over small molded pieces of vinegared rice.
nihon-shu	specific word for rice wine (sake).
nimono	foods stewed in sake and soy sauce.
noren	split curtain placed in a door entry. Commonly found in eateries.
nori	dried seaweed which comes in very thin sheets.
nuka	rice bran (used to pickle vegetables).

O

oden	fish, fish cake and vegetables simmered in broth.
oishii	word meaning delicious.
okonomiyaki	egg "pancakes" containing diced seafood, vegetables, or meat, that are grilled and topped with a savory sauce.
oshinko	pickles ("fresh fragrence").
onigiri	rice ball.
osechi ryoori	traditional New Year's food.

P

ramen	Chinese style egg noodles.
renkon	lotus root.
ringo	apple.
robatayaki	restaurant specializing in grilled foods.

S

saba	mackerel.
sakana	generic word for "fish".
shake	salmon.
o-sake	rice wine ("nihon-shu"), the -o is an honorific.
sarada	salad.
sashimi	raw fish served without rice.
sato	sugar.
sato-imo	a small, round, pototo like taro root ("country potato").
shabu-shabu	thin slices of beef quick cooked in broth with vegetables.
shiitake	Japan's best known mushroom.
shio	salt.
shiso	the green perilla leaf, usually served with sashimi (also called "beefsteak leaf). Purple shiso leaf is highly prized for it's use in pickles.
shoyu	soy sauce.
shungiku	chrysanthemum leaves, edible and used in stews. Quite tasty.
soba	buckwheat noodles. A favorite served hot or cold.
somen	very thin, white flour noodles served cold in summer.

T

tabemono	food
takenoko	bamboo shoots
tako	octopus.
tamago	egg.
tara	cod.
tekka-maki	rolled sushi made with raw tuna.
tendon	rice topped with tempura fried shrimp.
tenpura	lightly batter-fried seafood and vegetables.
tofu	soy bean curd. A delicious and healthy alternative to meats.
tori	chicken (meat)
tsukemono	Japanese style pickled vegetables.

W

wakame	a variety of seaweed.
wan	bowl (of soup)

waribashi	throwaway wooden chopsticks.
wasabi	very hot, green Japanese horseradish.

Y

yaki	grilled.
yasai	generic term for vegetable.
yose-nabe	a stew made from whatever is available.
yudofu	tofu simmered in hot water along with kombu seaweed.
yushoku	dinner.
yuzu	A highly prized and expensive lemon like citrus.

JAPANESE MENU GUIDE AND INGREDIENTS

Arare	crisp rice crackers seasoned with soy sauce
Azuki	sweetened red or black beans
Daikon	a member of the turnip family (similar to radish)
Kamaboko	fish cake made from white fish
Kanten	gelatin dessert made out of seaweed
Katsudon	fried pork cutlet
Kuromame	black beans
Manju	sweet bean paste buns
Mirin	sweetened rice wine
Miso	thick fermented soybean paste
Mochi	also called sweet or sticky rice (made into cakes)
Musubi	rice ball wrapped in seaweed
Namasu	salad of vegetables in a vinegar sauce
Nishime	vegetables with pork or chicken
Nori	dried, compressed seaweed
Okazu-ya	Japanese delicatessen
Panko	flour meal used for breading
Sake	rice wine
Sashimi	thin slices of very fresh salt water fish
Sekihan	rice and red beans
Senbei	sweet rice crackers
Shabu Shabu	meat and vegetables in a simmering broth
Shiitake	large mushrooms with dark caps

Shira Ae	vegetable and tofu salad
Shumai	small steamed dumplings
Soba	slender buckwheat noodle
Somen	thin and delicate rice noodles
Sukiyaki	meat, bean curd, vegetables cooked in soy sauce and sugar
Sushi	cold vinegar rice garnished with raw fish
Takuwan	pickled daikon or turnip
Tempura	vegetables, meat, or seafood quick-fried in light egg batter
Teppanyaki	style of dining where chefs cook food at your table
Teriyaki	soy based, sweet and salty flavoring used on beef, chicken and other foods
Tobiko	orange-reddish roe of the flying fish
Tofu	white soybean curd
Tonkatsu	breaded, deep-fried pork cutlet
Tsukemono	pickled vegetables
Udon	thick wheat noodles
Wasabi	similar to horseradish but green and hotter
Yaki Tori Kushi	chicken on a stick

LEARNING OUTCOME

Japanese cuisine has developed over the past 2,000 years with strong influences from both China and Korea. During Japan's development tea, chopsticks and a number of other important food related items were also introduced from China. The taboo against the consumption of meat developed further when the Japanese indigenous religion, Shinto, also adopted a philosophy similar to that of the Buddhists. Milk and other dairy products have failed to enjoy the same popularity in Europe as they do in Japan. The only Japanese dairy product known to history was produced between the eighth and fourteenth centuries. Preserving fish also became popular and sushi originated as a means of preserving fish by fermenting it in boiled rice. Japanese food is no longer considered as one of the world's unsolved mysteries it once was,In fact, more number of people are recognizing Japanese food as one of the world's healthiest cuisines

LESSON END ACTIVITY

- Collect the mor information on japenese food items.

- Collect the data base on Japanese restaurants in India.

QUESTIONS FOR DISCUSSION

1. Explain in detail about Japanese cuisine.
2. Explain the term dashi.
3. Explain the term short grain rice.
4. Explain the term nori.
5. Explain the method of Japanese cooking.
6. Explain ant 10 Japanese culinary term.
7. Explain Japanese menu guide.
8. Explain the term wasabi.

KEY TERMS

- Bean
- Dashi
- Menu guide
- Mirini
- Nori
- Term
- Wasabi

Chapter 28

European Cuisine

After studying this chapter, the student must know :

- Introduction and division of European cuisine
- French cuisine introduction
- French culinary regions
- Italian regional food
- Italian meal course
- Italian basic ingredients
- German cuisine introduction
- German cuisine region and specialty of German cuisine.

EUROPEAN CUISINE

European cuisine, or alternatively Western cuisine is a generalized term collectively referring to the cuisines of Europe and other Western countries. European cuisine includes that of Europe and to some extent Russia, as well as non-indigenous cuisines of North America, Australasia, Oceania, and Latin America.

Central and Eastern European cuisines

- Belarusian cuisine
- Bulgarian cuisine
- Czech cuisine
- Georgian cuisine
- Hungarian cuisine
- Jewish cuisine

- Lithuanian cuisine
- Moldovan cuisine
- Polish cuisine
- Romanian cuisine
- Russian cuisine
- Serbian cuisine
- Slovak cuisine
- Tatar cuisine
- Ukrainian cuisine

Northern European cuisines

- Danish cuisine
- Estonian cuisine
- Finnish cuisine
- Icelandic cuisine
- Lappish cuisine
- Latvian cuisine
- Lithuanian cuisine
- Norwegian cuisine
- Swedish cuisine

Southern European cuisines

- Bosnian cuisine
- Croatian cuisine
- Cypriot cuisine
- Gibraltarian cuisine
- Greek cuisine
- Italian cuisine
- Sicilian cuisine
- Macedonian cuisine
- Maltese cuisine
- Montenegrin cuisine
- Portuguese cuisine
- Slovenian cuisine
- Spanish cuisine

- Andalusian cuisine
- Asturian cuisine
- Aragonese cuisine
- Balearic cuisine
- Basque cuisine
- Canarian cuisine
- Cantabrian cuisine
- Castilian-Manchego cuisine
- Catalan cuisine
- Extremaduran cuisine
- Galician cuisine
- Leonese cuisine
- Valencian cuisine
- Turkish cuisine

Western European cuisines

- Belgian cuisine
- British cuisine
- English cuisine
- Scottish cuisine
- Welsh cuisine
- Anglo-Indian cuisine
- Dutch cuisine
- French cuisine
- German cuisine
- Irish cuisine
- Luxembourgian cuisine
- Swiss cuisine.

FRENCH CUISINE

Ingredients and dishes vary by region. There are many significant regional dishes that have become both national and regional. Many dishes that were once regional have proliferated in variations across the country. Cheese and wine are a major part of the cuisine, playing different roles regionally and nationally with their many variations and Appellation d'origine contrôlée (AOC) (regulated appellation) laws. French cuisine has evolved extensively over the centuries. Starting in the Middle ages, a unique and creative national cuisine began forming. Various social movements, political movements, and the work of great chefs came together to create this movement. Through the years the styles of French cuisine have been given different names, and have been codified by various master-chefs. During their lifetimes these chefs have been held in high regard for their contributions to the culture of the country. The national cuisine developed primarily in the city of Paris with the chefs to French royalty, but eventually it spread throughout the country and was even exported overseas .France can be divided into 13 culinary regions :

1. North-Picardy (Nord-Pas-de-Calais, Picardy, western Champagne-Ardenne).
2. Normandy (Normandy).
3. Brittany (Brittany, northern Loire).
4. Ile-de-France (Il-de-France, central Champagne-Ardenne).
5. Anjou-Touraine-Berry (Pays-de-la-Loire, Loire Valley).
6. Burgundy-Lyons (Burgundy, western Rhone-Alpes).
7. Jura-Franche-Comté (Franche-Comté).
8. Savoie-Dauphiné (Eastern Rhone-Alpes).
9. Languedoc-Provence-Corsica (excludes northern Languedoc).
10. Auvergne-Limousin-Périgord (includes northern Languedoc).
11. Grand South-West (southern Pays de Loire, Poitou-Charentes, Aquitaine except the northeast, Pyrennees except the Pays Basque).
12. Basque (southern Aquitaine, south-west Pyrenees).
13. Alsace-Lorraine (eastern Champagne-Ardenne, Lorraine, Alsace

Normandy

A land of lush pastures and orchards that produces pungent soft cheeses and cider, this region also includes the harbors, cliff walks and windy beaches of the Cotentin peninsula and the wooded valleys of the Seine. Well-known attractions include the island of Mont-St-Michel, Monet's garden at Giverny, and the Bayeux 'tapestry' (strictly, a giant piece of embroidery).

Since Normandy has always had both farmers and fishermen, its food reflects the working diets of these people. Expect to see cream or cider in dishes with plenty of good farm vegetables. Meats include rabbit, and various products derived from offal. Seafood is fresh and served simply, in generous portions. This is the home of Tarte aux Pommes, and older families will offer you Calvados at any time of day. This is apple brandy, sometimes home-brewed under ancient licences, and they'll offer stronger brews as the day progresses - from 36° in the morning to a fiery overproof 46° in the evening. Traditionally, a long, heavy meal includes a break for a 'Trou Normand' - a small glass of Calvados - to settle the stomach and prepare it for the next course.

Brittany

Think of the Bretons being to the Normans what the Cornish are to the people of Devon - to an outsider the one is like the other but even more so. But there are more Bretons than Cornish who can still speak their ancient languages.

They are fishermen and farmers who live on a peninsula with the English Channel on one side and Biscay on the other. The details of their Celtic ancestry are delightfully portrayed in the Asterix cartoon stories.

Leeks, potatoes and cauliflower are the traditional vegetables. Saint-Jacques (scallops) are the favorite shellfish, and you'll often find ray on the menu. Large wheels of shortbread-like galettes are favorite gap-fillers during the day. White wine and calvados are common ingredients. 'Soupe de Roscoff' is a creamy cauliflower and onion soup. 'Saint-Jacques à la bretonne' are cooked with leeks, shallots, carrots, herbs, butter and muscadet. Try the coarse farmhouse pâtés for something with both taste and texture.

Ile-de-France

Paris and the surrounding countryside form a comparatively wealthy region. Dishes include plenty of egg, cheese and onions. Sauces are lighter and less creamy than in the farming regions, and you'll find exotic spices such as vanilla. 'Lapin sauté chasseur' uses a sauce with the tang of lemon.

Anjou-Touraine-Berry

Expect some vegetables from warmer climates, more 'gamey' meats and more garlic. 'Poulet en Barbouille' uses additional blood from chicken giblets.

Burgundy-Lyons

You'll see sausages, Dijon mustard, rich deserts. Compare the peasant dish 'andouilles à la lyonnaise' (tripe sausages in pork fat and vinegar, with onions) with 'vacherin glacé au caramel' (a rich desert containing egg yolks, sugar, cream, rum and vanilla-flavored meringues)

Jura-Franche-Comté

A lush, hilly land of dairy cattle and soft comté cheese. Expect both peasant food (local sausages, etc.,) and lighter, sophisticated dishes (frogs' legs, coq au vin using a local 'yellow' wine). On two successive winter holidays in the Jura, I saw sucking pig in the charcuterie window.

Savoie-Dauphiné

Both foothills and real Alps. Peasant food uses local cheeses. Look for trout, and alcoholic fondues. The saucisson sec is excellent (salt-cured pork sausage with peppercorns - far preferable to Italian salami, in my opinion). Use it, with soft cheese and a baguette, for snacks.

Languedoc-Provence-Corsica

All the Mediterranean regions have food characterised by olive oil, olives, tomatoes, capsicum and herbs. The west shows Spanish influence, and Corsica a hint of southern Italy. The Languedoc is home to bouillabaisse, originally a fishwife's meal made from what her man couldn't sell, enlivened with garlic and white wine. A group of restaurants in and around Marseille, determined to uphold standards, sells 'the only varies bouillabaisse de Marseille' at steep prices. They created this to counter the bad impression given by uninspiring dishes served as 'our version' of the dish by cheap restaurants - but this turns it into haute cuisine, which is not how it originated.

Auvergne-Limousin-Périgord

The land of foie gras, sangliers (wild boar), chestnuts and a vast selection of forest mushrooms, with some excellent cheeses. Everything from peasant food to 'escalopes de foie gras' - foie gras sautéed in goose grease, served with white grapes cooked in strong, sweet white wine. Try soupe de châtaignes (chestnut soup with onion, celery, leek and garlic) on a chilly autumn evening.

Grand Sud-Ouest

This is the Biscay side of France. Bordeaux wines, plenty of seafood - and everyone has heard of entrecôte bordelaise. Try 'cailles au foie gras' (quail, foie gras, white grapes, white wine), or 'soupe aux huitres' (oysters floating in a rich soup made from egg, shallot, leek, butter and cream.

Basque

The food of the western Pyrenees reminds me slightly of Portuguese cooking. Colorful peppers and tomatoes, olive oil, garlic. Although the region only has a very short coastline adjacent to the Spanish border, it has several fish dishes. 'Thon à la basquaise' features tuna cutlets with garlic imbedded in the flesh, garnished with onions, peppers and tomatoes.

Alsace-Lorraine

This region is strongly influenced by southern Germany. Veal and game meats combine with the fruits and fungi of temperate climes. 'Omelette farcie de Nancy' features slices of blood sausage (the 'black pudding' of Scotland and northern England).

ITALIAN REGIONAL FOOD

Italian Regional Specialties

About Regional Italian Food and Wines

- Northern Italy Regional Food
- Central Italy Regional Food

- Southern Italy Regional Food

First-time travelers to Italy may be surprised on finding such a diversity of regional food. Unlike your typical Italian restaurant in the States, Italian food has much more variety than spaghetti and meatballs or Eggplant Parmesan. Even though you can find Italian specialties like pizza and tortellini all over Italy, it is well worth sampling the local dishes for a bit of authenticity. When eating foods grown or raised in the surrounding countryside and complemented with the local wine, both your Traveling and eating experiences are taken to a whole new level. The pride that Italians have in their locally grown produce, regional specialties and exceptional wine is something you cannot find in a supermarket.

ITALIAN REGIONAL SPECIALTIES: THE NORTH

Northern Italian cuisine is characterized by less use of olive oil, pasta and tomato sauce and more use of butter (or lard), rice, corn (for polenta) and chesses for cream sauces. Of course there are exceptions to these rules such as the olive oils of the Liguria and the Lakes regions. Pasta in the north is by no means non-existent, but it does have to share time with delicious risotto and polenta. Northern Italian main courses often reflect the people's pride in their unspoiled countryside and are likely to include some sort of game or wild fowl such as rabbit, quail or grouse. Seafood and shellfish are very popular on the coasts and rivers and streams provide carp and trout. Of course the overall rule being if it grows well in the area, it will usually be on the plate.

Val d'Aosta

The region produces Fontina cheese and is used in local specialties like Costoletta alla Valdostana - a veal chop covered in Fontina. Capriolo alla Valdostana is a hearty venison stew made with wine, vegetables and grappa. The rocky crags of the Alps help make Aostan wines unique and the region is home to the DOC recognized Reds Donnas, Chambave Rosso and Nus Rosso. Whites include the simply named and crisp Bianco and the Blanc de Morgex with its hints of alpine meadows. Val d'Aosta is also home to the dessert wine Nus-Malvoisie Fletri as well as locally made Grappa.

Piedmont- Piemonte

A popular dish is fonduta, a melted cheese dip of milk, eggs and white truffles (tartufi bianchi). Fine cheeses include Robiola, Caprini and Tumin electric, a white mountain cheese soaked in red peppers. Cardi alla Bagna Cauda is a dish of locally grown chard served with hot sauce, anchovies, garlic and white truffles. Other regional dishes include local game such as rabbit and boiled meat dishes like Vitello Tonnato (veal tongue) and ox tail. Grissino are thin and crispy breadsticks that have become popular throughout the country. Piedmonte is also the home to two wild fungi that are prized the world over: Porcini mushrooms and white truffles. Piemonte produces the Asti white wines that include Moscato and sparkling Asti Spumante. The region is also home to full-bodied reds that include Barbera, Barolo and Barberesco.

Lombardy

This region is known for its rice dishes including Minestrone alla Milanese, made with vegetables, rice and bacon. Risotto alla Milanese is a creamy dish of braised short-grain rice blended with meat stock, saffron and cheese. Other favorites include ravioli with a pumpkin filling from Montova, small quails with polenta from Bergamo. Osso bucco is a traditional main course of a knuckle of veal with the marrowbone intact and braised with rosemary and sage. The excellent cheeses of the region include the rich blue Gorgonzola, Grana Padana (a rival of Parmigiano-Reggiano), the alpine Bitto creamy Crescenza and gluttonous Mascarpone. Lombardy wines hail from the Valtellina area, known for its well-aged reds that include Valtellina Superiore, Lombardy best. Franciacorta is the home to sparkling white wines in the tradition of the Champagnes of France, but with the character of Italy.

Veneto

As in the Po River Plain, cooking in the Veneto incorporates polenta and rice in their dishes along with wild fowl, mushrooms, or seafood. Traditional courses include Risi e Bisi (rice and peas), and Fegato alla Veneziana (calf's liver fried with onions). Seafood ranging from prawns, shrimp and clams to fresh fish and eels play an important part of the local diet and are proudly displayed in the markets and restaurants. Wild game such as rabbit, duck, pigeon and guinea fowl are also favorites, found in the protected marshes of the Lagoon. Radicchio di Treviso is a bitter red chicory served as a salad but more often grilled and served with salt and olive oil. Asparagi di Bassano are white asparagus that are boiled and served with vinaigrette or eggs. Asiago is the best and most popular cheese that comes from the Veneto. Pandoro, a star-shaped cake delicately flavored with orange-flower is a specialty of Verona. The region is known for some of Italy's best known reds such as Valpolicella and Bardolino. The whites include Soave, Gambellara, Bianco di Custoza and

Vigne Alte. Trentino-Alto Adige

This region shares culinary traditions from both the Italian and German sides of the border. Canederli is made with bread and flour and served in a broth is just one of several types of gnocchi (dumplings) popular in Trentino-Alto Adige. Polenta is very popular around Trentino along with wild fowl, river trout and Germanic sauerkraut. Speck is a salumi style cured meat that is similar to bacon and has become available throughout Italy. The most popular cheeses include the fresh Tosela, Spressa delle Giudicarie (DOP) and Puzzone di Moena. Red wines include the full-bodied Marzemino and the fruity Teroldego White wines excel in this pre-alpine climate and include Nosiola, Pino Blanc, Chardonnay the Spumante Talento Trento and the traditional sweet dessert wine Vin Santo.

Friuli-Venezia Giulia

The region is known for its vast cornfields, which feed the areas demand for polenta. Prosciutto di San Daniele is a sweet cured ham that is hung to absorb the fresh mountain air. Montasio is a aged hard cheese that is sold at different levels of maturity. The cuisine of the Venezia Giulia portion, especially around Trieste reflects German/Slavic traditions. Iota is a soup made of beans, potatoes and white cabbage. Porcina is a mix of boiled pork with sauerkraut, mustard and horseradish. Slavic goulash and dumplings are also local favorites. The coastal areas love their seafood including cuttlefish (sepia), mixed fried fish and Boreto Graesano, a fish and white polenta soup. Regional desserts have a Germanic touch such as apple strudel, Cuguluf (a ring cake) and Gubana (made from dried fruit and raisins). Friuli wines are well known, with Ramandolo protected by a DOCG designation. Other reds include Refosco dal Peduncolo and Schiopettino. Friuli is best known for its whites with the very popular Tocai, Malvasia Istriana, and Ribolla gialla. Vitoska is a white wine served as an aperitivo and Picolit is a white dessert wine.

Liguria

The most famous of all culinary masterpieces from Liguria is its basil Pesto sauce, served with either Trofie (favored in Cinque Terre) or Trenette (favored in Genoa) pasta. The olive oil of the region is an exception to most of Northern Italian cooking and plays an everyday role along the rocky coast. Seafood plays a large role in the local diet with fresh caught anchovies being a favorite as well as Swordfish, Tuna, Sardines and Sea Bass. Zuppa di Datteri is a shellfish soup made in the port of La Spezia. Popular meat dishes including Tomaxelle (Veal rolls) and Coniglio in Umbido (Rabbit stew). Ligurian desserts include Pandolce Genovese, a sweet bread made with candied fruit, raisins and nuts, and sweet pizzas made with walnuts, chestnuts and candied fruit. Red wines include Rossese di Dolceacqua, Ormeasco, and the dessert wine Sciacchetra Rosso. The white wines of Liguria are ideal for seafood and include Cinque Terre, Sciacchetra and Colline di Levanto. Sprits range from Grappa to the citrus based Limoncello Ligure to walnut-infused Nocino.

Italian Regional Specialties: The Center

Much of what the rest of the world considers Italian food hails from the central regions of Italy. Velvety smooth olive oils, world-famous cheeses, savory cured meats and rich tomato sauces grace the tables of this sun-scorched . Beef dishes can be found more often here and the hills of Tuscan and Umbria are known for their wild boar. Both coasts share their love of locally caught seafood and the rugged interior is known for hearty mountain fare.

Emilia-Romagna

The region has a fine gastronomic reputation with stuffed pasta including the Tortellini of Emilia and the Cappelletti of Romagna, served with the famous Bolognese meat sauce (Ragu). The "king of all cheeses" Parmigiano-Reggiano has found its way into recipes around the world but its production is strictly enforced to ensure a continued tradition of quality. Pork products include Parma's famous Prosciutto, Zibello's time-honored Culatello, Bologna's Mortadella and the Zamponi (stuffed trotter sausage) of Modena. Romagna is home to fish and seafood dishes, with eels being a favorite of Comacchio. The area of Modena is also the home of the coveted Balsamic vinegar of Modena, yet another masterpiece of Emilia Romagna that is often imitated, but never duplicated. For wine, the sparkling red Lambrusco Salamino di Santa Croce barley resembling the inferior mass produced version available in the US. White wines include Albana di Romagna and Trebbiano di Romagna, both enjoyed since Roman times.

Tuscany

It can be argued that this is where Italian cooking was born - at the court of the Medici. The region is home to excellent olive oils, sheep milk cheeses and delicious roasted meat dishes. Florence offers its famous "alla fiorentina" steak and specialties that include: Ribollita, a thick vegatable soup, Fagioli all'uccelletto (beans sauted in Garlic and Sage with tomatoes) and Fagioli al Fiasco with oil, onions and herbs cooked in a round bottle (fiasco) on a coal fire. Seafood cooking includes triglie (red mullet) and a delicious fish soup known as Cacciucco alla Livornese. Siena offers Panforte, a cake containing almonds, honey and candied fruit. Tuscan wines sell worldwide, including Chianti, which comes in both red and white. Brunello di Montalcino is rightfully praised as well as the Vino Nobile di Montepulciano. The DOCG protected Vernaccia di San Gimignano is probably the most well-known Tuscan white wine.

Umbria

Norcia in the Apennine foothills is the home of Italy's best black truffles (tartufo nero), which are served over everything including local pecorino cheese. Many types of hand-made pasta like Strozzapreti (priest stranglers) are offered in a decadent black truffle sauce not easily found outside Umbria. Norcia is also home to excellent pork products such as their Prosciutto and various Salame. Besides delioucs home made fresh pastas made with egg, the region of Umbria is responsible for the production of much of the dried pasta consumed throughout Italy. The wines of Umbria include many excellent whites like the famous Orvieto, as well as higly praised reds such as Torgiano Rosso and Montefalco Rosso.

Marche (Marches)

The Le Marche versions of the famous fish stew known as Brodetto include red and gray mullet, cuttlefish or squid (or both), oil, garlic and saffron. The port of Ancona is known for Stoccafisso (stockfish), sole, bream, clams and mussels. Vincisgrassi is made with ground pork, mushrooms, tomato and béchamel sauce and topped with local truffles. Favorite meats include veal, rabbit, game birds (quail, pigeon), chicken and goose. Both meats and fish are usually done either in a porchetta style using fennel, garlic and rosemary or potacchio (with onion, tomato, white wine and rosemary). Young Pecorino cheeses and the Casciotta d'Urbino is also popular. Le Marche's wines include the reds Rosso Conero, Rosso Piceno and Vernaccia di Serrapetrona. Le Marche is home to standout white wines like Verdicchio (dei Castelli di Iesi or di Matelica) and Bianchello del Metauro, both excellent with seafood.

Lazio and Rome

There are many Roman pasta specialties: Bucatini all'amatriciana with tomato, onion, bacon and a dash of cognac, Spaghetti alla carbonara with a creamy egg and cheese sauce dusted with black pepper "coal flakes", Gnocchi alla Romana and Rigatoni alla Pagliata (rigatoni with calf's intestine). Meat dishes include Abbacchio al forno (roast lamb) or alla cacciatora (lamb with an anchovy and rosemary sauce) and Saltimbocca - a fillet of veal rolled in ham and flavored and served in a Marsala sauce. Favorite vegetable dishes include artichokes (carciofi) done either alla Giudia (Jewish style) or alla Romana - cooked in oil with garlic and parsley. The white wines of Montefiascone and the Castelii (Frascati) will satisfy the most discerning gourmet. Perhaps the most well known roman specialties (now available all over Italy and mostly everywhere) is th Bruschetta. Bruschetta is very simple : take a fingerthick slice of home made bread, toast it and then rub a clove of garlic over the surface and sprinkle some good olive oil and salt. (You can aslo add tomatoes pieces on top). Panzanella is another simple to prepare bread dish. Not quite as well known as the bruschetta (but it is a lot tastier than what it sound from the description). Panzanella: Take a slice of home made bread, moisten ligthly with some water, split open a nice ripe tomato and rub it over the bread until the juice is absorbed. Season with some olive oil, salt, a few drops of vinegar and a few basil leaves.

Abruzzi and Molise

These two regions share similar cuisines, with Molise being a little more rustic. Among the pasta, note the Maccheroni alla chitarra, made by hand and cut into strips. Pecorino, Caciocavallo, Scamorza and Latticing cheeses are all popular. In the mountainous interior lamb, kid, mutton and ewe are all favorite meats and are the basis for Molisian specialties like Cacio e Uova, cooked in an earthenware pot and served with egg and sharp cheese. Pork is used for local Prosciutto (including a smoked variety) and various types of Salami. Molise and Abruzzi also share a love for Porchetta (roast suckling pig). Molise is known for it's fiery diavolino red peppers, used in the traditional tomato ragu. The olive oil of Molise is some of the best but is not generally made in large amounts for export. The coast of Abruzzi and Molise famous for their Broddetto, which uses the local favorite red mullet. Other popular seafood includes fresh anchovies, swordfish, mussels and clams. The gutsy Montepulciano d'Abruzzo is one of Abruzzi's most popular and affordable export wines. Biferno comes in Rosso, Rosato and Bianco varieties and are all considered dry. Pentro di Isernia also is found in dry whites and reds

ITALIAN REGIONAL SPECIALTIES: THE SOUTH

From the Pizza of Naples to the countless types of dried and fresh pasta, the food of the south is the soul of Italy. Here you will find rich and spicy tomato sauces and the almost exclusive use of olive oil in cooking. In fact some of the best olive oil comes from this region, but very little of it is exported. The south is home to citrus fruits, fields of durum wheat for pasta, olive groves and vineyards. The sea is used to its fullest extent with all manner of seafood enjoyed from tuna to anchovies, clams to sea urchins.

Campania

Italian food would not be the same without Campania's Spaghetti topped with Pommarola, the famous tomato sauce. Campania is also the birthplace of the modern Pizza, with the world's first Pizzeria (still in business) started on the streets of Naples. The volcanic soils of Campania grow some of the best produce in Italy, including San Marzano tomatoes, peaches, grapes, apricots, figs, oranges and lemons. Campania's most famous cheese is the Mozzarella di Bufalo Campania, made from the milk of local water buffalos. Other popular cheeses include sheep's milk Pecorino, Scamorza, Ricotta (both cow and buffalo versions), and Mascarpone. Parmigiano Reggiano has also found its way into the recipes of Campania, with meat and vegetable dishes served "alla Parmigiana" Seafood is a staple of Campania's coastline with fish fried in olive oil a favorite of Naples, while other specialties make use of local octopus, cuttlefish, squid, clams and mussels. The standout wines of Campania include the reds Taurasi and Vesuvio and white Lacryma Christi and Greco di Tufo.

Puglia, Basilicata, and Calabria

The meat of choice in these Southern Italian regions is either lamb or kid and can be roasted, baked or grilled on skewers. Calabria is home to Capretto Ripieno al Forno, a roast kid stuffed with herbs. Pork is popular for local Salami with rabbit and beef also being popular. The Catanzaro area is home to Nduja, a soft spicy salami that can be spread on bread. Caciocavallo, Canestrato, Ricotta and Mozzarella are the most popular cheeses in these southern regions. Along the coast seafood plays a major role in the diet with favorites including mussels, oysters, octopus, red mullet and swordfish. Vegetables include fava beans, artichokes, chicory and various greens including rucola ("rocket"). Eggplants, peppers, lampasciuoli (a bitter type of onion), cauliflower, olives and olive oil are all southern staples. Regional pastas include Orecchiette and Bucatini, both served with tomato sauce or with olive oil, garlic and cauliflower. Apulia is home to moderately priced wines such as the reds Castel del Monte, Primitvo and Salice Salentino.

Sicily

The island is rich in fruit with lemons, blood oranges, tangerines, olives, almonds, and prickly pears in abundance. Caponata is an antipasto made with eggplant, olives, capers and celery. The ceci or chick pea has played an important role in Sicilian history and is well represented in the diet. Panella is a thin paste made of crushed ceci and served fried and Maccu is a creamy soup made from the same bean. Pasta is an everday staple in Sicily and often served with a rich spicy tomato sauce. Sicily also loves their seafood with popular dishes including grilled swordfish or snapper, Finocchio con le Sarde (fennel with sardines) and Sepia (cuttlefish) served in its own black sauce with pasta. The best known Sicilian meat dish Vitello al Marsala (veal marsala) and is just one of many regional meat specialties that can also involve lamb, kid or rabbit. The best-known wine is Marsala which is dark and strong, but Malvasia and the white wines of Etna and Lipari are also delicious.

Sardinia

Sardinia's bread is an excellent antipasto and really good with Sardinian sausages and sweet green olives. Spicy fish soups called Burrida and Cassola along with lobsters, crabs, anchovies, squid, clams and fresh sardines are all very popular along the Sardinian coast. Favorite Sardinian pasta dishes include Spaghetti con Bottarga, with dried gray mullet roe shaved on top, Malloreddus is a gnocchi flavored with saffron and served with a tomato sauce. Culingiones are round ravioli stuffed with spinach and cheese. Sardinia is known for its rustic sheep and goat cheeses like Pecorino Sardo and Fiore Sardo, which can either be served fresh or aged. The Sardinian interior produces some of the best lamb in all of Italy and known for being very lean. Sardinians enjoy their meats roasted and Porceddu, (Sardinian version of Porchetta) suckling pig or kid (suckling goat) is a favorite roasted outdoors over aromatic woods. Wines include the red Cannonau and Monica di Cagliari, with the most well known Sardinian white being Vernaccia di Oristano.

HOW TO EAT ITALIAN-STYLE

Italians believe that God keeps an Italian kitchen, and so everyone should enjoy la cucina italiana. The following advice will help you do it in style.

Dealing with Italian waiters is similar to crossing Italian streets: you can do it if you are brazen enough, showing skill and courage and looking all the time as though you own the place. A good waiter should explain the dishes on the menu and help you select the wine. But if you order coffee or tea during the meal, ask for the ketchup, bottle, or request a doggie bag... watch out, you will be in big trouble.

Cocktails before dinner are not popular and are associated negatively with Americans and the three-martini lunch. However, an aperitif, such as a flute of sparkling wine to sip as you are deciding what to order, is often served.

You do not have to order all of the courses in an Italian meal, but you will be expected to have more than a pasta and salad in a nice place. When you add the cover and service charges, fine dining will not be a Cheap Eat. If you want a true Cheap Eat, go to a cafeteria, snack bar, or dine al fresco with a picnic you have put together yourself.

A guiding principle in Italian dining is that you eat one food at a time and that every food has its place. If you order a light supper of pasta and salad at an informal trattoria, you will be served the pasta first and the salad after. If you want to start your meal with a salad, the key word is come, as in come antipasto, vorrei un insalata mista (as an antipasto, I would like a mixed salad), or comme secondo, vorrei un contorno (as a second course, I would like a vegetable).

If the waiter does not bring the Parmesan cheese, it probably does not go with what you are eating. Parmesan is never used on pasta with fish or lots of garlic, but it is offered with many types of soup.

Bread is served with all Italian meals and is part of the pane e coperto charge. Butter is seldom served except with breakfast.

The container of olive oil on the table is for more than sprinkling on your salad. A plain broiled or grilled fish is enhanced with a few drops of olio, and maybe some lemon.

Coffee is served after a meal, never with it.

Italian course is as follows:

- **Appetizers**
- Pasta

- Meat / Fish (with Vegetables or salad)
- Salad
- Cheese
- Fruit
- Sweets and coffee
- Ammazzacaffe (Grappa or Amaro

ITALIAN BASISC INGREDIENTS

Virgin Olive Oil

Virgin Olive Oil is made exactly like Extra Virgin, but their acidity, in terms of oleic acid is allowed to reach 1 ½%, 3%, and 4%. An oil with more than 4% is not suitable for consumption.

Pure Olive Oil

Oil that exceeds 4% oleic acid may be adjusted to edible levels by adding such solvents like trichloroethylene that reduces the acid, then it is blended with some virgin oil to improve its taste. It can then be called Olio d'Oliva or as most producers label it, Pure Olive Oil.

Nutmeg - Noce moscata

Nutmeg is a pungent spice which should be used with discretion, grated straight onto the dish in which it is required. When grated it releases a delicious aroma and flavour. It can be used in both sweet and savory dishes, especially in ravioli and tortellini fillings and often flavors hot punches and other warming drinks. I always add a touch of nutmeg to my bolognese meat sauce!

Anchovies (Alice, Acciugha) - Storing and Using

A jar of salted anchovies will keep almost indefinitely provided they remain covered by liquid and are always taken out with a clean spoon or fork. Canned and oiled anchovies last well if covered in oil.

Basil (Basilico)

Basil is a lovely aromatic herb with a spicy and aromatic scent. Many say that basil is the most important herb in Italian cooking, and I'd have to agree. In Italy basil leaves are best known in pesto, but is also used to flavour tomato sauces, salads and in minestrone and vegetable soups. Fresh basil, of course, is the best thing to use, and it is very easy to grow — dry basil has practically no flavour. If there are times when fresh basil is not available, do use dry basil (definitely Not for pesto, though) Use it in soups, salads and tomato sauces. Fresh basil can also be stored by layering in a jar with olive oil.

Garlic (Aglio) - Crushing techniques

Garlic is a must in my kitchen and it should be in yours, too. It is an important ingredient in Italian cuisine, especially in sauces, roasts and, of course, pesto. To crush garlic, sprinkle salt on the peeled clove and crush with the broad side of a large knife; or without using salt, crush the garlic with the blunt top side of the knife; or put the garlic on a flat surface and pound lightly with the back of your fist...the clove should split slightly, making it quite easy to remove the skin. When sautéing, be careful not to burn the garlic, as it will turn bitter

Olive Oil - Buying Quality

The quality of olive oil depends very much on the region it was produced in. The best olive oils come from the southern region of Apulia or the central regions of Latium, Umbria, and Tuscany.

Unfortunately in Italy the law does not require that an olive oil packer use only the oil produced in his area. Therefore, the geographic name on a label may sometimes relate only to the address of the plant, not to the region of production. The contents of the bottle or can, although legitimately labeled "extra virgin" may be a lesser quality oil from elsewhere. Your best bet is to try different oils and let your taste buds tell you which flavour you prefer. When you find one or two that you really like, stay with them. A good olive oil should "coat with flavour, not with grease".

German cuisine

German cuisine is a style of cooking derived from the nation of Germany. It has evolved as a national cuisine through centuries of social and political change with variations from region to region. The southern regions of Germany, Bavaria and Swabia share many dishes. Ingredients and dishes vary by province. There are many significant regional dishes that have become both national and regional.While the various regions of Germany were independent and autonomous communities until relatively recently, it is not surprising that they also developed special regional foods. There is a common factor: almost everywhere, these regional foods are based on the country's favorite staples of beer, pork, potatoes, and cabbage, yet they are different in the technique of cooking , seasoning, or the way they are served. German cuisne region divided into the followings :

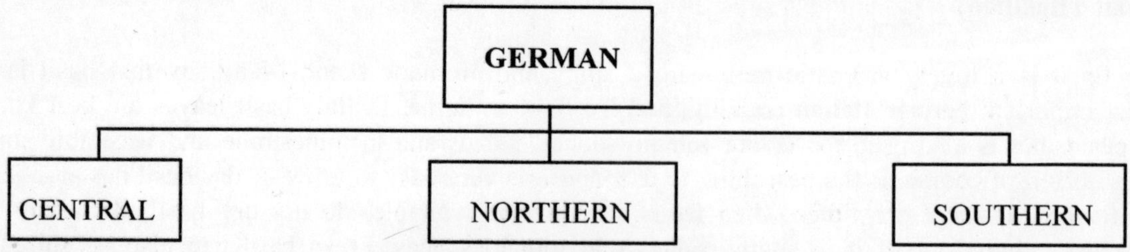

Fig 28.1 German culinary region

Central Region

- The Central region also includes hearty meals and foods, especially the famed Westphalian ham and dark heavy pumpernickel bread.
- Gravies are thickened with dried bread crumbs more often than with flour.

Northern region

- The Central region also includes hearty meals and foods, especially the famed Westphalian ham and dark heavy pumpernickel bread.
- Gravies are thickened with dried bread crumbs more often than with flour .
- Most interesting is the traditional North German meal of labskaus: a one-dish meal of meat and fish plus vegetables which became a sailor's specialty and earned the name lobscouse
- Slaughter plate is also a Northern specialty of a variety of meats and sausages – the byproducts of a slaughtering day – served with bread and pickles.
- Berlin, considered part of the Northern cuisine district, is famed for its ground meat dishes.

Southern region

- Southern German cuisine has a characteristically lighter touch .
- Here, dumplings are called knodel, and some very special potato dishes are prepared: puddings, pancakes, diced potatoes and bacon

LEARNING OUTCOME

Ingredients and dishes vary by region. There are many significant regional dishes that have become both national and regional. Many dishes that were once regional have proliferated in variations across the country. Cheese and wine are a major part of the cuisine, playing different roles regionally and nationally with their many variations and Appellation d'origine contrôlée (AOC) (regulated appellation) laws. French cuisine has evolved extensively over the centuries. French culinary region divided into 13 regions. Normandy has always had both farmers and fishermen, its food reflects the working diets of these people. Expect to see cream or cider in dishes with plenty of good farm vegetables. Italian food has much more variety than spaghetti and meatballs or Eggplant Parmesan. Even though you can find Italian specialties like pizza and tortellini all over Italy, it is well worth sampling the local dishes for a bit of authenticity. When eating foods grown or raised in the surrounding countryside and complemented with the local wine, both your Travelling and eating experiences are taken to a whole new level. Northern Italian cuisine is characterized by less use of olive oil, pasta and tomato sauce and more use of butter (or lard), rice, corn (for polenta) and chesses for cream sauces. German cuisine is a style of cooking derived from the nation of Germany. It has evolved as a national cuisine through centuries of social and political change with variations from region to region. The southern regions of Germany, Bavaria and Swabia share many dishes.

LESSON END ACTIVITY

- Collect the information on French food festivals in India.
- Collect the information on German food festivals in India.
- Collect the data base on French restaurant in India.
- Collect the data base on Italian restaurant in India.

QUESTIONS AND DISCUSSION

1. Explain in detail about European cuisine.
2. Explain the classification of European cuisine.
3. Explain in detail about French cuisine and their regions.
4. Explain in detail about the Italian regional food.
5. Explain the eating style of Italian and there Italian course.
6. Explain in detail about German cuisine with their region specialty.

STATE TRUE AND FALSE

- Pizza from German.
- Basil is common used in German cusine.
- Rosemary is common used in french cuisine.
- Extra virgin olive oil is puree olive oil.
- Olive is used mostly in European cuisine.

KEY TERMS

* Bitter	* Olive oil
* Cuisine	* Polenta
* Meal	* Slaughter
* Olive	* Staples

Chapter 29
Arabic Cuisine

After studying this chapter, the student must know :

- Introduction and its features
- Common ingredients
- Culture influence on Arabic cuisine
- Common element of Arabic cookery
- Glossary of Arabic cuisine.

ARABIC CUISINE

Arabic cuisine has its roots in tent cookery. Nomadic tribes could use only transportable foods such as rice and dates, or ambulatory stock like sheep and camels in their recipes - which tended to be rough sketches rather than strict formulae. "Tafathalo" means "Do me the honour". It is an invitation to come to the table.Sharing a meal with others is an old honoured tradition in the Arabic World and an expression of hospitality. Arab cuisine is defined as the various regional cuisines spanning the Arab World from Iraq to Morocco to Somalia to Yemen, and incorporating Levantine, Egyptian and others. It has also been influenced to a degree by the cuisines of Turkey, Pakistan, Iran, India, the Berbers and other cultures of the peoples of the region before the cultural Arabization brought by genealogical Arabians during the Arabian Muslim conquests.

The Arabic cuisine is mainly a combination of Mediterranean, Middle Eastern, and Indian food. It has been affected by the mingling of Arab and non-Arabs over the centuries. European cultures such as the Spanish, Italian, French and Greek also had impact on the Arab cooking. Turkish cuisine had impact on the entire Arab world, Persian and Indian cuisine had impact on the eastern side of the Arabic countries

As the caravans journeyed throughout the Middle East, new seasonings and vegetables were discovered and added to the existing repertoire. Each new discovery was incorporated into the diet in quantities palatable to a particular tribe - a fact that many cooks believe is responsible for the anomalies found in some Arabic dishes today.

The nomadic Bedouin influence is broadened by other cuisines from the Arab world, notably from Syria, Lebanon, Palestine and Egypt, resulting in a highly diverse food and drink culture.

Lebanese contributions have been the greatest influence on modern Middle Eastern cuisine, in no small part due to the entrepreneurship of the Lebanese that has helped to spread Arabic cuisine throughout the world from its centre in the Levant in such areas as Aleppo, Damascus, Beirut and Nablus. Lebanese culinary influence and business skills provide the framework for the exotic cuisine recognised internationally as Arabic.

Hospitality in the Arab world is second to none, and nowhere is it better expressed than in the age-old custom of serving freshly-brewed coffee or mint tea to every guest, whether the gathering be business or social.

The foreigner who takes time to learn and experiment with this excellent cuisine will be immediately won over and rewarded with many wonderful surprises. Arabic food can rival any international gastronomy for originality and good taste, and, because it basically comprises simple, natural and easily digested foodstuffs, it ranks high in nutritional value with today's fitness-conscious society.

INGREDIENTS

The Arabic cuisine contains a combination of a rich diversity of Mediterranean, Middle Eastern, and Indian food. You will find the following items most of the time:

Cinnamon, Curry powder, Fish (in coastal areas), Garlic, Lamb (or veal), Mild to hot sauces, Mint, Onion, Rice, Saffron, Sesame, Yogurt, Spices (similar to the Indian cuisine) due to heavy trading between the two regions. Tea, Thyme (or oregano), Turmeric, Variety of fruits (primarily citrus), Variety of vegetables such as cucumbers, eggplants, lettuce, tomato, green pepper, green beans, zucchini and parsley

CULTURE OF THE ARABIC CUISINE

The essential concept in the Arabic cuisine is hospitality.

Formal dinners and celebrations normally include large quantities of lamb (or veal), chicken, rice, stewed vegetables with tomato sauce and dishes seasoned with a variety of herbs and spices. Several other side dishes and salads are included.

Tea is inescapable and is the favourite hot drink and is constantly consumed. Coffee would be included as well.

The Middle Eastern diet consists of many ingredients not normally used in the American kitchen, such as lentil soups, fava beans, olive and sesame seed oils, olives, feta cheese, and dates.

Some of the Arabic dishes need a lot of preparation time, such as the stuffed grape leaves, stuffed zucchini, green peppers or cabbage.

Muslim Arabs do not consume pork meat or alcohol. Although, the Arabic market in many Arabic countries, such as Iraq, Lebanon, Egypt and Syria, sell pork meat and a variety of liquors and alcohol because the Christian Arabs consume these products.

The word "halal" means "allowed", is a way of describing the meat product which has been ritually slaughtered, similarly to the Jewish "kosher" tradition.

COMMON ELEMENTS OF ARABIC COOKERY

Bread

Bread is highly regarded in the Arab world. If anybody notices a scrap of bread on the street, they would pick it up and put on the side where no one can step on it accidentally. Bread is an essential ingredient on the table in the Arabic cuisine. It is used on the side, in salads, or in certain dishes such as the "fatteh"

Dairy

Yogurt made from sheep, cow or goat's milk is used in many ways;

- Diluted with water as a refreshing drink.
- Drained and thickened as a condiment.

Meat

Lamb is used in most of the Arabic countries, although some countries use veal more than lamb. The most prized dish an Arabic house can serve to their guests is baby lamb stuffed with spiced rice. The Bedouins use sheep and camel meat too.

Fruits

Fresh and dried fruits and nuts are widely used. Example of the fruits and nuts used are; pomegranates, lemons, dates, apples, figs, oranges, apricots, mango, almonds and pistachios.

Grains

Rice is a staple in all the Arabic countries. It is cooked in countless ways. It served alongside meat, fish, and stewed vegetables. Wheat is another staple and is used as whole grain, cracked or as flour for bread and a variety of pastries. Bulgur is another favorite grain in some Arabic countries and is used in breakfast in North African countries and cooked similarly to rice in Iraq.

Oil

Olive oil is the most common for cooking and dressing. It is produced in Lebanon, Syria, Palestine and parts of North Africa. Sesame oil is also used in some countries where olive oil is scarce.

Salads

Salads are always available whether at lunch or dinner. They are made with a variety of fresh vegetables and simple fresh dressing of lemon (or lime) juice, salt (and pepper) and olive oil.

Spices

Spices are the essence of the Arabic cuisine. The most common spices used include but not limited to; cinnamon, allspice, anise seeds, nutmeg, sumac, cardamom, cloves, cumin, caraway, black pepper, saffron, and turmeric. The Arabs have been long known in history for their spice trade with other countries.

Vegetables

Vegetables are used raw and cooked. A wide variety of vegetables is used. The favorites are eggplant, zucchini, cauliflower, okra, green beans and spinach. A variety of fresh and dried beans and legumes is also used such as peas and lentils.

Mazza (or Mezzah)

Mazza are side dishes or appetizers that are made of assortment of little tidbits in small plates. They accompany the main dish. They typically include salads, grains, pulses and vegetables.

GLOSSARY OF ARABIC CUISINE

Arabic Glossary	*English meaning*
Arabic Bread (Khubz Arabi, pita)	Flat, round bread, which can be easily split to make a sandwich, or broken apart and used as a utensil for scooping food
Arayess	Deep-fried lamb sandwich
Ataif (gatayef, kataif)	Small pancakes stuffed with nuts or cheese and doused with syrup
Baba Ghanoush	Char-grilled eggplant, tahina, olive oil, lemon juice and garlic purée - served as a dip
Baharat (bjar)	Arabic mixed spices
Bamia	Baby okra and lamb in tomato stew
Baklawa (baklava)	Dessert of layered pastry filled with nuts and steeped in honey-lemon syrup - usually cut into triangular or diamond shapes
Basboosa	Semolina tart soaked with syrup

Arabic Glossary	*English meaning*
Bukhari Rice	Lamb and rice stir-fried with onion, lemon, carrot and tomato paste
Burghul (bulghur wheat, bulgar)	Parboiled and dried wheat kernels processed into grain, used in tabbouleh and mixed with lamb in kibbeh
Cardamom	Aromatic spice, member of the ginger family, used to flavour Arabic coffee, yoghurt and stews
Coriander (cilantro)	Lacy, green-leaf relative of the parsley family with an extremely pungent flavour akin to a combination of lemon, sage and caraway.
Ejje	Arabic omelette
Falafel	Small deep-fried patties made of highly-spiced ground chick-peas
Fatayer	Pastry pockets filled with spinach, meat or cheese
Fattoush	Salad of toasted croutons, cucumbers, tomatoes and mint
Foul (ful)	Slow-cooked mash of brown beans and red lentils, dressed with lemon, olive oil and cumin
Gahwa (kahwa)	Coffee
Haleeb	Milk
Halwa (halva)	Sesame paste sweet, usually made in a slab and studded with fruit and nuts
Hamour	Red Sea fish of the grouper family
Hommus	Purée of chickpeas, tahina, lemon and garlic - served as a dip with Arabic bread
Jarish	Crushed wheat and yoghurt casserole
Jebne	White cheese
Kabsa	Classic Arabian dish of meat mixed with rice
Kebab	Skewered chunks of meat or fish cooked over charcoal
Kamareddine	Apricot nectar used to break fast during Ramadan
Khubz Marcook	Thin, dome-shaped Arabic bread
Kunafi (kunafah)	Shoelace pastry dessert stuffed with sweet white cheese, nuts and syrup

Arabic Glossary	*English meaning*
Kibbeh (kibbe)	Oval-shaped nuggets of ground lamb and burghul
Kibbeh Naye	Raw kibbeh, eaten like steak tartar
Koshary	Cooked dish of pasta, rice and lentils to which, onions, chillis and tomato paste are added
Kouzi	Whole lamb baked over rice so that rice absorbs the juice of the meat
Kufta (kofta)	Fingers, balls or a flat cake of minced meat and spices that can be baked or charcoal-grilled on skewers
Laban	Tangy-tasting sour milk drink widely used in cooking as a substitute for milk
Labenah	Thick creamy cheese, often spiced and used as a dip
Lahma Bi Ajeen	Arabic pizza
Loubia (fassulya)	Green beans cooked in tomato sauce
Ma'amul	Date cookies shaped in a wooden mould called a tabi
Makloubeh	Meat or fish with rice, broad beans and cauliflower
Mai	Water
Mantou	Dumplings stuffed with minced lamb
Markok	Lamb and pumpkin stew
Mehshi	Means stuffed - aubergines, courgettes, vine leaves or cabbage may be stuffed with a mixture of minced meat, rice and onions
Melokhiyyah	Green, spinach-like vegetable
Mezze (mezza, meze, mezzah)	The Arabic word for appetiser
Mish mish	Apricots
Mouhammara	Mixture of ground nuts, olive oil, cumin and chillis, eaten with Arabic bread
Moutabel	Eggplant dip made with tahina, olive oil and lemon juice
Mubassal	Onion pancakes
Muhalabiyyah	Silky textured semolina pudding served cold
Musakhan	Chicken casserole with sumac

Arabic Glossary	*English meaning*
Mutabak	Sweet or savoury pastry turnovers usually stuffed with cheese, banana or meat
Najil	Saddle-back grouper
Rocca	Aromatic salad green with a peppery mustard flavour, used in salads or mixed with hot yoghurt
Sambusek	Triangular pies filled with meat, cheese or spinach
Sayyadiya	Delicately-spiced fish dish served on a bed of rice
Seleek	Lamb and rice dish where the rice is cooked in milk rather than the juice of the meat
Shai (chai)	Tea
Shaour	Red Sea fish from the emperor family
Shawerma	A cone of pressed lamb, chicken or beef roasted on a vertical spit where the meat is shaved off from the outside as the spit keeps turning. Saudi Arabia's most popular sandwich is Arabic bread filled with shawerma meat, salad, hot sauce and tahina
Sheesha (hubbly bubbly)	Pipe for smoking tobacco leaves or dried fruit through a water filter
Shish Taouk	Skewered chicken pieces cooked over charcoal
Shourba	Soup
Snober	Pine nuts
Sukkar	Sugar
Sumac	Ground powder from the cashew family, used as a seasoning
Tabbouleh	Salad of burghul, tomato, mint and parsley
Taklia	Spice consisting of ground coriander and garlic
Tahina	An oily paste made from ground sesame seeds, used in hommus, moutabel and baba ghanoush
Tamr	Dates
Taratour	A thick mayonnaise of puréed pine nuts, garlic and lemon, used as a sauce or dip

Arabic Glossary	*English meaning*
Um Ali	'Ali's mother' is a pastry pudding with raisins and coconut steeped in milk
Warak Enab (warak dawali)	Stuffed vine leaves
Yansoon	Hot spiced tea, used for medicinal purposes
Zatoon	Olives
Zattar	Blend of spices including thyme, marjoram, sumac and salt

Lebanese menu

Here is a suggested menu for a Lebanese meal. Most of these dishes are easily recognized and can be found on menus worldwide.

— Mezze (appetizers):

Hummus bi Tahini (Garbanzo Bean Dip)

Khubz Arabi (Pita or Flat Bread)

— Salad:

Tabouleh (Burghul and Parsley Salad)

— Soup:

Shourabit Batata mah Adas (Potato-Lentil Soup)

— Entree:

Kibbeh (Ground Lamb and Burghul)

— Dessert:

Baklawa (Phyllo pastry with nuts)

— Beverage:

Ahweh (Arabic-style coffee)

LEARNING OUTCOME

The Arabic cuisine is mainly a combination of Mediterranean, Middle Eastern, and Indian food. It has been affected by the mingling of Arab and non-Arabs over the centuries. European cultures such as the Spanish, Italian, French and Greek also had impact on the Arab cooking. Turkish cuisine had impact on the entire Arab world, Persian and Indian cuisine had impact on the eastern side of the Arabic countries. Lebanese contributions have been the greatest influence on modern Middle Eastern cuisine, in no small part due to the entrepreneurship of the Lebanese that has helped to spread Arabic cuisine throughout the world from its centre in the Levant in such areas as Aleppo, Damascus, Beirut and Nablus. Lebanese culinary influence and business skills provide the framework for the exotic cuisine recognized internationally as Arabic.

LESSON END ACTIVITY

- Collect the information on Arabic restaurant in India .
- Collect the most popular dishes of Arabic cuisine in India.

QUESTIONS FOR DISCUSSION

1. Explain in detail about Arabic cuisine.
2. Explain the brief the culture environment of Arabic cuisine.
3. Mention the common elements of Arabic cuisine.

KEY TERMS

- Exotic
- Cuisine
- Nablus
- Hummus
- Tabouleah
- Shawrama

Chapter 30

Mediterranean Cuisine

After studying this chapter, the student must know

- Introduction
- Lebanese cuisine introduction and their specialty
- Thailand cuisine introduction and their specialty
- Essential Thai ingredients.

MEDITERRANEAN CUISINE

The Mediterranean is the deep, blue heart that gives life to the countries that surround her. To speak of "Mediterranean Cooking" — to make one language describe the couscous and dried fruit of Morocco, an Egyptian breakfast of ful, cool yogurt soup from Syria, Greek octopus salads, Italian prosciuttos, Niçoise pissaladières, and Catalan seafood stews — may seem a fool's errand. However, the various countries around the sea share more than a beach. From a western perspective, control of the world began with control of the Mediterranean, and thus it has been the seat of empires for millennia. The many powers that have ruled over large parts of the Mediterranean range from the Phoenicians to Alexander; the Romans to the Arabs; the Turks to the Venetians. This long history of imperial colonization, not to mention that of international trade, has rendered a deeply shared culture and agriculture among the Mediterranean countries.

The Mediterranean can be crudely divided into three culinary regions: North African (especially Morocco), eastern Mediterranean (Egypt, Greece, Israel, Lebanon, Syria, and Turkey), and southern European (Italy, France, Spain). Wine and herbs are central to Southern European cuisine, while spices intricately and boldly flavour North African foods.

The climate and terrain are constant throughout the region. Dry, hot summers give way to lovely, cool winters. The soil is dry, the light clear and white. Even the plants wear a protective dusting of white which gives much of the landscape a softened outline of pastel green, limned only by the severe blue sky from above and the bright blue water below:

Food is integral to the effusive hospitality which is imperative everywhere in the region and has been since ancient days when Abraham ran to slaughter a calf for the Lord, and Odysseus embarked on his famous house-tour of the Mediterranean. Flavours are robust and clear, unfettered by complicated sauces and heavy dollops of cream and butter. Home cooking is dominant as hautes cuisines bow before the traditional genius of the home and hearth.

The land's bounty, nurtured by the gentle climate, is reflected in the primary role vegetables play in dishes throughout the region. Onions, garlic, and tomatoes, surrounded by olive oil, begin many dishes. Eggplants abound, as do squashes, peppers, mushrooms, cucumbers, artichokes, okra, and various greens and lettuces. Legumes too are ubiquitous: lentils, chickpeas, fava beans in Egypt, green beans in France, white kidney beans in Tuscany. Fresh herbs include rosemary, basil, cilantro, parsley, mint, dill, fennel, and oregano.

Though the Mediterranean is increasingly fished-out and polluted, seafood remains at the core of the cooking heritage. All manner of shellfish erupt magnificently from soups, stews, and pastas. Anchovies, fresh and cured, are widely eaten, as are various white-fleshed fish like sole, flounder, and grouper. Other fish served in the region include swordfish, monkfish, eel, cuttlefish, squid, and octopus. Smaller animals, like lamb, goats, sheep, pork, rabbit, and fowl, provide most of the meat. Sheep and goats give forth dairy for rich yogurts and cheeses. Beef, however, is rare in Mediterranean cuisine, for the land cannot support large herds.

LEBANESE CUISINE

At one time the mere mention of the country Lebanon would conjure up images of sun-drenched beaches, snow-capped mountains and a cultured, hospitable population bearing a vibrant, healthy cuisine. With its world class museums, universities and exciting nightlife, Beirut was often referred to as "the Paris of the Middle East." Unfortunately, because of the war most only remember the violence and destruction that came close to annihilating this beautiful little country.

Lebanese food can be found throughout the Middle East and Mediterranean no doubt spread by the Lebanese sailors, merchants, and adventurers over the years. Lebanese dishes across the region may be prepared or seasoned somewhat differently. Because of this, the cuisines of the Middle East are often sadly lumped into one homogenous category but to view the cuisines of the Middle East as one is like proclaiming that all cuisines of Europe are alike. Lebanese food is unique in that it combines the sophistication and subtleties of European haute cuisines with the exotic ingredients of the orient.

The cuisine of Lebanon is the epitome of the Mediterranean diet. It includes an abundance of starches, fruits, vegetables, fresh fish and seafood; animal fats are consumed sparingly. Poultry is eaten more often than red meat, and when red meat is eaten it is usually lamb. It also includes copious amounts of garlic and olive oil and hardly a meal goes by in Lebanon that does not include these two ingredients. Most often foods are either grilled, baked or sauteed in olive oil; butter or cream is rarely used other than in desserts. Vegetables are often eaten raw or pickled as well as cooked. While the cuisine of Lebanon doesn't boast an entire repertoire of sauces, it focuses on herbs, spices and the freshness of ingredients; the assortment of dishes and combinations are almost limitless. The meals are full of robust, earthy flavors and much of what the Lebanese eat is dictated by the seasons.

With the recent emphasis on the health benefits of Mediterranean cuisine, people across the world are discovering and embracing authentic Lebanese food. The awareness of this ancient cuisine has also inspired professional chefs and restaurateurs across the world to feature exciting Lebanese items on their menus.

Situated between the east and the west, Lebanon is a culinary and cultural crossroads. Lebanon is located on the eastern most shore of the Mediterranean in the Fertile Crescent, where western civilization is said to have begun. The cuisine of this ancient land is diverse and steeped in history; both the eastern and western influences in its cookery are apparent. Though its mainstream popularity is relatively new, the cuisine is not; the cuisine of Lebanon has been in the making since pre-biblical times. The influence that Lebanon has had on the world is totally out of proportion to its size; culinary contributions from this tiny country have had the greatest impact on modern Middle Eastern cuisine. Roughly encompassing an area of land the size of Connecticut or New Jersey, the people and cuisine of Lebanon are known throughout the world-Lebanese cuisine is a true reflection of its welcoming culture.

Lebanon has two national dishes, Tabouleh (Tabouli) and Kibbeh. Tabouleh is a salad made of fresh cut parsley, minced tomatoes and onions. Mixed with cracked wheat (bulgur wheat) and seasoned with olive oil and lemon juice. Kibbeh is an emulsified paste of the freshest lamb and bulgur wheat. Think of kibbeh as a sort of Lebanese pate. Originally, kibbeh was made by pounding lamb with a jorn (mortar) and modaqqa (pestle), then kneading in spices and soaked bulgur. To some, that are unaccustomed to this procedure, this can be an unpleasant sight. The informative English food writer George Lassalle, in his book Middle Eastern Cuisine, East of Orphanides, describes kibbeh-making in the rural villages of Lebanon as "frightening." He found the incessant pounding and kneading of the meat and bulgur both dreary and alarming. With the advent of the electric grinder and food processor this ancient method of kibbeh-making has all but stopped, except in rural mountain villages.

Kibbeh can take on many forms, the famous being kibbeh nayee (raw kibbeh) which is somewhat like steak tartar. Two other common forms of the food are kibbeh bil-saneeyeh (baked kibbeh) and kibbeh mekliyeh (fried kibbeh), both of which usually contain a filling of cooked meat, onions, and pinenuts. Baked kibbeh is layered in a pan with its stuffing and drizzled with olive oil, while fried kibbeh is shaped into miniature hollowed out footballs and then stuffed before being fried. Both of these cooked kibbeh are often served with refreshing yogurt sauce. Despite advancements in modern technologies, kibbeh-making is still an arduous task.

Literally not a meal is eaten in Lebanon that does not include bread. It is seasoned with zahtar (thyme-sumac seasoning) and olive oil for breakfast, and utilized both as a foodstuff and eating utensil for virtually every meal or snack. In an area of the world that is steeped in biblical history it is easy to remember that in the Christian church bread symbolizes the body of Christ.

The entire Mediterranean rim is known for their anise-flavored liqueurs. In the South of France there is Pastis, in Italy you'll find Sambuca, in Greece Ouzo, and in Lebanon there is the ubiquitous

Arak. Arak is the national drink of Lebanon. Interestingly, these anise-flavored liqueurs came into existence around the turn of the century as a substitute-out of desperation actually-when the infamous beverage Absinthe became illegal. Absinthe was a bitter, anise-flavored liqueur that was popular with writers, painters and other freethinking types during the mid-to-late 1800's. It was originally produced about a century prior to treat malaria. However, the essential flavoring came from the bitter root of the wormwood plant and was reputed to have narcotic properties with disastrous side effects-prolonged consumption of the beverage caused lesions on the brain. When absinthe became illegal, manufacturers substituted anise for the wormwood, to supply the demand, and a number of close imitations were produced including Pernod, Sambuca and various brands of Arak and Ouzo.

In Lebanon, very rarely are drinks served without being accompanied by food. One of the more healthy and entertaining aspects of Lebanese cuisine is the manner or custom in which their food is often served, it's referred to as mezze. Similar to the tapas of Spain and antipasto of Italy, mezze is an array of small dishes placed before the guests creating an awe inspiring array of colours, flavors, textures and aromas. This style of serving food is less a part of family life than it is of entertaining. Mezze may be as simple as pickled vegetables, hummus and bread, or it may become an entire meal consisting of grilled marinated seafood, skewered meats, a variety of cooked and raw salads and an arrangement of desserts.

Although simple fresh fruits are often served towards the end of a Lebanese meal, there is also dessert and coffee. Baklawa, is a popular Lebanese dessert. The main difference between the Lebanese variety and its Greek cousin, is Lebanese baklawa often contains pistachio nuts and is drizzled with a rose-water syrup, the Greek variety usually contains walnuts and honey.This exquisite flavoured pastry has been made in Lebanon for thousands of years, its ancestor being a Phoenician dish consisting of dried fruit and nuts sandwiched between two layers of pastry and baked in an oven. Bakalwa was undoubtedly spread west across the mediterranean and found its way to Greece by Phoenician sailors and merchants. In the 9th century BC, the Assyrians invaded Lebanon and spread Baklawa east across their empire which centred in west Asia, developing around the city of Ashur, or Assur, on the upper Tigris River and south of the later capital, Nineveh. As a result Baklawa found its way to most Middle Eastern cities.

Coffee is a big deal in Lebanon. It is served throughout the day, at home and in the public cafes. Lebanese coffee is strong, thick and often flavored with cardamom. It is also usually heavily sweetened. When guests arrive at one's home, they are invariably persuaded to stay for a coffee, no matter how short their visit.

The food of Lebanon is a celebration of life; it is fresh, flavourful, diverse and invigorating. The genius of it is in its complex simplicity, and that the food is a product of both the earth and the sea. There is a natural bond that all of the Mediterranean cuisines share, from the tip of Spain to the Levant as the same waters equally kiss the countries of the Mediterranean, waters that the Phoenicians of old sailed and spread Lebanese culture and cuisine and left their permanent mark through their colonies. The legendary journeys of the Phoenicians not only spread the best of Lebanon across the seas but also brought back home the best of the cultures they encountered. Despite similarities of Mediterranean foods, the cuisine of Lebanon is without doubt in a class of its own

THAILAND CUISINE

Thailand is a small country in Southeast Asia, sharing a peninsula with Burma, Cambodia, Laos, and Vietnam. Like all local and national cuisines, the food of Thailand reveals a great deal about the country — it is a palimpsest of its political history, its trade, and its geography. Thailand sits between the cultural and political powers of India and China, and its food is clearly influenced by both. Yet Thailand's food, like her people, has maintained its own distinct identity.

As with meals throughout Southeast Asia, a Thai meal has no courses. And like most cooking of the region, the Thai meal is built around rice. Southern Thai people eat long-grain rice, while the northerners favor short-grain or 'sticky' rice. Noodles, probably introduced from China, also play a role in Thai cooking. Of course, Americans usually don't realize that rice is the main course, not the side dish—curries and other hot dishes are eaten by the Thai more as sauces than entrees, flavoring the cool rice. Meat is very expensive, and beef- or pork-based recipes often call for much less meat than would satisfy the average American carnivore. It is worth noting that the Thai eat with a spoon, fork and knife. In Southeast Asia, only the Vietnamese eat with chopsticks, so next time you'll know why your waiter in the Thai restaurant coughs when you ask for chopsticks.

Because Thailand forms a crescent around the Gulf of Thailand and the country is etched with hundreds of miles of rivers and canals, fish is a staple of the Thai diet. Fish sauce (nam pla) and/or shrimp paste (kapee) appear in nearly every recipe. The other distinct flavors of Thai cooking come from the indigenous spices and produce: coconut milk, lemon grass, tamarind, ginger, black pepper, galangal, garlic, cilantro, basil, palm sugar, turmeric, cumin, shallots, and green onions. Last but not least is the chile, a late influx into Thai cooking, having arrived with Portuguese traders early in the 16th century. The chile has become a central player and much Thai food is fiery hot.

Thai food is either stir-fried or steamed—primarily in a wok. Some foods are grilled, but, as in the rest of the region, a lack of fuel precludes baking. Chiles and other spices are ground into powder or paste with mortar and pestle or, for the convenience-oriented cook, with a coffee grinder.

ESSENTIAL THAI INGREDIENTS

Lemongrass. Lemon Grass is a plant that looks like grass, smells minty and tastes similar to lemon (hence the English name Lemongrass). The thick, woody base of each leaf has long been a key ingredient in Thai cooking. You can easily grow your own by putting a few stems in one inch of water, set in a sunny area, then transfer to your garden after roots start to grow.

Kaffir lime leaves. There is nothing like kaffir lime leaves in the world, as these leaves are just packed with a wonderful strong citrus fragrance. Kaffir lime leaves are used in a wide range of Thai cuisine, notably soups. They contribute astringency as well.

Fish sauce. If there's any one key ingredient that is critical to cooking Thai cuisine, it is fish sauce—for that reason alone, it's difficult to find vegetarian recipes that actually taste like Thai cuisine. Fish sauce provides the salty dimension in Thai cuisine, and it's high in protein as well as minerals and vitamins. It's made from small fish, salt-fermented for a long time, then the juice is extracted and boiled. Good fish sauce should be clear and brownish in colour.

Garlic. Most Thai recipes start with sliced garlic frying in oil, and go from there. It would be hard to eat a Thai meal without having garlic in one form or another.

Thai chile peppers. Thais cannot imagine food without chile—they sometimes eat them as a snack. Chiles come in different types and sizes. Phrik Khee Noo is the smallest kind, about a centimetre long, but also the hottest. Chopped up in fish sauce, it makes a sauce Thais add to almost any dish.

Coconut milk. Coconut milk is the rich base for many Thai curries and sweet dishes. Coconut milk or 'ga-ti' is traditionally made by mixing the grated meat of a ripe coconut with warm water and then squeezing out the juice. Now there are machines that grate and press coconut to produce the white, sweet-aroma coconut milk. Coconut milk comes in a can for convenient use.

Galanga. A type of ginger, but it's milder and looks different than the usual form of ginger found in supermarkets. Galanga interacts well with the other essential Thai ingredients found on this page. It gives a distinctive, lightly acid taste and helps reduce the smell of meat. Slices of galangal are added to many kinds of curry and soup. Some people crush the bulb and boil it in water as a preparation to cure indigestion or stomach upsets.

Palm sugar. Seeet is a key taste in Thai food, and many recipes use palm sugar. The sugar is harvested from a sugar palm tree, produced from the sweet, watery sap that drips from cut flower buds. The sap is collected each morning and boiled in huge woks on the plantations until a sticky sugar remains. This is whipped and dropped in lumps on cellophane, or filled into containers.

Jasmine rice. Also known as "fragrant rice", Thailand produces rice that's considered the very highest quality in the world. Indeed, much of the rice exported around the world is from Thailand.

LEARNING OUTCOME

The Mediterranean can be crudely divided into three culinary regions: North African (especially Morocco), eastern Mediterranean (Egypt, Greece, Israel, Lebanon, Syria, and Turkey), and southern European (Italy, France, Spain). Wine and herbs are central to Southern European cuisine, while spices intricately and boldly flavour North African foods. Lebanese food can be found throughout the Middle East and Mediterranean no doubt spread by the Lebanese sailors, merchants, and adventurers over the years. Lebanese dishes across the region may be prepared or seasoned somewhat differently. Because of this, the cuisines of the Middle East are often sadly lumped into one homogenous category but to view the cuisines of the Middle East as one is like proclaiming that all cuisines of Europe are alike. Lebanese food is unique in that it combines the sophistication and subtleties of European haute cuisines with the exotic ingredients of the orient. The entire Mediterranean rim is known for their anise-flavored liqueurs. In the South of France there is Pastis, in Italy you'll find Sambuca, in Greece Ouzo, and in Lebanon there is the ubiquitous Arak. Arak is the national drink of Lebanon. Thailand is a small country in Southeast Asia, sharing a peninsula with Burma, Cambodia, Laos, and Vietnam. Like all local and national cuisines, the food of Thailand reveals a great deal about the country — it is a palimpsest of its political history, its trade, and its geography.

LESSON END ACTIVITY

- Collect the more information of mediterrian cuisine
- Collect the information on mediterrian restaurant in India

QUESTIONS FOR DISCUSSION

1. Write a short note on Mediterrian cuisine.
2. Explain in detail about Lebanese cuisine.
3. Explain in detail about Thailand cuisine.
4. Mention the main ingredients of Thailand cuisine.

KEY TERMS

* Lemon grass
* Galangal
* Lime leaves
* Fish sauces
* Palm sugar
* Stir fried
* Kafir lime

Chapter 31

Mexican Cuisine and Spanish Cuisine

After studying this chapter, the student must know

- Introduction
- Key element in Mexican diet
- Regional cuisine of Mexican
- Spanish cuisine introduction
- Ingredients and typical food
- Typical Spanish ingredients lists.

INTRODUCTION

Covering the bottom third of North America and made up of thirty-one states and one very large capital. Mexico is probably the best neighbour a food-lover could have, when you consider the natural bounty of this rich and varied country. That's no doubt what the Spaniards thought when they landed on the shores of the Yucatan in 1521, much to the dismay of the Aztec, Maya, Zapotec and other natives populating this vast stretch of land. Hernan Cortes and his crew set the stage for three centuries of Spanish rule which finally started to unravel in 1810, when a village priest, Miguel Hidalgo, uttered his famous grito.The ensuing hundred years were filled with invasions (most notably from the U.S.) and fitful leadership, whereas the dawn of the twentieth century saw the beginning of the Mexican Revolution in earnest, with the likes of Pancho Villa duking it out with his countrymen. When the dust had settled, the Mexicans were in control, but hardly united. This was, after all, a country comprised of three distinct groups: native peoples, the descendants of the Spanish and mestizos, the result of intermarriage between the first two.

The melding of cultures contributed significantly to the melding of foods and food preparation in Mexico, often referred to as mestizaje, or "mixing." Corn, a staple for over 4,000 years, is the backbone of the diet. The kernels are softened in water and lime and then ground and fashioned (most commonly) into tortillas. Protein-rich beans and an infinite variety of chilies round out this holy trinity of Mexican cookery. The Spanish liked what they saw in Mexico and added a few things of their own, among them domestic animals, sugar and cheese. Mexican cuisine is further enhanced by an incredible array of fruits and vegetables which seem to taste better in Mexico than anywhere else: tomatoes, squash, sweet potatoes, avocado, coconut, pineapple, papaya and prickly pear cactus, to name several of the best. Herbs and spices also flavour the pot: cinnamon, clove, anise and cumin are all frequently-used spices, while cilantro, thyme, marjoram and the pungent epazote are popular herbs.

Good ingredients certainly count for a lot, but the Mexicans are also gifted cooks and seem to know how to give a dish that extra zing that makes it special. A simple salsa Mexicana is taken to new heights with a touch of cilantro and lime, while a complex mole sauce is always heavenly thanks to over thirty carefully-chosen herbs and spices which are added in and left to slowly simmer in the pot. Whether it's humble tacos de pollo or a regal cochinita Pibil, the Mexican kitchen is filled with honest, flavorful food which is prepared in a host of interesting ways.

MEXICAN CUISINE

Undoubtedly, an important part of the Mexican culture is its varied gastronomy. When Christopher Columbus in 1492 went out on his search for India and for the valuable black pepper, instead he found America, sparking off the conquest of countries which, like Mexico, opened the world to new culinary horizons with its universal donation of vanilla, chilli peppers, avocado, corn, tomato and chocolate, among others.

Mexican food is popular throughout the world. But the kind you might be used to – tacos, nachos with guacamole, quesadillas, and enchiladas - is only a small part of this country's culinary repertoire. The fundamental Mexican food is based on corn, black beans and chillies, but due to the variety of cultures and communities in Mexico, each region is marked by a distinct aroma, taste and texture. Due to their great gastronomic variety, the States of Puebla, Oaxaca and Yucatán stand out; however one must not forget the recipes from Bajío (central part of the country) or the cuisine of the border states.

In central Mexico you will find a blend of Aztec and Spanish food. Typical is the centuries old mole poblano, a thick, dark sauce made with dried chilli peppers, nuts, seeds, spices, Mexican chocolate, etc. Southern Mexico, with its variety of dried peppers and chillies, is famous for its savoury herbed stews and sauces. Seafood, garnished with tomatoes and herbs followed by strong coffee is the basic meal along the Pacific Coast. And in the Peninsula of Yucatán, dinner is likely to be a Mayan delicacy like cochinita pibil, which is pork meat cooked in banana leaves, served with the famous achiote-sauce.

The Mexican Diet

The Mexican table is filled with an assortment of foodstuffs. Sauces, soups and stews are common and expected, while preparations range from a quick-fry to slow roasting.

The following is a list of key elements in the Mexican diet.

Corn: most commonly used for tortillas, the warm, flat rounds which accompany or enhance many a dish. Also used for tacos (tortillas stuffed with chicken, beef, fish or cheese) and tamales (steamed and stuffed with meat or vegetables).

Chilies: used both fresh and dried, it's the white veins and seed pods that are the hottest part and pack a punch. Mexicans like to distinguish between heat and flavour, something that can be lost on the untrained palate. Popular varieties of chilies are jalapeno, poblano, serrano, guajillo, chipotle, pasilla, habanero, ancho, mulato and cascabel.

Beans: they run the gamut from lentils to kidney beans and fava beans and are found in many soups and stews. Small beans are often served refrito (refried in lard, tasty but heavy) or de la olla (boiled and served in a light broth).

Tomatoes: the essential ingredient for a tasty salsa Mexicana and also used in sauces for both fish and beef dishes. Tomatillos are small green tomatoes encased in a stiff husk — they're more tart and often used for a kicky tomatillo salsa which is laced with spicy chilies.

Fruit: mango, papaya, coconut and pineapple are all eaten fresh as well as used in sauces and desserts. Nopales (prickly pear cactus paddles) are sauteed and eaten as a vegetable of sorts but can also be found sweetened in desserts.

Special ingredients: flor de calabaza (squash blossoms) are used in everything from soups to sauces. Huitlacoche is a small, dark fungus (!) which grows on a corn stalk and is surprisingly creamy and delicious. Crepas de huitlacoche (huitlacoche crepes bathed in a dreamy cheese sauce) are a singularly Mexican treat. Romeritos and epazote are two pungent herbs which add a special zest to fish, beef and chicken dishes. Pepitas (pumpkin seeds) are used in sauces, most commonly in pipian, which is used to top many chicken dishes.

REGIONAL CUISINES

It stands to reason that a country as large as Mexico would have a variety of regional cuisines. Some of the best can be found in the states listed below.

Puebla

Two hours south of Mexico City is where the first mole sauce was prepared. As the legend goes, an order of nuns was asked to prepare a special dish for a visiting dignitary. Unsure of what would constitute a worthy dish, the nuns literally emptied out their pantry and filled a pot with a combination of herbs, spices and chocolate, over thirty ingredients in all. Left to simmer for several days, the resulting thick, sweet mole sauce was served over turkey at the royal feast. Today, mole is most commonly served over chicken. "The nuns are the best cooks in Mexico," says Francisco Cisneros, chef at Guaymas restaurant in Tiburon, California. Anyone who has ever tasted a good mole sauce would have to agree. Coffee is grown in Puebla, a nice accompaniment to the area's many unique desserts, especially camotes, a sweet potato confection. Pastry shops are as common in Puebla as churches, no small feat since there are said to be over 300 churches in the city of

Cholula alone. Your meal is likely to be more attractively presented in Puebla than anywhere else in Mexico, since this area is known for its azulejos, or glazed blue and white pottery and tiles.

Yucatan

The land of the Maya is a welcome relief for anyone tired of chilies. Many Yucateco auces are fruit-based, chief among them a sauce made from brick-red annatto seeds (achiote) and flavored with Seville oranges, pepper, garlic and cumin. This sauce is spread over chicken (pollo pibil) or pork (cochinita pibil), the meats are then baked in a banana leaf, and the result is delightfully good. Pack a picnic and trek to the ruins at Chichen Itza for a meal in an unbeatable setting.

Veracruz

Fish is the dish of choice in seaside Veracruz, a busy port filled with salty folks who love life and a good meal. Any fish dish a la Veracruzana means it'll be topped with a sauce of tomatoes, olives, capers and chilies. Exotic fruits (guanabana, mamey, chirimoya) and coffee are also grown in this fertile region. Care for a taco? tamale? enchilada? It's bound to be filled with fish while you're in Veracruz.

Oaxaca

You might want to drink your dinner while you're in Oaxaca. Coffee is grown in this state and is usually prepared a la olla, which means it's laced with sugar and cinnamon and left to simmer in a large pot for hours. The resulting brew will definitely perk you up. Heartier sorts will gravitate to the region's mescal, a very sober cousin of tequila. Hungry folks should try anything topped with mole Oaxaqueno, a sweeter version of the Puebla original thanks to the addition of bananas. The Oaxacans are rightfully proud of the bounty of their vast state, which also includes beautiful artesania (hand-carved wooden animals and the black pottery of San Bartolomeo de Coatepec are especially nice) and lyrical Zapotec dances.

SPANISH CUISINE

Spanish cooking has popular roots. It is the people's cuisine. Most of it is down-to-earth, uncomplicated food, based on the ingredients available locally or the crops grown regionally. Mountains run through Spain in several directions, acting as natural barriers to communication and making transportation difficult until the last half of the 20th century. This is one of the reasons why cooking differs so much from region to region.

Many dishes are prepared today using the same cooking methods and ingredients as they were two or three hundred years ago. Other dishes sprung up from European and American influences and were adapted to the Spanish taste. One thing is for sure, food in Spain is fresh, abundant and full of taste and the Spanish love their food dearly.

INGREDIENTS AND TYPICAL FOODS

The two basic ingredients of all Spanish food are olive oil and garlic. However, because Spain has very distinct geographical regions, settled by different ethnic and cultural groups, and because the weather is so different from province to province, the regional cuisines are very different. Many times the only common ingredients are olive oil and garlic!

LIST OF TYPICAL INGREDIENTS AND FOODS

Olive oil – Spanish recipes either call for olive oil or lard, mainly olive oil. Extra virgin olive oil is worth the added expense. Spain is a leading producer of olive oil and olives are grown all over the south of Spain. Learn Tips for Frying with Spanish Olive Oil.

Ham - or as the Spanish say, jamón is a very prized food. Spaniards take their ham very seriously and will pay a high price for top-quality ham. There is even a denomination of origin for certain types of ham! So proud are Spaniards of their ham, that there are several museums of ham, or museo de jamon. You will see different types on menus or in supermarkets, but typically it will be jamón serrano or ham from the sierra or mountains. Learn all about jamón español in our introduction!

Fish and Seafood – Because Spain is surrounded on three sides by water, fresh seafood is always plentiful in the markets and is eaten daily. Everything from halibut to shrimp and even octopus is common to see in the markets and on menus.

Cheeses – Wonderful cheeses of every type can be eaten in Spain. Spanish cheeses are made from sheep, cow, goat milk and mixed. Types range from aged cheeses, such as the manchego variety from La Mancha, to the soft creamy cheeses such as tetilla from Galicia and everything in between. There are even blue cheeses that mature in limestone caves, such as Cabrales. Cheese can be eaten as a tapa as well as during meals and for dessert.

Sausages – Spanish love sausage, in particular their chorizo, a pork sausage made with paprika. Again, there are many types of chorizo, from fresh and soft to smoked and aged. Every local market offers a variety and Spanish families often make their own in the winter and hang them in the cellar or the attic to dry.

Beef, Lamb and Pork – All three meats are common and can be roasted, grilled over the coals or sautéed in a sauce. Generally, Spanish prefer veal and suckling lamb and pig. Roasted meats are a popular dish for holidays and festive occasions.

Eggs – Eggs are eaten daily either fried, deviled, or in a Spanish omelet. They are an essential part of many recipes, including desserts.

Chicken – Chicken is very popular and is eaten regularly. It is prepared in every way, but mostly commonly is fried, roasted or stewed.

Fruits and Vegetables – Spanish eat lots of fresh fruit as snacks or as the last course to their meals. A fresh fruit bowl sits in every kitchen. Simple salads and sautéed vegetables are eaten every day. Popular dishes often include eggplant and zucchini.

Legumes - Beans of all types are eaten regularly. Beans and chickpeas (garbanzo beans) have been a staple of the Peninsula for centuries and rivaled bread as the most commonly eaten food!

Nuts - Spain is one of the top producers of almonds, hazelnuts and walnuts. Almond-based and milk-based desserts are very common. Turron, the almond nougat candy eaten at Christmas is probably the best-known of these sweets. Many recipes of Arabic origin contain crushed almonds. Hazelnuts, not almonds are the most popular nut to be mixed with chocolate.

Herbs and Spices – Garlic, onions and herbs such as oregano, rosemary and thyme are used, but garlic more than the others.

Cooking Methods

Cocido, olla, pote, guiso, estofado or escudella are the Spanish terms for stew. This is one dish that could be called characteristic of Spain, although each region has its own version. Spanish do not only stew, they roast,fry and saute many foods. It is not as common to bake or broil, although they do grill meats on a metal plate or on a charcoal grill.

As the Spanish say to wish everyone a good meal, "Buen provecho!"

LEARNING OUTCOME

Mexican food is popular throughout the world. But the kind you might be used to – tacos, nachos with guacamole, quesadillas, and enchiladas - is only a small part of this country's culinary repertoire. The fundamental Mexican food is based on corn, black beans and chillies, but due to the variety of cultures and communities in Mexico, each region is marked by a distinct aroma, taste and texture.

Due to their great gastronomic variety, the States of Puebla, Oaxaca and Yucatán stand out; however one must not forget the recipes from Bajío (central part of the country) or the cuisine of the border states. Spanish cooking has popular roots. It is the people's cuisine. Most of it is down-to-earth, uncomplicated food, based on the ingredients available locally or the crops grown regionally. Mountains run through Spain in several directions, acting as natural barriers to communication and making transportation difficult until the last half of the 20th century. This is one of the reasons why cooking differs so much from region to region.

LESSON END ACTIVITY

- Collect the more information about Mexican cuisine.
- Collect the more information about Spanish.

QUESTIONS FOR DISCUSSION

1. Explain in details about Mexican cuisine.
2. What are the key element of Mexican diet?
3. Explain in details about Spanish cuisine.
4. Mention the typical ingredients of Spanish cuisine.

KEY TERMS

* Cocido
* Cuisine
* Tortilla
* Jalapeno
* Culinary
* Stew
* Salsa
* Poblano

Chapter 32
Indian Cuisine

After studying this chapter, the student must know :

- Introduction
- Different aspects of Indian cuisine
- Northern Indian Regional cuisine
- Southern Indian Regional cuisine
- Eastern Regional cuisine
- Western Regional cuisine
- Central Indian cuisine.

INDIAN CUISINE

Indian cookery is not the cuisine of a single nationality. It is, rather, the collective name give to the combination of different cuisines from many different countries. India is a vast subcontinent, divided from the rest of Asia by the Himalayas. It is about the same size as all the countries of Europe put together, and is home to a diverse amount of people, speaking 14 major languages and 100 dialects. It's hardly surprising that the cuisine is also varied. Indian food has evolved over centuries and has flourished under the many rulers that India had. Chefs varied with one another to create exotic delicacies for their rajah's. The result is centuries of patronage to the art of cooking and a large repertoire of delicious recipes. We want to share the history of Indian cuisine so the world may be more intimate with our cuisine.

The different aspects of Indian Cuisine

Indian Cuisine is becoming popular due to its exotic flavours and healthful preparations. The repertoire of Indian Cuisine is vast and the following are interesting aspects of the cuisine.

Cooking according to tastes

In India, their really aren't actual written recipes, so therefore the person cooking is encouraged to orchestrate a dish by using fresh, seasonal and local vegetables. Spices are used sparingly, and Indian dishes are not always hot. Other than spices, herbs and other natural seasonings offer the sweet, sour, salty, bitter, pungent and astringent senses.

Cultural Influences

Many Indians are vegetarians, having been influenced by Buddha (Indian King and founder of Buddhism), Mahavir (founder of Jainism) and King Ashoka. Our cuisine has been influenced by the Aryans settlers, the Arab and Chinese traders and conquerors such as the Persians, Mongolians, Turks, the British and the Portuguese.

Ayurveda

Created by India, this ancient science system is comprehensive of health, diet and nutrition. India's cuisine has been shaped by this science. Ayurveda is the common thread that runs through the various sub cultures/regions of India. Otherwise, the cuisine can be vastly different from region to region

Each region has it's own cooking traditions, based on that area's climate and soil. As a general rule, food is more spicy the further south one travels.

Northern India

The Punjabi and Kashmiri styles of cooking come from the northern region of India. The north of the country is famed for its subtly spiced cooking. The Punjabi's have the reputation of being gourmets and the best cooks in the country. The Punjab are famous for Tandoori cooking and for many of its sweetmeats. Keen wheat eaters, which they prefer to consume over rice. Influence by the Moghals, Kashmiri cooking is known for its meat cuisine. The curries that are produced in this area, mostly made without onion and garlic, are close to perfection. Ghee is the most commonly used cooking fat in this region. A good example of a Northern Indian Cusine are Naan for a more in-depth explanation of Moghul cuisine. The ultimate destination of foodies is the North Zone of India. There is absolutely no dearth of variety for a creative gourmet in this part of the country. The zone is fortunate to be the hub of some of the most exotic styles of cooking. Many of which are renowned all over the world and regarded as the most developed and refined of all culinary arts. Most famous of all is the Mughal Cuisine. National, capital, Delhi is the place to enjoy this style in its best form. Known for their love for life and lavish styles, Mughals treated their gastronomic requirement with a lot of seriousness. They added a touch of royalty to the food and produced mouth watering taste with the generous use of spices, sausages, dry-fruits and butter. Roasted in tandoors, the meat dishes taste out of this world. Thinking of yummy Tandoori Chicken and Seekh Kebab

Jammu and Kashmir

Jammu and Kashmir is blessed with the tradition of Wazwan, the fabulous aromatic banquet consisting of over 36 delectable dishes. Most of these are meat based and contain heavy dose of spices, condiments and curds. Rista, Tabak Maaz, Rogan Josh are just some names of the dishes from this awesome state.

Awadh Style of Cooking

The Awadh style of cooking, popular in the city of Nawabs, Lucknow in Uttar Pradesh does not have a smaller fan following. 'Dum Pukht' method is prevalent in Awadhi cuisine. In this food is cooked in handis on slow fire. The final result is rich in taste and aroma. The very famous Murg Mussallam and Shami Kebabs are prepared with the dum process.

Punjab and Haryana

Food from Punjab, needs no introduction. Have a bite of Makki di Roti with Sarson ka Saag and down it with the famous Punjabi Lassi and one will get the taste of food in this land. Food in Punjab and Haryana is cooked with love. It is rich in butter and ghee and contains lot of spices.

Himanchal Pradesh and Uttarakhand

Himanchal Pradesh and Uttarakhand are simple and extremely nutritious. Here one can find huge variety of dals cooked in labour intensive styles over slow fire. One can find a lot of variety in cooking pattern in this state as taste preference change from one region to other.

PUNJABI CUISINE

Punjabi cuisine (from the Punjab region of Northern India and Eastern Pakistan). Punjabi cuisine can be non-vegetarian or completely vegetarian. One of the main features of Punjabi cuisine is its diverse range of dishes. Home cooked and restaurant Punjabi cuisine can vary significantly, with restaurant style using large amounts of clarified butter, known locally as ghee, with liberal amounts of butter and cream with home cooked concentrating on mainly upon preparations with wheat and other ingredients flavoured with *masalas* (spices). Though wheat varieties form their staple food, Punjabis do cook rice on special occasions. During winter a delicacy, *Roh Di Kheer*, is cooked using rice. Rice is cooked for a long time in sugar cane juice.

Within the state itself, there are different preferences. People in the area of Amritsar prefer stuffed parathas and milk products. In fact, the area is well known for quality of its milk products. There are certain dishes which are exclusive to Punjab, such as *Mah Di Dal and Saron Da Saag* (*Sarson Ka Saag*). The food is tailor-made for the Punjabi lifestyle in which most of the rural folk burn up a lot of calories while working in the fields. The main masala in a Punjabi dish consists of onion, garlic and ginger. Tandoori food is a Punjabi speciality especially for non-veg dishes. Many of the most popular elements of Anglo-Indian cuisine - such as *Tandoori Naan, Pakoras* and vegetable dishes with *paneer* - derive from the Punjab.

Punjab, the land of the five rivers-Beas, Satluj, Chenab, Ravi and Jhelum, is also called the land of milk and honey. Perhaps it would be appropriate to call it the land of plenty. Punjabi cooking and eating is just like the Punjabis themselves. It is simple and forthright. Punjabis are a hard working and fun loving community by nature with food and merriment, very much of part of their lives. Punjabi cuisine is never complicated. Bhunao is one of the main techniques of Punjabi cuisine specially for non-vegetarian cooking. It brings to mind images of appetizing food. Being an agricultural state the staple food of Punjab is wheat and to accompany hot rotis and parathas are a variety of the most exotic vegetarian and non-vegetarian delights.

The earliest references to region's food are found in the Vedas, which document the lives of the Aryans in the Punjab. Amazingly the elements mentioned over 6000 years ago are still extant in this cuisine. This includes dairy-*dughd* (milk), *ghrit* (*ghee*) and *dadhi* (curd), *shak* (leafy green vegetables) and a variety of grain. Even today, the staple in the Punjab is grains and vegetablesin their basic form. Ayurvedic texts refer to *Vatika* - a dumpling of sundried, spice specked delicacy made with lentil paste called vadi. The art of making vadi reached its acme in Amritsar with the arrival of the merchants of Marwar, who were invited by Ram Das, the fourth *Guru* if the Sikhs, to stream line the trade in the sacred city. There is also reference to vataka or vadha made of soaked coarsely ground and fermented mash (husked) *urad daal*. The unhusked mash is the mother of all lentils. *Rajmah* derives from the word *raj mash* or the regal mash. Other pulses mentioned are *chanak* (*channa dal*) and *alisandaga* (identified as *kabuli* or large *channa*) that is stated to have reached India with Alexender the Great's troops who came to India via Afghanistan. Punjab - this side of the border or that - is situated at the crossroads of the Silk Route. This allowed the Punjabis - Sikh, Hindu and Muslim - to imbibe diverse culinary influences. The proximity with Persia, Afghanistan and Central Asia gave them a taste for fresh and dried fruits and exotic nuts. Punjabi cuisine has always been strongly influenced by Mughal invaders who brought with them the tradition of the great Tandoor and now Punjabi tandoori cooking is celebrated as one of the most popular cuisine through out the world.

Let's take a look at some of the sub-regions that have contributed to enriching the cuisine of Punjab.

Peshawar - The most NorthWestern of districts in British India is a Pathan country and the fare is akin to the food eaten in Afganistan. The market in Peshawar handled, besides large volumes of cambric, silks and indigo, spices that came from Hyderabad (Deccan), saffron from Kashmir, sugar, salt tea and asafetida from Delhi. The exports were raisins and dry fruits.

Rawalpindi - South of Hazara and east of Jhelum, separated from Kashmir with Attock to its west, the district of Rawalpindi is covered with groves of oak, olive and chestnut. The flora and fauna is the same as in the other parts of the lower Himalayas. This area has imbibed culinary influences from Kashmir, NorthWest frontier and the plains and the plains irrigated by the Indus.

Baluchistan-Bounded on South by Arabian sea and extending in the North to Afghanistan, Baluchistan touches Persia in the west, and Sindh and Punjab in the East.

Food in the region has been basic and robust. Breads are made with wheat and jowar (barley). Cheeses of different kinds are an integral part of the diet and among the vegetables onion, garlic and fresh asafoetida stalks are used. Rice and fish are the staple diet along the coast. Among the birds chakor and grouse relished.

Amritsar - Shaped like an oblong between the Ravi and Beas rivers, the districts northeast of Gurdaspur and south-west of Lahore. The forests of dhaak, baer, mango and jamun abounded in the district until recent timesurbanization decimated most of them. The chief crops are wheat, gram, barley, maize, rice, cotton, pulses and sugarcane. The region is famous for its buffaloes and its milk products

Kashmiri Cuisine - The history of modern Kashmiri cuisine can be traced back to the fifteenth century invasion of India by Timur, and the migration of 1700 skilled woodcarvers, weavers, architects, calligraphers and cooks from Samarkand to the valley of Kashmir. The descendants of these cooks, the Wazas, are the master chefs of Kashmir. The ultimate formal banquet in Kashmir is the royal Wazwan. Of its thirty-six courses, between fifteen and thirty can be preparations of meat, cooked overnight by the master chef, Vasta Waza, and his retinue of wazas. Guests are seated in groups of four and share the meal out of a large metal plate called the trami.

The meal begins with a ritual washing of hands at a basin called the tash-t-nari, which is taken around by attendants. Then the tramis arrive, heaped with rice, quartered by four seekh kababs and contains four pieces of methi korma, one tabak maaz, one safed murg, one zafrani murg, and the first few courses. Curd and chutney are served seperately in small earthen pots. As each trami is completed, it is removed, and a new one brought in, until the dinner has run its course. Seven dishes are a must for these occassions— Rista, Rogan Josh, Tabak Maaz, Daniwal Korma, Aab Gosht, Marchwangan Korma and Gushtaba. The meal ends with the Gushtaba.

The Wazwan is Kashmir's most formal meal: a ritual serving before the guest of all the food there is in the house. This taste of hospitality must in turn be fully appreciated by the guest, for the wazwan is not a simple meal but a ceremony. Hours of cooking and days of planning go into the making and serving of a wazwan. Normally restricted to occasions of celebration at homes,

Fig 32.1 Wazwam people eating style

the wazwan experience includes table settings for groups of four on the floor where choice dish after dish is served, each aromatic with herbs and the fresh produce of the region.

First the *Tash-t-Nari* is passed around, and diners wash their hands from warm water in a samovar. The *waza* (chief cook) personally supervises each dish which comes out of his kitchen. even the ingredients for the meal have been hand-picked, and effort has ensured that each dish in this rich cuisine is one-of-a-kind. Choice delicacies such as Methi and Tabakmaaz, Roganjosh and Rista, and a variety of Kababs and vegetable preparations are served.

METHODS

One of the most complicated recipes for stewed broth comes from Kashmir. Endless cutting, pounding and sautéing are done to produce Kashmiri delicacies like rista and gushtaba. However, thankfully for the everyday cooks and housewives, these intricate culinary miracles are not a part of the daily fare that Kashmir is have. For daily consumption, meat is cooked variously with tomatoes, potatoes, green peas, spinach, turnips, green lentils, and Kashmir's indigenous spinach greens called haq to produce mouth-watering results.

During the winter months, the vegetables dried in autumn are used, albeit sparingly, for making the various stews and curries. A smooth blend of onions and tomatoes to which spices and ver are added is the base of the gravy. Contrary to the general impression that is held outside Kashmir, no fruits, dry fruits or saffron is used in everyday cooking.

The excellent chutneys that accompany any Kashmiri meal are quite simple to make. Roughly, equal proportions of white radish and onion are pounded with green chilly for piquancy, fresh coriander, and a few walnuts to make the mixture 'heating' enough. Salt and a few spoonfuls of curd are then added to the mixture. For grander occasions, radish is omitted and a liberal quantity of walnuts is added. On the other hand, salads, which in Kashmiri cuisine are slices of carrots, cucumber and white radish, are nothing to write home about.

Tea with milk and sugar is almost a taboo in the Kashmiri kitchen as the only tea anyone wants is the indigenous salt tea or the kahva. The tea is made by boiling fresh cut-tear-curl Assam green tea in water for half an hour, then adding milk, salt, and soda, and cooking the mixture till it gets a pink cast. It is then poured into a copper samovar whose central "chimney" is filled with live coals. After this, a sip is poured out for the head of the family to approve and then the tea is served to the rest in shallow bowls without handles.

All this goes as far as the daily cooking is concerned. However, the wazwans are a different matter altogether. The repertoire and the methods adopted by the wazas or cooks are all the same, yet the results can be strikingly different. Given the importance of meat, the crucial task of carving the mutton goes to the head waza while the junior helper does chores like pounding chilies. The grinding and pounding goes on for hours together till the Wazwan is ready.

STAPLES AND SOURCES

Mutton and rice, in that order, are the staple diet of all Kashmiris. Chicken and fish too find a place, but the all-important ingredient for daily food is the sheep's meat. Almost every part of the mutton is used to make some delicacy or the other and people buy meat of the specific part of the sheep according to the dish to be cooked that day.

The importance of rice in Kashmir can be gauged from the fact that the Kashmiri word for food is the same as that for rice. The chief crop grown in the valley, the rice eaten for lunch and dinner by Kashmiris is not the long-grained basmati variety but one quite dense and sticky.

A preparation very close to a Kashmiri's heart is the Kashmiri salt tea. The morning and afternoon cups of the steaming kahva, as the tea is locally known, are quite refreshing. To go along with the kahva are an entire range of breads like the flat unleavened lavas, sweet and savory shortbreads, triangles of flaky pastry, the bakarkhani, sheermal, and girda that the local bakers keep ready all the time.

An important source of vegetables and fruits are the floating gardens. An ingenious method of layering rich soil and organic fertilizer onto a floating bed of bamboo and twigs ensures that the vegetables that are grown on these 'gardens' are always on the surface of the water. Tomatoes, spinach greens, turnips are some of the vegetables that are grown on the lake and sold every day at dawn in a unique floating market from one boat to another.

Though black or green cardamoms, cinnamon, cloves, red chilly powder, turmeric and powdered aniseed and other spices are widely used, the most common is a spice cake called ver, the recipe of which varies from kitchen to kitchen. Ver is made once a year by pounding together large quantities of the garlic and red chilly along with other spices and is used all the year round. Pran, a shallot-like onion having cooling properties, is commonly used in Kashmiri cooking but is not found outside the valley.

SPECIALITIES AND SWEETS

Some of the specialties that have their origins in the Kashmiri system of culinary experimentation are lotus stem with whole green lentils, dried rings with aubergines and fish with white radish.

Meat being the staple, most of the special dishes have mutton as a major ingredient. Nahari, a special breakfast dish, is a stew of trotters and tongue, seasoned with cassia buds, cardamom, sandalwood powder, vetiver roots and dried rose petals. The sheermal bread goes well with this stew. The methi maz, on the other hand, is a superb blend of mild tasting entrails and strong-flavored fenugreek leaves.

Tracing its roots to Kashmir is the ever-popular rogan josh, which is spiced lamb cooked in yogurt and aniseed, a spice not very commonly used in other regional cuisines. While tabak maz is spiced ribs fried to crispiness, for the qorma, a lightly sour creamy dish, shoulder of lamb and tail are cooked in milk and dried apricots, and the yakhni uses curd as the base for its sauce. Rista, the first gravy dish to make its appearance in a wazwan, is a meatball of pounded lamb that is silky in texture. After a whole range of dishes comes the gushtaba, a giant meatball made of the same, pounded meat, cooked in a curd based gravy.

A semolina pudding sometimes follows the main courses of the wazwan, but there are not too many sweet dishes in the Kashmiri repertoire. However, a different preparation, served to freshen the mouth after the wazwan, is the gota-a mixture of aniseed, sugar candy, bits of supari (optional), coarsely grated coconut and kernels of muskmelon seeds.

Another specialty of Kashmir is the delicately understated saffron. It is the world's most expensive spice because farmers would have to harvest 70,000 of Crocus sativus flowers to extract 210 thousand stigmas to make one pound, which is less than a kilogram of saffron. One of the beliefs grown around saffron cultivation is that just before farmers start planting the saffron bulbs, they go down to a revered spring and pour cow's milk into it. If the milk sinks into the water, the crop will be good. However, if it floats, it augurs ill for the saffron harvest.

AWADHI CUISINE

Awadhi Cuisine is from the city of Lucknow which is the capital of the state of Uttar Pradesh located in Central-South Asia and Northern India), and the cooking patterns of the city are similar to those of Central Asia, the Middle East, and Northern India as well. The cuisine consists of both vegetarian and non-vegetarian dishes. Awadh has been greatly influenced by Mughal cooking techniques, and the cuisine of Lucknow bears similarities to those of Kashmir, Punjab and Hyderabad[disambiguation needed]; and the city is famous for its Nawabi foods. The traditional capital of Awadh has been Lucknow, the capital of the modern day Uttar Pradesh. The modern definition of Awadh geographically includes the districts of Ambedkar Nagar, Bahraich, Balrampur, Barabanki, Faizabad, Gonda, Hardoi, Lakhimpur Kheri, Lucknow, Pratapgarh, Raebareli, Shravasti, Sitapur, Sultanpur, and Unnao. The region is home to a distinct dialect, Awadhi, spoken by Awadhis.

The bawarchis and rakabdars of Awadh gave birth to the dum style of cooking or the art of cooking over a slow fire, which has become synonymous with Lucknow today. Their spread would consist of elaborate dishes like kebabs, kormas, biryani, kaliya, nahari-kulchas, zarda, sheermal, roomali rotis and warqi parathas. The richness of Awadh cuisine lies not only in the variety of cuisine but also in the ingredients used like mutton, paneer, and rich spices including cardamom and saffron

The most populous state of India, Uttar Pradesh has the most exotic recipes of the country in its kitty. The state capital, Lucknow (erstwhile Awadh), in particular is the favourite haunt of the gastronomes as Uttar Pradesh inherited the secrets of the nawabi cuisines. Thus amongst many other things Lucknow boasts of the rich and world famous Awadhi cuisine.

Outstanding feature of Awadhi tradition of cooking is the the 'Dum Pukht' process of preparing food. In this unique style, food is sealed in large pots called handi and placed over slow fire, allowing the ingredients to be cooked in their own juices under the under a strict supervision of bawarchis (cooks). It takes about three days to prepare the meal in a traditional manner. Bewitching aroma emanates on opening the lid of the handis. Finesse is also apparent in the blending of the various spices in Avadhi cuisine. 'Dastarkhwan', the ceremonial tradition of laying food on the table and a celebrated tradition of nawabs transcends the traditional cuisine into a fine-art.

SOUTHERN INDIA

This is the strong hold of the Hindus. The Hindu faith teaches non-violence, and thus not eating meat. The cow is a sacred animal, and Hindu followers are prohibited from eating it. The staple foods are vegetables and rice. Mustard oil is used as the cooking medium, and coconut, coconut milk and tamarind are used in many of the local recipes. Curries from this part of India, which include the fierce vindaloo, are thin and fiery, and use plenty of chilies. A good example of Southern Indian cuisine Lamb Vindaloo. Cuisine from southern part of India offers a variety of popular dishes. South Indian cuisine is known to display a wide range of options to the vegetarian and non-vegetarian food lovers. Popular south Indian dishes like Idli, dosa and sambhar are the most savoured items loved across India.

Cooking pattern in the four southern states of India, namely, Kerala, Andhra Pradesh, Karnataka and Tamil Nadu largely remains the same. Rice is the staple food in most parts of the southern India. Rice, lentils, grains and vegetables along with chutneys, pickles and papaddams (papads) constitute a standard meal for the people of southern India.

Kerala

A typical Kerala meal for special occasions is referred to as 'sadya', it is served on banana leaves and is a very tempting mix of spicy vegetable like kaalan, olan, aviyal, thoran etc. Most dishes in Kerala are made from coconut and rich spices which add distinct flavour to these dishes. Kerala cuisine also has a rich variety of chutneys and pickles to spice up the taste buds. As for the Cuisine of Kerala, it is midly flavored, gently cooked and has a certain genteel delicacy on the stomach. An example is the rich biriyanis of the northern parts of Kerala. The Malabar Biriyanis. Pulaos, pilaffs and biriyanis are meats spices and onions slowly steam cooked in boiled rice. Malabar biriyani was brought across the Indian Ocean by Arab Seafarers. It should be eaten hot with crispy, crunchy pappads.

A favourite breakfast dish is Pootu. Rice flour dough is lagered with gated coconut and steamed in hollow bamboo cylinder. It is eaten sprinkled with sugar or with mashed bananas or with a spicy curry made of channa or chic peas. Iddlis or fluffy white steamed cakes and dosas which are thin golden pancakes are popular in Kerala. They are made up of yeasty rice and lentil batter. They are not strictly Malayali Cuisine. They came across from the vegetarian kitchens next door in the State of Tamil Nadu.

Kerala does have its own well developed vegetarian cuisine. If you visit the State during post harvest Onam season lunch with thoran or kaalan or pachadi or olen. Thorans are gravy-less dishes of finely chopped boiled vegetables and possibly meet and sea food. The mustard seed used in thorans gives them a pleasantly assertive flavour, while the lightly fried grated coconut adds the church. Avial, on the other hand, is mixed vegetable gravy dish thickened with coconut and yoghurt. Drumsticks, jack fruit seeds and slices of mango are often used. Olen is also a very gravy dish made of ash gourd and drum beans where the predominant flavour is that of coconut milk. It is a fairly thick liquid squeezed out from the white flesh of a fresh coconut. Bananas are very popular in Kerala Cuisine. Sliced finely and deep fried as chips, they are chewy snacks. Cut into bits, fried and dipped in jaggerey or sugar syrup, they are sweets. Cooked in thick yoghurt and seasoned with chilly, turmeric cumin seed and curry leaves, they become Kaalan accompainment to the main meal. Malayalee Pachadi is a fairly thick sauce made of sugar, yoghurt, grated coconut, mustard seed and a wide spectrum range of spices including green and red chillies. Sambar is a cross between a sauce and a broth. It contains smashed lentils, cooked vegetables and spices including the exotic and edible resin asafoetida.

For desert, there is the Pradhman or Payasam, porridge like sweets with a vermicelli of rice base, cooked in milk and sugar or jaggery. A favourite dish of Syrian Christians residing at Kottayam is stew. Chicken and potatoes are simmered gently in a creamy white sauce flavoured with black pepper, cinnamon, cloves, green chillies, lime juice, shallots and coconut milk.

The stew is eaten with Appams. Appams Kallappams or Vellayappams are rice flour pancakes which have soft, thick white spongy centres and thin golden crip lace like edge. Meen vevichathu or fish in fiery red chilly sauce is also another favourite item. Besides the chicken and fish there is also red meat, erachi orlarthiathu. Beef (or lamb) is boiled with roasted cirruabder seeds, red chilles, cloves, onions, cummins garlic, ginger, fried coconut chips and a little vinegar. Then with the water reduced, the, meat is almost fried dry in a little oil that has been flavoured with sliced shallots and highly aromatic curry leaves.

Andhra Pradesh

It is known to have the spiciest cuisine among the southern states and is very famous throughout India. Chutneys and pickles are a common addition to most of the dishes. Andhra Pradesh has a good mix of both vegetarian and non-vegetarian cooking. The Hyderabadi cuisine is very famous and largely revolves around non-vegetarian dishes. Dosa, Upma, Pulihara, Hyderabadi Biryani, Chekkalu, pulusu and chaaru are some of the popular offerings of the Andhra cuisine. Food lovers in the country enjoy the famous Hyderbadi Biryani. Andhra Pradesh is an ever enchanting state, which is all the more famous for its cuisine. Spiciest of all the Indian cuisines, the cuisine of Andhra has many delicacies to boast of. The 'Nawabi' style of the state reflects in its gastronomy too. Andhra dwellers usually prefer vegetarian diet. However, people residing in coastal areas rely mostly on sea-food. Coconut oil makes the regular cooking medium for Andhra gastronomy.

Andhra Pradesh is acknowledged for being the largest producer of rice in India. Moreover, rice is also the staple food grain that is consumed in large quantities in the state. Most of the traditional food and dishes in Andhra Pradesh are rice-based. Rice goes with both vegetarian and non-vegetarian meals also. Coconut, spices and fresh herbs are often added to flavour the basic dishes like rice, sambhar, other lentils and steamed vegetables.

Hyderabadi cuisine

Hyderabadi cuisine is another branch of Andhra cuisine that offers the royal recipes of the 'Nawabs'. Chilli powder, oil and tamarind are liberally used in it, making the food really spicy and tangy. Pesarattu, Pulihora (or pulihaara), Gongura, Avakkai (raw mango pickle) are the popular vegetarian delicacies of Andhra cuisine. In non-vegetarian delicacies, dishes like Kodi Iguru (fry), Kodi Pulusu (gravy), Chepa Pulusu and Hyderabadi Biryani, top the charts.

The most delightful delicacies of Andhra food include 'Murku' (roundels of rice flour paste deep fried) and 'Appadams'. Onion pakodas (fried), vadas (spicy lentil doughnuts soaked in hot sambar) and idlis (steamed rice muffin-like dumplings) are the popular snacks in the state. The main food is formed by 'Pulihara' that is actually tamarind rice with green chilies. The condiments like chutneys and pickles make a fundamental part of Andhra food.

'Putharekulu', 'Kakinada Kaja', 'Bobbatlu', 'Booralu', 'Payasam', 'Sheer Khurma' and 'Bandhar Ladoo' are the most popular sweets of Andhra Pradesh. Like other South-Indian states, a traditional Andhra meal is served on a banana leaf. This wholesome meal comprises five types of dishes with a variety of condiments and side-dishes. In Andhra Pradesh, each meal is accompanied by curd to provide respite from the hot spices of food.

Karnataka

Bisi bele bath, jola roti, idli, masala dosa, palya and gojju are very popular items on offer by the Karnataka region. Udupi is a famous cuisine originating from Karnataka and is considered to be the inventor of the famous 'Masala Dosa'. A chain of popular udupi restaurants all over India are also a testament to the huge popularity of this Karnataka cuisine. The cuisine of Karnataka is quite varied with each region of the state having its own unique flavours. A typical Karnataka or Mysore meal is pure vegetarian cooked in sesame and ground nut oil while the coastal areas have a simple, yet flavorsome cuisine with meat, fish and seafood varieties cooked in coconut oil especially Mangalore coast with their Goan influence have their own distinct fish and meat specialties cooked in coconut milk. The Bhakri meal of northern Karnataka based on Jowar is very different as is the raggi meal of the rural areas of Mysore. The Kodavas or Coorgis, who are culturally quite different from the rest of the state, have an equally distinct cuisine.

The three staple items of Karnataka's culinary culture are rice, raggi and jowar (millet). The people in the northern districts prefer millet rotis with spicy vegetable preparations while in rural Mysore the preference is steamed ragi balls served with hot chutney or 'huli', very similar to Sambhar.

The traditional Karnataka meal is served on banana leaf (Patravali) or 'muttuga' leaves stitched together. Rice is served with a number of delicacies such as 'Huli', 'Kosambari' a lentil salad, 'Playas' mixed vegetables cooked mildly, 'Kootu', 'Saaru' a clear pepper broth, 'obattu' and any payasa (Kheer) etc and finally 'chitranna' rice favoured with lemon juice, green chilli and turmeric powder and sprinkled with fried groundnuts and coriander leaves which is a must in the formal meal. Puris made from whole-wheat flour are also served along with pappads and pickle. Other popular Karnataka specialties are Bisi bele bath, Uppittu, Mysore masala dosa and sweet dishes such as Obbattu or Holighe which is flat, thin, wafer-like chappati filled with a mixture of jaggery, coconut and sugar and fried gently on a skillet, 'Kesari bhath' (a halwa made of semolina, sugar, and saffron), chiroti, Mysore pak etc.

Tamil Nadu

Chettinad cuisine is one of the famous of Tamil Nadu cuisines originating from the chettinad region of Tamil Nadu and offers a wide variety of spices and non-vegetarian dishes. 'Sappadu' means a full-course meal in Tamil Nadu which include dishes which are served in a sequential fashion on banana leaves. Idli, Dosa and Puliyodarai are the most popular inclusions in Tamil cuisine. Tamil cuisine is perhaps the oldest representative of the continuous vegetarian cultures of the world. The delicious dishes from the state are relished all over the country and abroad. The cuisine has important delicacies like dosa, idli and vada served with sambar and chutneys. There is a wide range of rice and vegetable preparations. The meals are traditionally served on banana leaves. "Tamil cuisine is known for its aromatic, flavourful and sometimes spicy food. These recipes create an unique blend of spices, that makes the food very appetising, nutritious and wholesome. Vegetables, Meats and Dairy products are the foundation. Cinnamon, Nutmeg, Cloves, Cardamom, Cumin, Coriander, Coconut, Rosewater etc, flavour the food and remind us of the sweetness of life. Curry Powder, Ginger, Garlic, Chillies, Pepper etc add the zest." Tamil Nadu provides the visitor with a wide variety of delicious food both for the vegetarians as well as the non-vegetarians, though most food in Tamil Nadu consists of grains, lentils, rice and vegetables. Spices are added to give a distinctive taste.

Breakfast or tiffin includes idly(steamed rice cakes), dosai (a pancake made from a batter of rice) and lentils crisp fried on a pan, vada(deep fried doughnuts made from a batter of lentils), pongal (a mish mash of rice and lentils boiled together and seasoned with ghee, cashew nuts, pepper and cummin seed), uppuma(cooked semolina seasoned in oil with mustard, pepper, cummin seed and dry lentils.)

There are several variations of the dishes mentioned above which are eaten with coconut chutney, sambar (seasoned lentil broth) and mulaga podi (a powdered mix of several dried lentils eaten with oil).

Lunch or meals consists of cooked rice served with an array of vegetable dishes, sambar, chutneys, rasam (a hot broth made with tamarind juice and pepper) and curd(yogurt). For a non-vegetarian lunch, curries or dishes cooked with mutton, chicken or fish is included. The meals is incomplete without crisp papads or appalam.

Chettinad cuisine is a speciality in Tamil Nadu and will be a delight for those who like hot and spicy non-vegetarian food. This type of food has several variations of fish, mutton, and chicken dishes of which the Chettinad Pepper Chicken is a speciality. The Tamil style of Mughali food can be savoured in the biriyanis and paya. The later is a kind of spiced trotters broth and is eaten with either parathas or appam. Tamil Nadu, especially Chennai, is famous for its filter coffee as most Tamils have a subtle contempt for instant coffee.

The making of filter coffee is almost a ritual, for the coffee beans have to be first roasted and then ground. The powder is put into a filter set and boiling hot water is added to prepare the decoction and allowed to set for about 15 minutes. The decoction is then added to milk with sugar to taste. The final drink is poured from one container to another in rapid succession to make the ideal frothy cup of filter coffee. The last process makes one wonder whether the brew could be bought by the yard.

EASTERN INDIA

Encompassing Bengal and Bihar, this region is surrounded by rivers and seas; therefore, fish is both plentiful and inexpensive. Again, mustard oil is principal cooking medium, giving the food a slightly sweet flavour. Foods are spiced with mustard, cumin, anise and fenugreek seeds. This fish and coconut soup is a good East Indian recipe to try. East Zone of India is a hot mix of vegetarian and non-vegetarian food. Cultural and lingual diversity along with rich histories and geographic heterogeneity of the encompassing states makes the cuisine of this zone unique and unsurpassable. Fetish of the people of West Bengal for fish, rice and sweet is legendary and contributes a significant lot to the popular cuisine of not just east zone but also the national cuisine of India. Part of Orissa also share the love for fish and rice with the state of West Bengal due to the long coastline the duo states shares on the Bay of Bengal. Fish and other sea food are in plenty in this region and so are the recipes.

People in Bihar and Jharkhand love their platter with all the colours of seasonal vegetables which grow in abundance and rich variety here. Influence of Buddhism is apparent here as majority of the population practice vegetarianism. The state came under the influence of mighty Mughals once and naturally the famous Mughal cuisine left its mark here too.

What unites Bihar, Jharkhand, West Bengal and Orissa is the magical mix of seeds used for tempering dishes. Known as 'Panch Phoran', the mix consists of aniseed, mustard, fenugreek seed, cumin seed and black cumin seed.

Sikkim has a completely different cuisine as compared to other states of this zone. Cuisine of this state shows apparent influence of food culture of neighbouring countries, especially Tibet. Momos of Sikkim are loved by people all over the coCuisine of Bihar

Bihar Cuisine

Bihari cuisine has a history that can be traced to the cultures that flourished and waned in this part of the globe.

Rice - Main Course of Food

References to rice abound in a variety of sources. During the days of the Buddha, rice was the staple food. The elite consumed the superior quality of rice while the inferior quality fell to the lot of the poor. At Nalanda, Hiuen Tsang was given mahasali rice to eat. Each grain was as large as a bean, and when cooked, was aromatic, and shining like no other rice.

Centuries later, presenting an account of the different varieties of rice around the Gangetic basin, Abul Fazal said that if a single grain of each kind of rice was collected, they would fill a large vase. The Mughal chronicler described the rice cultivated in Patna as being 'rare and unequalled in quality'. The shali rice was popular and much in demand in Europe, while Indians preferred the shahpasand and basmati variety of Patna rice. The Gangetic plain proved to be a fertile ground for litchis – a relatively new plant that arrived in India only during the end of the 17th century. Originally from China, Buddhist pilgrims brought the first saplings of this plant from China as a hommage to the land of the Buddha.

Bihari cuisine is a mélange

Bhat, *dal*, *tarkari* and *achar* (rice, lentil, vegetable and pickle) have been part of Bihari cuisine since the days of yore. With the advent of Jainism and Buddhism, its followers took to a vegetarian diet, while others preferred goat, pig, deer, peacock, etc. In fact offering meat to a guest was as meritorious as performing the *dvadasah* (twelfth day) sacrifice. Thus slaughterhouses thrived alongside the Jain and Buddhist philosophies of *ahimsa* (non-violence). A variety of meat was openly sold in the market, and lavishly consumed during festivals. After inviting the Buddha for breakfast (this was also the Buddha's last breakfast), Chunda, a blacksmith, served him a dish called sukaramaddava, that translates to tender pork. Unlike Mahavira, the Buddha sanctioned fish and flesh as lawful though with some restrictions. Mahayana Buddhism rejected this altogether. The followers of this denomination believed that the sukaramaddava was some aromatic mushroom. Speculations abound about the unusual breakfast that none of the Buddha's disciples were allowed to consume, and the remains of which were buried.

Bihari cuisine has innumerable rice-based dishes.

The Buddha was usually offered rice cooked with milk, and mixed with honey. The Jatakas (legends on the Buddha's previous lives) mention pua (prepared from the mixture of powdered rice, milk, sugar, ghee, or clarified butter, and honey), pitta (rice cake), khajjaka (also known as khaja, the finest variety of this sweet prepared from wheat flour and sugar, is sold at Silao near Rajgir), palala (modern day tilkuta made from pounded tila, or sesame seeds). Sariputta, one of the disciples of the Buddha was very fond of palala. Gaya is famous for tilkuta, that can be found only in winter, and the finest shops selling tilkuta are located at Ramna. Another delicacy from Gaya is lai, prepared with sugar and beaten rice. Along with the peras (sweetmeat made of sugar and milk) of Mathura, the ones prepared in Gaya continue to be popular.

The Mithila Brahmins who take great pride in their Vedic culture considered themselves to be 'Aryanised' much before other parts of Bihar. Most of their festivals and religious rites are in strict accordance with the *shastras* (ancient scriptures). A fine variety of beaten rice or chiwra, with a heavy coat of curd and cream continues to be a favorite dish in *Mithila*. *Makhana*, a water fruit, (gorgon or fox nut) prepared from lotus seeds, is considered pure enough to be offered even to the gods. According to a popular adage in *Mithila*, betel leaves and makhana are not found in heaven. So one should relish them on earth so as not to regret later. Makhana is eaten in various forms, the commonest being salted puffs. *Kheer* (a dessert usually prepared with milk and rice) prepared with makhana is a mouth-watering delicacy.

Favourite Morning Meal

The people of northern Bihar realy heavily depend on the energy-giving *sattu* (powdered gram), and a number of preparations like *litti*, *parantha* (a sort of Indian bread) etc. are stuffed with sattu and spice. For breakfast in Bhagalpur and Patna, people often prepare drinks with sattu, salt, chopped onions and chilly. Litties come in a large variety and are often roasted on hot coals.

Muslim's Delicacy - The Biryani

Some seventy years before the Muslim conquest of North India, the Turks had consolidated their hold in Maner (22 miles from Patna). Around this time, the region came under the sway of the Sufis (Muslim saints and mystics who came to India once the Turks had established themselves here. Of the three chief orders of Sufism in India, Firdausi's Sufism particularly influenced Bihar). The influx of the Afghans, Mughals, Persians, and much later, the Bengal Nawabs, and the Europeans followed this. Certainly there was a synthesis of the local culinary genius and the art of the newcomers. Possibly this is called Mughlai. Otherwise the term in its true sense sounds hollow, for the Mongol nomads, associated more with warfare, hardly ever cooked good food.

Biryani, for instance, is a Persian world that means 'a dish of meat and rice in which the meat is roasted or fried. Usually referred to as a Mughlai dish, biryani has regional variations, and tastes different in Bombay, Lucknow, Calcutta, Hyderabad and Bihar. Today one can spot even vegetarian biryani on a menu! Likewise, Bombay sells boti kebab (meat pieces), Calcutta offers kathi kebab (meat roasted on wooden skewers), Hyderabad is famous for choti ki kebab (plaited kebab), while Bihar is reputed for its voluminous seekh kebab. Other Non-Veg Delicacies

Some of the dishes of Arabic origin like keema (minced meat), murgh masallam (a chicken delicacy), *naahari* (broth with chunks of meat, cooked overnight). *Halwa*, a dessert, is popular all over India, with slight regional variations. Persian delights like the *kebab*, *zardah*, *biryani*, *sheer maal* are available in all those cities of India that had a brush with Persian nobles. Baqarkhani is even named after one of the Persian governors in India, Baqar Khan. Some of the Bihari dishes like the curries, *shahi tukra* (a sort of French toast) and khichdi are supposed to be of European descent! While opinions are divided on whether the Mughal emperor, Jehangir, or Wajid Ali Shah is to be credited with the original recipe of the *kichdi*, the broth of rice, lentil and other left-overs seems to be a creation of Indian chefs at the behest of their white masters. The Pre-requisites of Mughal Preparations

Mughal recipes at their best would require a variety and quantity of ingredients that would simply cripple a modern housewife's budget. When Nur Jahan, the wife of the Mughal emperor, Jehangir, was in the Rohtasgarh Fort during the birth of her third son, she requisitioned 60 pounds of *ambergris* of the sea, 160 pounds of *khus*, 2000 pods of musk, 2000 bottles of the essence of Egyptian willow, essence of flowers, 10, 000 bottles of rose water from Yazd and 4000 pounds of saffron.

Saffron rice went well with Mughlai fare. One still finds pulaos (a rice, vegetable and spice dish, often served with meat or fish) painted in rich saffron colour without its slightest flavour. Wedding menus continue to display dishes like halwa-i-maquti, muzaffar, etc. A man of fine tastes, Maulana Abul Kalam Azad, the founder of the Nationalist Muslim Party, judged Bihari dishes to be the finest.

The Tribal Cuisine

Situated in the southern half of Bihar, Chota Nagpur is home to numerous aboriginal tribes that differ from each other in their food habits and cuisine. Their general daily diet consists of boiled cereals, millet and a curry of boiled vegetables or meat, or edible roots and tubers seasoned with salt and chillies. Some of the tribal specialities of Chotanagpur are asur pittha (cake) prepared from the flour of mahua (a tree that yields the hallucinogenic mahua flower), rice, or maize. Similary, asur khichdi is cooked by adding mahua flour when the rice is half cooked. When maize is crushed and cooked like rice, it is called sauria ghata. It takes two days to prepare the korwa lata, which is cooked by mixing the seeds of mahua to sarai (sakhua fruit). Korwa jatangi is another dish for which jatangi is fried, pounded and its oil extracted. The residual cake is fried in earthen pots and eaten as a mixture with mahua. No other tree is as valued for its flowers as the mahua. March-April is the season for collecting mahua since at that time the leafless branches are laden with flowers.

The Handia - The Tribal Beverage

The handia is an important tribal beverage that still sells on the roadsides of Chotanagpur. Most of the tribes cannot think of any occasion or function without a fairly good stock of Handia. It is made by fermenting rice with the help of biro – a medicinal cake that incorporates a dozen herbs (the manufacturers keep the ingredients a secret). The rice or millet to be fermented is first partially cooked over fire in a handa (earthen cooking pot). Only the amount of water that the rice can absorb is added. Next, it is cooked and mixed thoroughly with powdered biro. The new pot is then placed in a cool place for about a week following which the beverage is ready.

Bengal Cuisine

Fish and rice are the main ingredients that typically describe the cuisine of Bengal. Yet that doesn't mean there is nothing more to the state. The people here also eat a variety of vegetables that are grown there in suitable weather conditions. The main ingredient of the meals of the native people here is fish, cooked in different varieties. It is steamed, fried or stewed with a variety of different vegetables and also boiled with spices to add a unique flavour to the dish. Mustard oil is the all time favorite medium of cooking in the Bengali cuisine. Panchphoran is a spice that is very common and widely used in this state's cuisine. Panchphoran is a blend of five basic spices namely aniseed, mustard, fenugreek seed, cumin seed and black cumin seed. The state is also fond of sweets and curds making them a tradition through out the state. It is believed that a meal without a sweet or curd normally is incomplete. Sweet delicacies of this state are enjoyed and relished by all around the country. An aspect that makes Bengali food unique and different from the rest of the country is the fact that the Bengalis love to experiment with different cultures and try out new ways of cooking. Other famous cuisines of the state include Rassagolla (cottage cheese in sweet syrup), Sondesh, Began Bhaja, Luchi, Machcher Jhol, Doi Machch (sea food), Mishti Doi (sweetened curd) and Kosha Mangsho. Cuisine plays a huge role in defining the culture of Bengal. The love affair of Bengalis with food and drinks is famous in all corners of India. Be it a non vegetarian dish or a simple rice dish, the care and detailing that goes into its preparation is worth admiring. A Rice and fish dish seems to be the favorite of Bengali people. Even if the ingredients used in the dishes here might not vary drastically to dishes of neighboring states, but it is the use of unique spices that set Bengali cuisine in a different league altogether. The widows in the past, who were not allowed to step outside their homes or indulge in their interests, were confined to kitchen and household works. They experimented with different spices and came out with exquisite mixes of spices and new cooking techniques. Over the ages, dishes here have been under many outside influences as well like European, French and Islamic; but the biggest of them was Anglo Indian or Raj cuisine. The most important part of the meal comes last, after the main course, the delicious sweet dishes. Rosogolla, Sondesh and Mishti Doi are the most famous of all.

A True Bengali Meal

Just get a glimpse of a regular meal of a Bengali family, and you will know that people here don't eat to live; they live to eat. However, dont' consider them as over-eaters; it is the flavour, exquisiteness and variety of the dishes here that gets them the 'living to eat' tag. The meals on a normal day are simple and set for balanced nutrition. Rice and fish curries are the main dishes. All the meals start off with a bittersweet preparation like deep fried bitter gourd or shukto which is a soupy blend of many vegetables followed by steamed leafy vegetables. They work more like appetizers rather than a main meal.

Then comes the most significant course eaten with dal (lentils). Large proportions of rice are had with dal along with other curries. Machh Bhaja (fried fish) is the most common of all. For Machh bhaja, ruhu and hilsa fishes are used as ingredients. It is generally covered in chickpea flour (beshon) or poppyseed (posto). Fish and meat curries are the most favorite of Bengali people. Most famous fish curries are machher jhol, machher jhal, doi machh and chingri macch. In other meat delicacies, chicken, goat meat and beef are important. Though beef is still not eaten in many parts of West Bengal. The main meal is finished with delicious chutneys which are another specialty of Bengal. Chutneys made of mango, tomatoes and tamarind are popular their tangy taste

WESTERN INDIA

The cuisine of western India comes mainly from Goa and Bombay. Goan food tends to be hot and spicy, using a lot of coconut milk, vinegar and tamarind juice. Dishes are cooked at a low heat for a long time, giving them a wonderfully rich flavour. Bombay is famed for fruit ice creams and refreshing cold drinks, made from fruit juice and yogurt, known as lassi. Variety is the spice of life and also the hallmark of cuisine of the West Zone of India. Diversity in the geographical area in this zone from the most arid to the wet and coastal makes this zone most versatile in terms of cuisine. Smorgasbord of this zone contains a wide range of both simple vegetarian and delectable non-vegetarian inclusive of the exotic and world famous sea food. Mouth waters even at the very name of Maharashtra's bhel puris, Gujarat's dhoklas, Rajasthani bati choorma and Goa's vindaloo. Staple diet of the people of this zone is rice. Wheat, bajra and jowar are also consumed in regions such as in Gujarat and Rajasthan. A bounty of sea food in Goa and Maharashtra ensures that the fish and other sea food is the invariable part of the meal for the non-vegetarians. Subzi, dals along with rice and *rotis* constitute a vegetarian plate.

The state of Gujarat excels in the preparation of vegetarian dishes. The recipes are known for the subtle use of spices and rich texture. The greatest asset of the cuisine here is the unparalleled variety of snacks called '*farsan*'. Most of these are a hot selling constituents of the menu in restaurants and hotels all over India.

Picturesque Goa has stolen the heart of lovers of sea food across the country and even beyond. Recipes of chickens, prawns, fish, pork and even pastries of these land of beaches are simply mind blowing.

Cuisine from Rajasthan tells the tale of the struggle of its inhabitants who had to combat the harsh climate of the region. Facing the scarcity of water and almost nil agriculture, it is praiseworthy to note that people have devised recipes which fulfill the needs of the people of high energy food, takes care of the geographical compulsions and are still appreciated by gourmets of repute.

Cuisine of the state of Maharashtra is extremely versatile. Presence of multifarious communities in the state has helped Maharashtra to be innovating in recipes and rich in variety. Vast coastline ensure that there is no dearth of sea food in the state

Gujarati cuisine

Gujarati cuisine is a vegetarian gourmet's dreams come true. It is a vegetarian wonder with complete nutrition derived from leafy vegetables prepared in innumerable variations and subtly flavored with spices. Simple, practical, down-to-earth and wholesome, Gujarati cuisine truly reflects the heart of the state. Gujarati cuisine refers to the cuisine of the people from the state of Gujarat in the Western Region of India. It is primarily vegetarian, due to the influence of Hinduism and Jainism. The typical *Gujarati thali* consists of *roti* (a flat bread made from wheat flour), *daal* or *kadhi*, rice, and *sabzi/shaak* (a dish made up of different combinations of vegetables and spices, which may be stir fried, spicy or sweet). Cuisine can vary widely in flavour and heat, depending on a given family's tastes as well as the region of Gujarat they are from. North Gujarat, Kathiawad, Kachchh, and South Gujarat are the four major regions of Gujarat that all bring their own style to Gujarati food. Many Gujarati dishes are distinctively sweet, salty, and spicy at the same time

Situated on the western coast of India, the name of the state is derived from Gujjaratta, which means the land of Gurjars, who had migrated to India around the 5th century AD. The real cultural history of these people, however, is believed to have begun much earlier when Lord Krishna arrived here with the Yadavs, some 3, 500 years ago. Gujarat has three distinct regions. One is Gujarat proper and the other two are Saurashtra and Kutch. Communities practicing religions like Jainism, Islam, Zoroastrianism etc. can be found in the state. Gujarati cuisine is primarily vegetarian, the main reason for which is the Jain and Buddhist influences. However, the goodness of millet, yogurt, buttermilk, coconut, groundnut, sesame seeds and jaggery makes sure that this non-meat cuisine is not lacking in proteins. Gujarat is a place where both health and taste are derived from leafy vegetables and spices in a number of ingenious preparations. Surprisingly, there are some famous beef preparations too that have their origin in the state.

Staples

In Gujarat, the staple food is millet, which is known to have more protein, vitamin E and iron than wheat, while having less carbohydrate and fat. Millet flour is the mainstay of any meal and rotlis (bread) form an essential part of the harvest celebrations in the state. Sugarcane, wheat, millet, peanuts, sesame are native to the Saurashtra region, where the food is dominated by pulses and accompanied by sweets made from *gur* (molasses) or jaggery. In comparison to the dry region of Saurashtra, southern Gujarat is blessed with plenty of rainfall. Green vegetables and plenty of fruit therefore, dominate Surati food. On the other hand, Kutch cuisine is relatively simpler. Rice and pulses form the staple diet of the people of this region, who combine these two ingredients with spices in a variety of ways to dish out delicacies par excellence. In contrast to the majority Hindus who are pure vegetarians, the Bohras, a community of Muslim traders, are famous for their beef preparations They are also famous for their great variety of soups - hot and cold, clear and liberally mixed with cashew nuts and diced vegetables.

Specialities

A Kathiawari favorite is debra. Made with wheat flour mixed with spinach, green chilies, a dollop of yogurt and a pinch of salt and sugar, these are eaten with chudo-a thick sweet chutney made with raw man-goes, cardamoms, cloves, saffron and sugar. Yet another specialty is methia masala, a dry powder made from fenugreek seeds, chili powder and salt. This is sprinkled over raw vegetables and salads for a piquant flavour. A peanut fudge made from gur is another specialty, which is quite delicious.

In Gujarat, during winter when green vegetables are available in plenty, a delicious vegetable concoction called undhyoo is made using potato, brinjal, and green beans amongst several other vegetables. Paunk, another winter favorite in this region, is a dish that is a blend of tender, roasted cereal, jowar, and sev (a type of farsan), savory twists, garlic chutney and sugar balls.

Gujarati specialties like the nankhatais, kesar biscuits, khari biscuits, ghebar, gharis, a rich, round sweet made with condensed milk, ghee and dry fruit and the saglu baglu mithai are sold in bakeries and confectionery shops in Surat.

The main dish of Kutch cuisine is the khichdi, a simple lentil and rice mixture. It is eaten with kadhi-a savory curry made with yogurt using bay leaves, ginger, chilies and finely chopped vegetables as garnishing-onions and pickle.

Using the same lentils and rice, Kutchi kitchens produce delectable items like the khaman dhokla, a salty steamed cake made from chickpea flour; doodha pak, sweet, thickened milk confectioned with nuts, and srikhand, a dessert made of yogurt, flavored with saffron, cardamom, nuts and candied fruit which is eaten with hot, fluffy pooris. These three delicacies have made their way into the favorites list of the rest of India too and can be found in restaurants all over the country.

In contrast to the majority Hindus who are pure vegetarians, the Bohras, a community of Muslim traders, are famous for their beef preparations called malai tikka and malai wa khalija. An exclusive beef dish is the sagle bagla - exclusive because it is available only in a particular shop in Surat.

Methods

The state of Gujarat is renowned for sophisticated, light, vegetarian meals and there are slight variations in eating habits and modes of preparation in its three component regions.

Kathiawari and Kutch food both use red chili powder to make the cuisine spicy. The cuisine in south Gujarat too, is spicy but here green chilies add 'life' to the food. The Suratis also use far more sugar in their cooking and as a result the cuisine has a sweet, tangy flavour.

CENTRAL INDIAN CUISINE

Central Zone of India consists of both sweet and salty dishes. People of this part of the country do not have a distinct cuisine of their own, but they have beautifully imbibed the best of the food cultures from the neighboring states. This amalgamation of popular food cultures has resulted in the cuisine which is quite popular in its own right.

Chhattisgarh, which is an independent state today was till very recently a part of the larger state Madhya Pradesh. Popular choice of food in Chhattisgarh is hence very similar to that of Madhya Pradesh.

Food pattern in this zone differ from region to region. In some regions people take wheat and meat as their staple diet, but in other regions rice and fish is more common. Indore, the capital of Madhya Pradesh, offers the best of of the food of this zone and is quite popular amongst foodies.

Culinary Delight of Madhya Pradesh

Many of the things of Madhya Pradesh are different from the rest of the country. And the cuisine of this Malwa region state is no exception. Once you taste the numerous mouthwatering dishes, rest assured, you will have a hard time stopping your hands and satisfying your heart. Many who have not visited Madhya Pradesh might not have heard about the dishes in the state. That is because the major population in the state is of tribal people and they are not that outgoing. That is why their specialty generally remains within their own lands. Festivals are the time when the best of dishes are made and served.

Vegetarian Cuisine

The cuisine in Madhya Pradesh has a small tinge of Rajasthani and Gujrati cuisines. Earlier, Jowar was the most important cereal here. But now, Wheat is the staple food of Madhya Pradesh. Major share of the dishes in the state are vegetarian. The most famous of all the dishes is 'bhutte ki kees'. Corn and milk are the major ingredients in the meal. The corn is first grated and then roasted in ghee. It is then cooked in milk and few spices are mixed. The resulting meal is something that will make you want it again and again. Chakki ki shaak is another dish that has made it to list of supremely sumptuous. It is made up of wheat dough which is steamed and is used with a gravy of curd. Tapu is a different variety of wheat with which, special sweet cakes are made. You won't find them always as they are generally made during festival seasons. Madhya Pradesh is also famous for many sweet dishes like 'mawa-bati', 'khoprapak', 'shreekhand' and 'malpua'.

Non-Vegetarian Delicacies

Non-veg lovers are also in for a great time in Madhya Pradesh. Bhopal is the place where you will find few of the most delicious meat and fish items. The most favored is the spicy rogan josh that will make you crave for more after you have it once. Other delectable non veg items that made their mark in the hearts of many foodaholics are korma, seekh kabbab and shami kabbab. These items have become an inseparable part of all grand feast.

Indore Feast

When cuisine of Madhya Pradesh is takked about, how can one not mention Indore, the street food capital of India. Evenings at the famous streets like Sarafa Bazaar and Chhappan Dukaan is a dream come true for snack and sweet lovers. The many shops that put up their stalls offer exquisite items that you probably won't find anywhere else, at least not as good as here. 'Poha jalebi' and 'bhutte ka kees' are the most popular ones among the crowd. The chaat corners and sweet shops put so much on display itself that crossing them without having anything from there is simply unimaginable. People of Madhya Pradesh are very passionate about their food. And this is visible in the way they enjoy the process of making the exquisite dishes and the way they relish every slice of their meal. They are also known to be hospitable. And when you are served such exceptional delicacies with such love and care, the taste of the food doubles. So don't get surprised if you see everyone licking their fingers after the feast.

People of Madhya Pradesh have truly perfected the art of cooking. The cuisine of Madhya Pradesh is reputed to be the hottest and varied of all in the Indian sub continent. The specialty of their cuisine here is the use of wheat and milk with various items. Here You will find dishes that are hard to find outside Madhya Pradesh. Come and traverse through the streets of Madhya Pradesh to let your tongue know of a new high.

LEARNING OUTCOME

Indian Cuisine is becoming popular due to its exotic flavors and healthful preparations. The repertoire of Indian Cuisine is vast and the following are interesting aspects of the cuisine. Indian cookery is not the cuisine of a single nationality. It is, rather, the collective name give to the combination of different cuisines from many different countries.

India is a vast subcontinent, divided from the rest of Asia by the Himalayas. It is about the same size as all the countries of Europe put together, and is home to a diverse amount of people, speaking 14 major languages and 100 dialects. It's hardly surprising that the cuisine is also varied. Indian food has evolved over centuries and has flourished under the many rulers that India had. Chefs vied with one another to create exotic delicacies for their rajah's. Many Indians are vegetarians, having been influenced by Buddha (Indian King and founder of Buddhism), Mahavir (founder of Jainism) and King Ashoka. Our cuisine has been influenced by the Aryans settlers, the Arab and Chinese traders and conquerors such as the Persians, Mongolians, Turks, the British and the Portuguese. The Punjabi and Kashmiri styles of cooking come from the northern region of India. The north of the country is famed for its subtly spiced cooking. The Punjabi's have the reputation of being gourmets and the best cooks in the country. Jammu and Kashmir is blessed with the tradition of Wazwan, the fabulous aromatic banquet consisting of over 36 delectable dishes. Most of these are meat based and contain heavy dose of spices, condiments and curds. Rista, Tabak Maaz, Rogan

Josh are just some names of the dishes from this awesome state. Himanchal Pradesh and Uttaranchal are simple and extremely nutritious. Here one can find huge variety of dals cooked in labour intensive styles over slow fire. Awadhi Cuisine is from the city of Lucknow which is the capital of the state of Uttar Pradesh located in Central-South Asia and Northern India), and the cooking patterns of the city are similar to those of Central Asia, the Middle East, and Northern India as well. The cuisine consists of both vegetarian and non-vegetarian dishes. This is the strong hold of the Hindus. The Hindu faith teaches non-violence, and thus not eating meat. The cow is a sacred animal, and Hindu followers are prohibited from eating it. The staple foods are vegetables and rice. Mustard oil is used as the cooking medium, and coconut, coconut milk and tamarind are used in many of the local recipes. Curries from this part of India, which include the fierce vindaloo, are thin and fiery, and use plenty of chilies. A typical Kerala meal for special occasions is referred to as 'sadya', it is served on banana leaves and is a very tempting mix of spicy vegetable like kaalan, olan, aviyal, thoran etc. Most dishes in Kerala are made from coconut and rich spices which add distinct flavour to these dishes. Andhra Pradesh has a good mix of both vegetarian and non-vegetarian cooking. The Hyderabadi cuisine is very famous and largely revolves around non-vegetarian dishes. Dosa, Upma, Pulihara, Hyderabadi Biryani, Chekkalu, pulusu and chaaru are some of the popular offerings of the Andhra cuisine. Hyderabadi cuisine is another branch of Andhra cuisine that offers the royal recipes of the 'Nawabs'. Chilli powder, oil and tamarind are liberally used in it, making the food really spicy and tangy. Pesarattu, Pulihora (or pulihaara), Gongura, Avakkai (raw mango pickle) are the popular vegetarian delicacies of Andhra cuisine. In non-vegetarian delicacies, dishes like Kodi Iguru (fry), Kodi Pulusu (gravy), Chepa Pulusu and Hyderabadi Biryani, top the charts. Karnataka cuisine. The cuisine of Karnataka is quite varied with each region of the state having its own unique flavours. A typical Karnataka or Mysore meal is pure vegetarian cooked in sesame and ground nut oil while the coastal areas have a simple, yet flavorsome cuisine with meat, fish and seafood varieties cooked in coconut oil especially. Tamil cuisine is perhaps the oldest representative of the continuous vegetarian cultures of the world. The delicious dishes from the state are relished all over the country and abroad. The cuisine has important delicacies like dosa, idli and vada served with sambar and chutneys. Fish and rice are the main ingredients that typically describe the cuisine of West Bengal. The cuisine of western India comes mainly from Goa and Bombay. Goan food tends to be hot and spicy, using a lot of coconut milk, vinegar and tamarind juice. Dishes are cooked at a low heat for a long time, giving them a wonderfully rich flavour. Gujarati cuisine is a vegetarian gourmet's dreams come true. It is a vegetarian wonder with complete nutrition derived from leafy vegetables prepared in innumerable variations and subtly flavored with spices. Simple, practical, down-to-earth and wholesome, Gujarati cuisine truly reflects the heart of the state. The cuisine in Madhya Pradesh has a small tinge of Rajasthani and Gujrati cuisines. Earlier, Jowar was the most important cereal here. But now, Wheat is the staple food of Madhya Pradesh. Major share of the dishes in the state are vegetarian. The most famous of all the dishes is 'bhutte ki kees'. Corn and milk are the major ingredients in the meal. People of Madhya Pradesh have truly perfected the art of cooking. The cuisine of Madhya Pradesh is reputed to be the hottest and varied of all in the Indian sub continent

LESSON END ACTIVITY

- Collect the information about Indian cuisine and there specialities.
- Collect the information on Indian speciality restaurant in out side the India.
- Collect more information about south India cuisine.
- Collect more information about Central India cuisine.

QUESTIONS FOR DISCUSSION

1. Explain the detail about Indian cuisine and there different aspects.
2. Explain in detail about northern Indian cuisine with their regions.
3. Explain in detail about south Indian cuisine with their regions.
4. Explain in detail about Punjabi cuisine with their regions.
5. Explain in detail about Awadhi cuisine.
6. Explain in detail about eastern Indian cuisine with their regions.
7. Explain in detail about Tamil Naidu cuisine.
8. Explain in detail about Karnataka cuisine.
9. Explain in detail about Madhya Pradesh cuisine.
10. Explain in detail about Bihar cuisine.
11. Write a short note on West Bengal cuisine.
12. Write a short note of Guajarati cuisine.

KEY TERMS

* Cereal
* Culinary
* Masala
* Paratha
* Rooti
* Tamarind
* Cooking
* Kodi
* Naan
* Regions
* Staple

Recipes on International Cuisine

THAI MENU

Chicken Satay (Satay gai)

Ingredients	*Quantity*
For marination	
Boneless chicken	300 gram
Vegetable oil	80 ml
Lime juice	20 gram
Salt and pepper	8 gram
Lemon leaves	2 no.
Galangal	5 gram
Lemon grass	5 gram
For dip	
Vegetable oil	30 gram
Onion	50 gram
Green chilies	10 gram
Garlic	20 gram
Peanut butter	100 gram
Lime juice	20 gram
Water	40 ml
Lime leaves	2 no.
Galangal	5 gram.

Method

1. Combined both the oil and the lime juice in a bowl. Add grated galangal chop lemon leaves, chop lemon grass and chicken cubes, marinate for at least one hour.

2. To make a dip, heat the oil in a pan and sauté the onion, chili and garlic over low heat, stirring occasionally, for about five minutes until just softened. At the peanut butter, water, lime leaves galangal and Lemon Juice and simmer gently, stirring constantly, until the peanut butter is softened enough to make a dip- you may need to add extra water to make a thinner consistency.
3. Meanwhile drain the chicken cubes and thread them on to a wooden skewers.
4. Put under a hot broiler or barbecue or shallow fry in a pan. Turning frequently for about 10 minutes until cooked and brown. Serve hot with the warm dip.

**Cooking Tip: Soaked the wooden skewers in a cold water for 45 minutes before threading the meat to help keep them from burning during cooking.

Cottage Cheese Satay

Ingredients	*Quantity*
For marination	
Cottage cheese	300 gram
Vegetable oil	80 ml
Soya sauce	20 ml
Salt and pepper	8 gram
Lemon leaves	2 no.
Galangal	5 gram
Lemon grass	5 gram
For dip	
Vegetable oil	30 gram
Onion	50 gram
Green chilies	10 gram
Garlic	20 gram
Peanut butter	100 gram
Lime juice	20 gram
Water	40 ml
Lime leaves	2 no.
Galangal	5 gram.

Method

1. Combined both the oil and the Soya sauce in a bowl. Add grated galangal chop lemon leaves, chop lemon grass and cottage cheese cubes, marinate for at least one hour.

2. To make a dip, heat the oil in a pan and sauté the onion, chili and garlic over low heat, stirring occasionally, for about five minutes until just softened. At the peanut butter, water, lime leaves galangal and Lemon Juice and simmer gently, stirring constantly, until the peanut butter is softened enough to make a dip- you may need to add extra water to make a thinner consistency.
3. Meanwhile drain the cottage cheese and thread them on to wooden skewers.
4. Put under a hot broiler or barbecue or shallow fry in a pan. Turning frequently for about 10 minutes until cooked and brown. Serve hot with the warm dip.

   ****Cooking Tip**: Soaked the wooden skewers in cold water for 45 minutes before threading the meat to help keep them from burning during cooking

Thai Cucumber Salad

Ingredients	*Quantity*
Cucumber	350 gram
Lemon Leaves	2 No.
Fresh Red Chilies	4 No.
Lemon Juice	20 ml
Cilantro	10 gram
Sesame Seed	10 gram
Salt and pepper	5 gram
Basil	10 gram
Grated Galangal	10 gram
Fish Sauce (Optional)	10 gram
Oil	10 ml

Method

1. Diced the cucumber.
2. In a bowl add oil, lemon juice, shredded basil, grated galangal, chop cilantro, chop fresh red chilies, fish sauce. Mix thoroughly.
3. Add cucumber in a bowl mix thoroughly.
4. Serve with sprinkle of sesame seed and cilantro

Vegetable and noodle paste (*Guay tiaw nam sai puk*)

Ingredients	*Quantity*
Vegetable Oil	30 ml
Onion	125 gram

Ingredients	*Quantity*
Garlic	50 gram
Carrot	100 gram
Cauliflower	100 gram
Pumpkin	100 gram
Vegetable stock	1 litre
Coconut Milk	200 ml
Soya Sauce	4 tbsp
Red Curry Paste	2 tbsp
Glass Noodles	100 gram
Fresh Cilantro	1 bunch
Bean Sprout	50 gram

Method

1. Heat the Oil in a wok and stir-fry the onion and garlic for two to three minutes. At the carrot pumpkin and cauliflower and stir fry for three to four minutes until just tender.
2. Pour in the stock and coconut milk and bring to boil. Add the soya sauce, curry paste and noodles and let simmer for two to three minutes, until the noodle have swelled. Stir in the bean sprout and cilantro and serve immediately.

Green chicken curry (Kaeng khiao wan gai)

Ingredients	*Quantity*
Vegetable Oil	30 ml
Onion	100 gram
Garlic	20 gram
Green Curry Paste	75 gram
Coconut Milk	100 ml
Chicken Stock	100 ml
Lime Leaves	4 no.
Boneless chicken	350 gram
Fish Sauce	20 ml
Thai soya Sauce	10 ml
Thai Egg Plant	20 gram
Lemon Grass	10 gram
Jaggery or palm sugar	20 gram
Cilantro	20 gram

Ingredients	*Quantity*
Basil	10 gram
Cream	50 ml

Method

1. Heat the oil in a wok and stir- fry the onion and a garlic for one to two minutes, until starting to softened. Add the curry paste and stir fry for 1-2 minutes.
2. Add the coconut milk, stock, egg plant, basil lime leaves bring to boil, add the chicken. Reduce the heat and let simmer gently for 15 to 20 minutes until the chicken is tender.
3. Add the fish sauce, soya sauce, lime juice and jaggery. Cook for 2 to 3 minutes. Finish with cream and garnish with chop cilantro.

Vegetable with tofu and spinach *(Pud pak sat tao hu)*

Ingredients	*Quantity*
Vegetable oil for (deep fry)	300 ml
Tofu	350 gram
Onion	100 gram
Garlic	10 gram
Fresh red chili	4 No.
Celery Stalks	10 gram
Mushroom	100 gram
Capsicum	100 gram
Carrot	100 gram
Red /yellow bell pepper	2 No.
Coconut Milk	100 ml
Red curry paste	50 gram
Jaggery	50 gram
Soya Sauce	2 tbsp
Spinach	150 gram
Lemon Leaves	2 No.
Basil	20 gram
Galangal	10 gram

Method

1. Heat oil in a wok and deep fry the tofu cubes until crisp and brown.
2. Heat 2 tbsp of the oil in a wok and stir fry the onion, garlic and chili for 1 to 2 minutes,

until they start to soften. Add the celery, lemon leaves, basil, chop galangal, mushroom, carrot, capsicum, bell pepper and stir fry for 3 to 4 minutes until they soften. .

3. Stir in the curry paste and coconut milk and gradually bring to boil. Add the sugar/ jaggery and soya sauce and then spinach. Cook, stirring constantly, until the spinach has wilted. Serve immediately topped with tofu.

Stir Fried Rice With Vegetables (Khao Phat Puk)

Ingredients	*Quantity*
Rice	250 gram
Vegetable Oil	2 tbsp
Green Curry Paste	1 tbsp
Onion	100 gram
Garlic	20 gram
Carrot	100 gram
Pumpkin	100 gram
Beans	100 gram
Green Chillies	20 gram
Fish Sauce	2 tbsp
Basil	20 gram
Galangal	10 gram
Cabbage	100 gram

Method

1. Cook the rice in lightly salted boiling water for 12 to 15 minutes, drain well, then cook thoroughly and chill it in refrigerator.
2. Blanch all the vegetable.
3. Heat the oil in a wok and stir fry the curry paste for 1 minute. Add the onion and Garlic and stir fry for 1 minute.
4. Add all the vegetable, break up the rice and added it to the wok. Cook stirring constantly for 2 to 3 minutes until the rice is hot. Stir in the fish sauce and basil leaves. Serve hot.

Mini Coconut Crepes (Kanum Buang Ma-Prow Oon)

Ingredients	*Quantity*
Fresh coconut (grated)	50 gram
Flour	300 gram
Powder Sugar	80 gram
Eggs	2 Nos

Milk	100 ml
Desicated coconut	50 gram
Butter	50 gram
Melon	30 gram

Method

1. Put a flour in a bowl and stir in the sugar. Beat in the eggs and half the milk. Gradually beat in the remaining milk and then coconut mixture to make a creamy better, add desiccated coconut in it.
2. Melt a dotted -butter in a non-stick pan, add 3 or 4 tbsp of better, spacing them well apart as they will spread during cooking.
3. Cook for 1 to 2 minutes, then flip over to cook the second side.
4. Remove from the pan and keep warm and serve warm with melon slices.

CHINESE MENU

Hot and sour soup

Ingredients	*Quantity*
Red Chili Paste	2 tbsp
Corn flour	30 gram
Soya Sauce	2 tbsp
Vinegar	2 tbsp
Capsicum chopped	50 gram
Carrot Chopped	50 gram
Cabbage chopped	50 gram
Black pepper powder	1 tsp
Sugar	50 gram
Salt	10 gram
MSG	10 gram
Vegetable stalk	1 litre
Cilantro	30 gram
Spring Onion	50 gram
Onion	50 gram
Garlic	30 gram
Oil	20 ml
Cottage cheese	30 gram

Method

1. In a wok add oil, put onion and garlic sauté it add all vegetables except cabbage and cottage cheese.
2. Add chilly paste and Soya sauce sauté it add vegetable stock, bring to boil.
3. Dissolve corn flour in water add to the boiling soup.
4. Adjust seasoning and add cottage cheese, cabbage and garnish with cilantro and serve hot.

Kimchi Salad

Ingredients	*Quantity*
Cabbage	450 gram
Green Onion	30 gram
Garlic	20 gram
Ginger Chopped	10 gram
Red chili Paste	20 gram
Soya Sauce	10 ml
Sugar	20 gram
Cilantro	20 gram
Tomato ketchup	20 ml
Salt	5 tbsp
Vinegar	10 ml
sesame Seed	10 gram
Oil	20 ml

Method

1. Take off the cabbage leaves one by one and wash them thoroughly and cut the leaves in dice and sprinkle with salt.
2. Chop the green onion, garlic, cilantro and ginger finely.
3. Wash the salted cabbage dices and brain them well.
4. Put all the seasoning in a bowl. Mix them well by hand. Add the dice cabbage and mix them well together. Transfer to a serving bowl.

Vegetable Manchurian

Ingredients	*Quantity*
Grated cabbage	50 gram
Grated Carrot	50 gram

Chopped onion	30 gram
Chopped green chili	10 gram
Crush Garlic	10 gram
Corn Flour	30 gram
Refined flour	2 tbsp
Oil	250 ml
Soya Sauce	2 tbsp
Salt	10 gram
Pepper powder	1 tsp
Sugar	1 tsp
MSG	10 gram
Ginger	10 gram
Vegetable stock	1 litre

Method

1. Mix grated cabbage and carrot and squeeze water out from them.
2. Now in a bowl take the squeeze cabbage and carrot and mix one tbsp corn starch and cube chop chilies grated ginger and little salt into it.
3. Make a small bowls (like Koftas) of the mixer.
4. Heat the oil in a wok and deep fry the balls till golden brown, drain and keep a side.
5. Now in a separate pan heat to tbsp oil.
6. Saute garlic, green chilies and spring onion.
7. Add vegetable stock, salt, pepper powder, MSG, Sugar and soya sauce and bring it to a boil.
8. Mix one tbsp corn flour with half of cup of cold water and stir into it.
9. Gently add the fry balls to the gravy.
10. Cook the vegetable Manchurian 3 to 4 minute and serve hot garnish with chopped coriander.

Chili chicken

Ingredients	*Quantity*
Boneless Chicken	350 gram
Soya Sauce	2 tbsp
Egg	2 No.
Corn Flour	2 tbsp
Refined flour	2 tbsp

Green Chilies	10 gram
Onion	100 gram
Garlic	20 gram
Salt	10 gram
Sugar	10 gram
MSG	20 gram
Chicken Stock	350 ml
Oil	350 ml
Red Chili paste	30 gram
Cilantro	20 gram
Capsicum	50 gram

Method

1. Cut the boneless chicken into one inch cubes.
2. Take one tbsp soya sauce, tbsp corn flour, salt, Egg in a bowl and marinate chicken pieces in the mixture for about 10 to 15 minutes.
3. Oil and deep fry the marinated chicken pieces till golden brown.
4. Now in a separate wok 1 tbsp oil and add chop garlic, red chili paste add onion and capsicum dice and sauté for few second. Add chicken stock.
5. Bring to boil and add sugar salt, MSG and remaining soya sauce. Add fried chicken pieces to it and cook for a few minutes.
6. Dissolve the remaining corn flour in half cup of water and add to a curry stirring constantly to avoid lumps.

Sweet and sour potatoes

Ingredients	*Quantity*
Potatoes	500 gram
Soya Sauce	1 tbsp
Vinegar	1 tbsp
Sugar	1 tbsp
Tomato Ketchup	2 tbsp
Green Onions	50 gram
Ginger	20 gram
Garlic	20 gram
Oil	350 ml
Chili Paste	30 gram
Fresh Coriander	30 gram

Method

1. Cut the potatoes into thin strips, the size and the thickness of a double the match stick
2. Fry the potatoes in a hot oil.
3. Chop the green onion, ginger and garlic.
4. Heat the wok over medium heat. Add oil, add the ginger, garlic, chili paste, vinegar, soya sauce and tomato ketchup.
5. Add the fried potatoes in it. Mix it well. Stir in the green onion and coriander. Mix everything together and serve hot.

Chinese fried rice

Ingredients	*Quantity*
Rice	350 gram
Oil	3 tbsp
Beans (Burnoise)	100 gram
Carrot (Burnoise)	80 gram
Spring Onion	50 gram
Green Chilies	4 Nos.
Ginger Chopped	20 gram
Garlic Chopped	20 gram
Soya Sauce	2 tbsp
Vinegar	2 tbsp
Salt and pepper	10 gram
Coriander	20 gram

Method

1. Pick, wash and soak the rice in enough water for ten to 15 minutes and drain.
2. Boil water, add rice and little water.
3. Cook uncovered on a low heat till rice is tender. Take care not to overcook the rice, each grain of rice should be separate.
4. When rice is done, grain and put in refrigerator.
5. Boil all the vegetables.
6. Heat oil in a wok add ginger and garlic and stir fry all vegetable, take care that all vegetable are not over done, they should be crisp.
7. Add the cooked rice, salt and pepper, vinegar, soya sauce and mix it well and garnish with chopped coriander.

Banana-Apple Toffee

Ingredients	*Quantity*
Banana / Apple	2 No.
Egg	1 No
Flour	100 gram
Oil	250 ml
Sugar	250 gram
Sesame Seed	50 gram

Method

1. Beat the egg and flour, blending into a smooth batter.
2. Dip apple and banana into a batter.
3. Heat oil until it is very hot, add banana and apple at a time.
4. Fry for 2 to 3 minutes until golden brown.
5. Drain on absorbent paper.
6. Place sugar, water in a sauce pan over a moderate heat until goes to thick consistency.
7. Add sesame seed into the mixture.
8. Add banana and apple to the sugar mixture to coat it., and put it into a cold water and remove from water and serve immediately.

INDONESIAN MENU

Teriyaki chicken

Ingredients	*Quantity*
Boneless chicken	350 gram
Onions	50 gram
Teriyaki Marinate	30 gram
Salt and pepper	10 gram
Oil	20 ml

Method

1. Cut chicken into bite size pieces.
2. Pour enough marinade to coat chicken and mix together.
3. Refrigerate at least 20 minutes.
4. (To retain moisture during high temperature cooking) You can refrigerate over night before cooking.

5. Heat a heavy wok or skillet and drizzle oil down sides and coat bottom.
6. It is important to have sufficient oil so the meat does not stick to be pan.
7. Excess will drain off.
8. Allow it to heat until it is slightly smoking.
9. Keep heat high and cook small batches of one cup or less of chicken pieces at a time.
10. Allow pan to heat for a few seconds between batches.
11. Cook each batch until barely done.
12. Chicken should be "blackened" If your heat is high enough..
13. When all chicken is cooked return it all to the pan and make sure it is completely one.
14. Dip out the chicken leaving the excess oil in the pan and quickly stir-fry the onion and add it to the chicken.
15. Salt and pepper to taste.
16. Serve with fried rice and egg rolls, if desired.

Teriyaki Cottage Cheese

Note: In cottage Cheese Teriyaki all ingredients are same but addition of mustard is added to the marrination.

Teriyake

Ingredients	*Quantity*
Soya Sauce	100 ml
Oil	50 ml
Molasses	2 tbsp
Minced ginger	1 tbsp
Mustard Powder	1 tbsp
Garlic minced	1 tbsp
White paper	5 gram
Honey	1 tsp
Tabasco sauce	1 tsp

Method

1. Mix all the ingredients thoroughly in a bowl.
2. or let it sit for several hours and strain the solid and use as a dipping sauce.

Sop Ayam

Ingredients	*Quantity*
Vegetable stock	2 litre
Butter	1 tbsp
Onion finely sliced, fried	100 gram
Nut meg	½ tsp
Clove	2 No.
Pepper	½ tsp
Potatoes	200 gram
Carrot	150 gram
Spring Onion	50 gram
Parsley	One sprig
Cabbage Leaves	100 gram
Peas	100 gram
Garlic	100 gram
Flour	1 tbsp
Salt	1 tsp
Mustard	1 tsp

Method

1. Simmer vegetable stock in a pot.
2. Heat butter and sauté onion, nut meg, cloves, pepper, mustard and garlic. Add to the boiling stock.
3. Add potatoes, carrot, spring onion and peas.
4. Just before removing from heat, add cabbage and flour.
5. Simmer until cooked and season to taste.
6. Garnish with fried onions and serve hot.

Gado Gado

Ingredients	*Quantity*
Ice berg	100 gram
Beans	50 gram
Cabbage	50 gram
Cucumber	50 gram
Tofu	30 gram

Egg	4 No
Fresh Red Chili	5 gram
Green Chili	5 gram
Onion	50 gram
Peanut	30 gram
Lemon	1 No.
Sugar	5 gram
Salt	5 gram
Potatoes	50 gram
Beans sprout	20 gram
*Peanut sauce	50 gram

Method

1. Fry Egg and Tofu.
2. Cut into small pieces.
3. Boil one egg and slice it.
4. Boil cabbage beans and sliced them.
5. Sliced onion and chili pepper.
6. Mix and grind all these with sugar, lemon, salt and pepper and boil with little bit of water (except fry egg and tofu.)
7. In another pan boil all the vegetables, except potatoes.
8. Boil potatoes in separate pot until tender, then peel them.
9. Cut potatoes, egg and cucumber into slice
10. Heat peanut sauce on low heat. Arrange the green vegetable on a platter.
11. Pour the peanut sauce over a platter.

Kepiting Kari

Ingredients	*Quantity*
Crab	4 No.
Onion	100 gram
Lemon grass	30 gram
Tamarind	2 tsp
Boiling Water	250 ml
Coriander leaves	1 bunch
Garlic	30 gram

Galangal	30 gram
Chilies	20 gram
Candle nut	4 No
Turmeric	1 tbsp
Salt and Pepper	10 gram
Oil	3 tbsp
Coconut Milk	100 ml

Method

1. Cut the 4 crabs into quarters with a cleaver or large knife. With a hammer, gently crack the claws and harder sections of shell.
2. Finely clop 6 shallots and 2 stalks lemon grass. Steep 2 teaspoons tamarind in half a cup of boiling water. Chop a handful of fresh coriander leaves.
3. In a food processor, grind together 2 cloves garlic, 1 tablespoon fresh galangal, 2-3 birdseye chilies, seeded, 4 candlenuts (or substitute 8-10 cashews) and 1 teaspoon blachan (hard dark brown shrimp paste), 1 teaspoon turmeric and salt and pepper to taste. Heat 3 tablespoons oil in a large wok or pan, and fry and paste until fragrant. Add shallots, lemon grass, crab pieces and 2 cups coconut milk.
4. Simmer for quarter of an hour. Strain the tamarind water and add half to the sauce. Taste and add more if you wish. Ladle curry into a serving dish and scatter the fre3sh coriander on top. Serve with plain rice.

Sayur Tumis

Ingredients	*Quantity*
Carrot	100 gram
Beans	100 gram
Cabbage	100 gram
Peas	100 gram
Spring Onion	100 gram
Potatoes	100 gram
Ginger	50 gram
Garlic	50 gram
Onion	100 gram
Curry Leaves	30 gram
Salt	5 gram
Soya Sauce	10 gram

Method

1. Cut all the vegetables in diagonal shape and blanching in hot water. Remember all the vegetable are crunchy.
2. Heat oil in a wok and fry the garlic onions and curry leaves over medium heat. Stirring constantly until onions is soft.
3. Add the vegetables and stir fry until lightly cooked but still crispy.
4. Add salt and soya sauce and serve immediately.

Nasi Goreng (vegetable variation)

Ingredients	*Quantity*
Long grain rice	250 gram
Onion	100 gram
Red chili paste	50 gram
Vegetable Oil	20 ml
Salt	To taste
Soya Sauce	2 tsp
Tomato Ketchup	2 tsp
Eggs	2 Nos.
Beans Sprout	50 gram

Method

1. Boil the rice a good long time before you intended to fry it. Two hours is the satisfactory interval.
2. Heat the oil in a wok.
3. Saute Onion chili paste for a minute at season with salt, soya sauce and tomato ketchup.
4. Put in all the rice, and stir it continuously. It is well heated, remove from the fire add beans sproute Serve with fried egg on top.

Note:- Basically in Nasi Goreng addition of Sea food and chicken instead of vegetables.

Pandan cake

Ingredients	*Quantity*
Egg Yoke	8 No.
Egg white	6 No
Sugar	175 gram
Flour	180 gram

Coconut Milk	¾ cup
Semolina	3 tbsp
Green spinach Puree for colour	10 gram

Method

1. Boil coconut milk and semolina extract in a low heat.
2. Beat egg yolks and egg white and sugar. Add food colouring.
3. Slowly add the cooked coconut milk, mixing it evenly.
4. Butter the cake pane mixture inside. Bake until till done

FRENCH MENU

Champaignon-farcis

Ingredients	*Quantity*
Mushroom	300 gram
Onion	10 gram
Butter	50 gram
Breadcrumbs	25 gram

Method

1. Peel and remove the stalk and wash well.
2. Retain 8-12 of best of mushroom. Finely chop the stalk of the mushroom and onion
3. Cook shallots in a little fat, do not colour.
4. Add chopped mushrooms and cook for 3-4 mints (duxelle)
5. Grill mushroom.
6. Place duxelle in the centre of each mushroom.
7. Sprinkle with a few bread crumbs and melted butter.
8. Reheat the oven or under the salamander and serve.

VICHYSSOISE SOUP

Ingredients	*Quantity*
Leeks	450 gram
Butter	55 gram
Onion	55 gram
Vegetable stock	2 litre
Potatoes	55 gram

Cream	175 ml
Parsley and chives	20 gram
Seasoning	To taste
Garlic	30 gram

Method

1. Cut leeks fine.
2. Chop onion sauté leek in butter without browning.
3. Add seasoning and add thinly slice potato.
4. Cook till vegetable are tender.
5. Pass through a sieve and more seasoning if necessary.
6. Stir cream, reheat, garnished with chop parsley and chives and serve chill or hot

Poulet a la king

Ingredients	*Quantity*
Chicken	400 gram
Butter	30 gram
Mushroom	75 gram
Lemon Juice	10 ml
Capsicum	60 gram
Bell pepper	100 gram
Chicken veloute	400 gram
Heavy cream	150 gram
White wine	50 gram
Egg yolk	1 No.
Seasoning	To taste
Parsley	5 gram.

Method

1. Debone chicken cut into ¾ inch pieces and seared it.
2. Wash mushroom, deseed capsicum and bell pepper and cut into 1 "inch dice.
3. Chop parsley.
4. melt butter in a pan add mushroom lemon juice and capsicum over medium heat for 1 min.
5. Add chicken and sauté over min., add wine increase to high heat and sauté for a min.

6. Add chicken veloute bring it to a boil and simmer for 2-3 min. Now add cream and bring to a boil again and add bell pepper and seasoning 7 stir.
7. Add liaison of one egg and 50 ml of cream to the chicken and add parsley and adjust seasoning.
8. Serve with pilaf.

Chicken Veloute

Ingredients	*Quantity*
Chicken Stock	1.3 litre
Seasoning	To taste
Butter	20 gram
Roux	100 gram

Method

1. Bring stock to a boil, add roux gradually whisking and until the sauce become smooth.
2. Reduce to a low heat and simmer for 30 min. stirring occasionally.
3. Bring to a boil again adjust seasoning.
4. Spread 20 g of melted butter on top to prevent skin formation.

Legumes Au Paprika

Ingredients	*Quantity*
Carrot	100 gram
French Beans	100 gram
Mushroom	100 gram
Baby corn	100 gram
Asparagus	50 gram
Butter	40 gram
Paprika Powder	20 gram
Tomato puree	80 ml
Béchamel	30 mll
Heavy cream	90 ml
Seasoning	To taste
Parsley	20 gram
Garlic	50 gram
Onion	100 gram

Method

1. Peel wash and cut carrot into ¾ inch cubes, string beans and cut into cubes into ¾ "cubes, cut the stalk of the mushroom, par boiled corn and cut asparagus into 2 " sizes clean was and chop parsley.
2. Melt butter in a pan add vegetable and sauté over medium heat for a min add paprika and tomato puree.
3. Add béchamel sauce and cream, bring to boil and simmer for a min. adjust to a seasoning.
4. Transfer to a deep serving dish garnish with parsley served with pilaf.

Braised Pilaf

Ingredients	*Quantity*
Butter	50 gram
Chopped Onion	25 gram
Rice	100 gram
White stock	200 ml
Salt, mill pepper	To taste

Method

1. Place 25 grams butter in a small sauteuse, add the onion.
2. Cook gently without colouring for 2-3 mins. Add the rice.
3. Cook gently without coloring for 2-3 minutes.
4. Add twice the amount of stock to rice.
5. Season, cover with a buttered paper, bring to boil.
6. Place in a hot oven 230-250 c for approximately 15 mints until cooked .
7. remove immediately into a cool sauté use.
8. Carefully mix in the remaining butter with a two pronged fork.
9. Correct mix in the remaining butter with a two-pronged form.
10. Correct the seasoning and serve.

Roasted Potatoes

Ingredients	*Quantity*
Potatoes	1 kg
Oil	200 gram
Garlic	50 gram
Herbs	20 gram

Salt	10 gram
Black pepper	20 gram
Parsley	10 gram

Method

1. Preheat oven to 450° F.
2. Cut the potatoes into the quarters and blanch in a water
3. Marinate the blanch potatoes with salt, garlic and herbs.
4. Put in a oven and bake it till its colour to golden brown.

Chocolate Bavarois

Ingredients	*Quantity*
Gelatine	10 gram
Eggs separated	2 nos
Castor Sugar	50 gram
Milk	¼ litres
Whipping or double cream	125 ml

Medhod

1. If using leaf gelarine, soak in cold water.
2. Cream the yolk and sugar in a bowl until almost white.
3. Whisk on the milk which has been brough to the boil, mix well.
4. Clean the milk saucepan which should be a thick based one, and return the mixture to it.
5. return to a low heat and stir continuously with a wooden spoon until the mixture coats the back of the spoon. The mixture must not boil.
6. Remove from the heat, add the gelatin and stir until dissolved.
7. Pass through a fine strainer into a clean bowl, leave in a cool place, stirring occasionally until almost setting point.
8. fold in the lightly beaten cream.
9. fold in the stiffly beaten whites.
10. Pour the mixture into a mould (may be very lightly greased with oil.)
11. allow to set in the refrigerator.
12. Shake and turn out on to a flat dish.

ITALIAN MENU

Suppli (Fried Rice Balls Stuffed With Cheese)

Ingredients	*Quantity*
Small grain sticky rice	250 gram
Onions	50 gram
Proceeds cheese	20 gram
Fresh breadcrumbs	100 gram
Oil	200 ml
Basil	10 gram
Flour	30 gram
Parsley	10 gram
Seasoning	20 gram

Method

1. Cook the rice and allow the rice to cool.
2. Saute Onions, mix in cook rice, add shredded basil, flour seasoning, parsley, mix them thoroughly.
3. Use your hand to form the rice mixture into the balls, the size of a walnut.
4. Poke a hole into the centre of each ball, fill it with cheese mixture and close the hole over again with the rice mixture.
5. Heat the oil until a small piece of bread sizzles.
6. Spread some flour on a plate. Beat the flour mixture or egg in a shallow ball. Coat the ball in that mixture, sprinkle with breadcrumbs. Roll the ball in the flour then in egg and finally in the breadcrumbs.
7. Fry them a few at a time in the hot oil until golden and crisp

Minestrone Soup

Ingredients	*Quantity*
Carrot	50 gram
Beans	50 gram
Onion	20 gram
Garlic	10 gram
Tomatoes	100 gram
Macroni	30 gram
Parsley leaves	10 gram

Potatoes	50 gram
Bake beans	30 gram
Cabbage	50 gram
Parmesan Cheese	20 gram
Oil	20 gram

Method

1. Heat oil in a large sauce pan. Saute onions and garlic. Add all vegetables except cabbage. Cook over low heat.
2. Add tomato paste and vegetable stock and baked beans. Cook of low heat until all vegetables are cooked.
3. Add macroni and seasoning, check the consistency.
4. Serve hot, sprinkle with plenty of parmesan cheese.

Tagliatelle With Bolognese Sauce (Tagliatelle Alla Bolognese)

Ingredients	*Quantity*
Onion	30 gram
Carrot	30 gram
Celery	30 gram
Garlic	20 gram
Minced Lamb	350 gram
Tomato purie	100 gram
Salt and pepper	10 gram
Basil	20 gram
Parmesan Cheese	10 gram
Tagliatelle	500 gram
Oil	30 ml

Method

1. Heat oil in a large sauce pan. Add the onion, carrot, celery and garlic and cook gently.
2. Add the minced lamb to the pan with the vegetables and cook over a midium heat until the meat change colour, stirring constantly and breaking up any lumps with the wooden spoon.
3. Pour in the wine. Stir frequently until it has evaporate then add tomato puree and seasoning.
4. Boil Tagliatelle till a la dente stage.
5. In a sauce pan. Add oil, garlic and put tagliatelle and sauté it with seasoning.

6. Put sauté pasta in a plate and pour sauce on the top.

Pasta Al l' Arrabbiata

Ingredients	*Quantity*
Penne	500 gram
Dry Red Chili	20 gram
Tomatoes	1 kg
Oil	20 ml
Basil	30 gram
Garlic	30 gram
Salt pepper	10 gram
Parmesan Cheese	20 gram
Oregeano	10 gram

Method

1. Blanched the tomatoes, remove the seeds and roughly chopped the tomatoes.
2. Boil the pasta.
3. Heat oil in a pan add garlic and chop tomatoes with their juice, add chili flakes, cook the sauce.
4. Add the boil pasta to the sauce, toss it, add seasoning and herbs. Serve hot sprinkle with parmesan cheese.

Baked Vegetable Lasagne

Ingredients	*Quantity*
Lasagne	10 No
Oil	20 ml
Seasonal Vegetable	100 gram
Bechammel sauce	100 ml
Tomato Sauce	100 ml
Chili Flakes	10 gram
Cheese	50 gram
Butter	50 gram

Method

1. Boil the lasagne sheets.

2. Cook all the vegetables, add some béchamel sauce and tomato sauce and add some seasoning and cheese.
3. In a baking tray, greese that tray with butter, put Lasagne sheet add some vegetables pours white sauce on it and dotted with tomato sauce. Alternate this thing until the baking tray is full. Final layer is with lasagne sheet and pour the upper layer with white sauce and sprinkle some cheese and dot with butter.
4. Bake in a oven until cooked. Remove from the oven and allow to send for five minutes before serving.

Risotto With Vegetables

Ingredients	*Quantity*
Risotto rice	250 gram
Seasonal Vegetable	100 gram
Onion	50 gram
Garlic	20 gram
Vegetable Stock	500 ml
Salt and pepper	10 gram
Butter	20 gram
Cream	20 gram
Parmesan Cheese	20 gram

Method

1. Heat oil in a pan. Saute onion and garlic. Add all vegetables. Saute it. Add rice and stir it continuously without browning the rice.
2. Add hot water cup by cup and stir continuously until it cooks.
3. At last add butter and parmesan cheese and serve hot.

Tiramisu

Ingredients	*Quantity*
Egg	3 Nos
Mascarpone Cheese	450 gram
Sugar	50 gram
Coffee	20 gram
Coco powder	10 gram
Chocolate	100 gram

Spounge	100 gram
Vanilla essence	10 gram

Method

1. Put the egg white in a grease free bowl and mix whisk it until stiff and in peaks.
2. Mix the mascarpone, vanilla essence, sugar and egg yolks in a separate large bowl and mix with until evenly combined. Fold in the egg white then put a few spoonful mixture in the bottom of the large serving bowl and spread it out evenly.
3. Mix the coffee, liquor together in a shallow dish. Dip a sponge finger in the mixture, turn it quickly so that it becomes saturated but does not disintegrate, and place it on top of the mascarpone in the bowl. Add five more dipped sponge fingers, placing them side by side.
4. Spoon in about one- third of the remaining mixture and spread it out. Make more layers in the same way, ending with mascarpone. Level the surface, then sift cocoa powder all over. Cover and chill overnight. Before serving, sprinkle with cocoa and grated chocolate.

GERMAN MENU

Zweibel suppe (onion soup)

Ingredients	*Quantity*
Onions	500 gram
Butter	50 gram
Apple	100 gram
Flour	20 gram
Vegetables stock	1 litre
Salt and White Pepper	To taste
Dried Marjoram	5 gram
Fresh Chives	50 gram
Grated Processed cheese	75 gram
Beer	50 ml

Method

1. Peel, halve and slice the onion.
2. Melt butter in a sauce pan and sauté the onion in it until translucent.
3. Peel, quarter and core the apple and slice thinly.
4. Stir the apple into a sauté onion, allow to swear for a few minutes, then sprinkle flour.
5. Add stock and beer, season to taste with salt, pepper and marjoram and simmer over a medium heat for about 20 minutes.

Just before sewing sprinkle with chives and grate cheese

Creamy Cole Slaw

Ingredients	*Quantity*
Carrot	100 gram
Cabbage	200 gram
Mayonnaise	100 gram
Cream	50 gram
Sugar	20 gram
Mustard	20 gram
Salt and Pepper	To taste
Vinegar	10 ml
Celery	29 gram
Onion	100 gram

Method

1. Slice the cabbage as thinly as possible on a cutting board, then place it in a large bowl. Add the salt and rub the cabbage between your hands, working the salt into it until you can not feel any more salt granules in the mix. Place the salted cabbage in a large colander and drain in the sink for 1 hour.
2. Whisk the mayonnaise, cream, mustard, vinegar, and sugar in a large serving bowl.
3. Rinse the cabbage to get rid of the excess salt; squeeze it dry in batches between paper towels. Add it to the dressing.
4. Add the celery and shallot. Toss well.

Kartoffel Knoedel

Ingredients	*Quantity*
White Bread	2 No.
Butter	10 Gm
Parsley leaves	20 gram
Potatoes	1 kg
Salt	10 gram
Corn flour	100 gram
Egg yolks	2 Nos
Freshly grated nutmeg	10 gram

Method

1. To make the filling for the dumplings, cut the bread into small cubes. Toast the bread cubes in a pan with the butter. Toast until golden brown. Leave to drain on kitchen paper and mix with the parsley leaves.
2. To make the dumplings, wash the potatoes and boil in enough salt water with the cloves until the potatoes are tender. Drain the potatoes and scope them when they are cool enough to handle. Press through a potato ricer.
3. Weigh out 1 kg from the pressed potato mixture and mix with the corn flour, egg yolks, brown butter, salt and nutmeg to form a smooth potato dough.
4. With damp hands, form 8 rounds from the dough. Flatten them slightly and then fill with the toasted bread. Then form into a smooth dumpling. Place the dumplings into a pan of salted, simmering water for about 20 minutes. Remove with a slotted spoon.

Reibekuchen(potato pan cakes)

Ingredients	*Quantity*
Potatoes	500 gram
Onions	100 gram
Eggs	3 No.
Salt	To Taste
Black pepper	To Taste
Oil	To fry

Method

1. Boil potatoes up to ¾ doneness.
2. Grate that potatoes and squeeze in a muslin cloth to remove extra moister.
3. Put the grated potatoes in a bowl and add chopped onion egg and salt and mix thoroughly.
4. Heat the fat made a cake by pressing both hand and fry it on pan until both side are golden brown.

Apple Strudel

Ingredients	*Quantity*
Flour	400 gram
Oil	10 ml
Luke warm water	200 ml
Apple	100 Gm

Sugar	60 gram
Raisin	20 gram
Cinnamon	10 gram
Butter	50 gram
Breadcrumbs	50 gram
Lemon Juice	10 gram.

Method

1. Start preparing Apfelstrudel by creating the crust, knead flour, salt, oil and water into a slightly stiff dough and divide into three small loaves, lightly coat the surface of each loaf with butter and let stand for an hour.
2. Preheat oven to 400 degrees. Butter a baking dish and set aside. The pan can also be lined with parchment. Dust a large 4 by 4 foot clean cloth with flour. Filling Ingredients vigorously to mix thoroughly.
3. Roll each of the three loaves as thin as possible, Stretch the dough sheets onto the clean cloth. The dough sheets should reach approximately 3.5 by 2.5 feet in size. Coat 2/3 of the dough sheet with the buttered breadcrumbs. Spread the remaining 1/3 of the rolled out sheet of dough with the filling mix. Trim away excess dough to form a regular shape.
4. Use the cloth to roll the dough into a roll like a jelly roll. Place the Apfelstrudel in a horseshoe shape on the baking pan. Brush the Apfelstrudel with the remaining butter and place in the oven.
5. Bake for approximately 35 minutes. Remove from oven and serve and serve warm.

JAPANESE MENU

Sushi

Ingredients	*Quantity*
Nori Sea Weed	4 No.
Short grain rice	250 gram
Cucumber	100 gram
Capsicum	50 gram
Salmon	150 gram
Rice Vinegar	70 ml
Wasabi	10 gram
Sesame Oil	10 ml
Sesame Seeds	10 gram

Method

1. Boiled rice and cool in a refrigerator.
2. In a suitable size of mixing bowl, combine the rice vinegar with Sesame Oil.
3. Add the Cucumber strips, capsicum and carrot. Stirring gently and allow to marinate for about 4 hours.
4. Remove from the marinate and drain.
5. Place a nori sheet on a mat, put a rice on the top spread over the sheet add cucumber strips, capsicum and salmon on alternative layers and put wasabi paste on it.
6. Roll the mat and tight with hands and put in a refrigerator for half an hour. Cut the Sushi from Japanese knife.

Japanese clear soup (Tofu to osui mono)

Ingredients	*Quantity*
Vegetable stock	500 ml
Soya sauce	2 tbsp
Mushroom	50 gram
Carrot	50 gram
Cabbage	50 gram
Green onion	50 gram
Lemon Juice	10 ml
Tofu	20 gram
Oil	20 ml
Garlic	20 gram
Onion	50 gram
Japanese Vinegar	50 gram

Method

1. Heat oil in a pan, sauté, onion and garlic
2. Add all vegetables except cabbage and add soya sauce, vinegar in it.
3. Cook it on slow fire, add tofu and lemon juice, adjust the seasoning and serve it hot.

Chicken and Leeks Yakitori (Negi-ma)

Ingredients	*Quantity*
Chicken Boneless/Mushroom	½ kg
Leeks	200 gram

Bamboo skewers	12 Nos
Soya Sauce	10 gram
Salt and Pepper	10 gram
Sugar	5 gram
Yakitori Sauce	40 gram
Garlic	20 gram
Oil	50 ml
Ginger	10 gram

Method

1. Marinate the Chicken. With Soya sauce, salt, pepper, garlic, oil and ginger and Sugar.
2. Thread the chicken and leeks alternatively on to the skewers and brush with yakitori sauce. Grill, basting regularly.

Curry udon

Ingredients	*Quantity*
Glass Noodle	100 gram
Vegetable stock	1 litre
Seasonal Vegetable	200 gram
Onions	50 gram
Corn Starch	20 gram
Soya Sauce	10 gram
Garlic	20 gram
Oil	10 ml
Seasoning	10 gram

Method

1. Heat oil in a pan. Saute onion and garlic.
2. Add all vegetables. Add soya sauce and seasoning and let it boil until all vegetable are cooked.
3. Add glass noodle in it. Add corn starch, adjust the seasoning and serve hot.

Japanese fried rice (cha-han).

Ingredients	*Quantity*
Rice	350 gram

Oil	3 tbsp
Beans (Burnoise)	100 gram
Carrot (Burnoise)	80 gram
Spring Onion	50 gram
Green Chilies	4 Nos.
Ginger Chopped	20 gram
Garlic Chopped	20 gram
Soya Sauce	2 tbsp
Vinegar	2 tbsp
Salt and pepper	10 gram
Coriander	20 gram

Method

1. Pick, wash and soak the rice in enough water for ten to 15 minutes and drain.
2. Boil water, add rice and little water.
3. Cook uncovered on a low heat till rice is tender. Take care not to overcook the rice, each grain of rice should be separate.
4. When rice is done, grain and put in refrigerator.
5. Boil all the vegetables.
6. Heat oil in a wok add ginger and garlic and stir fry all vegetable, take care that all vegetable are not over done, they should be crisp.
7. Add the cooked rice, salt and pepper, vinegar, soya sauce and mix it well and garnish with chopped coriander.

Dorayaki

Ingredients	*Quantity*
Egg	3 Nos
Sugar	80 gram
Baking powder	20 gram
Water	3 tbsp
Flour	100 gram
Kidney beans	100 gram
Vegetable Oil	100 ml

Method

1. Boil the kidney beans and put in a two consistency.
2. Put a egg and sugar in a bowl and mix very well.

3. Dissolve baking soda in the water add the water in the egg mixture, add stiff flour in the egg mixture gradually. Make a smooth batter.
4. In a non-stick pan, pour a scoop of batter into the pan.
5. Turn over when bubbles appear on the surface.
6. Repeat this process to make, 8 to 10 pan cake.
7. Make pair of pan cakes and put a scoop of kidney beans between them.

MEXICAN CUISINE

Tortilla chips with mango salsa

Ingredients	*Quantity*
For tortilla chips	
Corn flour	100 gram
Salt	10 gram
Warm water	50 gram
Refined flour	50 gram
For Mango Salsa	
Mango	250 gram
Red Chilies	20 gram
Green Chilies	20 gram
Onion	20 gram
Coriander	20 gram
Lemon Juice	20 ml

Method

1. Make a tortilla dough and cut each tortilla in six triangular wedges and fry it.
2. Peel the mango and onion.
3. Chop green chilies.
4. In a bowl cut mangoes and onion mix with seasoning, chilies, lemon juice and coriander.
5. Serve with tortilla chips

Burritos with chicken

Ingredients	*Quantity*
Rice	50 gram
Oil	10 ml
Onion	1 No
Cloves (ground)	2 No.

Oregano	10 gram
Tomatoes (chopped)	2 No.
Chicken breast (b/l)/kidney beans	2/200 No. /gram
Processed cheese	100 gram
Sour cream	40 ml
Flour tortilla	200 gram

Method

1. bring a saucepan of lightly salted water to a boil. Add the rice and cook for 8 minutes. Drain, rinse and then drain again.
2. Heat the oil in a large saucepan. Add the onion, with the ground cloves and oregano, and fry for 2-3 minutes. Stir in the rice and tomatoes and cook over low heat until all the tomato juice has been absorbed. Set the pan aside.
3. Put the chicken breasts in a large saucepan, pour in enough water to cover and bring to a boil. Lower the heat and simmer for about 10 minutes or until the chicken is cooked through. Lift the chicken out of the pan, put on a plate and cool slightly.
4. Preheat the oven of 325 degree F. Shred the chicken by pulling the flesh apart with two forks, then add the chicken to the rice mixture, with the grated cheese. Stir in the sour cream, if using.
5. wrap the tortillas in aluminum foil and place them on a plate. Stand the plate over boiling water for about 5 minutes. Alternatively, wrap in microwave-safe plastic wrap and heat in a microwave on full power for 1 minute.
6. Spoon one-eighth of the filling into the center of a tortilla and fold in both sides. Fold the bottom up and the top down to form a parcel. Secure with a toothpick.
7. Put the filled burrito in a shallow dish or casserole, cover with foil and keep warm in the oven while you make seven more. Remove the toothpicks before serving, sprinkled with fresh oregano.

   Note: In Kidney beans salsa, add chop onion, greed chilies, tomatoes and coriander, mix together lemon juice and salt pepper

Mexican rice

Ingredients	*Quantity*
Rice	150 gram
Tomato (chopped)	2 No.
Onion (chopped)	1 No.
Garlic (chopped)	4 cloves
Oil	40 ml

Vegetable stock	200 ml
Salt (t.t.)	15 gram
Chiles (fresno)	3 No.
Peas	100 gram
Black pepper	10 gram
Tomato puree	100 ml

Method

1. Put the rice in a large heatproof bowl and pour in boiling water to cover. Stir once, then let stand for 10 minutes. Transfer to a strainer over the sink, rinse under cold water, then drain again. Set aside to dry slightly.
2. Meanwhile, pour the tomatoes and juice into a food processor or blender, add the onion and garlic and process until smooth.
3. Heat the oil in a large, heavy pan, add the rice and cook over medium heat until it becomes a delicate golden brown. Stir occasionally to ensure that the rice does not stick to the bottom of the pan.
4. Add the tomato mixture and stir over medium heat until all the liquid has been absorbed. Stir in the stock, salt, whole chilies and peas, if using. Continue to cook the mixture, stirring occasionally, until all the liquid has been absorbed and the rice is just tender.
5. remove the pan from the heat, cover it with a tight-fitting lid and let it stand in a warm place for –10 minutes. Remove the chilies, fluff up the rice lightly and serve, sprinkled with black pepper. The chilies may be used as a garnish, if desired.

Fried potatoes

Ingredients	*Quantity*
Chilies	20 gram
Vegetable Oil	20 ml
Onion chop	200 gram
Potatoes	500 gram
Oregano	20 gram
Coriander	30 gram
Red chilies	30 gram

Method

1. Cut the potatoes in dice and fry it.
2. Heat oil in a pan, add onion, sauté it at, add fried potatoes, oregano, Red Chilies, Green Chilies, Coriander.
3. Adjust seasoning and serve hot.

Drunken plantains

Ingredients	*Quantity*
Banana	6 Nos
Butter	100 gram
Rum	100 ml
Orange Juice	100 ml
Cinnamon Powder	20 gram
Dark Brown Sugar	100 gram
Mint	10 gram
Almond	10 gram
Heavy Cream	20 ml

Method

1. Preheat the oven to 350 F. Peel the plantains and cut them in half lengthwise. Put the pieces in a shallow baking dish, dot them all over with butter, then spoon on the rum and orange juice.
2. Mix the orange zest, cinnamon and brown sugar in a bowl. Sprinkle the mixture on the plantains.
3. Bake for 25-30 minutes, until the plantains are soft and the sugar has melted into the rum and orange juice to form a sauce.
4. Meanwhile, slice the almonds and dry-fry them in a heavy frying pan until the cut sides are golden. Serve the plantains in individual bowls, with some of the sauce spooned on top. Sprinkle the almonds on top, decorate with the fresh mint sprigs and pass crème fraiche or heavy cream separately.

ARABIC CUISINE

Falafel

Ingredients	*Quantity*
Chickpeas	250 gram
Garlic	5 gram
Parsley	10 gram
Coriander	10 gram
Green chilli	20 gram
Flour	20 gram
Baking soda	2 gram
Cumin	2 gram
Coriander seeds	2 gram

Vegetable oil	1 Litre
Pepper	0.5 Table spoon
Salt	0.5 Table spoon

Method

1. Prepare the chickpeas. Take a large bowl and put in the chickpeas. Then, pour over enough water to cover the chickpeas and an additional 2 cm more. Leave to soak overnight. In the morning they will look plump and swollen.
2. Drain and puree chickpeas. Hold the chickpeas over the sink and drain off the water with your hand over the bowl. Now spoon the chickpeas into the blender bowl. Don't overfill the blender ! If the blender is small, you will have to do it in batches. If you have a bigger mixer you can do it all at once. Close the blender and pulse a couple of times, then blend on full power until you create a breadcrumb like mixture. Check the consistency by stirring with a spoon. If necessary, blend again on full power until you create a fine puree. Then transfer into a bowl.
3. Puree the rest of Ingredients. Introduce the parsley, coriander, chilli, garlic along with 2 tablespoons of the pureed chickpeas into the bowl of the blender. Put the lid on and blend until well combined.
4. Mix and season. Spoon the blended mixture into the bowl of pureed chickpeas. Then add the flour, the cumin, the crushed coriander seeds, the baking soda and about one and a half tablespoons of salt. Finally, add some pepper. Combine it all together thoroughly with a spoon. If it looks too dry, a few drops of water can be added.
5. Preheat the oil. Place the saucepan on the hob and add the oil. Then heat it up on a medium high setting.
6. Make the Falafel balls. Take a small amount of the blended mixture in your fingertips and mould into small balls. Then place onto a baking tray. This amount of Ingredients should make around twenty five to thirty balls. Kept covered, this mixture will keep for one day in the fridge.
7. Fry the Falafel balls. The oil should now be hot enough to fry. Individually, spoon half the batch of falafel balls into the oil. Allow to fry for 2 minutes until golden brown, stirring with the slotted spoon, so they brown evenly. Then remove and drain on a tray prepared with some kitchen towel. Now repeat the process with the remaining falafel balls.
8. Serve and enjoy. The falafel balls are now ready ! They are usually served inside pitta bread with tahini, humus, or chopped salad.

Tabbouleh

Ingredients	*Quantity*
Tomatoes	200 gram

Green onion	100 gram
Parsley	100 gram
Onion	100 gram
Fresh mint	50 gram
Burgle(soaked)	100 gram
Dry mint	2 gram
Salt	2 gram
Lemon juice	2 gram
Olive oil	100 ml.
Cayenne pepper	0.5 Table spoon

Method

Rinse and finely chop parsley and fresh mint leaves and place in a bowl. Add chopped tomato, green onion, yellow onion, and soaked burgle and combine with parsley. In a separate small bowl combine salt, dry mint, lemon juice, olive oil and cayenne pepper then add to parsley mixture and let sit for 5 minutes before serving to allow burgle to absorb some of the dressing.

Fattoush

Ingredients	*Quantity*
Romain lettuce fine chopped	100 gram
Cabbage shredded	50 gram
Red pepper diced	50 gram
Green pepper diced	50 gram
Cucumber diced	50 gram
Radish diced	50 gram
Tomato diced	50 gram
Carrot shredded	50 gram
Green onion chopped	50 gram
Red onion chopped	25 gram
Parsley chopped	30 gram
Dry mint	10 gram
Lemon juice	4 gram
Garlic minced	4 No.
Olive oil	40 ml.
Pita chips (bread)	1 No.

Method

Chop up the first 12 Ingredients and place in a large bowl. In a small bowl mix the mint, sumac, garlic, lemon juice and olive oil. Piece the toasted or fried pita chips into ½ inch bits. When ready to serve, mix all of the vegetables then add the dressing and mix. Top with pita chips.

Hummus

Ingredients	*Quantity*
Chickpeas (soaked)	125 gram
Tahini	75 ml.
Lemon juice	2 gram
Water	0.5 Litre
Salt	30 gram
Cumin	30 gram
Paprika	15 gram
Olive oil	50 ml.
Parsley, chopped	40 gram
Green chilly, chopped	30 gram

Method

1. **Soak the chickpeas**. Take a large bowl and put in the chickpeas. Then, pour over enough water to cover the chickpeas and an additional 2 cm more. Leave to soak overnight. In the morning they will look plump and swollen.
2. **Cook chickpeas**. Place a saucepan on the hob and add the chickpeas with their water. Then, add a little more water and turn on to a high heat. As the chickpeas begin to simmer, foam will rise to the top, skim off this foam into a bowl with a spoon and discard. Then, turn down the heat to a very slow simmer and cover with the pan lid leaving an opening. Cook for an hour and a half, adding more water through out the cooking if needed. Once cooked the chickpeas should be plump and soft. You should be a able to squash them with a spoon.
3. **Make the hummus**. Place two spoonfuls of the chickpeas into a bowl and set aside for later on. Then spoon the remaining chickpeas into a blender. Put the lid on and puree until it becomes a fairly smooth paste. Repeat the process until all the chickpeas are used. Then. Spoon the blended paste into a bowl. Really authentic humus is made in a bowl with a pestle!
4. **Finish the Hummus**. Take the juice from the squeezed lemon and add it to the bowl of blended chickpeas paste. Add in the tahini, season with salt and whisk well. Then, add a little water to moisten the mixture. Whisk again until it is all well combined. Check that the amounts of salt and lemon juice are to your liking.

5. **Make chickpea garnish**. Add the paprika to the bowl with the reserved chickpeas. Follow with the cumin, the tablespoon of lemon juice, the olive oil, the chopped green chilli, the chopped parsley and some salt. Then mix it all together.
6. **Serve and enjoy**. Place two big spoonfuls of hummus onto a serving plate. Then, using the back of the spoon, spread the humus around in swirls creating a hollow in the middle. Then, place the chickpea garnish in the centre. Your hummus is now ready. It can be served with fresh pitta bread, a drizzle of olive oil and baba ganoush. A versatile vegetarian dish, Hummus goes with almost anything. It will keep in the fridge for 2-3 days in a sealed container.

Tzatziki sauce

Ingredients	*Quantity*
Yogurt (thick)	200 gram
Cucumber	50 gram
Garlic (minced)	4 No.
Dry mint	2 gram

Method

If you are making the tzatziki in advance, salt the cucumber first so that most of its juices drain away as opposed to making the appetizer watery. Mix the above Ingredients and keep chilled in the refrigerator.

Tahini sauce

Ingredients	*Quantity*
Garlic minced	4 No.
Lemon juice	2 Tea spoon
Tahini	100 gram
Chopped parsley	30 gram
Chopped green onion	20 gram

Method

1. In a bowl add the first 5 Ingredients and mix with a wire whisk until well combined. Mix in the parsley.
2. Garnish with fresh chopped green onion.

Lamb moussaka

Ingredients	*Quantity*
Lamb mince	450 gram
Onion fine chopped	25 gram
Garlic fine chopped	14 Clove
Cinnamon powder	0.5 gram
Sweet corn	100 gram
Tomatoes chopped	150 gram
Tomato puree	100 gram
Parsley chopped	40 gram
Aubergines, thinly sliced lengthways	300 gram
Yoghurt	100 gram
Egg (beaten)	1 No.
Parmesan cheese (grated)	40 gram

Method

1. Prepare the Ingredients. Preheat the oven to Gas mark 4, 180° C., 350° F. Heat a large non-stick frying pan and cook the mince, onion and garlic for 5-7 minutes. Add the cinnamon, sweet corn, chopped tomatoes, tomato puree and seasoning. Bring to the boil, reduce the heat and simmer for 10-15 minutes. Stir through the parsley.
2. Prepare the moussaka. Arrange half the aubergines in the bottom of a large ovenproof dish and spoon over half the mince mixture. Repeat. Instead of making a white sauce in a small bowl mix together the yogurt, egg and seasoning and stir in half the Parmesan. Pour over the dish and sprinkle with the remaining cheese.
3. Cook. Bake for 40 minutes or until brown.

Baba ghanoush

Ingredients	*Quantity*
Egg plant baked (peeled)	450 gram
Lemon juice	4 T. spoon
Garlic minced	8 Clove
Salt	15 gram
Tahini	50 gram
Parsley	40 gram
Cayenne pepper	15 gram
Olive oil	30 gram

Method

Roast the eggplant then place a plastic bag to cool, then you can peel and remove top, place in a bowl. Add garlic, lemon juice land tahini paste, blend in a blender or with a mortar. Spread in a place and garnish with parsley or mint and top with olive oil and a sprinkle of cayenne pepper or paprika.

Couscous

Ingredients	*Quantity*
Chicken breast	4 No.
Vegetable oil	40 ml
Salt	40 gram
Red pepper (ground)	15 gram
Apple- peeled and chopped	100 gram
Garlic fine chopped	4 No.
Curry powder	40 gram
Grated orange peel	30 gram
Chicken broth	150 ml.
Cornstarch	10 gram
Couscous (cooked)	60 gram

Method

1. Remove excess fat from chicken; cut chicken into 1 inch pieces.
2. Heat 2 teaspoons vegetable oil in 10 inch nonstick skillet until hot.
3. Cook and stir chicken, salt, and red pepper in oil over medium heat until chicken is done, about 5 minutes. Remove chicken.
4. Add 1 teaspoon vegetable oil, apple, onion, garlic, curry powder, and orange peel.
5. Cook and stir until apple is tender, about 7 minutes.
6. Stir in chicken broth and chicken. Heat to boiling, stirring constantly.
7. Mix cornstarch and water; stir into chicken mixture.
8. Boil and stir until mixture slightly thickens, about 1 minute. serve over couscous.

Basbousa

Ingredients	*Quantity*
Sugar	300 gram
Water	100 ml

Fresh lemon juice	2 T. spoon
Coconut	150 gram
Yogurt	100 gram
Vegetable oil	50 ml.
Heavy cream	50 ml.
Semolina	150 gram
Egg	2 No.
Baking powder.	20 gram

Method

1. For the Syrup. Prepare syrup by putting the sugar and water in a heavy saucepan. Bring to a boil while constantly stirring to dissolve the sugar. Let it boil until it appears clear. Add few drops of lemon and let it boil for minutes or so. Remove from saucepan and let it cool completely.
2. For the Basbousa. Preheat the oven to 350 F. In a bowl combine all the Ingredients (sugar, coconut, yogurt, oil, cream, semolina, eggs, and baking powder) and stir until well mixed. Grease 2 9-inch round pans and divide batter among them. Decorate the surface with whole blanched almonds, pistachios, or pine nuts.
3. Bake until golden (30 minutes). Remove from oven and pour some syrup on the whole pan or on each small muffin size and return the pan to the oven for a few minutes (5 minutes) to dry the surface. Allow to cook; cut into squares like brownies.

Pita bread

Ingredients	*Quantity*
Dry yeast	10 gram
Lukewarm water	100 ml.
Flour	150 gram
Salt	10 gram
Sugar	10 gram

Method

1. Mixing bowl, rolling pin (or use a bottle). Paddle or similar to transfer bread to and from oven, pizza stone or baking sheet, oven. Dissolve yeast in ½ cup lukewarm water, add one tsp sugar, stir and let stand for 10 minutes until frothy.
2. In a large mixing bowl combine the flour and salt, mix thoroughly using your hands or a rubber spatula; make a well, add the yeasty water and about ½ the lukewarm water; mix and gradually add more water a few TBSP at a time using a rubber spatula (it can be very

sticky until well mixed) until firm and elastic and just a little sticky (may adhere slightly to your hand- you want the dough to be as soft and 'fluid' as possible so it can 'pop').

3. Turn dough on to a lightly floured working surface and knead for 10 minutes or until dough is smooth and elastic. Return to the bowl, cover with a plastic wrap and leave in a warm, draft-free place to rise for 2-3 hours (much less if you are using 'rapid-rise' yeast).
4. When dough has nearly doubled in size, punch down, knead lightly, roll out a 'rope' and pinch off hand fulls to form into balls about the size of tangerines-between a ping-pong and a tennis ball.
5. Put pizza stone or baking sheet in oven on lowest rack; remove any other racks to ease access, pre-heat oven to 450 deg. F.
6. Place balls on a lightly floured surface a few inches apart, cover and let rest for 10-15 minutes.
7. On your lightly floured working surface, squash a ball flat and round with your hand and then roll out, flipping and turning, a round of the desired thickness-less than ¼ inch thick and about 5" across. This will take experimentation, until you achieve the kind of bread you like. I like it very thin, but suit yourself.
8. Now the interesting part: baking the bread. Middle Eastern bread ovens are cavernous affairs (even wood-fired from time to time) and are very hot, with a very hot floor. The bread is put on long paddles (same as pizza) and deployed in the oven until it puffs and browns slightly on top.

RAJASTHANI CUISINE

Mirchi vada

No of portions: 4

Ingredients	*Quantity*
Large green chillies	8 no
Boiled Potatoes	250 gram
Red Chilly powder	1 tsp
Garam Masala pd	½ tsp
Chat masala	1½ tsp
Green coriander (chopped)	1 tbsp
Salt	1tsp
gram flour	150 gram
Baking Powder	A pinch
Salt	½ tsp
Red chilly powder	½ tsp

Method

1. Slit green chilies and remove the seeds.
2. Mash the potatoes and add red chili powder, Garam Masala Powder, chaat masala, green coriander and salt. Mash and mix well
3. Divide this into equal portions.
4. Stuff a little of this mixture into the green chilies and also cover the chilies with this potato mixture.
5. Now prepare a thick batter using gram flour, baking powder, red chili powder, salt and about 1 cup of water.
6. Keep the batter for about 10 minutes.
7. Heat oil in a Kadhai.
8. Dip stuffed green chilies into the gram flour batter and deep fry until golden brown.

Gatte ki subzi

No of portions: 4

Ingredients	*Quantity*
Besan	150 gram
Coriander Powder	1 tsp
Ghee	50 gram
Yoghurt	200 gram
Oil	50 gram
Red chilly powder	1 tsp
Turmeric	½ tsp
Salt	15 gram
Cumin Seeds	1 tsp

Method

1. Mix besan while adding ½ tbsp salt, ½ tbsp red chilli powder, ½ tbsp coriander powder and *ghee*. Make a stiff dough.
2. Make 5-6 thing and long strips of out of the dough. Put these strips in boiling water and cook for 5 minutes. Cut these guttas in small pieces.
3. Strain the yoghurt through a strainer. Add ½ tbsp salt,½ tbsp red chilli powder and ½ tbsp coriander powder and turmeric to yoghurt. Mix well.
4. Add the gatta pieces. Heat oil in a *kadhai*.
5. Put the tadka of cumin seeds and add yoghurt mixture. Cook it for 5-6 minutes while stirring continuesly and bring it to boil.

6. Add besan gattas and simmer the flame and cook for another 5-7 minutes.
7. Finally put tadka of red chilli powder and garnish it with fresh, chopped coriander.

Laal Mass

Ingredients	*Quantity*
Mutton Leg	800 gram
Onions (chopped)	100 gram
Tomato (chopped/paste)	300 gram
Ginger Paste	20 gram
Garlic Paste	30 gram
Curd	100 gram
Red Chili Powder	20 gram
Turmeric powder	5 gram
Coriander.	10 gram
Cooking Oil	50ml
Cloves	2 gram
Cardamom Black	2 gram
Black Peppers (crushed	10 no
Bay Leaves	2 no

Method

1. Wash the mutton and remove all fat.
2. In a pan put cooking oil. When the oil is hot, add chopped onions and fry them until golden brown.
3. Keep aside a little of the brown onions to use for garnish.
4. Add the garlic and ginger paste, cook for 15 min.
5. Add cut portions of mutton and let it cook for 30 min.
6. Now add bay leaves, black pepper, red chili powder, cardamom black, turmeric powder and curd, then add salt to taste.
7. Cook until the spices are well-cooked and mixed.
8. Add tomato paste and cook on low fire for 40 min.
9. When ready, remove lal maas from the fire and garnish with finely chopped coriander leaves and fried onions before serving

Mangori papad ki subzi

No. of portions: 4

Ingredients	*Quantity*
Mangoori	100 gram
Papad	8 no
Tomatoes	150 gram
Ginger	15 gram
Jeera	1tsp
Oil	3 tbsp
Salt	1 tsp
Green Coriander	1 tbsp(chopped)
Green Chillies	3-4 no
Turmeric	½ tsp
Coriander Seeds	1 tsp
Red Chillies	1 tsp
Hing	1 pinch

Method

1. Deep Fry the Mangoories and Papad
2. Heat Oil add Jeera,Crushed Corianda seeds, Whole Red Chilli and Choppes Ginger,Sault it
3. Add Fine chopped Tomatoes and for Tomatoes puree cook it add Hing then Masala.
4. Add Water and simmer it.
5. Mix the Mangori and Papad.

Lahsooni Dal

No. of portions: 4

Ingredients	*Quantity*
Moongdal	200 gram
Garlic	25 gram
Oil	30 ml
Corianda Leaves	1 tbsp(chopped)

Method

1. Heat Oil in a Kadhai and in another Bowl Dal with Turmeric.
2. In Heating Oil Garlic Brown it add Dal Cooled for few Minutes add Salt and garnished with fresh coriander leaves.

Bajre Ki Roti (Millet flour bread) recipe

Ingredients	Quantity
Millet flour	400 gram
Salt	5 gram
Ghee	30 gram
Water	As required

Method

1. Sift the millet flour and salt together. Gradually add enough warm water and knead with greased palms to make a semi-soft dough. Knead the dough 5 minutes before making the roti.
2. Divide the dough equally into lemon-sized portions. Flatten each portion with your palms pressing the edges together to make 5 - 6 inch. - diameter discs. This has to be done carefully so that the edges do not break. Avoid using the rolling pin.
3. Heat a griddle (tawa); lay a disc flat on it and roast both sides. Then put it directly on a coal fire to make it crisp. Smear 2 tbsp ghee on the disc, crumple lightly between both palms and serve hot. Repeat with the other discs.
4. Serve immediately with yoghurt, jaggery, onion, and sangar ka saag or lasan chutney.

Churma

Ingredients	*Quantity*
Wheat flour	200 gram
Khoya	100 gram
Ghee	400 gram
Sugar(pwd)	200 gram
Almonds	50 gram
Cardamom	4no
Dalchini(pwd)	1no

Method

1. Melt 150 gram ghee and mix it in wheat flour. Make a stiff dough using very little water.
2. Heat the rest of the ghee in a kadahi. Make about 15-20 balls with the dough. Fry it on low flame till it becomes golden brown. Churn it in grinder after it cools down. Mix khoya.
3. Heat 1 tbsp. ghee in kadahi. Add cardamom seeds and dalchini. Add the above mixture of wheat flour and khoya. Fry it for one minute. When it cools down, add sugar and chopped almonds. Mix well.
4. Serve in a plate. You can enjoy the taste of churma for 8-10 days if you keep it in an airtight box.

MAHARASHTRIAN MENU

Tomato Saar

No. of Portions : 4

Ingredients	*Quantity*
Tomatoes	500 gram
Rice Flour	40 gram
Coconut milk	200 ml
Vegetable Oil	20 ml
Cumin Seeds	15 gram
Green Chillies	10 gram
Red Chilly Pd	10 gram
Salt	10 gram
Sugar	10 gram
Black Pepper	15 gram
Green Corriander	25 gram
Water	1 litre

Method

1. Wash, Boil, Peel and puree the tomatoes.
2. Put the rice flour in a bowl slowly add the coconut milk and mix this paste with the tomato puree.
3. Heat oil in a handi over a medium flame, add first the cumin seeds then green chilies, stir and and the tomato mixture, the RCP, Salt, Sugar and the pepper.
4. Stir and bring it to simmer, cook till done.
5. Sprinkle some chopped fresh coriander while service

Kolhapuri Chicken

No. of Portions : 4

Ingredients	*Quantity*
Chicken	1 No.
Coriander seeds	10 gram
Ginger	20 gram
Garlic	30 gram
Cumin	5 gram
Onions	300 gram
Pepper corn	10 gram
Turmeric	10 gram
Red chillies	10 gram
Salt	15 gram
Oil	30 ml
Tomatoes	500 gram
yoghurt	200 gram
Cloves	2 No.

Method

1 Cut the chicken into medium pieces
2 Put the chicken in a bowl and marinate it with yoghurt, grated ginger and crushed garlic, salt and turmeric.
3 Broil some red chillies, coriander seeds, cloves, and grind them.
4 Slice the onions and some tomatoes.
5. Heat fat, add sliced onions, and cook till it turns brown.
6. Add ginger garlic, spices, marinated chicken and stir fry.
7. Add tomatoes followed by salt, some water and cook till it is done.
8. Garnish with ginger juliennes and coriander

Masala Chi Vangi

No of Portions: 4

Ingredients	*Quantity*
Brinjal	½ kg
Coconut	01 No.

Onion	500 gram
Corrianderseeds	10 gram
Peppercorn	5 gram
Turmeric powder	5 gram
Red chilly powder	10 gram
Cloves	2 gram
Sugar	10 gram
Corriandar seeds	5 gram
Salt	15 gram
Oil	30 gram

Method

1. Grate the Coconuts,chop onions.
2. Wash and cut the Brinjals into cubes.
3. Roast the whole masalas and grind them.
3. Heat oil into a vessel,sauté onion + Brinjals + salt + sugar + turmeric.
4. Add some water if it start sticking into the pan.
5. Fry it well then add sufficient water to cook it.
6. Sprinkle the grated coconuts and garnish it with chopped corriander

Tomato Bhat

No. of Portions : 4

Ingredients	*Quantity*
Rice	350 gram
Coconut	1/2
Onions	250 gram
Garlic	10 gram
Ginger	10 gram
Peppercorn	5 gram
Cloves	5 gram
Salt	10 gram
Fat	10 gram
Corriander Green	10 gram
Water	As Required

Method

1. Pick, wash and soak the rice.
2. Make paste of ¾ th of tomatoes. Slice the onions and remaining tomatoes.
3. Heat fat in the heavy – bottom pan.
4. Add whole masalas, when it crackles add sliced onions and cook till it turns brown
5. Add rice and sauté till it become transparent.
6. Add tomatoes and water and cook till it gets done.
7. Garnish with brown onions and coriander.

Amti (dal)

No of Portions: 4

Ingredients	*Quantity*
Moong Dal	300 gram
Onion	250 gram
Turmeric	10 garm
Red chilly powder	10 gram
Green Chillies	10 gram
Tamarind	10 gram
Jaggery	10 gram
Garam Masala	15 gram
Oil	50 gram
Salt	10 gram
Curry Leaves	20 (approx)
Water	As required

Method

1. Clean,Wash and soak the dal.
2. Chop the onions and slit the green chillies.
3. Soak the Tamarind in water.
4. Cook the dal with salt and turmeric powder.
5. Heat oil in a pan,Add Mustard seeds andcurry leaves when it crackles add,green chillies, chopped onions then add chilly powder and turmeric.
6. Now add the cooked dal followed by jaggery and Tamarind pulp.
7. Adjust the seasoning and serve hot

Coconut Poli

No of Portions: 4

Ingredients	*Quantity*
Maida	1/2 kg
Fat	30 gram
Coconut	1/2
Cardomom	5 No.
Rose Essence	5 No.
Sugar(b/f)	50 gram
Dried Fruits	30 gram

Method

1. Grate the coconuts and chop the dried fruits.
2. Make the mixture for stuffing by cooking grated coconut,sugar and chopped dried fruits on slow fire.
3. Sieve the maida,salt and powder sugar.
4. Rub some ghee with the maida and Make a firm daugh using sufficient sugar.
5. Divide the daugh into equal parts
6. Roll into small chapaties and fill the mixture in the centre and cover it with other chapatti

Goan Cuisine

No. of Portions : 4

Ingredients	*Quantity*
Flour	200 gram
Baking powder	10 gram
Salt	20 gram
Ground coriander	2tbs
Ground cumin	4tbs
Grounded coriander seeds	2tbs
Ginger chop	100 gram
Lemon juice	20 ml
Water	200 ml

Corn	300 gram
Onion chop	200 gram
Curry leaves	20 gram
Green chillies	20 gram
Fresh corriander	30 gram
Potatoes	100 gram

Method

1. Wash the corn and potatoes and boil it.
2. Sieve the flour.
3. Sift together the flour, baking powder, salt, ground coriander, and ground cumin in a medium bowl. Add egg, lemon juice and water. Stir vigorously with a wooden spoon until smooth. Add the corn, onions, and cilantro. Stir until just combined.
4. Heat a large frying pan on medium high heat. Add enough oil to generously coat the bottom of the pan. When oil is hot (shimmering not smoking), spoon about 2 heaping tablespoons worth of fritter batter into the pan to form one fritter, patting it down with the back of the spoon as soon as it is in the pan. Work in batches. Leave about 1/2 inch between the fritters in the pan. Let cook about 2-3 minutes on each side, flipping the fritters when they are nicely browned on one side. When browned on the other side, remove the fritters to a plate lined with paper towels to absorb the excess fat.
5. Add oil as needed to keep the bottom of the pan well coated. Note that the fritters will likely splatter a bit as you are cooking. So, either use a screen splatter guard, or wear long sleeved clothes while you cook

Mutton Vindaloo

No. of Portions : 4

Ingredients	*Quantity*
Mutton [Lean goat meat]	800 gram
Chopped onion	300 gram
Tamrind extract	4 tbsp
Vinegar	2 tbsp
Potatoes	300 gram
Oil	200 gram
For the masala paste	
Whole cardamom	2 no
Cumin seeds	1 tbs

Garlic	200 gram
Whole red chillies	6no
Clove	2 gram
Coriander powder	2tbs
Chopped ginger	100 gram
Salt	20 gram
Turmeric	1tbs
Cinnamon	4no
Tomato chopped	200 gram

Method

1. Clean the fat of the mutton and wash it
2. Clean the vegetables
3. Grind all the Contents of the masala into a smooth paste, with water
4. Heat oil in a pan
5. Sauté the chopped onion till it turns transluscent.
6. Now, add the masala paste and mutton and mix well.
7. Add water, cover the pan and let it cook for a while.
8. Now, add the tamarind extract, vinegar and boiled potatoes and simmer for 3-4 minutes.
9. Mutton Vindaloo is ready to serve.

Mushroom Xacuti

Number of Portion 04

Ingredients	*Quantity*
Mushroom	500 gram
Ghee	50 gram
Onions	75 gram
Coconuts	1/2 no
Lime	1/2 no

For Masala

Coriander seeds	1 tbs
Peppercorns	10 gram

Dry red chillies	5 no
Turmeric powder	2 tbs
Cloves	1 no
Cinnamon	2 tbs
Cumin seeds	4 no
Garlic	200 gram
Star anise	1 no.
Caraway seeds	2 tbs
Cardamom	4 no.
Aniseed	2 tbs
Poppy seed (khuskhus)	30 gram

Method

1. Wash the mushrooms and vegetables
2. Grate the two coconuts separately. Take first (thick) and second (thin) extract of milk from one grated coconut by adding water and keep it aside.
3. Roast the other grated coconut with two sliced onions in a pan with a little ghee, until the coconut is pale brown. Then grind it finely and keep aside.
4. Roast the Ingredients for masala in 1-2 tbs of ghee and grind well.
5. Heat the remaining ghee. Chop four onions and fry it in ghee till light brown. Add chicken, turn over on all sides till brown. Add the ground masala, fry for a minute. Add salt and second extract of coconut milk. Cook until chicken is tender.
6. Cut the remaining onions into quarters and add it to the mushroom along with the coconut-onion paste kept aside. Simmer for a few minutes and then add the first extract of coconut milk. Add salt if required. Keep on a slow fire until the sauce has thickened.
7. Sprinkle lime juice over the xacuti before serving.

Goan Pulaoo

No of portions: 4

Ingredients	*Quantity*
Rice	400 gram
Whole garam masala	5 gram
Tomatoes	50 gram
Onion	50 gram
Curry leaves	5 no

Red chillies	2no
Coriander	10 gram
Salt	20 gram
Ghee	30 gram

Method

1. Heat oil in a pan, add the cinnamon, cloves, cardamoms, chilies and fry for 1 minute.
2. Then add the onions and fry until they get golden in colour.
3. Now add the tomatoes.
4. Add salt, turmeric and cook for 7-10 minutes.
5. Add rice, 3 cups of water and cook by covering the pan till done.
6. Garnish with chopped cilantro and serve hot.

Dodol

No. of portions: 4

Ingredients	*Quantity*
Rice flour	100 gram
large coconuts	1no
Jaggery	100 gram
Sugar	2tbs
Cashew nuts, chopped	20 gram

Method

1. Grind the rice or powder it and blend it with a little water or coconut juice and keep aside.
2. Grate and grind the coconuts coarsely.
3. Extract about one and half litres of thick coconut juice and around 8 litres thin juice.
4. Keep the thin coconut juice on the fire, preferably in a large copper vessel, and bring to the boil stirring continuously. Add the rice mixture, a little at a time, continuing stirring.
5. Let it boil for around two hours. Add coconut jaggery and sugar and salt and continue stirring. When the mixture begins to thicken, add the thick coconut juice.
6. The Dodol will start leaving the sides of the pan stainless steel container. Decorate with chopped cashew nuts. Serve sliced.

BENGALI CUISINE

Ghugni Recipe

No. of persons: 4

Ingredients	*Quantity*
White Peas	150 gram
Chopped onion	100 gram
Tomato	100 gram
Garlic	2pods
Ginger	10 gram
Cumin seed	5 gram
Garam masala	5 gram
Oil	20 gram
Salt	5 gram
Green chillies	4no
Lemon	1no
Green coriander	10 gram
Coriander powder	5 gram

Method

1. Soaked and boil white peas till it turns soft.
2. Heat the oil.
3. Fry onion, ginger and garlic.
4. Fry it till onion gets brown.
5. Add tomatoes and stir it properly.
6. Now mix this with cooked peas.
7. Add cumin seed powder and coriander powder.
8. Add garam masala And lemon juice
9. Adorn with coriander and chopped onion.

Machher Jhol Recipe

No. of persons: 4

Ingredients	*Quantity*
Rohu fish	800 gram
Garlic	50 gram

Green chilli	10 gram
Turmeric	5 gram
Black mustard	25 gram
Panch phoron	15 gram
water	500ml
Mustard oil	300ml
Salt	20 gram

Method

1. Wash and cut the fish
2. Marinate the fish with salt and turmeric.
3. Heat oil in a kadhai or wok and fry the fish for 20 minutes. Set aside.
4. Make a fine paste of ginger, chili, turmeric and mustard seeds, with a little water, in the food processor.
5. Heat oil in a pan and add panch phoron.
6. When the seeds crackle, add the mustard paste and salt.
7. Cook for 5 minutes, stirring all the while.
8. Add fish and rest of the water. Simmer for 5 minutes.
9. Serve hot with boiled rice.
10. Machher Jhol is ready.

Aloo Posto

No. of persons: 4

Ingredients	*Quantity*
Potatoes	500 gram
Poppy seeds	50 gram
Onion	100 gram
Redchilli	4 no
Turmeric	5 gram
Ginger	10 gram
Garlic	20 gram
Oil	50ml
Water	As required
Green chillies	4 no
Bayleaf	2 no

Salt	20 gram
Panch phoram	15 gram

Method

1. Cut the potatoes into long slices of about 2 in x ¼ in × ¼ in wide and keep aside.
2. Soak poppy seeds in warm water for about an hour. Grind poppy seeds, green chilies and salt with enough water in a grinder to make a smooth paste. Preparation
3. Heat oil in a pan and add bay leaf to it. Add all the Ingredients mentioned under"paanch phoran" and allow them to crackle.
4. Now add sliced onion and sauté.
5. Add ginger-garlic paste and sauté until it turns golden brown.
6. Add potato pieces, turmeric powder, coriander powder, red chili powder and salt to the above.
7. Fry it for 3-4 minutes and then, add the poppy seeds paste to it. Fry for another 3-4 minutes and pour water into it.
8. Lower the flame and cover the pan. Allow the dish to cook for a few more seconds till the water evaporates.
9. Aloo Posto is ready to savor. Serve with freshly cooked basmati rice.

Cholar Dal Recipe

No. of persons: 4

Ingredients	*Quantity*
Chana dal	150 gram
Cumin seeds	5 gram
Cloves	2 no
Green chillies	4no
Garam masala powder	5 gram
Cinnamon	5 gram
Sugar	5 gram
Salt	10 gram
Ghee	10 gram
Oil	20 gram
Coconut	½ no
Green coriander	10 gram

Method

1. Wash the dal properly.
2. Add turmeric powder and garam masala.
3. Boil the daal till it turns soft.
4. Heat the oil.
5. Add cumin seeds, and green chilies.
6. Mix boiled daal and water.
7. Now add salt, sugar and ghee.
8. Boil it for few minutes.
9. Adorn with fried coconut.

Bengali Pualo

No. of persons: 4

Ingredients	*Quantity*
Rice	400 gram
Onions	50 gram
Cashew nuts	20 gram
Raisins	20 gram
Sugar	10 gram
Ghee	50 gram
Salt	15 gram
Dry coconuts	25 gram
Water	As required
Garam masala whole	15 gram

Method

1. Chop onions and break the cashew nuts finely.
2. Wash the rice and soak in water for 20 minutes.
3. Heat ghee in a pan, add the whole garam masala, chopped onions and fry till onions are soft.
4. Add soaked rice, fry for about five minutes. Add enough water and salt, bring it to boil.
5. Add sugar, cashewnuts, raisins and mixed dry fruits. Stir well, cover and cook till done.
6. Serve hot with favourable side dishes.

Luchi

No. of persons: 4

Ingredients	*Quantity*
Maida	400 gram
Ghee	50 gram
Water	As required
Salt	5 gram
Oil (for frying)	1/2 litre

Method

1. Mix ghee, salt with flour.
2. Add water to prepare dough.
3. Roll out rounds balls and fry till they turn golden brown.
4. Serve with curry.

Kalakand

No. of persons: 4

Ingredients	*Quantity*
Milk	2litre
Sugar	100 gram
Citric acid	5 gram
Dry fruits	30 gram

Method

1. Chop dry fruits
2. Boil the milk and reduce to half
3. Add the citric acid ones the milk curdle continuous reducing it till its become thick add sugar and continue to cook. string till softly thicken in a lump.
4. Set in a tray and garnished with chop dry fruits and nuts.
5. Cut it into diamonds and served.

Unit 6
BAKERY

Unit 6

BAKERY

Chapter 34

Introduction to Bakery

After studying this chapter, the student must know:

- History of bakery
- The art and science of baking
- Ingredients and their functions
- Temperature and baker.

HISTORY OF BAKING

There is no doubt that baking has always being and will continues to be one of the most important and colourful areas of culinary development. The ties of baking to agriculture lies in its quest your improved texture and refined flavours of baked goods as well as other confectionery. The originated production of wheat by Egyptians is consider by most histories to be true beginning of bread which are produced today, many century ago Egyptians the Greeks where preparing 50 different kinds of bread by about 400 BC or all of these were baked in closed oven. The Romans then developed system to man produce breads which helped them to get many victories has bread could be made in advance and cooked. It was during reigns of emperors Augustus and Julies Ceasor (100-44 BC) that public baked shop begin to be establish, owner of baked shop were either Politian or retained army officials who were able employ slave labour. The slave came from all parts of world. The result these blend was exchange of ideas and methods of culinary preparation ready to further development of baking. This was made better by creation brick oven and mechanical means of milling flour.

The restless population of some was spending a lot of money and time on testing. The banquet lasted for a days. In order to satisfy the corrupted Roman society. Pastries of various kinds were created. During games in the coliseum these were sold to spectators as these days Popcorns and hot dogs are sold in today's football games. Knowledge of Baking was developed and preserved in monasteries – the intellectual store has of Europe. The monks practice the art of baking and enclosed guarded their secret knowledge later the monks gives bread instant of taxes to feudal barols. This was the situation in 13th centuries when Phillips II of France gave bakers the right to build their own ovens. These industries continue until the discovery of America when the export of sugar becomes steady – it's was as if lightning has structed the pastry trays and ovens of Europe. Until than honey had only being sweating agent, other bit of magic of America was the invention of Cocoa after which there was no limit for the pastry Chef is.

In 1675 this art was given another boost when a Sicilian Pastry Cook by the name of Procopio went to Paris and open the first ice cream parlour this was so successful that within five years another two hundred parlour are set-up. The distinguish between the pastry cook and baker begin to become more prominent they separated because of argument about oven temperature since bread required much stronger heat than delicates pastry. After this baking school open to trained professional.

THE ART AND SCIENCE OF BAKING

Bringing together the balance quantity of various ingredients in a proper form. This is the definition of art and science of baking when you mix and blend many dry ingredients liquids and leavings together and exposes the mixture to heat a variety of actions combined as one unit for example butter and sugar melt eggs coagulated, liquid makes steam and starches start swelling – baking powder, baking soda and yeast for gasses. It's very important that the baker learn the performance of each ingredients in the preparation of quality baked goods many thing can go it's important to pay attention and follow the instruction of formula by step by step when something goes bring must always find your mistake or else you were repeat it. The mistake must become a opportunity to improves become more professional.

INGREDIENTS AND THEIR FUNCTIONS

(1) Fats and Oils:

(A) **Lard**:- The fat of hags (Pigs) has a unique flavour and makes a flaky Pie crust.

(B) **Butter:**- Fresh butter consist of 80 to 82% of butter fat, 13 to 15% water and 3 to 5% milk solid. It's available salted and unsalted. It's considered replaced for its quality and flavour.

(C) **Margin**:- The product is made from a variety of vegetable and animal fat it's compossed of 80 to 82% fat 13 to 15% water and 3 to 5% milk solid plus salt, colour and flavour. It's a shortening often used to replaced butter. It must be remembered that it does have different flavour and melting properties.

(D) **Vegetable Shorting**:- These are derived from nuts, seeds and drains. Specially shortening are available for whip topping cakes, batter and dough's are available as regular or Plain with an emulsifier or with a stabilizer with a higher or lower melting Point. They have been developed to gain greater adaptability of product improve shell life reduce cost and greater stability.

(E) **Oil**:- It's often used in chiffon cakes quick breads normal breads and soft rolls dough. It's used for deep frying dough nuts and other pastries.

(2) Sugar and Sweetener:-

(A) **Granulated Sugar**:- This sugar has been refined into crystal either Sugar cane or Sugar Beats super fine granulated sugar is preferred in baking because of its ability to dissolve faster in cake batters and other mixture. It's often used for making margins.

(B) **Powder sugar**:- This also knows as confectionary sugar. It has very fine texture, the same as flour and must also be sifted and before added to other Ingredients. It's should also be stored in air tight container.

(C) **Raw Sugar**:- It less refined than other sugar having a coarse of temperature sugar. It has not been bleached and so it's retained light brown or blend colour.

(D) **Brown Sugar**:- It's available in light and dark colour. The higher the percentage of molasses and other solids the darker it's in colour and more intense in flavour. It's should be stored in air tight container. To keep brown sugar soft place a slice apple or potatoes in an open plastic beg inside the container with a brown sugar.

(E) **Granulated Brown Sugar**:- Is not compact like brown sugar. Moisture is removed during the processing and refining allowing the granulation it's not possible to replaced brown sugar with granulated brown sugar because of moisture content. The resulting product will have a different texture it's used most often as a topping for pancakes and fruits.

(F) **Molasses**:- This is a thick brownish liquid by product derived from the refining of granulated sugar. The lighter the colour the sweater the molasses.

(G) **Maple Sugar**:- It is a refined maple sap (bark juice) and has a rich wonderful flavour it's highly priced product which is very expensive maple sugar is a great topping for Danish pastry and special desserts and cakes.

(H) **Maple Syrup**:- Is a reduce maple sap it will darken with agent but retain it's flavour. It's best should under refrigeration.

(I) **Corn Syrup:-** Are available in varying texture intensity and flavour it's used in cakes, icing fruit filling and topping the formula being used will indicated the type of corn syrup needed.

(3) Leaving Agents

(A) Baking Soda:- Act as a leavening agent when mixed with an acid such as sour cream, sour milk, butter milk, molasses or citrus juices. The chemical reaction of leavening agent and acid produces gasses which makes the mixture rise. Baking soda is mainly used in cakes using coco powder or chocolate.

(B) Baking Powder:- They are basic three types of baking powder. Double action baking powder release one third of its carbon dioxide at room temperature and the rest during baking. Tartarate baking powder reacts quicker as soon as liquid is added Phosphate, baking powder is slower and only heat release its gasses.

(C) Yeast:- This is a tiny leaving fungus which thrives (Leaves) on sweetness warm and moisture. Yeast release gasses that make bread dough rise making the bread light. Given sufficient time yeast will not only make dough rise it will also act on the gluten in the flour to give flavour as well as texture. The primary key to effective use of yeast is control of temperature. Compressed fresh yeast should be dissolve into 205° F in milk or water. When using the newer type of instant yeast please follow the manufacture direction.

(4) Flour:-

(A) Cake Flour:- This is selected soft wheat flour which is very finally mild cake flour contain more starch and less gluten than a hard wheat bread flour. It's more expensive then APF (All Purpose Flour) it makes it's possible to produce a cake with a lighter smother texture.

(B) All Purpose Flour:- This is mixture or blend of hard and soft wheat flour. This type of flour is used for home baking because of it versatility (different function). It's can be used for cake baking and all type of soft dough's.

(C) Bread Flour:- Is made from hard wheat. It has a high gluten content and is generally used in hard rolls and bread dough's. It may be used in combination with APF in Danish or sweet dough.

(D) Pastry Flour:- It's made from soft wheat flour but not finally mild as cake flour.

(E) Corn Meal:- It's coarsely ground kernels of corn and its available in white or yellow colour.

(F) Whole Wheat:- This contain all Ingredients of the cleaned whole wheat grain.

(5) Eggs:- Fresh are used in large quantities in baking served as a leaving agent in cakes and soufflés as thickening agent in sauces and custard as binding agent in batters and dough's. The eggs consists of the yolk and the white. The yolk is high in fat, Protein and emulsifier called lecithin, the yolk is valued by the baker for its rich flavour and which it contributed to the baked product. The white is primarily composed of Albumen protein which is valued for its ability to act as binder and it ability hold air to create light product.

One of the forms in which egg white are often used by the baker is beaten. The manner in which the eggs whites are to be used in a recipe decides what there are 3 stages of beaten eggs white:-

1. **Soft Peak**:- it's a stage at which they are beaten to fluppy and creaming stage. If the recipe calls for sugar. This is the point at which it should gradually added.
2. **Glossy Peak**:- The second stage is the "glossy peak" it's beating egg white until reform glossy peak when the beater is lifted from the bowls. At this stage they hold shape and a stiff but not dry. It is best for folding in soft batter chiffons pies mousse soufflés and pudding. To fold beaten egg white into the butter pie all white on the top of the batter and proceed to blend gently cut down to the bottom of the mixture and then return in a upward motion. Until a prefect blending is achieve do not ever mixed your aim is to incorporate the air capture in the beaten eggs white if you over fold or over mixed the tinny air pockets will be flatten.
3. **Stiff Peak**:- This comes after the second stage the result it is stiffer larger peaks generally used for margin, pie, toppings frosting and similar item continue beating in excess of the third stage yield the dry useless egg white.

(6) Varieties of Milk:

(a) **Whole Milk**:- This milk contains 3.5% butter fat and is used for baking for rich flavour.

(b) **Low Fat Milk**:- 1 to 2% butter fat.

(c) **Skim Milk**:- 0.1 to 0.5% butter fat suitable for replacement of whole milk.

(d) **Butter Milk**:- This a product remaining after sweet or sour milk has been churned as fat removed. It has distinctive flavour cultured butter milk. It's soured product produced in the making of pasteurized skim milk after treatment with a suitable lactic acid bacteria cultural. This product has distinctive flavour texture and high acid content.

(e) **Evaporated**:- This whole cows milk from which 60% of water is removed. Its homonoized, pasteurized and sealed in canned.

(f) **Sweetened Condensed Milk**:- Made by evaporates half of a water from milk and adding sufficient quantities of cane or cone sugar to act as preservative. It's than heated cooled and canned. This is not suitable for replacing other milk produce due to its high sugar content.

(g) **Dried Whole Milk Solid**:- There are reaming dried solid after all the later is has been removed from whole milk.

(h) **Yoghurt**:- Milk which has been fermented with introduction of bacteria.

(i) **Heavy Cream:-** This product contain 35 to 45% of butter fat. There is little which replace the richness of heavy cream.

(j) **Light Cream**:- This product contain less than 30% of butter fat.

SPICES

All Spices:- The flavour are blend of these (Cinnamon nutmeg and clove) come from West Indies and its used for cake.

Anises:- This tinny valued of oval seed of parsley family taste laicorice comes from Middle Casts Mexico.

Caraway Seeds:- Tinny oval seeds used bread:- rolls, cookies

Cinnamon:- Oldest Spices, bark of trees uses deserts, pastries and cookies.

Cloves:- Dried Flower buds, used in cookies, pudding etc.

Ginger: Cakes, pie, pudding

Nutmeg: pie, cakes, cookies

Poppy seeds: Bread rolls, cookies

Seasame seeds: bread, cookie.

CHOCOLATE

It is important that you understand the composition of chocolate. It made from roasted coco beans. The nib or meat inside of the beans are rich in coco butter. The heat created in grinding process cause the coco beans to meat into dark mask called chocolate liquor

1) **Dark chocolate** : The most versatile chocolate are dark, sweetened varieties, better sweat, semi sweet and sweet chocolate. Vary a amount of sugar is added to chocolate liquor to create these types of chocolates.
2) **Milk chocolate** : The chocolate contain more coco butter but less chocolate liquor compared to dark chocolate. It has mild taste and softer texture. It must contain 12% dry milk solids to meet the standards
3) **White coco butter coatings**: White coco butter coating does not contain chocolate liquor that is why it not called chocolate. This popular coating has a sweet very mild chocolate flavour and is ideal for delicate dessert and decorative works.
4) **Compound coating** : The product is frequently confused with white coco butter coating and dual chocolate it is flavoured and coloured compound which contain no coco butter. It is vegetable oil based coating which cant be a consider a chocolate, it is often contain palm kernels or sugar, dry milk solids, lecithin, flavorings, coco and good colouring.
5) **Coco butter**: This is a natural fat contain with in the coco beans
6) **Unsweetened chocolate**: This is 100 % chocolate liquor are called bitter or baking chocolate

TEMPERATURE AND BAKER

A baker use dry heat. Manipulation of that heat determines the success or failure of that product.

Three important guidelines are:

1. Don't crowed the items too closely together in the oven. The air flows around the product is very important.
2. Improper loading of oven can cause hot or cold spob with in the oven and therefore uneven baking.
3. Always pre-heat the oven and check it proper temperature.

Oven temperatures

Degree F	Degree C	Description
250	120	Very slow
300	150	Slow
325	165	Moderately low
350	180	Moderately
375	190	Moderately Hot
400	205	Hot
450	230	Very hot
500	260	Extremely Hot

LEARNING OUTCOME

There is no doubt that baking has always being and will continues to be one of the most important and colourful areas of culinary development. The ties of baking to agriculture lies in its quest your improved texture and refined flavours of baked goods as well as other confectionery. The originated production of wheat by Egyptians is consider by most histories to be true beginning of bread which are produced today many century Egyptians the Greeks where preparing 50 different kinds of bread by about 400 BC or all of these were baked in closed oven. Bringing together the balance quantity of various Ingredients in a proper form. This is the definition of art and science of baking when you mix and blend many dry Ingredients liquids and leavings together and exposes the mixture to heat a variety of actions combined as one unit. It is very important to know the function of each Ingredients which are used in bakery.

QUESTIONS FOR DISCUSSION

1. Explain in details about history of bakery ?
2. Explain the art and science of baking ?
3. Explain the functions of fats and oils with their used in bakery ?
4. Explain the functions of sugar with their used in bakery ?
5. Explain the functions of leavening agent with their used in bakery ?
6. Explain the functions of chocolate with their used in bakery ?

KEY TERMS

* Agent
* Baker
* Dough
* Pie
* Baking
* Cookies
* Leavening

Chapter 34
Yeast, Bread and Dough

After studying this chapter, the student must know

- Components and their contribution to whole
- Method of preparation
- Forming loaves
- Storage and handling of breads
- Types of mixture and quick breads
- Bread, Scones and buns introduction
- Recipes of breads
- Scones introduction
- Scones recipes

YEAST, BREAD AND DOUGH

Components and their contribution to whole:-

1) **Yeast** : As yeast extracts the gas of CO_2 and alcohol. This gas cause rise in a baked product. The alcohol evaporated during baking the since yeast is living organism but you remember it will die. The primary cause of death is excess of heat Yeast will mature according to its own timetable and it should not be in hurried. Premature bread death cause your bread not to rise. yeast will never be done in hurried. Yeast compressed or dry is usually stirred into small amount of warm liquid and allowed to stand for at least 5 minutes to dissolve. If you have any doubt on its freshness, it has to be proofed. Dissolve it in ¼th cup of warm water, 1table spoon of sugar and 2 table spoon of flour. If the yeast is alive an active, it will be spurred by the sugar and fed by the flour, with in the 10min. it should begin to expand foam.

The temperature of liquid in which the yeast is dissolve is critical

WATER TEMPERATURE FOR YEAST

Compressed yeast: (100-105° F)

Dry yeast (105-115° F)

Note: New types of yeast are being developed which do not require dissolving in water. They can be mixed with their Ingredients of bread and used.

Yeast food/dough conditioners: Their major function is to condition the water and to assist in the proper fermentation of the dough. Improperly fermented dough will not rise properly. This is cause by the improper generation of yeast and sugar interaction with the flour. It may rise too rapidly not allowing proper development of gluten. This can result in over all soft texture or it may yield bread which has a strong yeasty flavour and heavy texture. Yeast food contains three type of functional Ingredients :

1. **Ammonia Salt**: - Supply yeast with nitrogen, they used for growth.
2. **Calcium salt**: Produce correct amount of hardness in the dough water to firm the gluten.
3. **Oxidant Agents**: Result in firmer less sticky dough.

The use of yeast foods is determined by the strength of flour and the fermented period desire. These product are used mainly in large quantity of bread and roll production. They help to give a bread, a batter grainy texture and appearance. Access amount of yeast food will give a product which is low in volume and coarse in texture.

FLOUR

Wheat flour with its rich protein called gluten which gives dough its strength and elasticity. Gluten is capable of expending greatly. It creates a net work 100 of air pockets. These pockets trap gases produce by the yeast which would otherwise escape. Whole wheat flour contains a kernel that is bran and germ. All purpose white flour is made from the inner part of the white kernel known as endosperm. It's the endosperm which contain the highest quantity of gluten. Gluten rich wheat produce a good eating bread. Unbleached flour has more food value but don't produce very white bread.

LIQUID

The liquid terms into a steam during baking which helps to create a texture of the bread Water, milk even bear can be used as liquid each of these will provide the moisture as needed to create the dough and the steam. Milk Provides a richer bread with more tender crust. The natural fat content of the milk shortness and softens the strength of Gluten and enriches the breads, the natural sugar also adds to richen proportion of liquid added changes with recipe variations.

SWEETENERS

Sugar makes the rise quickly and help brown the crust the bakes shouldn't assume that it a little bit good than a whole lot is better too much sugar with inhibit the action of the yeast. There granulated sugar is more commonly used sweetener there are other which will add variety in flavour texture and colour. Honey, molasses, corn syrup or brown sugar can be used to sweeten bread as can raisins and date, hence the flavour of other Ingredients in the bread.

SALT

It has three primary function in bread dough:

1. It adds flavour and brings out the flavour of other Ingredients used.
2. The Second function of the salt in the dough has both positive and negative aspects. Salt control the fermentation process of the yeast and other Ingredients in the dough, this is beneficial when temperatures are not controlled. Salt reducing the gassing power of yeast allowing the development of more uniform rise in the product. The amount of salt in the dough must be balance to achieve proper fermentation of dough.

   Excess salt will give dense bread with under develop volume. Too little salt can yield a dough which has too much volume and shape looking uniformity the best range of salt is 1½ to 4% of flour weight.
3. The third function of salt in the dough is strengthening and tightening of Gluten as the dough ferments enzymes in the flour begin to react with the gluten, restricting the gluten formation. The formation of gluten is critical to the texture and flavour of the bread. Salts inhabit the enzymes action allowing the gluten to develop.

SHORTENING

It is often added to enrich bread. It gives flavour to bread and makes it tender. Bread with shortening stays longer and better.

EGGS

Not required in bread but when added it provides richness, texture and flavour. It also improve keeping quality.

METHOD OF PREPARATION

There are many formulas some are rich and some are lean dough don't have enriching Ingredients, other have a high % of Ingredients like eggs fats sugar these are rich dough's. There are two types method:-

1. **Straight Dough Method:-** In this method the yeast is combined with a portion of the water the reminder of the water salt, sugar non fat dry milk is place in a mixing bowl the flour is than added and the mixture is mixed for one minute the yeast solution is than added to the mixture and is mixed for one minute. The shortenings is added at last and then the dough is mixed for 10 to 15 minutes or until it's smooth and elastic.

   At this point to things needs to be pointed out first the shortening is added last to prevent its infrastructure with incorporation of the yeast and to help produce a good blend of all Ingredients.

The last mixing stage allows the gluten in the dough to stretch and develop. It must develop enough elasticity to allow the yeast to do its work latter.

In making straight dough after the dough has been mixed, it's customary to let the fermentation (rising to proceed) until the mass has expanded to nearly full capacity. This should be done before it has risen to a point where it becomes to sag (not high) near the centre of the dough. Ones the dough has been punched it's than folded the coolers protein of the dough is folded towards the centre and the warm portion is cooked up and over. This process equalized the temperature of the dough retarding the continued fast action of the yeast for a short period. The dough is now ready to be benched and formed.

2. **Sponge Dough Method:-** Used extensively for large quality bread product it produces a very tightly texture sponge bread, the sponge dough method is done into two stage:-

(A) The yeast is dissolved using full amount of liquid than part of the sugar and flour are also added to this mixture this combination is mixed to a thick batter or very soft dough. The mixture is covered and allows fermenting until at least double its sizes.

(B) The mixture is then punched (this is the pushing of the dough / mixture down to release part of the carbon dioxide which has develop). The remaining Ingredients making a uniform smooth dough (there are several ways to ferment your dough along fermentation off 5 to 6 hours at a control temperature of 15° C or lower improves the flavour and texture of your final product greatly. As with the straight dough this dough is punch and folded when the fermentation is complete it than ready to bench and formed.) For both dough method control of the fermentation is the key. Otherwise you can make a yang under write dough or otherwise old dough there must be proper balance of Ingredients mixing temperature and time.

(C) **Raising Dough:** - The dough should never be dissolved during rising period. At that time the yeast is producing the little gas bubbles the stretch the gluten in the flour and make the dough expand. Most bakers test the dough pressing the dough lightly with the finger tips when the finger is removed the dough may receded slightly around the area pressed or the imprint made may simply closed, if the imprinted received slightly the dough is ready to punch and folded. If the imprint closed the dough doesn't raised it's not ready to punch when it's ready the dough is punched down. This releases large quantity of CO_2.

The time required for dough to rise is very considerably depending upon the number of factors these factors include the type of yeast, fat content and temperature.

If you oven proof your dough. The bread may have a yeasty flavour or texture or have a separation between crumb and crust.

If you product has over risen in the final phase, most likely it will sinks in the oven.

Bending: - After fermentation work done on bench is calls bending (dough is on the take and working that.) have an yeasty flavour and aroma. It may lack good flavour of texture or have a separation between the crumb and the crust. If the product has ever risen final phase most likely it will sink in the oven. If you don't give dough sufficient time to rise the product will be to most or heavy.

Always let your product rise to the desire bulk in warm and humid place. The best environment is 80° F and away from the drafts. Depressed the raised dough with your finger, and if the indentation remains the dough has full risen.

FORMING LOAVES

After the dough has developed properly it's than benched and formed. Benching simple means the handling of the dough on the baker's table. There are three steps of foaming loaves. There are scaling, rounding and make-up. Benching must be done rapidly to prevent over fermenting the dough. Additionally rise in the dough on the table can result in poor finished product. If it's not possible to bench the dough rapidly enough to prevent further rise portion of the dough should be retread. It can be bench latter on Retarding means placing the dough in a coolers place to slow down the action of the yeast.

Retarding the dough: - You make the dough and get into the refrigerator for 24 hrs. This process is called Retarding the dough (for prevent from over ferment).

Scaling:- Is the division of the dough into the size pieces needed. This is done by the use of weight and scales to ensure correct portioning.

Rounding:- Is the primary steps in shaping the loaf or roll. Each scale piece of dough is shall into a smooth round ball. This is done by rolling the piece of dough between your two hands. The roll is then placed down. It's covered to a cloth to prevent formation of crust. Let the piece rest for 15 to 20 minutes. This allows the gluten to relax prior to final make-up. If the gluten is not allow to release the final shape of the product is distarted as the gluten relaxes proper make-up with yield and evenly balance product when not done properly rolls began to resemble football and basketball. Always keep dough ream down on the baking sheet or bread pastry the piece must be properly molded duping the finally proofing and taking. A pieces with crease cracks and reams into surface will not proof and bake well.

Proofing:- A proofing described earlier was proofing the yeast prior to mixing the bread dough. The proofing we will discuss here. Has a some different purpose this proofing allows the yeast to inflate and forms gas one least time. The dough will adjust and release itself in this final proofing varies from 50 to 75 minutes this applies when the temperature 90° F.

Baking:- The actual baking of the product requires consideration of the desire finished product. A hard crusted bread is baked with baked injection into the oven during first part of baking. The amount of steam must be controlled too much steam tends to produce a shinny extremely tough crust. During baking process whether injected or natural created by the product it should be water vaporizes at oven temperature. As the moisture on the surface of the baked product vaporizes its cause's caramelization of sugar starches or other Ingredients. This provides the golden crisp crust that is so highly valued in breads.

The oven temperature required for baking will vary according to the loaf of bread, if large in size make sure the temperature should be such that surface should not burn before the bread is cooked inside for a small loaf. The temperature must be raised to that the loaf will brown before the loaf is over baked. The types of bread dough also effect the temperature the time required for proper baking, then there are three points.

1. Rich dough formulas are usually baked at lowers oven temperature 350-400° F.
2. Lean dough required longer baking time at higher temperature for thick hard crust 385-420° F.
3. Extremely lean dough like bench bread needs even higher temperature 413-465° F.

Washes

Most yeast product is brushed with a wash before baking. This is done to improve the finished appearance of baked bread. The type of wash used will depend upon the intended uses of the final product.

1. **Water**: - use for hard rusted bread if not or little steam is available. This assist in the production of browning the formation of the texture of the crust.
2. **Egg Wash**: - Should be applying very evenly to avoid the item browning with sticks and highlight. The egg wash is mainly used for Danish before cakes and soft tolls.

   Two types of egg wash may be used, whole egg or egg white when using whole egg normal mixture 1 egg to 1 cup of water. A wash prepared of egg white only bring less cholesterol and fat to the finished product. The normal mixture is 3 egg white to one cup of water.
3. **Sugar Based Glazes**: - They give the product high shine and help to seal in moisture. Examples are honey and sugar syrup glazes and fruit puree based glazes such as a thin apricot glazes on a Danish or other sweet dough produce.

STORAGE HANDLING

Cooling baked breads

It is as important a procedure as proofing one's baked bread or rolls should be removed from pan because the pan retains heat which induces to over cooking. Perfectly baked bread may be destroyed by carry over cooking. After removal from pan keep bread in a cool area free from drafts. Breads dries out quickly if the air is either too warm or too dry any bread is best serve within 8 hours of begin baked however for longer storage wrapped your bread in a moisture proof plastic bag. It's a popular belief that refrigerated breads keep a longer but this not true. The refrigeration in a circulation of cold air techniques. As we have said earlier any air remove moisture from bread storing bread in cool areas keep them test. Bread produces in large commercial kitchen or bakery have mould inhibitors and moisturizing agent added to them which extended their shell life.

Quick Breads

Are speedy and easy bakes they are made without yeast from dough and batters it doesn't have to rise (Proof) before going into the oven. They raise quickly ones they are in the oven baking powder baking soda, beaten eggs and egg white or other combination of leavening agent. Provide Steam, Air and CO_2 gasses to leaven the product. The quick bread have cake like appearance and a lighter texture than yeast breads and mostly contain fruit, nuts or other seasoning.

Types of Mixture

Two main grouping are batter and dough batter is again grouped as Pour and drop Pour batter are thin to Pour from mixing bowl into baking pan to griddle. A drop batter is thick enough to required spooning into your baking pan.

Dough is defined as a mixture which is stiff enough to roll out.

Ingredients

Batter and dough are made from dry ingredients like flour, baking powder, baking soda, salt sugar, fat, eggs and liquids as used as needed.

Mixing method

When making quick bread all ingredients should be evenly mixed at one time. Development of gluten in the flour is controlled in mixing quick bread. It's the stirring and the leading that develops the gluten for quick breads stirring and kneading should be kept to a minimum.

TYPES OF QUICK BREADS

(a) Muffin: - Basic Ingredients are flour, fat (butter), eggs, liquids, baking soda. Salt and baking powdered to this basic mixture can be added, fruits such as blue berries, dates, raisins or bananas and nut meets such as Pecan walnut and almonds, other items are poppy seeds and many other type of cereals.

Mixed flour baking powder salt and sugar blend milk, soft or melted butter and eggs. If an acid liquids (butter milk) and baking powder has been used and combined them shortly before blending in moist ingredients. Make a well in the centre of dry ingredients and pour a liquid mixture into it. The batter should appear lumpy not smooth. If over mixed boneless formed in the produce during baking result will be a product with tough texture.

(b) Baking Powder Biscuits:- Made from dough which contain more flour than liquid in the first step evenly distributed salt and leavening agent in the flour. Next is cutting of the fat into dry ingredients can be done with a pastry blenders or mixture and will resemble corn meal when done. After this liquid is added dough is made working the mixture as little as possible. The dough is placed on a flour surface and folded a few times until it's soft but not sticky. It's than rolled out and biscuits of fancy shaped cut and placed on greece baking Pan and baked brush the top lightly with oil or egg Biscuits should be baked as soon as possible after mixing.

Variations are butter milk biscuits cheese, biscuits, currents biscuits and drops biscuits.

(c) Corn Bread:- Famous and Northern Southern American bread, basic ingredients for corn bread are cornmeal flour, sugar, baking powder, eggs, fats and liquids. Mixing method as for muffins can be baked in a muffin pan or sheet pan.

(d) Yeast Dough Nuts:- Are made by using simple straight dough mixing processors. All ingredients are mixed and dough made. It's than bench and fry.

(e) Cake dough nuts:- The major difference between cake and yeast dough nuts is in the leavening agents used. Cake dough nuts are usually leaven with baking powder. The result is product which has with a muffin requires no fermentation period slight lower temperature are used for frying there.

Note : Dough nut icing:- The icing used for dough nut is flow icing. It's combination of blended syrup, salt, powder, sugar baking powder, water, eggs white and flavouring. It can be used as spread over coffee cakes sweet rolls or dough nuts.

Griddle cakes and waffles:- For there its important that the protein of liquid (including eggs) to dry ingredients be adequate the portion should produce either hearty porous thick cakes or a thin moist light grained cake. Basic ingredients are all purpose flour, sugar, baking powder salts eggs fat and milk and cream.

Mixing Procedure

Beat eggs and milk, mix butter lightly in a mixing bowl, mixed the flour, baking powder, sugar and salt together combined the two mixture stirring just enough to damping the mixture so can makes a lighter fluffier product by separating the eggs beating the egg whites folding it last.

BREAD, SCONES AND BUNS

Breading making was at one time part of the week's work in every household, but home-made bread nowadays is a luxury in most families. There is no reason why it should be, for bread does not present any great difficulties in the making. A change of bread is good for us all, and there are so many delicious kinds, we can provide with a little trouble. A little knowledge is necessary before we can make yeast bread to perfection. There are two kinds of yeast, compressed and brewer's. There is a tinge of bitterness with brewer's yeast, and also it is difficult to obtain. An ounce of compressed yeast has about the same "raising" effect as two large tablespoons of fresh brewer's yeast. There are one or two points to be considered when using yeast. It should not come in contact with anything that is very cold; so warm all the utensils and let the Ingredients stand in a warm place for a while before you begin to make bread. Then you must remember that the dough must be set to rise in a warm place, not too hot nor in a draught. The plate rack over a Kitchener or gas stove or in front of a fire, if not draughty, is an excellent place. The oven must be hot when the bread is put in. To "cream" yeast, stir it with a little sugar until it becomes liquid. Dried eggs and household milk may be used in place of fresh eggs and milk in any of the following recipes:

White bread 3½ lb, 1 tablespoon salt, 1 oz yeast, 1 level dessertspoon, Castor Sugar 1½ pints and water.

Time: About 1 hour, Electricity, 450° F.

Method

Warm all the utensils before you begin to make the bread. Mix the flour and salt together and pass them through a fine sieve. This ensures that the flour is free from lumps, and also mixes the salt evenly with it. Put these into a bowl, not a large one, but one about a foot across, as the flour must be in a heap, otherwise you cannot make a "hole" in the centre. Now cream the sugar and yeast together. That is, put them in a cup and stir with a spoon until they are a smooth liquid. Make the water just lukewarm and add it to the yeast and sugar. Then with a wooden spoon make a hole in the centre of the flour and pour all the liquid gently into the hole. The hole must not go to the bottom of the bowl, as there must be a layer of flour under the liquid. Now, with the spoon, stir a little of the flour into the liquid, sufficient to form it into a fairly stiff batter that will just drop from the spoon. Sprinkle a little dry flour over the batter and leave the remainder of the dry flour in a wall round it.

Cover the bowl with a cloth and stand it in a warm place for the "sponge", as it is called, to rise. This will take about half an hour. When the yeast has risen through the flour and is a mass of bubbles, it is ready to knead. To do this, just mix the remainder of the flour with the batter, then turn it on to a board. Press your knuckles well in, while kneading. It will take about a quarter of an hour. When it is a smooth dough, put it back in the bowl and cover again with the cloth. Leave it in a warm place for one and a half hours to rise. It should then have doubled its original size. If you are baking the bread in tins, make them quite warm and then there will be no need to grease them. Half fill each tin with the dough and put them in a warm place to "prove" them for a quarter of an hour. Then put them in a hot oven, after about ten minutes and reduce the heat to moderate. They will need about one and a half hours. If you like a richer bread, use half milk and half water, and if you are not baking the loaves in tins, make them either co-burgs or cottage loaves. For the former, make the dough in round loaves, then cut across the centre both ways. For a cottage loaf, take two pieces of dough, one about twice the size of the other. Press the smaller on the larger, and make a hole through the centre of the two with a thick wooden skewer.

Wholemeal Bread

1 lb. white flour, 2½ lb. wholemean flour, 1 oz. Yeast, 1 large teaspoon castor Sugar, 1 table spoon salt or 1½ pint water and, 3/4 pint milk.(Wholemeal flour absorbs more water than white flour, and if sufficient liquid is not used, the bread is dry and hard.)

Method

Mix together the two flours and salt, and see that they are evenly blended. Put them into a bowl, and cream the sugar and yeast as described for white bread. Make half the milk and water lukewarm and mix it with the yeast. Make a hole in the flour and pour the yeast gently in. Mix enough of the dry flour round to form a batter, and cover with a sprinkling of flour. Sprinkle the salt on the dry flour of the wall "surrounding the batter.

Cover the basin with a cloth and stand in a warm place for one hour, then mix with a wooden spoon, and make the remainder of the milk and water lukewarm and add. Then knead on a board to a smooth dough, return to the bowl and leave in a warm place for one and a half hours. Half fill the tins with the dough and leave for fifteen minutes in a warm place. Bake as white bread. All wholemeal flour can be used; it is a matter of taste, some people preferring a coarse bread, others one of finer texture. Then, again, sometimes it is a case of obeying doctor's orders.

Milk Loaves (Small)

1½ lb. flour, 3/4 pint Milk, 2 oz. Butter or Margarine, 1 Egg, small teaspoon Salt, 1 teaspoon Castor Sugar and ½ oz. Yeast.

Time: 20 to 30 minutes. Temperature: Gas, regulo Mark 6. electricity, 425° F.

Method

Make the milk lukewarm. Cream the yeast and sugar in a basin, add the milk to it, also the well beaten egg. Put the flour into a bowl add the salt and mix well. Rub in the butter or margarine until evenly mixed. Pour in the yeast mixture and beat to a dough. Put it in a warm place to rise for one and a quarter hours, then form the dough into little cottage loaves, miniature coburgs, horseshoes or twists or just plain rolls. Leave them in a warm place for ten minutes. Brush over the beaten egg and bake in a good oven.

Nut Loaf

½ lb. Plain Flour, ¾ oz. Granulated Sugar, 1 heaped dessertspoon Baking Powder, 1 Egg, ½ pint Milk, ¼ lb. shelled Nuts, good pinch of salt.

Time : about 45 minutes. Temperature: electricity, 450° F.

Method

Chop the nuts finely or put them through a mincer or nut mill. Beat the egg well with the sugar. Mix the flour with the baking powder and salt, and put them twice through a fine sieve. Mix the milk with the beaten egg and sugar, and gradually add in the sifted flour and the nuts. Mix thoroughly to an even dough. Turn into a hot tin and bake in a hot oven.

Raisin Loaf

1 lb. Flour, good pinch of Salt, 2 oz. Butter or Lard, 2 oz. Granulated Sugar, 4 oz. Raisins, 1oz. Yeast, teaspoon Castor Sugar, 1 Egg, ½ pint Milk.

Time: about 45 minutes. Temperatur4e: Gas, Regulo Mark 7. Electricity, 450° F.

Method

Mix the salt with the flour, rub the fat in lightly until it is evenly mixed with the flour. Stir in the sugar and the raisins stoned and cut in halves. Cream the yeast with the castor sugar. Well beat the egg and make a hole in the centre of the flour mixture, pour in the yeast, egg and milk. Mix a little of the flour with the liquid and leave to rise for twenty minutes in a warm place. Then beat until thoroughly mixed. Cover with a cloth and leave in a warm place for one and a half hours. Bake in a hot tin in a moderate oven.

SCONES

How to Use the Girdle or Griddle

In Scotland the girdle is in daily use, and scones in a great measure take the place of bread. In many of the farmhouses may be seen a little crane attached to the kitchen stove, with a chain to hook the girdle on; by this means it can be raised to different heights from the fire, according to the degree of heat desired. A peat fire is considered the best for cooking girdle cakes and scones, but they can be cooked quite well on an ordinary kitcheners, gas or electric stove, using the girdle without the hook. If the heat is too great, use an asbestos mat under the girdle. As a substitute for a girdle a very thick frying pan may be used, or even an iron plate. The girdle should be heated slowly then well floured before the scones are put on, the flour brushed off, and more added before cooking each fresh batch of scones. If the flour burns, the girdle is too hot and the flour must be brushed off, the girdle cooled a little and fresh flour added. When cooking potato and drop scones the girdle is first greased with butter or lard and regreased between each batch.

Afternoon Tea Scones

1/2 lb. flour, 1 small teaspoon Baking Powder, 3 oz. Butter, 2oz. Castor Sugar, 2oz. Currants, teaspoon Mixed Spice, 1 Egg and 2 oz Milk.

Time: 20 minutes. Temperature: electricity, 450° F.

Method

Mix baking powder, flour and spice and sift them. Rub in the butter until the mixture looks like breadcrumbs and there is no plain flour left. Stir in the currants and sugar. Mix to a dough with a well beaten egg mixed with the milk (reserve a little of this). Form into three round cakes and bake for twenty minutes on well greased tins. Brush over with egg and milk and sprinkle with castor sugar when almost done. Cut into small scones when cooked.

Almond Rolls

1/2 lb. flour, 1 teaspoon baking powder, 1 oz. Sweet Almonds, 1 oz. Ground Almonds, 1 oz. Butter, 2 oz. Castor Sugar, 1 Egg, and tablespoons milk.

Time: 15 to 20 minutes. Temperature: electricity, 450° F.

Method

Blanch the almonds and cut them in fine strips. Mix the baking powder with the flour, rub in the butter, add the sugar, sweet and ground almonds and mix in the well beaten egg and milk. Roll out lightly on a floured board, cut into three-inch squares, and roll each square. Put them on a well greased tin and bake at once in a hot oven fifteen to twenty minutes.

Berkshire Tea Cakes

1/2 lb. Self-raising flour, 3 oz. Butter or lard, good pinch of Salt , 1/4 teaspoon Vanilla Essence, Milk to mix.

Time: about 20 minutes. Temperature:. Electricity, 450° F.

Method

Sift the flour with the salt, rub in the butter or lard (half of each is very good), add the vanilla and enough cold milk to form a soft dough. Roll out on a floured board, cut into cakes with a flut4ed cutter, and bake for about twenty minutes in a moderate oven. Cut through the centre, butter and serve hot or cold, with jam or marmalade. (two ounces of currants or sultanas can take the place of the vanilla.)

Breakfast or Tea Rolls

1/2 lb. Self-raising flour, 1 teaspoon Salt, 1 oz. Butter, Milk to mix.

Time: 20 minutes. Temperature: Electricity, 50° F.

Method

Rub the butter into the flour until it is quite evenly distributed. Stir in the salt. Add enough milk to form a stiff dough. Form lightly into rolls. Place them on a floured tin and bake twenty minutes in a hot oven. A little cinnamon or mixed spice is nice in these rolls.

Buttermilk Scones

1 lb. fine pastry flour, 1 oz. Butter or Margarine, pinch of salt, 1-heaped teaspoon Bicarbonate of Soda, 1 level teaspoon Cream of Tartar, ½ pint Buttermilk.

Time: 6 to 8 minutes. Temperature: Moderate.

Rub the fat into the flour, stir in the salt, bicarbonate of soda and cream of tartar. Mix to a rather soft but not sticky dough with buttermilk. Roll out thinly. Cut into rounds and cook on a hot girdle that has been well floured. Cook about four minutes on one side, then turn and cook on the other side.

LEARNING OUTCOME

Yeast will mature according to its own timetable and it should not be in hurried. Premature bread death cause your bread not to rise. yeast will never be done in hurried. Yeast compressed or dry is usually stirred into small amount of warm liquid and allowed to stand for at least 5 minutes to dissolve. Wheat flour with its rich protein called gluten which gives dough its strength and elasticity. Gluten is capable of expending greatly. It creates a net work 100 of air pockets. These pockets trap gases produce by the yeast which would otherwise escape. Shortening is often added to enrich bread. It gives flavour to bread and makes it tender. Bread with shortening stays longer and better. There are many formulas some are rich and some are lean dough don't have enriching Ingredients, other have a high % of ingredients like eggs fats sugar these are rich dough's. There are two types method - Straight Dough Method and Sponge Dough Method. There are three steps of foaming loaves. There are scaling, rounding and make-up. Benching must be done rapidly to prevent over fermenting the dough. Additionally rise in the dough on the table can result in poor finished product. If it's not possible to bench the dough rapidly enough to prevent further rise portion of the dough should be retread. It can be bench latter on Retarding means placing the dough in a coolers place to slow down the action of the yeast. It is as important a procedure as proofing one's baked bread or rolls should be removed from pan because the pan retain heat which induce to over cooking. Perfectly baked bread may be destroyed by carry over cooking. After removal from pan keep bread in a cool area free from drafts. Two main grouping are batter and dough batter is again grouped as Pour and drop Pour batter are thin to Pour from mixing bowl into baking Pan to griddle. A drop batter is thick enough to required spooning into your baking Pan. Beat eggs milk, method butter lightly in a mixing bowl mixed the flour baking powder sugar and salt together combined the two mixture stirring just enough to damping the mixture so can makes a lighter fluffier product by separating the eggs beating the egg whites folding it last.

LESSON END ACTIVITY

- Visit a bakery and learn the mixing method.
- Visit a bakery and learn the different types of bread.

QUESTIONS FOR DISCUSSION

1. Explain the contribution of yeast and flour in the bakery.
2. Explain the method of preparing dough.
3. Explain the process of foaming loaves.
4. Explain the term washes.
5. Explain the procedure of storing and handling of breads.
6. Explain the type of mixture.
7. Explain the types of quick breads.
8. Mention the recipes of bread.

KEY TERMS

Breads	Dough	Fermented	Griddle
Loaves	Recipe	Retard	Washes

Chapter 36

Pastry Dough

After studying this chapter, the student must know

- Types of dough
- Preparation and ingredients of dough
- Mixing procedure of various dough
- Cookie dough, ingredients and its types
- Ingredients making puff pastry
- Pastries, savoury and sweet
- Savoury fillings for choux buns
- Vol-au-vent, Éclairs, Choux buns
- Pastry horns or cornets

PASTRY DOUGH

This chapter discusses the primary type of dough used in making pastry- There are four basic types. They are:

1. Sweet dough.
2. Pie Pastry dough
3. Puff pastry dough
4. Cookie dough.

1. Sweet dough is most common used for making breakfast rolls and coffee cakes.

(a) **Flour**: - Hard wheat flour is needed needs longer fermentation but has better tolerance for extended work on bench. Best for Danish because it takes multiple rolls and folds.

(b) **Sugar**:- Granulated sugar is used 9 to 20% sugar is used, when 9% is used its yield dough's good for sweet buns with good volume and softness when more % of sugar is used it give low volume product but they will be sweeter more tender and with more shell life.

(c) **Shortenings-** 16% to 24% fat tender and short in texture rolls available too much fat will make it grease and low volume.

(d) **Eggs**: - Improve handling quality use in whole eggs in amount 16 to 22%.

(e) **Milks**: - Fresh milk is expectable. Non fat dry milk is used commercial 3 to 6 %.

(f) **Yeast**: It contain increases in sweet dough because of high sugar contain sugar slow down yeast action by increasing the viscosity of the dough making it more difficult for yeast producing gasses to raised 3 to 6% depending on richness of formula.

(g) **Spices**: All varieties flavour to baked product mace in Danish dough.

PREPARATION OF SWEET DOUGH

There are two types of Sweet dough

1. Regular and
2. Danish Pastry.

Product will differ in each case. Regular is fine even texture where as danish dough is flaky texture. Special points in mixing sweet dough- mix using the straight dough method until the dough is smooth and elastic.

Fermentation of Sweet Dough

Normal fermentation for sweet dough and danish pastry differ the fermentation to tolerance of sweet dough is less critical than bread dough since the time for makeup will vary for sweet rolls and coffee cake it's advisable. To keep the dough young. This allows for longer bench tolerance a regular sweet dough is given a normal fermentation. This means that its allow first full rise before make up proofing and baking. The fermentation of Danish pastry dough is retarding. The dough is chilled after mixing and the bitter or margin is folded into layers in the dough. The dough is chilled again. Before make up proofing and baking. The chilling period is necessary to keep the fat from melting soaking into the layers of the dough.

Retarding Sweet Dough

Retarded dough is yeast dough that's refrigerated for a long time before baking this is done to lengthen the amount of time the product may be held before being baked if left at room temperature. The yeast will continue to be highly active and product many over rise before it's to be baked. Refrigeration temperature returns the fermentation process but don't affect the quality of product the ideal temperature is retarded sweet dough is 35° F dough's which are to be held as long as 24 hours, have to be shared below 40° F. Refrigeration can also cause the exterior of the dough to form a crust and dry out if you have a humidity control in your refrigerator keep it up 85%, if not rapped the dough in plastic firm before to dry.

Retarding Danish pastry

A key factor in making excellence Danish pastry is the rolling out of the fat and the temperature at which it's done. It should be cold enough to keep the roll in butter and firm cool dough rolls out easily. Before make up bring the dough temperature and room temperature not above.

Proofing Danish pastry: - The correct degree of proofing will yield a flaky buttery danish. Under proof dough will not be flaky and the oven temperature should not be to low.

Baking sweet dough:- Needs full proofing before baking fast caking required. Should be egg washed before proofing most baked sweet dough product are glazed or iced white warm.

Puff pastry dough:- Refers to has the pastry of thousand leaves. This is rolled in dough like croissants or Danish pastry its one of the most difficult to make the rising of puff pastry. It is truly a magical performance which request number of step process of rolling folding and turning will create 100 of alternative sheets of fats and dough. The heat of the oven melt the butter and creates steam which puffs the dough in flaky layers.

Ingredients

(a) **Flour:**- Hard wheat bread flour since high % of fat is used the flour should to hard the amt if rolling the dough which stands requires a flour higher in gluten content. A suffer flour will breakdown by rolling.

(b) **Shortenings**: - In used in relating short quantities reason for using less shortenings is because a large quantity of rolling fat is used.

(c) **Acid:**- Cream of tartar lemon juice or vinegar- is used by many bakers in preparation or puff pastry dough. Its assists in relaxing the gluten.

(d) **Salt**:- Improves flavour.

(e) **Eggs**:- Yolks lubricate the gluten in the dough eggs white contribute the volume of dough.

(f) **Rolls in fat**:- Percentage fat to flour should not be less 50 % rolling fat should be of same consistency as dough. Fat most often used as butter or margin shorting or puff paste (This is a fat specialty blended to used in puff pastry). If the fat is at right consistency and the temperature correct its possible to distributed the fat evenly in the dough without tearing. Butter is preferred because of its low melting point. Leaving agent is not used in this dough it's the fat which raises the layer.

The fat of roll in must contain a certain amount of moisture as the dough is folded and rolled with the fat multiple layer of days sealed around fat are formed when the dough is placed in the hot oven the fat being to melt, enriching and lubricating the tough surrounding it. The fat thereby creates a small pocket in the dough. The moisture release by the fat evaporates as it heated, creating, steam this steam pushes up the pocket that has been formed the same action is created with 100 of pocket with in the pastry creating a volume a minimum of 8 times its original thickness.

PASTRY AND PIES

Pie is an American dessert of light brown flaky crust holding fresh fruit custard or cream.

Pie Crust Ingredients

Hard wheat bread flour is normally used because its less lightly to absorb fat. Then soft wheat flour, there by yielding a pie dough that's easier to rolled and pan.

Shortening is responsible for the tenderness, taste and shell life of pie crust. Solid fat yields flakery pies than melted or soft fat. A solid fat will not blend readily with the flour allowing development of layers in the rolled dough similar to these in Danish and puff pastry.

Liquids is the most critical Ingredients in a pie dough the quantity of water used shall be adequate to form a dough than handles well not sticky or wet, not dry. The amount of water that a pie dough mixture will need depends on how thorough the flour and shorting are blended. The more thorough the blend the less water required because there is no flour left free to absorb it. A dough which under mix or wet will shrink as it bakes and may be difficult to brown. Is to small quantity of liquid is used the result will be a flour and shortenings mixture which is to crumbles and difficult to handling no development of gluten take place.

Salt has binding effect on the dough it help the development of flavour and enhance the flavour of other Ingredients.

MIXING PROCEDURE FOR PIE DOUGH

1. Refrigerate Ingredients to improve the handling of pie dough, particularly if store rooms are warm flour and shorting should be above 60° F for best mixing. Water however shall be 40° to 45° F.
2. Blend all the flour and fat using a pastry blender, cutting fat into small places until it resemble a coarse corn meat.
3. Dissolve salt in the water and add it to the flour and fat mixture. Mix slightly until the desire consistency is obtain. Over mixing will produce a tough crust with considerable shrinkage.

Make-up of the dough

When mixing is complete rolled pieces of the dough into 3 inch thick cylinder. Allow to rest for 4 hours under refrigeration. Resting increases stretching properties so that it can be handle property when rolled and made up.

Dividing the dough

When ready to make a pie, at dough into size pieces needed for top bottom for a normal pie, top pieces should be seven ounce and bottom pieces 8 ounce, this is suitable for a 9 inch pie plate.

Rolling the dough

Dust each chilled pie dough pieces lightly with flour flatten each pieces with a palm or our hand before rolling with a dusters rolling pin when rolling used thick stroke start from centre and rolled toward the edges. Rolls, do not force the dough cut making a circular shop should be rolled into a circle all. One to two inch large than sized needed. Thickness of the pie should be 1/8 inch do not Greece pie pans. Pie dough have enough fat to prevents sticking. Fold the rolled dough in half lift to the pie pan and unfold it, carefully. Do not stretch dough. Fit carefully so that there is no air space between pan and dough. Gently push the dough down into the bottom of the pan and. Pet out any air packet that is form.

One crust pie

If you are making a pie shell for a single crust or open face pie form the shell in the pan as follows.

1. Fold the extra ¾ inch dough under along the rim of the pie plate so that its double in thickness.
2. Crimp using your 2 fore-fingers press and pleat intervals to make a stand up scalloped edges.

Two crust pie

First fold the extra 3 fold of an inch of dough of the bottom crust under, fill the shell with appropriate filling- egg wash the edge, than carefully placed for crust on top crimp the two pieces of crust together seen pie will usually washed to removed excess flour given high sheen wash can be either water, milk and melted butter egg wash or other washes. Allow wash to dry on crust before baking.

Lattice top crust

Make a beautifully finished specially shiny berries pies. Roll out your dough as for top crust cut in two strips 1 to ¾ inch wide place the strips on filled pie. Weaving them in and out of each other trim the strips even with the over hangings between crust fold the edges of the bottom crust up over the ends of the strips and press together. Lattice strips, may also be twisted to give a spiral effects.

Cobblers

Are sheet type pies the bottom and top crust are made of regular pie dough or a cookie or tart dough, the filling are usually fruit. Make up of a cobblers are same as for two crust pie.

Novelty pie crust

In addition to regular pie dough the graham crackers, vanilla cookies, gingers snap or other dry cake or cookie, crumbs may be used in making a crust for cream type filling these items are crushed or blended with butter or margin and nuts or spices than mold it into a pie pan. This type of pie crust should be chilled before using, or may be baked if the firmer crust is dryer.

Turn over

Pie dough or puff pastry may be used to make turnovers. Turn over filling are like these used for regular pies-the dough it rolled in rectangular sheets and than at into 6 inch square the edges of each square are brushed with water or egg wash (these helps to ensure a tight sealed of the turnover). About 2oz. of filling are place in the centre of the square of dough the edges are than folded forming a triangular shaped then sealed and you should than cut a vent to allow the steam from the filling to escape during cooking.

Storage

Unbaked pie dough will keep in the refrigerate and highly wrapped for about 4 days. It may be frozen for at least 3 months, if it is tightly wrapped and scaled.

Cookie dough:- Cookies are often referred to a small sweet cake items they are very similar to cakes in the type of Ingredients used and the method to mix them they differ from cakes in the proportion of Ingredients and panning method, ***the primary difference Between cakes and cookies is the amount of moisture in the mixture***. A balance of the other Ingredients is needed to accomate the lack of offer moister in the mix.

Ingredients

Sugar: Sugar is the most major Ingredients in cookies mixture. The type of sugar used and the quantity both effect the spread of the cookies as its cook (spread of the cookie is a major concern in the production of cookies. Particular those which are to have a particular design). A coarse sugar will cause a cream cookie to spread a great deal in cooking and extremely fine sugar, confectionary sugar may restrict the spread of cookie too much and may also cause the fat to separate from the mix if the cookie is to begged (pressed from a pastry bagged)finally granulated sugar is best for most the cookie.

Fat: Fat is also a major Ingredients in many cookies it's the fat that gives the cookies its richness. This type of fat chosen can effect the flavour and handling characteristics of the cookies dough, butter gives the best flavour however it has the low melting point and may not stand up to the handling. For a rolled cookie dough shortening has a better elasticity at normal temperature, shortenings has a higher melting point and has expectable flavour but not the rich flavour of butter the best result will achieved with the blend of better and shorting.

Eggs: Eggs are important for structure and flavour of the cookies. Increase egg content will reduce the spread and increase flavour, they also assist in holding the sugar in the mixture.

Flour: Flour is the primary source of structure in the cookies. The majority of cookie formula required the blend of hard and soft wheat flour. The high fat and sugar content of cookie formula cannot be properly contained by the soft flour such as cake flour, causing excessive spread-However used of strictly hard wheat flour can yield a tough cookies, the gluten in the flour should not be developed when cookie dough is mixed when its, result will be tough cookie, the exception to the used of hard wheat flour is in the preparation of cookie dough with egg whites. These require the use of soft wheat cake flour.

Milk: Milk or water are the liquids most commonly used in cookie dough when water is used a non fat milk powder is added to the formula the flavour of the cookie benefit from the milk liquid, must be used cocessially a slack mixture will have a great spread.

Type of cookies dough

Cookies dough are classified all to the method by which they are mixed.

They are placed in three categories.

1. Stiff dough,
2. Soft dough and
3. Refrigerated dough.

Formula of stiff dough:- Continues less liquids, egg and flour then soft cookies. These cookies are often referred to as slices or rolled cookies. The desirable finished provided is crisp when humidity been excessive this cookies become moist and tends to soften up using its crispness this type of cookies include peanut butter cookies and sugar cookies crisp cookies keep best when stored in a container loose fitting cover.

Soft dough batter: - Has a high moisture content and requires a great percentage of egg to build structure. The desirable finish product is a soft moist cookie it's best stored or packed in a container with tight fitting cover cookies, in the category are dropped cookies if all bought such as butter scotch and chocolate cookies.

Refrigerated dough: - Are mixed in the same manner as when dough expect the dough is very stiff, as the resulting cookie is very brittle. After mixing is completed the dough is weighted of into pieces of convinces sizes. The dough is than formed into rolles which may be wrapped and refrigerated to cut into cookies as needed. The roll of dough may be sliced into individual cookies which are panned wrapped and than refrigerated ready to placed directly into the oven when needed or cut cookies. Can be spread in bulk and pan as needed- the advantage of the dough is that it can be made and stored in the refrigerator until needed. This eliminates waste and provided a ready sources of dessert in a short notice.

Mixing of cookies.:- Primary factor is proper mixing and temperature control. Cookies dough is often chilled after mixing to facilitates shaping the convential of creaming method, it is the one most commonly used for cookies, cookie dough should be mixed just enough to blend the Ingredients thoroughly. The longer the creaming of shortening and sugar the less spread the final product will have because the sugar will be most finally distributed through out the mixing - when the mixing is over creamed the cookies will not spread as much due to the dissolving of the sugar crystal.

Under creaming will give the cookies a coarse structure and will result in a baked product that's has spread. Its important to have a correct balance in the creaming process not only does it effect, the spread of the cookies but also the baking quality. If lump of the sugar are left in the dough during mixing sticky is likely to occur. The syrup form during of baking become hard and solidify on the baking pan. Ones the creaming is complete the flour is added to the mixture here again you have the opportunity determined the quality of your cookies. Over mixing develop the gluten in the dough. This retards the spread of the cookies in the baking the longer the mixing after blending the flour and water the most developed the structure. A highly developed structure reduce the spread of cookies in baking.

Baking cookies

Right temperature baking for cookies 385° to 400° F a cool oven produce pale colour, while a hot oven may produce to dark a colour. Too hot an oven will set a cookie before it has a chance to spread to any extend. Steam has a softening effect upon the cookies in the oven giving them greater chance to spread become they set. Cookies should be on soft sides when remove from the oven, the heat in the cookies and the pan will continue to cook the cookie during the cooking period, over baking drying out the cookies and reduces flavour and taste.

PASTRIES, SAVOURY AND SWEET

To be able to make good pastry is a great asset, for pastry is the foundation of so many dishes, both savoury and sweet. Even the very last remnants of a joint become a dainty dish, if nicely flavoured and served in a pastry case or minced and disguised in a roll pudding. The beginner should start with short pastries, for these are so simple to make and success is sure if the directions are carefully followed. Then continue with flaky pastry before attempting the more ambitious puff, for puff pastry sometimes presents difficulties to beginners; but a little practice and particular care over the various processes of mixing, rolling, folding and baking will soon ensure success. When, upon opening the oven, you find it has risen to twice its original size, and looks truly professional, the thrill you will feel at having created something perfect will make the trouble seem well worth while. And if, when making some pastry dish, there are scraps over, which is very often the case, do not waste them or just put that piece of dough in the oven. Use it for one of the recipes for small pastries, for it takes very little to make a dainty dish of tarts that will be a pleasing change for dinner or tea.

CHOUX PASTRY

Choux pastry is not really difficult to make, but like many other things it needs practice. It makes such dainty sweets and savouries that it is well worth a little trouble.

½ lb. Flour, 1 teaspoon Cornflour 2 oz., Fresh Butter ½ pint, Water, Good pinch of Salt, 2 Eggs.

Temperature: electricity, 400° F.

Method

Mix together the flour, corn flour and salt, and sift them. Put the butter in a saucepan with ½ pint of water, and bring to the boil. Then take it off the fire and stir in quickly the flour mixed with the salt and corn flour. Then stir quickly over gently heat, until the paste will leave the sides of the saucepan quite clean. Remove from the fire, let it cool for a minute or two, then beat in the eggs one at a time—do not whisk them first, just break them into the paste. When the eggs are all beaten in and the mixture is quite smooth, it is ready.

Flaky Pastry

½ lb. flour, Good pinch of salt, 5 oz. Butter or Margarine 5 gram, Cream of Tartar, cold water.

Temperature: Electricity, 450° F.

Method

Mix the cream of tartar and salt with the flour, and sift them well. Pat the butter into very small marbles, and drop them into the flour. Stir, but do not rub them in, then add a little cold water; stir whilst you add it until you have used enough to form rather a firm paste. Be careful not to add too much water. Roll it out lightly on a well floured board. Fold in three from the top and roll again. Repeat this, folding and rolling twice more, rolling only in one direction. Let the pastry stand for ten minutes between each rolling. After the third rolling, it is ready for use.

Flaky Dripping Pastry

1 lb. plain flour, teaspoon Baking Powder, ½ lb. Dripping, small teaspoon Salt, cold water.

Temperature: Electricity, 55° F.

Method

If the dripping hard, as it invariably is in cold weather, put it in a warm place for some time before you are using it. It must not oil, but should be quite soft. Then mix the salt with it on a soup plate and beat it to a soft cream, making it smooth and quite free from any lumps. Sift the flour into a bowl and add enough cold water to form a dough which is soft enough to roll easily, but not in the least sticky. Roll it out and spread the creamed fat on the centre to within half an inch of the edges. Sprinkle the baking powder on the fat and fold it over from either side, making three layers. Now roll it out as thin as possible, fold and roll again, fold and roll once more and it is ready to use. This pastry is particularly good for meat or fruit pies to be eaten hot. It needs a hot oven.

Puff Pastry

12 oz. Plain Flour, 8oz. Butter or Margarine or 4oz. Butter and 4oz. Margarine, pinch of Salt, very cold water.

Temperature: Electricity, 500° F.

The great point with pastry making is to keep it as cool as possible while mixing and rolling, so make it in a cool place and not near the kitchen fire. If you have naturally hot hands, wash them in very hot water five minutes before you begin to mix the pastry, and handle it as little as possible. Use pastry flour or good plain flour, not self-raising. See that it is perfectly dry. Add the salt to it, and put it through a fine sieve into a bowl—a sixpenny wire gravy strainer answers very well in place of a sieve. Use fresh butter or unsalted margarine—a mixture of the two makes very good pastry. All margarine may be used, but it will not, of course, have the butter flavour. Now cut the ½ lb. of butter or margarine into thin slices; a ½ lb. piece should cut eight slices. Fluff up the flour in the basin with an egg whisk or fork, so that it does not lie heavily. Put each piece of butter into it in turn and well coat it with the flour.

Lightly flour a pastry board or marble slab (the top of an old wash-stand makes an excellent pastry board) and roll out each slice of butter or margarine quite thinly; place them on a cold plate in a pile as you do them. Next form the flour in the bowl into light dough with very cold water. Use a knife for mixing, and add the water very gradually. Be very careful not to put in too much; the paste must be soft enough to roll easily, but it must not be at all sticky. You will probably find you have to use your hands to form the paste into a ball, but do not handle it more than you can possibly help. Use the tips of the fingers, for they are much cooler than the palms of the hands.

Roll out the dough as thinly as possible, then cover the centre of the dough with the rolled out butter; this should use four of the slices, leaving as equal space of uncovered pastry on either side. Fold over the plain pastry on the right side so that it covers the butter, and place the remaining four slices of butter on the piece of pastry you have folded over, and cover it by folding the plain piece of pastry over from the left side. Now roll it out, rolling away from you. Use the rolling pin lightly, giving short rapid rolls, and always rolling forward, not backward. Never roll right off the pastry—stop before you get to the edge. This is most important to remember, because your object is to keep the air in the paste, and if you roll off the edge you naturally push it out. Leave the pastry for ten minutes in a cool place. The pastry is now a long oblong shape. Cut it in half, put one half aside on a cold plate, and fold and roll the pastry in the same way as you did before—folding from either side to centre, and then rolling out to an oblong shape. Roll the second half in the same way. You will find this easier than rolling the whole piece; repeat this process of folding and rolling, then put it aside and do the same with the other half. Leave for ten minutes. Then put it on the other pastry on the board and cut through the two, making two halves again. Roll out thinly, fold and roll out onfce more, and it is ready. It is a good plan to cut off a small piece of the pastry and bake it to test if it has been rolled sufficiently; if it does not rise as well as it should, repeat the folding and rolling. This sounds a lengthly process, but when you have made puff pastry a few times you will find it quite easy and well worth while, for you can produce such a variety of dishes at a small cost with its aid.

Baking

Puff pastry can be spoilt in the baking quite as easily as in the making. If the oven is not hot enough the butter will melt and ooze out before the pastry begins to cook; if the oven is too hot, the pastry begins to cook; if the oven is too hot, the pastry will burn before it is done through.

If you are cooking in a gas oven, turn the regulator Mark 9 for ten minutes before you wish to bake. A temperature of 500° F. is needed. If cooking in an ordinary stove and without a thermometer, the oven can be tested in the following way: Place a piece of white paper or sprinkle a good pinch of flour on the shelf. Shut the door for thirty secondes and if the paper or flour by that time.

PUFF PASTRY MAKING

1. **Ingredients**: When making puff pastry, use pastry flour or plain white flour, not self-raising. It must be perfectly dry. Add to it the salt, and sift them through a find sieve. Use fresh butter or unsalted margarine, mixed together if liked. This will make very good pastry—of better flavour than if margarine alone were used.
2. **Preparing Butter and Flour**: Now cut the butter or margarine into thin slices; there should be about eight slices to the half-pound. Use an egg whisk or a fork to fluff up the flour in the basin. The flour should now lie quite lightly in the bowl. Well coat each piece of butter eith flour.
3. **Rolling the Butter**:- Dredge flour lightly over a pastry-board. A very good pastry board can be made from the marble top of an old wash stand. Roll out each slice of butter or margarine until it is quite thin. When this is done, pile the slices on a plate, until all are finished.
4. **Making the Dough**:- Form the flour in the bowl into a light dough with very cold water, using a knife for mixing, and adding the water gradually. Do not add enough to make the dough sticky. Form the dough into a ball, handling. It as little as possible, and using the tips of the fingers only.
5. **Spreading the Butter**:—The dough should now be rolled out as thinly as possible on the floured board. Put the rolled-out butter or margarine on the middle of the dough. Four of the eight pieces should be used, and an equal space of uncovered dough should be left all round the pieces.
6. **Arranging Butter and Dough**:- fold over the plain pastry on the right side so that it covers the butter. Now place the remaining four pieces of butter on the piece of pastry which has just been folded over. Cover them by folding the plain pastry from the left side; you will thus have three layers of pastry.
7. **Rolling the Pastry**:- Roll the pastry out, always rolling away from you. Hold the rolling pin very lightly, and give short, rapid rolls. Never roll right off the edge of the pastry. If you do so, you will push the air from the pastry, and the object is to keep it light and full of air.
8. **Folding the Pastry**:- Cut the pastry in halves. Fold and roll one half as before, folding from either side to the centre, and rolling out to an oblong shape.l Repeat with the second hall. Repeat alternately once more. Leave ten minutes. Now put the pieces together on the board, cut through, and repeat with these halves as before. Then roll into one piece.

Savoury Pastry

½ lb. plain Flour, ½ teaspoon Baking Powder, ½ lb. fresh Butter or unsalted Margarine, 1 Egg, cold water.

Temperature: electricity, 450° F.

Method

1. Mix the baking powder with the flour and put through a fine sieve.
2. Then rub in the fat until it is thoroughly mixed and there is no loose flour left in the bowl.
3. Next stir in the of form a still dough with a well beaten egg, and a little cold water. Add the water very gradually; it should be a stiff dough, not in the least sticky. Roll out the pastry and use for savoury patties or tartlets.

Short Pastry

1 lb. ordinary Flour, good pinch of Salt, 8 oz. Lard, margarine or clarified Dripping, very cold water

Temperature : electricity, 450° F.

Method

Mix the salt with the flour, and pass through a sieve so tht it is quite free from lumps. Then rub in the fat lightly with the tips of the fingers, and continue rubbing it in until the mixture looks like fine breadcrumbs and there remains no dry flour in the basin. Add cold water very gradually, until you have a soft dough. The dough should be soft enough to roll easily, but it must not be at all sticky—wet pastry means a heavy crust. Roll out lightly on a floured board, and it is ready. If you are using dripping and it is at all hard, which is often the case in cold weather, cream it first before rubbing it into the flour, otherwise it is difficult to get a smooth paste. This is an excellent short pastry for general use, and very quickly made. It can be used for roly-poly puddings, jam tarts, fruit tarts, cheese cakes, and meat pies or puddings.

Short Sweet Pastry

This is especially good for all kinds of tartlets, cheese cakes and flans.

½ lb. flour, 3 oz. Castor Sugar, 3 oz. Butter or Margarine, 1 Egg, pinch of Salt.

Temperature: Electricity. 450° F.

Method

Mix the salt with the flour and sift them into a basin. Rub in the margarine, add the sugar. Now stir in a well beaten egg, and add enough cold water to form a rather stiff dough. Roll out and use. This pastry can be flavoured in any way you wish. A quarter of a teaspoon of grated lemon or orange rind added to the dry Ingredients makes a delicious pastry for lemon or orange tartlets.

Vol-au-vent

This is a name given to deep puff pastry cases. They are quite easy to make and may be filled with either meat, fish or fruit. They make a pretty dish filled with fruit, and they are useful, too, for serving left-over meat or fish, a well flavoured mince may be a party dish if served in a vol-au-vent.

Time: 20 to 30 minutes. Temperature:. electricity, 500° F.

Cut an oval piece of puff pastry—a small dish is a very good guide if you have not an oval cutter-then cut two oval rings of pastry about an inch wide. Wet the edge of the oval piece and place a ring on it, then wet this also with cold water and place the other ring upon it. Bake in a hot oven.

SAVOURY FILLINGS FOR CHOUX CASES

Game and Mushroom

1/2 lb. cooked Game, 2 oz. Mushrooms, tablespoons liquid Aspic Jellyb 1 gill Game Gravy (made from bones or giblets), 1oz. Butter.

Method

Peel the mushrooms and fry them in the butter. Take out the mushrooms. See that the game is quite free from skin, bone and gristle. Chop the mush-rooms, mix them with the game, and put both through a mincer. Add this mince to the butter in which the mushrooms were fried, put in the gravy, stir together until thoroughly mixed and quite hot. Add the aspic (this can be bought in packets.) Mix well, turn into a dish and leave in a cold place until required. Cut a slice and put in each éclair or pastry case when required. If you wish to serve the game in pastry or soufflé cases, fill them with the mixture before it is quite cold and leave in a cold place until required. This mixture is very good hot in patty or soufflé cases. Use half the given quantity of aspic jelly.

ECLAIRS

Fill a forcing bag with choux pastry, screw on a plain tube and force the paste on to a baking tin in long strips. If you do not possess a forcing bag, three parts fill sponge finger tins with the paste. Brush them over with beaten egg and bake about half an hour in a moderate oven. Open them down one side with a knife while they are hot. Leave until cool on a wire tray or sieve. Then fill with custard or cream and ice with coffee or chocolate glace icing, or they may be filled with a savoury mixture.

CHOUX BUNS

Bake the choux pastry in patty pans or put spoonfuls on a baking tin. Bake as éclairs. Cut open while hot and fill when cool.

PASTRY HORNS OR CORNETS

Ordinary short or puff pastry may be used for these, or sweet short pastry for sweet fillings and savoury pastry for meat or fish fillings. You will require horn tins. Grease the outsides of them. Roll out puff or short pastry (as you prefer) rather thinly and cut it in strips; wind these round and round the outside of a greased cornet mould, allowing each round slightly to overlap the last. Place on a greased baking tin, and bake puff pastry in a hot oven, short pastry in a moderate oven.

LEARNING OUTCOME

There are four basic types of pastry dough. Sweet dough is most common used for making breakfast rolls and coffee cakes. Normal fermentation for sweet dough and danish pastry differ the fermentation to tolerance of sweet dough is less critical than bread dough since the time for make up will vary for sweet rolls and coffee cake its advisable. Retarded dough is yeast dough that's refrigerated for a long time before baking this is done to lengthen the amount of time the product may be held before being baked if left at room temperature. The fat of roll in must contain a certain amount of moisture as the dough is folded and rolled with the fat multiple layer of days sealed around fat are formed when the dough is placed in the hot oven the fat being to melt, enriching and lubricating the tough surrounding it. Cookies are often referred to a small sweet cake items they are very similar to cakes in the type of Ingredients used and the method to mix them they differ from cakes in the proportion of Ingredients and panning method, ***the primary difference Between cakes and cookies is the amount of moisture in the mixture.*** Continues less liquids, egg and flour then soft cookies. These cookies are often referred to as slices or rolled cookies. The desirable finished provided is crisp when humidity been excessive this cookies

QUESTIONS FOR DISCUSSION

1. Explain the basic types of dough.
2. Explain the method of preparation of sweet dough.
3. Explain the procedure of mixing pie dough.
4. Explain the term turnover in bakery.
5. Explain the term cookie and its main Ingredients.
6. Explain the types of cookie dough.
7. Mention the process puff making procedure.
8. Explain the term Éclairs.

KEY TERMS

* Buns
* Choux paste
* Dough
* Vol-au-vent
* Cakes
* Cookies
* Fermented

Chapter 36
Cakes

After studying this chapter, the student must know :

- Introduction
- Method of mixing the Ingredients
- Ingredients of cakes
- Chocolate and chocolate handling
- Types of cakes and its preparation
- Mixing of different cakes
- High altitude baking
- Storage of cakes
- Different cake recipes

CAKES

General Directions

When making cakes it is most important to have all the ingredients prepared before you start to mix them. A cake may be quite spoilt if you have to wait to blanch almonds or slice peel whilst you are beating. With regard to ingredients, use ordinary flour unless self-raising is specified in the recipe. Always sift flour before using; that is, pass it through a fine sieve. This is absolutely necessary in recipes where the fat and sugar are creamed and the flour added afterwards. You cannot produce a good creamy batter with lumpy flour. Unless otherwise directed, mix any small powders such as baking powder, spices and salt with the flour before sifting it; they will then be evenly distributed in the cake. See also that sugar is quite free from lumps. Beginners are frequently puzzled by the word "shortening," which is used in some recipes; it is simply another name for fat.

When making cakes, fats are either rubbed into the flour or creamed with the sugar, and successful cake making depends largely on the way this is done.

To Rub Fat into Flour:—Use the tips of the fingers, and mix evenly so that when finished every particle of four has some fat mixed with it. There should be no dry flour remaining in the bowl and the mixture should look like very fine breadcrumbs. If dripping is used, it should first be clarified unless it has been very carefully strained while hot.

To Clarify—Put it into basin, cover well with boiling water, stirring until the fat has quite melted. Leave until cold. Then remove the dripping from the water and carefully scrape the under part before using.

To Cream Fat.—Fat that is to be creamed should be neither oily nor hard. So put it in a very cold place or in cold water for some time before using in hot weather, and in a warm place or use a warm basin in very cold weather, but be careful not to make it in the least oily or the flavour will be spoilt. A wooden spoon is best for creaming. Put the fat in a bowl, flatten it with the spoon, then fold and flatten again. Now best until it is quite soft and creamy; so soft, in fact, that a metal spoon will fall in when placed upon it. The process is the same for butter, margarine, lard or clarified dripping. Buy Australian fruits—they are economical in price and excellent in flavour. Good fruit should not need washing. Look it over to remove any little stones or stalks, then put it on a sieve, sprinkle with flour, rub gently and shake. This method cleans the fruit and the tiny stalks will fall through the sieve. Also the flour that clings to the fruit will prevent it falling to the bottom of the cake.

Candied peel goes farther and looks nicer if sliced and not chopped. Raisins must be cut in halves and the stones removed, cherries cut in quarters when used for cakes. Almonds need blanching. Put them in a basin, cover well with boiling water, leave a minute, then remove the skins putting the almonds into a bowl of cold water as you skin them to preserve their colour. Dry well before using. With Brazil nuts the brown skin is scraped off with a knife. Dried. walnuts do not need skinning. When the peel of oranges or lemons is used for flavouring it should either be finely grated or it may be rubbed off on a hump of sugar, which is afterwards crushed to fine powder. Care must be taken to use only the yellow part of the rind as the white pith has a bitter taste. Eggs must be fresh; there is no economy in buying stale ones. One fresh egg will produce more lightness than two stale ones.

Some cakes depend entirely on eggs for their lightness, and when this is the case do not grudge time spend in beating them. Follow the directions exactly when time is given, for if there is not sufficient air beaten into the eggs the result will not be satisfactory. Cakes that contain baking powder or bicarbonate of soda—the two other "lightening" Ingredients—must be put into the oven as soon as possible alter the moister has been added or the "lightening" effect will work off and the result will be a heavy cake. Line tins with greaseproof paper when baking rich cakes; two thicknesses should be used for those that require several hours baking. For sponge cakes brush the tin over with liquid butter or margarine, then sprinkle a little flour and castor sugar mixed in equal quantities. Shake the tins to remove any superfluous flour. When baking, do not open the oven door except when necessary, and always shut it gently. It is impossible to give the exact time for the baking of various kinds of cakes, but a good rest is to insert a warm skewer in the centre of a cake and withdraw it quickly. If it is still clean and bright, without the least stickiness, the cake is done. Cakes should be kept in air-tight tins. Dried eggs and household milk may be used in place of fresh eggs and milk in any of the recipes.

Ingredients:- Use in most cakes are flour, sugar, shortening or butter eggs, salt, liquid and leaving formula balance is the key to producing a good cake of any type.

Flour:- Most cakes formulas called for bleached soft wheat flour. This flour produces fine cell structure, fine grains, smooth texture the low protein soft wheat flour is essential to quality production, reduces possibility of toughness, hard wheat flour contain more gluten and producer a coarse texture cakes.

Sugar:- Serves three purposes in cakes mixture - sweeten, tenderized and moisture. Sugar tenderized the softening of the flour protein and starches in the cakes mix. Its helps to return moisture in bake cakes making then moist and edible for several days. Type of sugar used in granulated brown and molasses. Molasses is used in ginger bread or spice cakes to add flour and moisture. Brown sugar enhances flavour and light molasses increase moisture retention.

Fat:- Cakes may contain butter or margin and hydrogenated shortening compound (With or without) emulsifier added or oil. The function of shortenings and other type of fat or oil is to lubricate the internal structure, this aids the incorporation or holding of air and moisture allowing production of a tender product to fulfil this function, fat must thoroughly mixed and dispersered throughout the batter. Butter and hydrogenated shortening compounds are easily mixed and yield cakes of maximum volume. Hydrogenated shortenings may contain an ingredients known as emulsifier. This adds the distribution of fat in a mixture enabling the baker to obtain a cake that's of large volume. Fine grain and pleasingly moistness. More importantly the emulsifier aids in creating off an even texture with less efforts and skills. A cake made with emulsified shortening does not require as much creaming action because the fat is disposed more efficiently. This type of shortenings are mandatory for high ratio cakes these are cakes which contain greater percentage of sugar than flour.

Salt:- Main purpose of salt in baking is in effect on taste and flavour its bring out the flavour of other Ingredients too much salt will create a unpleasant flour.

Eggs:- Egg in baking serve the number of purposes its contribute to be cakes structure by working in the gluten in the flour. Egg binds and helps stabilize the batter. Whipped egg holds air and allow it to expand during baking supply some leavening actions. Egg also act as an emulsifying agent because of less thin in the yolk which is an emulsifying agent. National emulsifying agent moisture, colour, flavour and eating quality are all control by the egg in cake baking.

The qualify and quantity has to be constantly presences although. Fresh egg are best they vary in size always weight the fresh eggs broken at of the shell for use in cakes.

Liquid:- Its need to combined and activate other Ingredients. It's the primary control for the consistency of the finished cakes : Batter. Milk, Water, Juice, Liquors or coffee can be used as the liquids in cakes baking.

Leavening:- Cakes are leaven in three ways incorporation of air in during mixing, chemical leaving agent such as baking powder or vapours pressure created in the oven. The kind of leaving used depends upon the richness of the formula consistency of the batter and baking temperature. All three leavening agent produces the lightness and porousness which given caked there characteristics texture.

I. **Incorporated Air**:- Air is naturally incorporated into cake batter during mixing how much are is incorporate will depend on many factor how many times. The flour is rifted the speed of hand or machine mixing, the mixing method tools used all effect the incorporation of air another factor is the temperature of cake batter. Formula instruction should be carefully, followed and attention paid to mixing times an Ingredients temperature. Cakes low in moisture, dough made with rich Ingredients such as pound cakes obtained most of leaving from mixing. Due to the incorporation of air they require less or no chemical leaving.

II. **Chemical leaving agent**:- Baking powder is the most common leaving agent used in cake baking. It liberate because gas when it comes to contact with the liquid, the amount and speed with its which releases gas depends on the type of baking powder used.

III. **Baking soda:** - Is used in many cakes its use to generate CO_2 and contributes to the lightness of the cakes when baking soda is the only leaving used the formula must also contain an acid Ingredients it's a combination of soda and the moist acid which produce CO_2 gas, sour milk, vinegar, butter milk, sour cream and molasses are common used in this manner.

Cakes made from lean formula high in moisture. Required more leaving ingredients.

Vapours (Water or Steam) : Some leaving action is produces by steam or water vapour given out liquid by the cake batter during baking. As the steam is release it expand the cells develops in the cake structure pushing the cake up.

Chocolate:- Possibly the most popular cake flavour is chocolate, the type of chocolate used in the cake baking vary from unsweetened to sweet the choice of chocolate with depend on the final product desire you must be conscious while substituting one chocolate from another called for in a formula. The variance in sugar milk solids and oil content can change the texture of the product varied.

Good chocolate handling

1. Remember chocolate burns easily. It should be melted over simmering water and bain-marie.
2. Keep and store chocolate will wrapped in cools place.
3. When chocolate is explored to air over a long period it sometimes takes on a harmless white discolouration and becomes crumbly. This does not mean that mean that its stale, this is perfectly usable.

Dry fruit and nuts

Contribute to flavour and texture. If the dry fruits are old and hard soften them by keeping in boiling water 5 to 10 minutes. Than drain thoroughly and pet dry. There are often floured before adding. This helps to keep from settling down to buttom of the cake during handling and baking.

Types of cakes

The promotion and type of ingredients used serve as a base for dividing cakes into 3 separate groups.

1. Batter cakes
2. Foam cakes.
3. Chiffon cake.

1. **Batter Cakes:-** There are many substitution of the three main group of cakes - These subdivision are based on the Ingredients in the mix and the way in which they are added to the basic formula. Its include:-
   a. *Pound cake*:- contain a high % of fat.
   b. *Plain layer cakes*:- contain a small % of fat.
   c. *Chocolate cake*:- layer cakes incorporated chocolate, coco powder and soda.
2. **Foam cakes**:- contain very little and no fat. This class of cakes is leavened by air whipped into the egg portion of the mixed. The expansion of air and the vapours pressure created by the heat in the baking process causes the mix to rise foam cakes includes.
   a. *Angle food cake*: in this egg white are used for foam.
   b. *Spung cake*: In this whole egg, egg yolks or combination of two are used for foam.
3. **Chiffon cakes**:- Contain both foam and butter the 2 component are mixed separately and folded together for final mixture.

PREPARATION OF CAKES

Preparing of cake pan: Use the correct size pan mention in the formula the pan should be greece and lightly floured- this prevent cake for sticking. If cake sticks to pan it will normally break before removing which makes it useless for proper finishing pan and moulds with design need special care. There are certain types of cakes which don't require greece or floured. The most prominent ones are angel food cake. The beaten egg white that leaven angle food cake will rise better or ungreased surface.

Mixing cakes batter

Selection of good high quality Ingredients is absolutely, necessary to produce a good high quality finish product. The Ingredients alone however will not guarantee a fine product. It's the balance of Ingredients, the mixing procedure the gravity butter or dough, the final temperature and final a taking process. The idea of mixing is to combined the items in a homogenous mix. This gets complicated with the nature of Ingredients for example liquid or fat do not readily mix its for this reason that closed attention must be given to mixing procedure.

1) To mix a cake property mise- en-place should be ready first gathered and measure all Ingredients called for in a formula.
2) Pre heat the oven- have all ingredient at room temperature the allows to produce a batter which is at the best temperature Ingredients to interact prefer temperature is 75 degree.

Beating a cake by hand needs more time gradually mixing normally cakes batter should be beaten only long enough to combined all Ingredients thorough.

PROCEDURE OR MIXING WILL VARY WITH THE TYPE OF CAKE

Mixing batter cakes

They require the batter or shortening to be soften first or creamed first. This allows it to blend more readily with other Ingredients. The sugar should than we added gradually beaten in well butter and sugar when properly creamed together will get light in colour will get creamy and fluffy consistencies.

The Egg and egg works are added next with vanilla and other flavouring. Be carefully to add the eggs one at a time or very gradually. Given the time the eggs will act as an emulsifying agent suspended the fat and sugar to that the final mix is a smooth blend. When the eggs are added two quickly or sugar and fat are in properly creamed the fat will separate from the rest of the mixture. The result will be a cake of improper browning and poor texture. If the batter cake formula calls a separated egg, the egg whites should be beaten separately and folded in just before baking.

After eggs flour is added remember at this point you only want to mix enough to combined a Ingredients. If the cake batter is over beaten the cake will have a coarse tough texture will large tunnels. Ones the mix is complete scale or major the batter into prepare baking pan.

Mixing foam cakes

These cakes specifically sponge cakes are very delicate and there Ingredients must be combined carefully. The egg yolk are beaten first than sugar and other flavouring are added the egg white which do the leavning should be carefully be beaten not over beaten. This should be done just before they are folded in. Its best to beat a little sugar into the beaten egg whites to help them hold the air.

Next, stir a little of beaten egg white into a egg yolk mixture to lighten it fold the remaining white alternatively with the stiffed flour gently into the mixture before to used a gentle hand and mixed only enough to blend the mixture.

Filling cakes pan:- Most cake pan should be filled not most than 2/3rds full this allows the cakes to have a room to rise, be sure to spread the batter up against the size of the pan and into the corner of a square pan. The filling of pan with cakes batter is termed as scaling.

Baking cakes:- Always baked in a preheated oven unless the formula says other wise, many cakes have be ruined with slow start with in a cold oven. Make sure that oven temperature is accurate, glass or darked coloured pan will retain more heat than shinny one. When using this type of pan used the same amount of baking time but reduced the oven temperature by 25° F. Crowding the oven will cause un even baking allow room for heat to circulate do not let pan touch each other. If the cake is baking unevenly turned the baking pan serval times.

Any discussion on when a cake is done must consider carry over cooking-. The heat remaining in the cake pan after its removed from the oven will continue to be transferred to the interior of the cake until the pan completely cooled. To retain a proper moister level in your bakes cake it requires that you remove it from the oven at right time- It also need to be removed from the pan at the right time. Being to test a cake. five to 10 minutes before its supported to be done-.This is done by pressing lightly with your finger tips on the centre of cake, most cakes unless they are very rich will spring back leaving little expression when done- additionally a cake that's done will shrinkage a bit away from the side of the baking pan.

High altitude baking:- A change in attitude is a real problem in making any type of leavened product,. At an attitude at 3500 feet or higher the amount of leaving a cake must be reduce also the oven temperature has to be raised if these changes are not made cake will dry coarse and crumbly decrease the amount of baking powder or baking soda by 1/3 all 3500 feet half at 5000 feet 2/3 above 5000 feel raised the oven temperature. 25° F do not beat the eggs egg white as much.

Cooling cakes:- Timely removal or cakes from its baking pan is important to the quality of cake. Let batter cake cook and shrink in there pan for about 5 min after removal from the oven that turn them out in a wire rack to cool completely. If the cake should stick to the pan use a spatula to loosen it gently.

Spung cake, angle food cake, chiffon cake should be allow to cool up side down in there pans. This is done by inverting the pan in which they are baked Air must be allow to freely circulated around the cake while its cooling. When the cake is cooled it can be unmolded.

Storage of cakes:- Cakes taste better when they are fresh no more a day too old. However if you plan a cake for several days. Wrapped in a foil or plastic wrapped.

BELGIUM CAKE

Time: 2 hours. Temperature: Gas,. Electricity. 400° F.

Ingredients	*Quantity*
Flour	450 gram
Dripping	450 gram
Demerara sugar	180 gram
Currants	120 gram
Raisins	120 gram
Salt	20 gram
Mixed spices	15 gram
Soda bicarbonate	5 gram
Warm water	350 gram

Method

1. Put the water into a saucepan with the dripping, sugar and fruit, and stir over gentle heat until it boils.
2. Let is continue boiling for five minutes. Leave until cold.
3. Then mix the flour, salt and spice, and sift them. Stir them into the mixture.

4. Add the bicarbonate of soda dissolved in a teaspoon of warm water. Turn into a well greased tin and bake for two hours in a moderate oven.

CARAMEL FOR DARKENING CAKES

Time: about 20 minutes. Temperature: Moderate.

Ingredients	*Quantity*
Demerara sugar	100 gram
Water	20ml

Method

1. Put the sugar in a saucepan and stir it over very gentle heat until it begins to dissolve.
2. Then add the water very gradually and continue to stir constantly until the sugar has quite dissolved and the mixture is stick and brown. Cover and store in a jar in a dry place.

CHERRY CAKE

Time:45 minutes. Temperature: Gas, Electricity, 400° F.

Ingredients	*Quantity*
Flour	150 gram
Castor sugar	90 gram
Butter	60 gram
Baking powder	2 gram
Glazes cherries	30 gram
Citron pee	30 gram
Eggs	2 no
Milk	1 tbsp

Fig 37.1 Cherry cake

Method

1. Cream together the butter, margarine and sugar.
2. Add eggs well beaten, and beat for five minutes.
3. Continuc bcating while adding the cherries, cut in halves and floured, and the sliced peel.
4. Then gradually beat in the flour, mixed with baking powder; last of all, the milk.
5. Place in a tin lined with buttered paper and bake in a moderate oven for about 45 minutes.

CHERRY AND LEMON CAKE

Ingredients	*Quantity*
Flour	250 gram
Castor sugar	120 gram
Butter	120 gram
Baking powder	2 gram
Glazes cherries	30 gram
Candied lemon peel	30 gram
Eggs	2 no
Milk	100 ml

Fig 37.2 Cherry and lemon cake

Method

1. Beat the eggs well. Then beat the sugar and butter to a very soft cream. Cut the cherries in quarters and dust them with flour.
2. To the beaten sugar and butter, add a little flour and egg alternately, beating briskly all the while.
3. Mix the baking powder with the last of the flour. Stir in the grated rind, the peel cut in thin strips and the prepared cherries.
4. Add the milk. Mix well. Turn into a tin lined with buttered paper and bake one and a half hours in a moderate oven.

CHOCOLATE FRUIT CAKE

Time: about 1 hour. Temperature: Gas, Electricity: 375° F.

Ingredients	*Quantity*
Flour	180 gram
Castor sugar	90 gram
Butter	120 gram
Baking powder	1 gram
Cocoa powder	30 gram
Sultanas	60 gram
Eggs	2no
Milk	1tbsp

Fig 37.3 Chocolate fruit cake

Method

1. Stone the raisins and cut them in quarters; see the sultanas are clean and free from stalks.

2. Mix flour, cocoa and baking powder together and put them through a fine sieve.
3. Beat margarine and sugar to a soft cream, drop in the yolk and white of one egg and beat four minutes, add another egg and beat four minutes more.
4. Continue beating while you add the flour, fruit and milk gradually.
5. When it is an evenly mixed batter, turn into a well greased tin and bake in a moderate oven for about one hour.

CHOCOLATE NUT CAKE

Time: about 1 ½ hours. Temperature: Gas, Electricity: 375° F.

Ingredients	*Quantity*
Flour	180 gram
Castor sugar	90 gram
Butter	60 gram
Baking powder	1 gram
Cocoa powder	30 gram
Sweet almonds	60 gram
Eggs	2no
Milk	100ml
Vanilla essence	2 gram

Fig 37.4 Chocolate nut cake

Method

1. Mix the cocoa and vanilla with the milk.
2. Beat the butter to a cream, add the sugar and the eggs gradually, and beat until smooth. Then beat in the flour and the almonds, blanched and sliced.
3. Add the milk and mix to a smooth batter.
4. Turn into a well greased tin and bake one and a half hours in a moderate oven.

CHOCOLATE RAISIN CAKE

Time: about 45 minutes. Temperature:, Electricity: 400° F.

Ingredients	*Quantity*
Flour	250 gram
Castor sugar	90 gram
Butter	60 gram
Baking powder	1 gram
Cocoa powder	30 gram

Raisins	60 gram
Eggs	2 no
Milk	100 ml
Plain chocolate	60 gram
Sweet almonds	20 gram

Fig 37.5 Chocolate raisins cake

Method

1. Stone the raisins and cut them in halves.
2. Grate the chocolate and melt it over boiling water.
3. Beat butter and sugar to a cream, add the yolks of the eggs well beaten and the melted chocolate.
4. Mix well, add the raisins, then beat in the flour gradually, the whites of the eggs and about two tablespoons of lukewarm milk with the soda dissolved in it.
5. Turn into a well greased tin and bake for about three-quarters of an hour. Blanch the almonds and, when the cake is nearly done, press the almonds on it and return to the oven.

CHOCOLATE SPONGE CAKE

Time : about 45 minutes. Temperature: Gas, Electricity: 400° F.

Ingredients	*Quantity*
Flour	90 gram
Castor sugar	90 gram
Eggs	2no
Plain chocolate	60 gram
Sweet almonds	20 gram
For the Icing	
Vanilla Chocolate	60 gram
Butter	90 gram
Icing sugar	50 gram

Method

1. Break the eggs into a basin, add the sugar. Stand the basin over a saucepan of hot water and whip the mixture for a quarter of an hour.
2. Take the basin off the saucepan, melt the chocolate, and stir it in. Stir in, also, the flour and the almonds blanched and sliced.
3. When it is a smooth evenly coloured mixture, turn it into a well buttered tin and bake in a moderate oven. Leave until cold.

4. Then grate the vanilla chocolate, put it in a basin over a saucepan of boiling water, add one dessertspoon of water and stir until the chocolate has quite melted. Cool.
5. Beat the butter to a cream, add it to the cooled chocolate, also the sieved icing sugar. Beat all together until smooth. Then spread it evenly over the tip of the cake. Leave for a few hours, then decorate with royal icing.

CHOCOLATE SWISS ROLL

Time: 10 to 15 minutes. Temperature: Gas, Electricity: 425° F.

Ingredients	*Quantity*
Eggs	2 no
Castor sugar	90 gram
Vanilla powder	5 gram
Plain chocolate	60 gram
Flour	60 gram
Filling	
Egg	2 no
Cream	2 tbsp
Milk	2 tbsp
Gelatine	10 gram
Castor sugar	60 gram
Vanilla essence	12drops

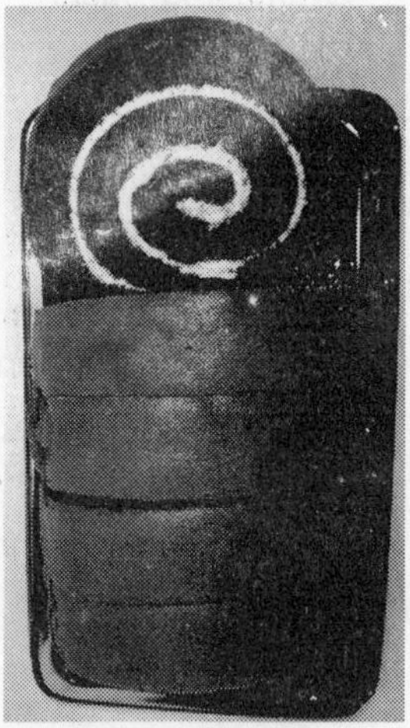

Fig 37.6 Chocolate swiss roll

Method

1. Put eggs and sugar in a basin, place over a pan of boiling water and whip for twenty minutes.
2. Stir in chocolate (previously method), add flour and vanilla. Stir until quite smooth.
3. Then pour the mixture into a shallow baking tin which has been buttered and dastard with sugar and flour. Bake in a quick oven.
4. When done, turn on to a paper dusted with sifted icing sugar.
5. Roll up loosely and leave until cool. When almost cold, unroll very carefully, spread with the following filling or with whipped cream, and re-roll
6. **The filling.**—Whip the white of egg quite stiff whip the cream until thick. Soak the gelatine in just enough water to cover it, then dissolve it in the milk made warm.
7. Cool, then mix with beaten white of egg, cream, vanilla and sugar. Mix well and use.

COCONUT CAKE

Time 1 ½ hours. Temperature: Gas, Electricity: 375° F.

Ingredients	*Quantity*
Flour	180 gram
Butter	120 gram
Desiccated coconut	60 gram
Ratafia essence	10 gram
Granulated sugar	90 gram
Egg	1no
Milk	50 ml

Method:

1. Beat the butter and sugar to a soft cream, add a well whisked egg and the ratafia, and beat until smooth. Now beat in the flour.
2. Add the coconut and, lastly, the milk. When thoroughly mixed, turn into a well greased tin and bake for an hour and a quarter in a moderate oven.
3. Use fresh coconut when procurable, it has a more delicate flavour than when desiccated. Grate it finely and allow 3 oz. Instead of 2 oz.

LEARNING OUTCOME

A cake may be quite spoilt if you have to wait to blanch almonds or slice peel whilst you are beating. With regard to Ingredients, use ordinary four unless self-raising is specified in the recipe. Always sift four before using; that is, pass it through a find sieve. This is absolutely necessary in recipes where the fat and sugar are creamed and the flour added afterwards. You cannot produce a good creamy batter with lumpy flour. Fat that is to be creamed should be neither oily nor hard. So put it in a very cold place or in cold water for some time before using in hot weather, and in a warm place or use a warm basin in very cold weather, but be careful not to make it in the least oily or the flavour will be spoilt. Use the correct size pan mention in the formula the pan should be greece and lightly floured - this prevent cake for sticking. If cake sticks to pan it will normally break before removing which makes it useless for proper finishing pan and moulds with design need special care. A change in attitude is a real problem in making any type of leavened product,. At an attitude it 3500 feet or higher the amount of leaving a cake must be reduce also the oven temperature has to be raised if these changes are not made cake will dry coarse

QUESTIONS FOR DISCUSSION

1. Explain the method of cake making.

2. Explain the procedure of rub fat in flour.
3. Explain in details about the cake Ingredients.
4. Explain the procedure of preparation of the cakes.
5. Difference between mixing cake batter and mixing foam cakes.
6. Explain the term high altitude baking.

KEY TERMS

* Altitude	* Batter
* Fat	* Foam
* Mixing	* Rub
* Sieve	

Chapter 37

Biscuits and Petit Fours

After studying this chapter, the student must know :

- Introduction
- Standards recipes of Biscuits
- Petit four introduction
- Shaping the mixture
- Short bread
- Shaping short bread
- Baking short bread.

BISCUITS

Biscuits are very easy to make, and can be kept for some time in airtight tins. With a fruit cake and a store of biscuits, we can always feel prepared for the unexpected guests dropping into tea. Most biscuits require a slow oven, as they need to cook well without getting too brown; if overcooked they lack flavour. Biscuit cutters in a variety of shapes can be bought for a few pence, and make the biscuits look far more attractive than just plain rounds. Queen cake tins can also be used as cutters. Soft mixtures such as those employed for richer biscuits can be made very dainty in appearance by putting the mixture through a forcing bag. Dried eggs can be used in place of fresh eggs in most of these recipes.

TO FROST

Beat the white of the egg to a stiff froth and add enough castor sugar to make it as thick as thick as cream. Brush the biscuits over with this and dry in a warm room or a cool oven.

BUTTER BISCUITS

Time: about 20 minutes. Temperature: Gas,. Electricity, 375° F.

Ingredients	*Quantity*
Flour	100 gram
Butter	120 gram
Castor sugar	50 gram

Method

1. Rub the butter lightly into the flour until the mixture looks like breadcrumbs.
2. Now stir in the sugar and when evenly mixed, add enough cold water to form a stiff dough.
3. Roll out thinly, about the thickness of two pennies placed together, and cut in rounds with a wineglass or biscuit cutter.
4. Place them on a well-buttered baking sheet, prick well with a fork, and bake in a slow oven for about twenty minutes until they are a very pale. Fawn.

CARAWAY BISCUITS

Add half a teaspoon of caraway seeds to the above mixture when mixing in the sugar.

CARAWAY ROCKS

Time: 10 minutes. Temperature: Gas, Electricity, 450° F.

Ingredients	*Quantity*
Flour	225 gram
Butter	180 gram
Castor sugar	90 gram
Caraway seeds	60 gram
Salt	2 gram
Egg	1no
Milk	20ml

Method

1. Mix the salt and flour, rub in the margarine, add the sugar, caraway seeds and sliced peel.
2. Mix to a very stiff paste with the well beaten egg and a little milk. Drop in little lumps on to a buttered tin and bake ten minutes in a quick oven.

CHOCOLATE BISCUITS

Time: 20 minutes. Temperature: Gas, Electricity, 350° F.

Ingredients	*Quantity*
Flour	225 gram
Butter	180 gram
Castor sugar	90 gram
Vanilla essence	5 gram
Salt	2 gram
Egg	1no
For the chocolate icing	120 gram
Icing sugar	90 gram
Plain chocolate	1tsp
Water	

Method

1. Mix the salt with the flour, rub in the butter, add the sugar and vanilla essence and well beaten egg.
2. Roll out thinly and cut in rounds with a biscuit cutter or small wineglass. Bake to a pale biscuit colour in a slow oven.
3. Leave until cold. Grate the chocolate and rub the icing sugar through a sieve.
4. Put them in a saucepan with the water, and melt over gentle heat. When quite dissolved, cool a little, then pour gently on each biscuit and leave until dry and set.

CINNAMON BISCUITS

Time: 20 minutes. Temperature: Gas, Electricity, 375° F.

Ingredients	*Quantity*
Flour	225 gram
Butter	180 gram
Castor sugar	90 gram
Cinnamon powder	10 gram
Salt	2 gram
Milk	20ml

Method

1. Mix the cinnamon and salt with the flour.
2. Rub the butter into it, add the sugar and then the milk, and knead on a board to a smooth paste.
3. Roll out. cut into biscuits with a wineglass, and bake in a slow oven.

PETITIS FOURS

Fig 38.1 Different varities of petitis fours

Traditionally Petits Fours is the name given to possibly the most popular of all fancy biscuits. They are made from a rich cake batter or an almond paste with flour or butter, and may be iced or glazed with coloured icing or garnished with crystallized fruits, angelica, almonds, etc. The chef will enjoy creating new designs, for these little biscuits are not difficult to make, although they may appear so to the inexperienced eye. The great point about them is to get the mixture the right consistency so that it will pass through the piping bag easily and yet retain the shape desired.

CAKE BATTER FOR PETITIS FOURS

6oz.	Flour
6oz.	Castor Sugar
4oz.	Butter
1/2 lb.	Ground almonds

beaten Egg to mix.

Time:10 to 15 minutes. Temperature: Gas, Electricity, 375° F.

Beat the butter to a soft cream, add the sugar and beat again. Mix in the almonds and the flour and blend all the Ingredients to a soft paste with well beaten egg. It should be just soft enough to pass through the forcing tube without being at all sticky.

ALMOND PASTE FOR PETITIS FOURS

This paste is made without flour or butter and is more in the nature of a sweetmeat than a cake.

1/2 lb.	Ground Almonds
1/2 lb	Castor Sugar
12 drops	Flavouring Essence
2 No	Egg

Time: about 4 minutes. Temperature: Gas, Electricity, 400° F.

Mix the ground almonds with the sugar and put them through a sieve, and the flavouring to a well beaten egg, and use to form the whole into a soft paste, adding as much more egg as may be necessary. The mixture may be divided into two or three parts and coloured mauve, pale green or pink by kneading into it a few drops of colouring.

SHAPING THE MIXTURE

Grease a baking tin well, or line it with wafer paper. The mixture may then be dropped on in small rocky mounds but the appearance is much improved if it is forced. Take a forcing bag and drop in a tin funnel. These may be obtained in a variety of shapes –rose, ribbon, etc. Turn back the top of the bag and three parts fill with the mixture, then fold over the top and gently force out the mixture into fancy shapes, in very much the same way as you would when icing a cake. If you are using the rich cake batter, bake in a moderate oven ten to fifteen minutes. If you are using the almond paste mixture let the shaped paste stand for twenty-four hours, then bake to slightly tint them in a hot oven for a few minutes. To glaze Petitis fours, brush them over with white of egg beaten with a little castor sugar and decorate with blanched almonds, glace cherries and angelica.

SHORTBREAD

The making of shortbread needs some experience and a great deal of patience. The best shortbread is made without any moister except the butter, and that means that patient kneading is necessary to form the soft dough that is required. Cool hands are not necessary, as a warm hand facilities the forming of the dough. Warm the basin to be used, and in cold weather the butter or other fat may be warmed also, just sufficiently to make it soft, but not hot enough to make it oily, or the flavour of the shortbread will be spoilt.. Flour, rice-flour and sugar should all be well sifted. Never omit to add a little salt. When all the Ingredients have been mixed together, rub the fat well in, then turn the dough on to a floured board and knead continually until it is a soft pliable paste that can be rolled out lightly without breaking. If, as you roll, the paste breaks and crumbles, it will require more kneading.

SHAPING SHORTBREAD

Roll the paste out lightly once, as you would short pastry, with a floured roller. Confectioners have round and square moulds for forming shortbread, but very much the same effect can be produced by placing a plate, dish or tin on the paste, according to the shape you wish to produce, and cutting round with a knife. After cutting, pinch the edges well all round with the thumb and first finger. Prick the centre of the shortbread well, so that it bakes evenly and does not rise at all in the middle, and then put it on buttered tins.

BAKING SHORTBREAD

Shortbread needs a very moderate oven; a quick oven dries up the butter and spoils the shortness. The oven must not be hot enough to brown shortbread; when done it should be a pale fawn biscuit colour. When shortbread is done it is quite soft; it only becomes crisp when cold. That is why beginners so often fail in the baking of shortbread, and over bake, expecting it to become crisp. Do not move the shortbread from the tins until it is quite cold; if moved when hot it is very liable to break. When cold, store in an airtight tin.

ECONOMICAL SHORTBREAD

Quantity	*Ingredients*
1 lb	flour
teaspoon	grated Lemon Rind
1/2 lb	Margarine
1/2 lb	White Sugar
pinch of Salt.	

Time: 30 to 45 minutes. Temperature: Gas, Electricity, 350° F.

Method

Warm the margarine slightly, put it in a bowl with the other Ingredients and knead thoroughly until it is a firm dough. Roll out on a floured board, cut into rounds, and bake in a slow oven to a pale golden brown.

RICH SHORTBREAD

Quantity	*Ingredients*
1 lb.	fine Pastry Flour
3oz	Rice-flour
1 lb	fresh Butter or unsalted Margarine
1/2 teaspoon	Salt
1/2 lb	Castor Sugar.

Time: about 45 minutes. Temperature: Gas, Electricity, 350° F.

Method

Sift together the flour, rice, sugar and salt and put them in a warm basin. Slightly warm the butter and rub it in. continue rubbing it in until it begins to bind, then turn on to a floured board and knead as you would bread until it is a soft, smooth, pliable dough,. Roll it out lightly and form it into the shape desired. Let it dry for one hour before baking, then bake on a buttered tin in a very moderate oven until it is a light biscuit colour. It will take three-quarters of an hour, or longer, if you are making a very thick cake.

LEARNING OUTCOME

Biscuits are very easy to make, and can be kept for some time in airtight tins. With a fruit cake and a store of biscuits, we can always feel prepared for the unexpected guests dropping in to tea. Most biscuits require a slow oven, as they need to cook well without getting too brown; if overcooked they lack flavour. Biscuit cutters in a variety of shapes can be bought for a few pence, and make the biscuits look far more attractive than just plain rounds.

Petits Fours is the name given to possibly the most popular of all fancy biscuits. They are made from a rich cake batter or an almond paste with flour or butter, and may be iced or glazed with coloured icing or garnished with crystallized fruits, angelica, almonds, etc. The making of shortbread needs some experience and a great deal of patience. The best shortbread is made without any moister except the butter, and that means that patient kneading is necessary to form the soft dough that is required. Cool hands are not necessary, as a warm hand facilities the forming of the dough. Shortbread needs a very moderate oven; a quick oven dries up the butter and spoils the shortness. The oven must not be hot enough to brown shortbread; when done it should be a pale fawn biscuit colour. When shortbread is done it is quite soft; it only becomes crisp when cold

QUESTIONS FOR DISCUSSION

1. Explain the term biscuits ?
2. Explain the term petit fours ?
3. Explainthe term short bread ?
4. Mention the procedure of shaping the short bread ?

KEY TERMS

* Biscuits
* Petit fours
* Short bread
* Crisp
* Shaping
* Moderate.

Chapter 38

Cake Icings and Fillings

After studying this chapter, the student must know :

- Introduction
- Decorating
- To use the syringe
- Different icing recipes
- Chocolate dipping
- Pastries, savoury and sweet
- Savoury fillings for choux buns.

CAKE ICINGS AND FILLINGS

There are many kinds of icings, cooked and uncooked. All are quite simple to make and to the number of fillings there is no end, as new varieties will constantly suggest themselves. You soon find that with a Genoese or ordinary sponge cake as a foundation you can make a hundred different kinds of fancy cakes, according to the flavouring and icing which you choose. One word about your Ingredients. See that they are of excellent quality the icing sugar fine and white, the eggs absolutely fresh. You may use cooking eggs for the actual cake, but it is essential to use new-laid ones for the icing as many are not cooked at all.

DECORATING

The fascinating work of decorating may be accomplished with an icing bag or syringe and some icing funnels. The syringe certainly is the easiest, as the bag needs some manipulation. Cotton bags may be bought, but a paper one answers very well. Take a piece of grease proof paper about a foot long and ten inches wide, cut it in two from end to end at opposite corners to form a triangle and fold it like a sugar loaf to a point. Cut a small piece off the point and drop in an icing funnel.

Three parts fill with icing, folding the top down to prevent it escaping that way and gently squeeze the icing through the tube. A whole icing set can now be bought very cheaply consisting of a revolving stand, a metal icing syringe and six funnels. There are about ferry different patterns in funnels, but about half a dozen will be sufficient for all ordinary purposes.

The funnel with the small round hole for writing names, greetings or forming narrow festoons or lattice work is most useful. The small round fluted hole answers the same purpose. The " rose" funnels have round serrated openings that form rosettes in various sizes. The straight flat openings, both plain and fancy, from which the icing comes out in a flat ribbon-like stream, are used to form garlands, bows and true lovers' knots.

TO USE THE SYRINGE

Take off the handle-end and fill it with the icing. Do not fill it too tightly or press the icing in, for if it is too full you will find it hard to work. Then selected the funnel you wish to use and screw it on to the other end. If royal icing is chosen it should be of the consistency of whipped cream. If it is too dry, and you find it difficult to work, add a little more beaten egg white. If, on the other hand, it runs out too easily and the patterns will not form well, it needs more sugar. You will soon get to know just the consistency required. First practice patterns on a boards or sheet of paper. Screw on the funnel with the small round hole and write some names or greetings. For the down strokes where the letter need to be thicker, pause slightly so that a little more icing comes out.

Now screw on a round rosette funnel and practice roles of various sizes. You must hold the syringe straight over where you want the pattern to appear, and not slanting as you would for writing. If you find it easier, the pattern you desire to make can be very lightly marked on the cake first. Icing is far easier than it looks, and as you work, new patterns will constantly be suggesting themselves to you. Piping is also done with butter icing or whipped cream.

TO ICE A CAKE

A cake should be made level at the top before it is iced and any rough edges removed with a sharp knife. Then turn the cake upside down and ice the bottom which will now be uppermost. The bottom of the cake is iced because the surface is more even. If almond icing is being used first, it should be left for twenty-four hours to dry before the royal icing is put on. A small revolving icing stand is a great help when icing, and it is quite inexpensive. If a cake, such as a wedding cake, is to be kept for some time. It is wise to give it a thin coating of lemon glace icing before the royal icing is put on, as this prevents the oil from the almond paste working through. Leave for a day, then put on a thin coating of royal icing; leave for twenty-four hours before covering it with the final coat. It should then be left until dry and firm before being decorated, and the surface should be as smooth as chine. This is only obtained by spreading the icing very evenly with a warm silver knife.

FROSTING ICEING

Ingredients used

a. **Fresh whipping cream**: Highly perishable item to butter when over whipped and separates if held too long, before serving most important fiction in making whipped cream its temperature, the cream should be whipped in a very cold bowl must remain cold during whipping and services. Although not a stable topping but taste wise it's the best.

b. **Pasteurized whipping cream**:- It has been proceeds to process his holding qualities similar like fresh cream.

c. **Dehydrated and frozen non dairy topping**:- They produces a very stable packing which have a good flavour replacement for whipped cream when temperature and time are a problem blended cold in a high speed mixture.

d. **Egg white**:- Act as a structure builder in cooked frosting. Its often used to achieve a texture desire in butter cream frosting. Primary ingredient for meringues. Its also mixed with powdered sugar in royal icing which is usely solely for decoration.

e. **Sugar**:- Sugar or some substance high in sugar is the basic in the all froasting- The principle sugar used in granulated sugar and powdered sugar and syrup. powder sugar is preferred in un cooked frosting. Granulated is used in the preparation of syrup for used in frosting like fudge type.

f. **Syrup**:- Bakers use simple syrup (equal amount of sugar and water) or blended syrup Glucose or invest sugar (blended sugar) are prepared for making cook frosting. These blended syrup prevent the formation of large hard crystal in the frosting. The amount of syrup a mixture can tolerate depends on the grinding of sugar and amount of fat in the frosting.. Too much syrup will obstruct the frosting for being hard.

g. **Liquid**:- Are necessary in froasting to make soft enough to spread. Most common liquid as in frosting are milk, water, coffee, various juices, flavouring and egg whites.

h. **Fat**:- Butter, margin and emulsifier short are all suitable for cream frosting But gives the best mouth feel. Emulsified shorting are more stable.

i. **Salt**: function of salt is only to enhance

j. **Colouring agent**: Approved artificial food coloured must be used preferable to used natural colour where possible soft pastel colours are the best rather than bright and loud colour

k. **Cream of tartor**:- This changes the chemical turn of sugar creating small crystal. This gives a creaming texture and act as a drying agent by forming a thin layer on the crust.

TYPE OF FROSTING AND TOPPINGS

1. **Whipped type frosting**:- Made from fresh whipping cream, pasteurized whipping cream and dehydrated or frozen non dairy topping to at maximum volume the cream should be handling cold and whipped quickly. The variety can be varied by addition of fruits flavouring coconut, spice and chocolate these addition are added after the topping has formed a peak.

2. **Fondant:-** Is a base for many things. Cooked sugar syrup compared of glucose compounds of granulated sugar and one pounds of water. Which has been cooked to 240 degree F between ball and hard ball stage. The cook texture is placed on a wet marble slab allow to cool. To approx. 110 degree F its worked with a bakers knife bringing the edges to the centre. This result in short even cooling preventing the outer edges becoming hard while forming the texture into constantly smooth creamy paste.

   Fondant is used both as a frosting and as an additive for other frosting- As a frosting fondant is used for frosting cake petit- four, coffee cake and other items. Its applied in semi liquid state which will set up into a shinny non-sticky coating.

3. **Butter cream**: Light and smooth mixture of butter or shortening with sugar or liquids. A balance of fat and sugar makes a good butter cream. Too much fat makes its greece its creamed enough to give a light fluffy product.

   Basic butter cream is a simple mixture of fat shortening or butter and sugar- Basic butter cream is often lightened by an addition of egg white a enriched with egg yolk.

   Meringue type butter cream are mixture of butter and meringue French butter cream are mixture are prepared by betting a boil syrup into beaten egg yolks and then whipping the mixture a light form. soft butter is them whipped to finished the frosting

4. **Pastry butter cream**:- are made by equal amount of butter and pastry cream powder sugar.

5. **Foam type frosting** are boiled frosting like meringue or marshmallow although gelatin is set them and hold there shape and they are not stable. This type of frosting is used when the product will be served in a short period of time.

6. **Fudge Type Froasting**:- Are heavy and rich mainly of them look and taste like candy they are stable frosting which hold there shape.

7. **Flat frosting:-** simple mixture of 5 pounds of powder sugar to 10 oz of water, 9 oz of com syrup and flavouring as desire. Use warm too ice coffee cake sweet rolls and danish pastry.

8. **Royal icing:-** Is a decorative frosting most from powder sugar egg white and cream of tartar. It has a creamy texture and is used to make decorative ornaments and other specialty cakes. This frosting is not eaten when dry its hard brittle.

Application of frosting and topping:- make the cake top uniform, spread uncooked frosting on cake room temperature. A cook frosting such as fondant may need to be warmed slightly before been applied to the cake thin frosting can be thicken by stirring in powdered sugar. Any frosting which is too thick can be thin by a gradually beating in few drops of water whipped toping are short lived so should be through chilled when topping are applied all frosting are remains well refrigerates but not frozen.

FOUNDATION ICINGS

Almond Icing (Cooked)

Quantity	*Ingredients*
3/4 lb.	ground Almonds

1 teaspoon	Lemon Juice
1 lb	best Icing Sugar
2	fresh Eggs.

Enough for a large Cake

Method

Roll the sugar until it is quite free from lumps, then rub it through a find wire sieve. Mix it well with the ground almonds and the lemon juice, turn it into a small saucepan into which has been poured about a dessertspoon of water, and stir in over gentle heat until it is a smooth mass. Take it off the fire, add the beaten egg, and stir it on the table until thoroughly mixed. Leave until nearly cold, then spread over the top of the cake or cakes with a hot knife, being careful to make it as smooth as possible. Leave in a warm place until it has set firmly. Then cover it with your royal icing.

Almond Icing (Uncooked)

Quantity	*Ingredients*
1 lb	ground Almonds
1 lb	best Icing Sugar or
1/2 lb	Icing sugar and
1/2 lb	fine Castor Sugar
1 tbs	Lemon Juice
1 dessertspoon	Orange flower Water or
1/2 teaspoon	flavouring Essence of any kind preferred
2 or 3	Eggs.

Method

This is the icing used under royal icing for birthday, wedding, Christmas and other rich cakes. Some people prefer the cooked variety as the texture is a little smoother. The success depends upon good kneading. Rub the icing sugar through a very fine sieve and mix the flavouring and lemon juice with it. Then gradually add enough whipped egg to form a soft dough. Knead well with the hand, as you would bread dipping the fingers in icing sugar occasionally. Whole eggs or whites only may be used, whichever is most convenient. Whether all icing sugar or half icing and half castor is used is a matter of taste. All icing sugar makes a firmer paste. To use this icing, spread it evenly on the cake, dipping the knife in hot water from time to time as necessary. If there is any difficulty in making the almond icing stick, brush the cake over with white of egg.

Royal Icing

Quantity	*Ingredients*
1 lb	Icing Sugar
1 dessertspoon	Lemon Juice
4 No.	Eggs

drop of liquid blue colouring if a very white icing is required.

Method

This is the firm icing suitable for rich cakes. It is also used for piping and all kinds of fancy decorations. It is important that the sugar should be rubbed through a very fine sieve until it is a fine as flour. The eggs must perfectly fresh. As they vary so much in size, the exact number needed cannot be given; but the icing should be a thick firm cream for coating and for piping it must be thin enough to flow easily through the icing syringe or bag. At the same time, it must be stiff enough to form and keep the patterns required. To make the icing, rub the sugar through a very fine sieve. If at all hard or lumpy, roll it first with a rolling pin, crushing out the lumps. Put it into a bowl, add the lemon juice and blue colouring, and mix well. Whip the white of egg and add it gradually, working it well all the time with a wooden spoon, then beat briskly until it is a perfectly smooth paste of the consistency you require. If your are not using your icing immediately, cover it with a damp cloth to prevent it hardening on the top. The clothe should be stretched tightly across, as the object is to prevent air entering.

BOILED ICINGS AND FROSTINGS

Boiled Icing Without Egg

Quantity	*Ingredients*
1/2 lb	Icing Sugar
1/4 pint	Water.

Time : 40 minutes. Temperature: moderate.

Method

This boiled icing is quite good and very quickly made, but not equal to the other variety. Put the sugar and water in a saucepan and stir over gentl heat until the sugar has dissolved. Then boil for four minutes without stirring. Pour it into a basin and beat with a wooden spoon until it is thick and white.

Boiled Chocolate Icing

Quantity	*Ingredients*
1/2 lb	Granulated Sugar
1/2 pint	cold Water
2 oz.	Unsweetened Chocolate
12drops	Vanilla or Almond Essence
1 No.	Egg.

Temperature 238° F.

Method

Break up the chocolate and melt it over hot water. Put the sugar and water into a saucepan. Stir over gentle heat until the sugar has dissolved, then boil steadily without stirring until the thermometer reaches 238° F. or it forms a very soft ball when a little is tested in cold water. Beat the egg white. When the syrup is ready, pour it in a slow stream on to the egg-white, then beat in the melted chocolate, and stir until smooth, creamy and evenly coloured. Finally, add the essence.

Boiled Icing or Frosting

Quantity	*Ingredients*
1 breakfast cup	Granulated Sugar
4 tablespoons	Water
1 teaspoon	Lemon Juice
1/2 teaspoon	Cream of Tartar
1	Egg white.

Method

Put the sugar and water into a saucepan and boil without stirring, until the syrup forms a thread when taken up on a skewer (240° F.). Add the lemon juice and bring to be boil again. Whip the white of egg until stiff, and then add the cream of tartar to it. Pour the syrup slowly on to the egg-white, and beat it well in. When white, thick and smooth, pour it gently on to the cake.

Coconut Frosting

This can be made by adding a ¼ lb. of grated coconut, or 2 oz. Of desiccatged coconut, to the above icing while it is hot.

Fluffy Frosting

Make this in the same way as boiled frosting, but use the white of two eggs instead of one, and beat briskly until the mixture is cold. Egg whites for this icing must be beaten until very stiff.

Fluffy Frosting (Chocolate)

Proceed as for " fluffy Frosting" recipe, but add 2 oz. Of melted plain chocolate during the beating.

Frosting For Buns

White of 1 Egg, Castor Sugar, Few drops of Vanilla.

Method

Whisk the egg-white until it is quite stiff, add enough castor sugar to make it as thick as cream. Add a few drops of vanilla. Brush the buns over with this when cold and leave in a warm place to dry. This quickly made frosting is excellent for all kinds of buns or small cakes.

VARIOUS BUTTER ICINGS

Butter Icing

Quantity	*Ingredients*
1/4 lb	fresh Butter or unsalted Margarine
6 oz	Icing Sugar

Vanilla flavouring.

Method

Beat the butter to a very soft cream. Rub the icing sugar through a fine sieve and mix it gradually with the butter. Add the flavouring, mix until evenly distributed. This icing can be flavoured in any way desired, also coloured; it is used either as a filling or as an icing. Keep it as cold as possible.

Chocolate Butter Icing

Break up 1½ oz. Unsweetened chocolate and dissolve it in a tablespoon of hot water. Beat smooth, cool, and when cold add it to the butter icing, working it in evenly.

Coffee Butter Icing

This is made by adding enough coffee essence or very strong coffee to the recipe for butter icing, to make it a pale fawn colour.

Fluffy Butter Icing

Quantity	*Ingredients*
2 oz	Butter or unsalted Margarine
1/4 lb	Castor Sugar
1 No.	Egg
12 drops	flavouring Essence or
1/4 teaspoon	Very finely grated orange or Lemon rind.

Method

Beat the butter and sugar to a soft cream with the flavouring. Beat the white of egg to a stiff froth. Stir it lightly into the butter until well mixed, and use.

Glace Icings

These are the shiny soft icings, almost transparent when only a thin coating is used. The chief point to member when making them is that the icing must not be made very hot. If it is, your iced cake will be dull and not possess that smooth satiny appearance which is so attractive. The icing sugar must be rubbed through a fine sieve, and the mixture when ready should be thick enough to form a thin coating on the back of a spoon. Be careful not to add too much liquid, as the icing will not be smooth or shiny if you have to thicken it with more sugar.

This icing is used for both large and small cakes; on very rich cakes, for weddings and other festivities, a coating is also put under the royal icing to give a smooth appearance. Gently pour the icing over large cakes, small ones should be placed on a wire sieve or tray and the icing poured over them with a spoon. Have a dish or plate underneath to catch any that falls through, as this can be used again. Tiny cakes can be dipped into the icing with a sweet fork or skewer, held for a moment to drain, and then placed on a sieve to dry.

Chocolate Glace Icing

Quantity	*Ingredients*
1/4 lb.	Icing Sugar
1/4 lb	plain Chocolate
1/4 teaspoon	Vanilla.

Method

Melt the chocolate over hot water; it quickens the process to grate it first. When melted, beat it with a wooden spoon to make sure there are no lumps. Stir in the sugar and vanilla and enough cold water to make a mixture like thin cream. Use when the sugar has quite dissolved and the icing is only just lukewarm.

Orange Or Lemon Glace Icing

Quantity	*Ingredients*
1/4 lb	Icing Sugar
1 tablespoon	Water
1 dessertspoon	Lemon Juice.

Method

See that the sugar is quite free from lumps, put it in a double saucepan with the liquids, and stir until the sugar has melted. Remember that it should be only just warm. Pour gently over the cake, or cakes. Make orange glace the same way, but use orange juice in place of both lemon juice and water. Tangerine orange juice gives a pleasant flavour. Strong coffee, or coffee extract diluted with water, in place of plain water and fruit juice, may be used,. With these and all other glace icings, success depends upon not over heating the mixture.

ICING A CAKE

1. ALMOND ICING:- When this icing is to be used, it is spread evenly on the top of the cake with a hot knife, as smoothly as possible. Sometimes the sides of a cake are almond iced also: for this, measure the circumference of the cake, then roll out a strip of the paste the length and width required. Turn the cake upon its side and roll it along the paste, pressing it lightly to make it adhere. Leave to dry for 24 hours.
2. ICING: A cake should be made level before it is iced and any rough edges removed with a sharp knife. If it is to be kept for some time before using, it is wise to give it a thin coating of lemon glace icing before the royal icing. Leave for a day and then put on a thin coating of royal icing. Leave another 24 hours before putting on the final coat. Spread the icing with a warm silver knife.
3. USING THE SYRINGE: A whole Icing set, consisting of a revolving stand, a metal icing syringe and six funnels can be bought very cheaply and this outfit will be found reasonably easy to manipulate. The bag and funnel method can be used if an outfit is not available, and although cotton bags can be bought a papper one will answer very well. Fold a triangle into a cone, nip off the point and drop in the icing funnel.
4. DECORATING: First practise patterns on a board or sheet of paper. Do not fill the icing bag too full, or you will find it hard to work. If royal icing is too dry, add a little more beaten egg white; if it runs too easily, It needs more sugar, Icing is far easier than. It looks and as you work, new patterns will constantly be suggesting themselves. Piping is also done with butter Icing or whipped cream.

PEPPERMINT GLACE ICING

Mix together 2 oz. Fine icing sugar, a good dessertspoon of cold water, twelve drops of lemon juice, twelve drops of peppermint essence, and proceed as previously directed.

UNCOOKED ICINGS

Chocolate Icing Made With Chocolate Powder

Quantity	*Ingredients*
2 oz.	Chocolate Powder
1/4 lb	Icing Sugar
2 tablespoons	warm Water

Vanilla or almond flavouring.

Method

Rub the icing sugar through a fine sieve. Put the chocolate powder in a basin with the water and stand it over a saucepan of very hot water. Stir until the powder has quite melted, then add the sugar gradually. Mix well and beat until smooth; to this add the flavouring.

Coconut Icing

Method

Mix together a tablespoon of cream with 6 oz. Of icing sugar that has been rubbed through a fine sieve; add 2 oz. Of fresh coconut cut in thin slices and a little whipped white of egg to bind it. It should be a thick paste.

Chocolate Coconut Icing

for this, add 2 oz. melted chocolate to the above and work it in until evenly tinted.

FILLINGS

Almond Butter Filling

Quantity	*Ingredients*
3oz	Ground Almonds
2oz	Plain Chocolate
2oz	Icing Sugar
1oz	Fresh Butter
1 No.	Egg.

Method

Well whisk the egg-white. Dissolve the butter. Rub the icing sugar through a fine sieve. See that the ground almonds are free from lumps. Mix well together the sugar and almonds. Melt the chocolate and add it, work it in evenly with a wooden spoon. Then add the butter, mix well with the whipped egg-white, and use. As a change from the chocolate flavour, use in its place a few drops of coffee essence, mixing it with the butter.

Apple Filling

Quantity	*Ingredients*
½ lb.	Cooking Apples
2 oz	Granulated Sugar
1 No.	Lemon
1 No.	yolk of egg.

Method

Peel, core and cut up the apples. Put them in a saucepan and cook very gently until quite soft, but be careful they do not stick or burn. Stir in the sugar and, when dissolved, take the pan off the heat, Add the juice and grated lemon rind, and the well whipped yolk of egg, and beat until quite smooth.

Banana Filling

Quantity	*Ingredients*
2 large or 3 small	Bananas
1	lemon or Orange
6oz.	Castor Sugar.

Method

Skin the bananas, remove the threads, and rub the fruit through a sieve. Add the strained juice of the lemon or orange and the yellow part of half the rind finely grated. Mix in the sugar and beat all together briskly for eight minutes.

Chocolate Cream Filling

Quantity	*Ingredients*
1/2 lb.	Icing Sugar
2 tablespoons	Cream

2 oz.	Plain Chocolate
6 drops	Vanilla.

Sift the sugar. Grate the chocolate and melt it in the oven or in a little stewpan. Add it to the sugar, also the vanilla essence and the whipped cream. Beat all well together.

CHOCOLATE DIPPING

For correct chocolate coating, chocolate co venture or best quality unsweetened chocolate and cocoa-butter must be used, allowing 1 oz. Of cocoa butter to every pound of couverture or unsweetened chocolate. You will need a saucepan and an enamel bowl that fits it closely so that no steam can escape. It is very important for successful dipping that no steam is in the room. A very dry atmosphere is essential, so do not try to dip in a damp atmosphere. Have all your centres ready before you start dipping. Never try dipping with a very small amount of chocolate as it will not keep a uniform temperature. Two pounds of couverture is a good quantity, though 1 lb. may be used. Any chocolate left over can be remelted and used, so there is not any waste.

Take the bowl from the saucepan, stand it in very cold water and stir the chocolate until it is cool and thick. If you use a thermometer it should register 82 to 84 F. Drop in the centres to be coated, one at a time, take out with a fork, let any superfluous chocolate drop off, and place on a perfectly dry marble slab. If the chocolate is the right temperature, it will set almost at once, and be shining and glossy in appearance. Continue dipping centres in this way, giving the chocolate a good stir between each dip.

It the mixture becomes too set and thick, place the pan in warm water again for a few minutes. Do not be disheartened if your chocolates are not perfect the first time you try to make them. Dipping needs practice—a business cannot be learned in an hour. But after a little experience you will learn to know how cool the chocolate should be. It is usually found that most beginners make the mistake of diping when the chocolate is too warm. It must be quite cool, or it will not be glossy when set and dull chocolates never look appetizing. Pack your chocolates in boxes when they are ready. They soon spoil if exposed to the air for any length of time.

Decorate the chocolates to match the centres. For instance, if the fondant is flavoured with rose-water, decorate each chocolate with a crystallized rose petal if flavoured with sweet violet essence put a violet on each one. Place a blanched almond on almond-flavoured fondant. Chocolates may also be decorated with an icing syringe, either with chocolate or fondant, made just liquid enough to work through the syringe easily. If when dry your chocolates are streaky or grey looking, they did not dry quickly enough. Do not attempt chocolate making on a very hot or very wet day.

Fancy shapes are made by beating the centre mixture until thick enough to form a shape, then force pieces through an icing syringe as you would icing when decorating cakes. Almost any kind of sweet can be chocolate coated. Here are a few suggestions, but as you work new ideas and combinations will occur to you. Almonds, brazil-nuts, pea-nuts, may be dipped as they are, or first covered with a coating of marzipan or fondant. Marzipan of different flavours is very good with a chocolate covering.

Fondants of very shape, colour and flavour are always popular. A very pretty chocolate is made if the cooked fondant is poured into rubber moulds left for a day to set well and then dipped into chocolate coating. When butterscotch, plain toffee and nut toffees are to be dipped, they should be set in very shallow tins, and marked in small squares. Caramels of all kinds, ginger cubes, glace pineapple, jellies, fruit pastes, nougat cut in squares walnuts in fondant, may all be dipped successfully.

LEARNING OUTCOME

There are many kinds of icings, cooked and uncooked. All are quite simple t5o make and to the number of fillings there is no end, as new varieties will constantly suggest themselves. You soon find that with a Genoese or ordinary sponge cake as a foundation you can make a hundred different kinds of fancy cakes, according to the flavouring and icing which you choose. One word about your Ingredients. The fascinating work of decorating may be accomplished with an icing bag or syringe and some icing funnels. The syringe certainly is the easiest, as the bag needs some manipulation. Cotton bags may be bought, but a paper one answers very well. Take a piece of grease proof paper about a foot long and ten inches wide, cut it in two from end to end at opposite corners to form a triangle and fold it like a sugar loaf to a point. Cut a small piece off the point and drop in an icing funnel. A cake should be made level at the top before it is iced and any rough edges removed with a sharp knife. Then turn the cake upside down and ice the bottom which will now be uppermost. The bottom of the cake is iced because the surface is more even. If almond icing is being used first, it should be left for twenty-four hours to dry before the royal icing is put on. A small revolving icing stand is a great help when icing, and it is quite inexpensive. For correct chocolate coating, chocolate co venture or best quality unsweetened chocolate and cocoa-butter must be used, allowing 1 oz. Of cocoa butter to every pound of couverture or unsweetened chocolate. Fondants of very shape, colour and flavour are always popular. A very pretty chocolate is made if the cooked fondant is poured into rubber moulds left for a day to set well and then dipped into chocolate coating

LESSON END ACTIVITY

- Go to the bakery shops and learn the different types of icings.
- Go to the bakery shops and learn the different ways to coat iceings on cakes.

QUESTIONS FOR DISCUSSION

1. What is cake icing?
2. Explain the procedure to use syringe.
3. Explain the procedure to ice a cake.

4. Explain the term frosting icings and what Ingredients are used in this ?
5. Explain the types of frosting and icings.
6. Mention the procedure of making fondants icings.
7. Explain the term chocolate dipping.

KEY TERMS

* Cocoa
* Dipping
* Fondant
* Frosting
* Fudge
* Funnels
* Iceings
* Sponge
* Whipped cream

Unit 7
KITCHEN MANAGEMENT

Chapter 39
Kitchen Designing

After studying this chapter, the student must know

- Introduction and meaning
- Kitchen layout and types
- Computer based kitchen layout design
- Steps in designing kitchen
- Kitchen layout and functions
- Equipment purchased guide lines
- Budget and time line
- Investment and space requirement
- Energy usage
- Equipment and energy
- Managing energy consumption
- Heating system and air conditioning
- HVAC equipment maintenance
- Special requirements
- Kitchen layouts.

KITCHEN DESIGNING

Commercial kitchen reflects the nature of the business in which one is involved. Kitchen is planned and designed as per the food offered by restaurants, cafeteria or hotels. Commercial kitchen should be built under the guidance of an architect and great importance should be given to the safety and security of the kitchen. Commercial kitchen should be carefully planed and designed as it is one of the most important parts that have to be perfect in each and every segment or it can leave one on the back foot from the very beginning. First important thing is that a kitchen should be built with proper ventilation and as per the codes of hospitality industry. Its design and construction should be meeting the health and safety norms.

The areas of the commercial kitchen where there is scope of smoke and steam should have sufficient ventilation. It not only ensures that one follows health and safety regulations but it also increase the productivity of the kitchen staff. Kitchen staff will be getting a better environment where they can stay cool and sweat free. This kitchen should have fire extinguishers because these kitchens are susceptible to accidents due to fire and smoke. Serious thought and planning should be undertaken while designing and constructing the commercial kitchen. The type of food offered is the key factor that helps in the designing of the commercial kitchen. Commercial kitchen should be installed with the equipment that will be helpful in preparing the food and the costly equipment should be avoided which barely get used. One should avoid installing the flashy cooking equipment if only simple food are been offered.

The commercial kitchen is a busy place where it has to handle orders of various customers at the peak hours of lunch and dinners, so there should be enough space for the waiters and waitresses to move around and meet the orders of the customers without creating any mess of the kitchen. The commercial kitchen should not be installed with stunning and elegant high tech gadgets instead it should be simple and efficient. For example slippery floor should be avoided in the kitchen as it can cause threat to the kitchen personnel. One should install quality equipment in the kitchen as it can cost in the long run and hamper the business prospect.

Providing comfortable and quality equipment to the kitchen personnel ensures smooth functioning of the kitchen work and also ensures safety to the kitchen staff. One should judiciously use the internet and e-books to find cost effective solution to enhance the design of the commercial kitchen, which will also result in the productivity of the hospitality business.

Here are some incredibly useful tips on commercial kitchen design, to make an arduous process a little more straightforward.

Start by sitting down and thinking about the kind of kitchen you're going to create. Whether you're serving top notch quality food or running a simple cafeteria, your commercial kitchen designs should reflect its purpose.

Now you know exactly what the purpose of your kitchen is, jot down the things you'll need in your commercial kitchen to make sure it runs smoothly. Only write down things you absolutely need to start off with and then consider whether you have the money and space to incorporate these things. Many commercial kitchen designs are doomed to failure before they even start because of improper planning. Don't fall into this trap, do your homework and enjoy the benefits later on down the road.

The next thing is to ensure that you have all the relevant papers completed. These include all of the health and safety issues that you'll have to conform with. If you're unsure, contact your local council for advice. They'll be able to divert you to the relevant people who can help you get everything sorted.

When you're ready to start actually investing in your kitchen, be sensible about the things you buy. It's so easy to spend huge amounts of money on the most high tech gadgets that look stunning but ask yourself, do you really need them? It's much better to have a simple, efficient kitchen and this can often be achieved with more standard equipment.

On the other side of the coin, don't be cheap with your kitchen appliances as it can cost you in the long run. If the people working in there don't have the right tools to do a good job, it can cost you in profits later on. Often its better to spend a little bit more to get things done quicker, so think about every appliance you put into your kitchen.

You'll also want to dedicate a decent amount of time towards deciding where you want everything positioned. For example, if you need dedicated service areas, then it's important you leave enough space for people to comfortably move around. Too many people complete their commercial kitchen design without planning for enough service space. This costs them later on when busy services grind their kitchen to a halt. The same principle needs to be applied to washing up areas. This is an excellent example of the kind of decision you'll have to make. Dishwashers can create a massive amount of steam so you need the washing up area to have plenty of ventilation. Again, these are things that most people don't take into consideration which is an awful mistake. The fundamental advice when it comes to commercial kitchen design is to think about every little detail and when you've done that think about the consequences. There are so many things that can trip you up and it's just not worth taking the risk

MEANING

Kitchen Design is all About Your Bottom-line.

With the high cost of rent, utilities, labor, construction and equipment purchases; it is necessary to have a good kitchen design that is functional and efficient. Mistakes made in the layout, design and equipment purchases can be extremely costly, hamper operations and the ability to effectively produce a quality meal. This guide can get you started in the right direction. If you would like more assistance; we offer a variety of design services that will help put more dollars back in your pocket.

Kitchen layout types

The efficiency of your kitchen can depend more on how it's laid out than the amount of space you have. When you begin your plan it's a good idea to think about the natural workflows between the primary activity areas: Oven, preparation area and food storage area. Read below to find out the five basic layout shapes that will provide a practical kitchen. Each layout type includes a black line symbolizing the working triangle, which helps to illustrate movement between each of the primary activity areas. To find out more about the working triangle, visit the section on ergonomics.

The single line kitchen

This is a smart and simple solution for narrow rooms, ideally with one wall over three yards long without windows or doors. However, this shape of kitchen causes the longest journey distances since you often have to walk from one end of the room to the other. Therefore, it can be a good idea to situate the sink in the middle of the line, with adequate space separating it from the cook-tops.

The galley kitchen

This shape offers the most efficient use of space, making it the choice of many professional chefs. The two rows allows room for lots of preparation space, and moving between activity areas can be as easy as turning around. However, this shape is not ideal if the corridor is open at both ends, as it can cause traffic congestion. Make sure there is enough room for opposite drawers to be open at the same time (at least 1.3yds). Another important consideration is to keep the cleaning and cooking areas on the same side in order to minimize the risk of accidents while moving hot pans between the sink and cook-top.

The L-shape kitchen

This is a very popular kitchen layout - ideal for a family kitchen or for entertaining guests as it can easily accommodate table and chairs in the same room. Using two adjacent walls, the kitchen also benefits from lack of through-traffic. The sink, stove and fridge should be separated by a preparation area.

The U-shape kitchen

Using three full walls of a room can offer the perfect working kitchen. The fridge, cooktop and sink can be spaced out for total efficiency and convenience. This is great news for those of you who take your cooking seriously, as it provides the best workflows with the shortest distances around the kitchen. This shape also allows for large amounts of worktop and storage space.

The Island kitchen

A very popular kitchen type, the island layout is perfect if you plan to entertain. An independent island unit can face a dining or living area, allowing the cook to socialize while preparing. A sink here provides the optimal arrangement in terms of the kitchen's working triangle. Otherwise, cook-tops with a canopy over the island can form a stunning focal point to the kitchen.

Computer based Kitchen Layout Design

The basic assumption in developing the kitchen layout design tool was that there exists common operational features in the kitchens of same type and same cooking process. To utilise these common features it is necessary to examine and divide these features into smaller parts and form a default data library. The basic menu offerings, serving times, size and number of portions and necessary sections with sufficient space requirements are all characteristics of the kitchen type. The process type, in turn, determines the space and equipment requirements for the facility. In the beginning of the kitchen design process the designer defines kitchen type and process type as an input. The layout design tool utilises the default data library and gives preliminary information regarding the type of menu, number of meals to produce in a day divided to different serving periods and size of portions. All default data library values are alterable if needed. In that way it is possible to specify preliminary values to get more detailed information. The menu serves as the source of information for the various food items to be prepared. The menu will guide the further design process. Default data libraries will facilitate developing the menu and also facilitates assessing the impacts of menu. After editing the library values characteristic to the kitchen and process type, the layout design application produces a list of cooking equipment required and performs preliminary space dimensioning. Equipment requirements will be determined from a complete analysis of typical menu. For each food item on the menu, information regarding anticipated number of portions to be prepared, portion sizes, main Ingredients, and the process to be performed are indicated. The total time that the equipment will

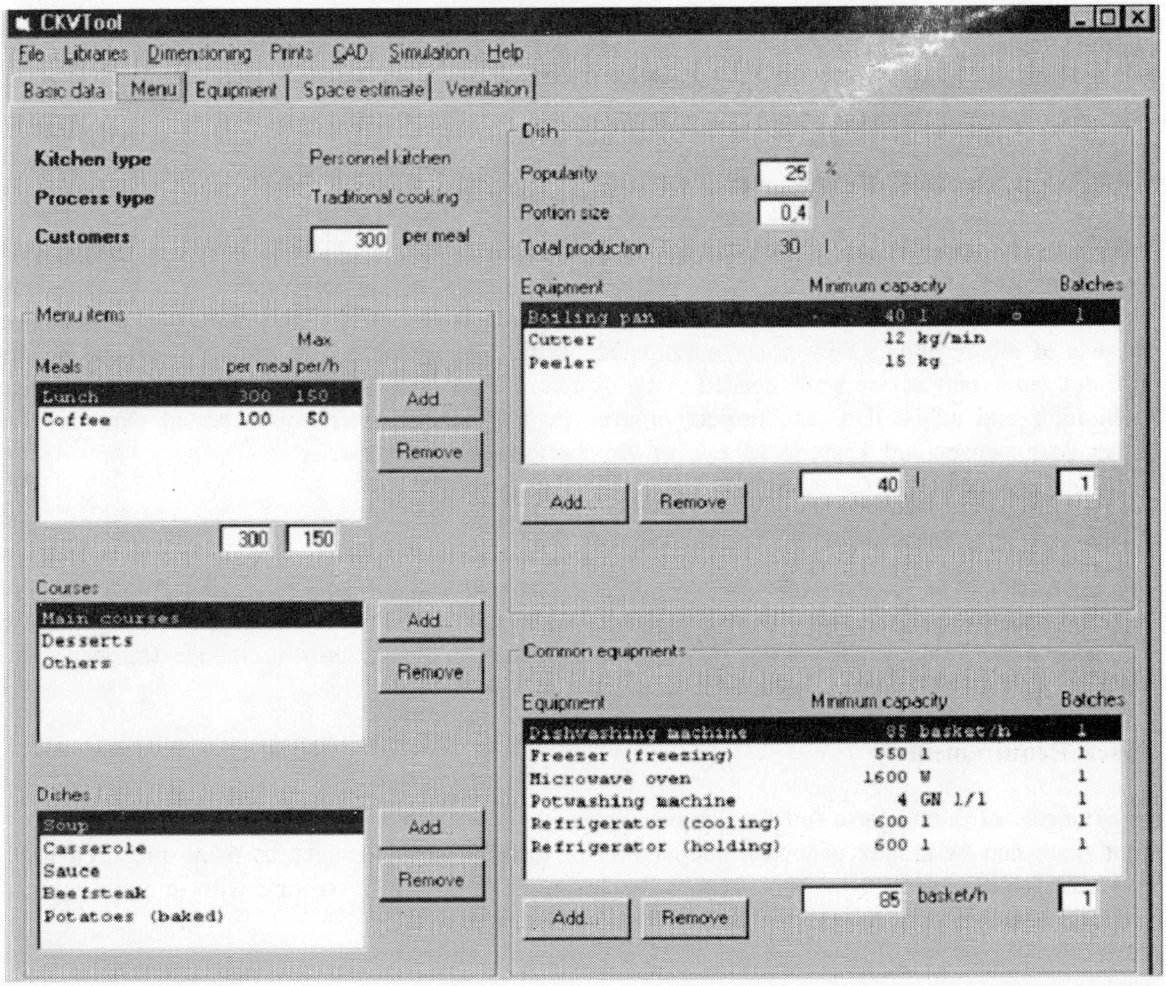

be used for each process is evaluated. After this is done for each process, the equipment usage is evaluated and final equipment capacity will be determined by the system. At this point in the design process, it may be found desirable to add, delete, or change some of the menu items or processing methods in order to achieve greater equipment utilisation. The preliminary space dimensioning includes room estimates for all functional areas, such as receiving, storage, preparation, cooking, and dish-washing, that are required to produce the menu items. The space required for each functional area of the facility is dependent upon many factors. The factors involved include the number of meals to be prepared, the functions and tasks to be performed, the equipment requirements and the suitable space for traffic and movement. Preliminary space dimensioning is also performed by the system in order to facilitate the layout designers detailed operational and workplace design. Accurate space dimensioning will be performed by the layout designer when the functions and tasks have been evaluated and grouping of equipment, including auxiliary equipment and material, tool and utensils storages, needed toper form the desired task has been done. To facilitate configuration and visualisation of the layout, the system utilises a general data library (3D-models of equipment) and as the final product of layout design process user will gain 3D-modelled layout solution. The 3D-model of the facility is valuable when visualising (Fig. 39.4) the layout solution to the owner or user of the facility. In addition, the 3D-model will be employed by auxiliary design solutions. For example, as an input data of building or kitchen geometry for energy- and simulation tools.

Establish a Realistic Budget and Timeline

There is an endless list of details that need to be taken into consideration on any commercial kitchen project. Needless to say; many entrepreneurs drastically underestimate their budgets and the work involved. It is common to find projects running out of money and months over schedule because of all the things they never anticipated. Avoid guesswork, pay attention to all the details and seek out expert advice when needed. After you have a good working budget you should continue to monitor and adjust it as the project progresses. Pay careful attention to actual expenses vs. projected expenses and keeping an eye on the bottom-line.

Invest Wisely

Remember your kitchen is the engine of your business and the goal is to take your restaurant on a long and successful ride. To help ensure your success you need the engine to be designed for optimal performance. Investing the time and money in the back-of-the-house (kitchen) will increase your overall performance and financial rewards over the years.

Space Requirements

The rule of thumb for a full service restaurant is aprox. 5'sq/ft of kitchen space for every seat. That space can be greater or smaller depending on several variables such as using prepared food, take out service and the type of restaurant. For example, a 60 seat restaurant with minimal takeout service, would require aprox. 300 sq/ft of usable kitchen space.

Energy Usage

Restaurants spend as much as 30% of their overhead costs on utility bills. A good kitchen design needs to be energy efficient to help reduce cooking, heating and cooling cost. The biggest and most common problems are found in the HVAC / hood system.

Steps in designing Kitchen

STEP I - It All Starts with The Menu

A common problem is building the kitchen first then designing the menu after. The menu needs to be established first and then the kitchen design should meet the specific needs. By starting with the menu and deciding just what you want your kitchen to be capable of producing, you will save on unnecessary expenses and labor.

STEP II - From Menu to Floor Plan

After you have your menu decided on, you need to focus on the kitchen layout and design. There are many important reasons why you want to take the time to develop a functional and effective kitchen design, before you begin work. First, you will need to decide whether you're going to use a professional designer, or try to do-it-yourself. Either way, it is vital that you're informed on the elements of good kitchen design.

STEP III - Seek-out Expert Advice

Whether you choose to do-it-yourself or use a designer; you will need reliable information to make smart and informed decisions. So do your homework. The more you know, the less likely you will foolishly or naively waste money. Working with a designer be careful in choosing a commercial kitchen designer, because choosing a designer is like choosing someone to manage your financial investments. Understand that the major part of your business start-up cost will most likely be spent in the kitchen. The goal is to achieve the best results for the money that you're investing. Typically, commercial kitchen designers are either an equipment salesperson, or an architect. However, they may or may not actually know how to design an efficient and functional kitchen. Either way, don't be influenced by a fancy/ professional looking blueprints or CAD drawings. Before you begin, ask about their experience in commercial kitchen design and ask for references from completed projects. Then hit the streets and visit the restaurants they designed. Talk to the chefs, cooks and wait staff. See for yourself how well the kitchen functions and ask the owner if the kitchen meets his needs and expectations. Below is a list of "Symptoms of Poor Design" you can use when checking references.

Step IV - Design Fees

Equipment salesmen will typically provide a free "footprint" or equipment layout, while architects' are known to charge fairly large fees that are based on the scope of the project and/or a percentage of the projects cost. It is important to understand what support services are included in the design work;

- Site Evaluation - Survey for potential problems, energy sourcing, capabilities and limitations.

- HVAC/Hood Design
- Kitchen and/or dining room floor plans
- Equipment layout - make sure the designer is knowledgeable on functionality to help save on energy and labor cost
- Detailed CAD Drawings
- Itemized equipment schedules
- Power loads /requirements
- Equipment cut-sheets - detail the specs on the equipment for proper installation
- Product comparisons
- Itemized budgets - which you can use in acquiring financing
- Blueprint and Mechanical drawings

Do-it Your-Self

Many restaurant owners are the "do-it-your-self" type and that's OK if you know what you're doing and don't do a patch-job. Too often restaurateurs cut corners to save on expenses and end up; *tripping over Rules to pick-up pennies.* Use this design guide to help avoid many common problems and costly mistakes.

Symptoms of Poor Design

If your restaurant's kitchen is already operational and experiencing any of these problems you may want to consider modifying your kitchen design to increase profits. Are you experiencing:

- High utility bills
- Higher then normal labor cost
- Slow or uneven food production
- Poor ventilation
- Bottle-necking or employees tripping over each other
- Disorganization
- Unsanitary conditions
- Unhappy kitchen staff
- Excessive heat or humidity
- Low profit margins
- Customer complaints.

STEP V - Attention to Details

Designing a commercial kitchen takes pre-planning and attention to details. Whether you are working with a designer or doing it yourself, these are some of the important issues that you should be considering:

- Budget and time restrictions.
- Cost effectiveness - original investment and the cost of operating, as related to projected income.
- Menu - What kind of equipment is needed?
- Style of Service
- Seating capacity – How much food?
- Turnover rates – How fast?
- Take-out, banquets or catering services
- Labor force – usage and flow
- Designated areas for the various kitchen functions (see list)
- Site considerations or limitations
- Available power supplies
- Inventory management - receiving, storage, security, usage
- HVAC - (heating, ventilation, air-conditioning)
- Energy efficiency - (Equipment and Energy)
- Codes and Regulations - building, sanitation, health and safety
- Flexibility for expansion and/or revisions.

Kitchen Layout and Function Traffic Patterns and Work-stations

The goal is to create smooth traffic patterns and clearly defined workstations that do not overlap. Employees' paths should not cross. To help achieve this fundamental goal, study the layout and use a marker to trace traffic patterns of specific kitchen jobs. Also, use the list below to establish designated areas and workstations in the kitchen and a smooth interaction between them. For example; a waitress with dirty dishes should not cross paths with waitresses delivering food. It is essential to create two doors to the kitchen; one for traffic "IN" the other for traffic "OUT". Where is the food picked-up and where are the dirty dishes dropped off. These paths/employees should not overlap or cross. The layout begins with dividing the kitchen into the following specific areas and workstations:

- Receiving Inventory
- Cold and Dry Storage
- Food Preparation
- Cooking Line
- Holding Area
- Waitress Pick-up
- Clean-up
- Garbage

- Recycling
- Employee Break Area

Equipment Purchases New Equipment

- Quality Used
- Refurbished
- Leasing Arrangements

It's important to get the best product for the best value that meets your specific needs.

Equipment

Is a big investment and each purchase will continue to effect your bottom-line over the years. So don't just look at the price tag, you need to also consider the all of the following;

- Quality - Life Expectancy
- What is it capable of doing and what is it limited on doing.
- Optional accessories and their cost
- Required Labor
- Energy Consumption
- Maintenance Cost
- Repair and/or replacement parts (filters, belts, accessories)
- Freight Charges
- Delivery and Installation Fees
- Manufacturers' Warranty

Quality vs. Pricing

If your budget is really tight, always ask if there's a cheaper alternative. As with any purchase you make, you need to be clear with your salesman if you're most concerned with quality or pricing. Also, consider buying quality used equipment. It may be wiser to buy a high-end used piece, rather then a cheap new piece. For example: Stainless steel shelving or worktables have an unlimited life expectancy, while galvanized units will last only 6+ years. However, shelving also varies by how much weight it can hold. Many big box discount stores are offering stainless steel units for less money, but they can't hold the same weight as more expensive commercial grade shelving.

Buyer Beware

Always compare your quotes and get the all the details in writing. Usually if there is a big difference in the pricing on a quote between dealers, you're probably not comparing graphs to graphs. There may be a difference in the quality of the product, hidden charges, or any of the above mentioned variables. Unfortunately, there are some less then reputable dealers who will deliberately substitute a cheaper product(s), believing the buyer won't know the difference. Make sure you are comparing Merlot Graphs.

Affordable Options

- Quality used or refurbished equipment that is built to last; can save you from 30% to 50% or more.
- Leasing new equipment to reduce out of pocket expenses. It often requires little or no down payment and low monthly fees. Ice Machines are a common piece that are easily leased.

Shipping and Delivery

Always check for possible hidden fees like added fees for freight, delivery or installation. Commercial kitchen equipment can require several men or special equipment to move. Therefore know the terms of delivery and inquire about any additional cost.

Terms of Delivery - Equipment Quotes or Invoices Should Specify

- Is the freight included in the purchase price?
- If the freight is included, then is it to your door or the dealers warehouse?
- Is there a delivery fee from the warehouse to the restaurant?
- Will the equipment be delivered to your door or will it be brought inside and set-in-place?
- Is set-up or installation included?
- If modifications are needed to the electric, gas or the site, who is responsible?
- Who is responsible for any damages? (Some freight companies refuse to be responsible for damages and don't provide insurance against it)

Damages/Wrong Item

Always thoroughly check every delivery for damages and verify that it is exactly what you ordered. Open each box. Refuse to accept damage goods/wrong item. If you accept the delivery of a damaged shipment or the wrong item, there is no compensation. If possible take a picture of the damage for your records, before letting them take it away.

Additional Expenses and Considerations

When developing a realistic budget and timeline for your commercial kitchen project make sure you consider the following:

- Fees and permits
- Electric, plumbing or gas-line modifications

- Delivery charges - Double check all quotes to verify if delivery or installation is included.
- Installation of equipment and materials
- Wall Coverings- Cooking lines require fire rated material. Always check local codes.

Choose from:

- Board (not recommended behind or near heat producing equipment)
- Ceramic Tile
- Stainless Steel Panels - glued or screwed to walls
- Durable/washable paint
- Non-skid floors and matting to prevent accidents Choose a product that is easy to clean, durable/commercial grade and resilient to water, grease, and acid.
- Proper lighting that is energy efficient and doesn't add to the heat in the kitchen.
- Hood systems for ventilation and make-up air
- Fire suppression system
- Food preparation equipment and worktables
- Shelving and storage - always check weight capacities of units
- Ceilings - should be easy to clean, tolerance to high levels of humidity, and firer ate do sheet-rock/plastero drop ceilings that are fire ratedo FRP lined ceiling tiles (durable and washable)
- Security - to prevent /reduce employee theft

Equipment and Energy

Ice Machines

- Refrigeration
- Dishwashers
- Cooking
- HVAC

Introduction

Energy Efficiency is Critical to Your Profitability

It is estimated that 1/2 of your total energy bill is related to refrigeration, food preparation and cooking. Furthermore, as the cost of energy continues to go up, profits margins continue to go down. In response, we have outlined some need-to-know information and strategies that can help you lower your utility bills by 30% or more. Better yet, many of these ideas require little or no real financial investment. Remember, even small changes in the way you manage your energy usage can make a big difference in your bills.

Need-to-Know Information and Strategies

Ice Machines

- Air Cooled
- Water Cooled
- Remote Air Cooled
- Ice Machines are energy guzzlers.
- Don't buy a unit that produces more ice then you need.
- Locate Ice-Machines in cooler areas away from anything that produces heat.
- If a unit is located outside, keep it out of the sun or build a sun screen/shelter. This can cut-operating cost by 50%.
- Investing in energy efficient units.

There are three types of Ice Machines:

1. **Least Efficient**: **Air Cooled** = Uses the MOST energy. 5.4-22.5 kW per/100lbs of ice.
2. **Semi Efficient:** : **Water Cooled** = More efficient then air cooled.
3. **Most Efficient:** Remote Air-Cooled = Condensers transfer, the heat generated by ice production to outside the building. Plus they are less noisy.

Refrigeration

- Walk-ins
- Reach-ins
- Display Cases

You Can Cut Energy Cost by 30% with Proper Maintenance

- Locate refrigeration away from any heat producing equipment, in a well-ventilated area.
- Refrigeration units should be 4" from the wall, to allow for proper airflow.
- The unit should be level both; front to back, and side-to-side.
- Clean coils and filters regularly.
- Maintain proper airflow to coils, condensers/evaporators.
- Check door seals and replace worn or leaky seals.
- Check evaporators for frost. Ice build-up over 1/4 inch robs energy.
- Set defrost cycles for off peak hours.
- In dry climates set the "Energy Miser" switch. This turns off the auto heaters used to defrost.
- Load and unload fridge/freezers quickly.
- Load new inventory quickly before it has a chance to warm.

- Let heated items cool before loading.
- Let frozen items defrost in the refrigerator.
- Install strip curtains to walk-ins.
- Monitor temperatures: Follow the recommended food safety guidelines, but don't over-chill and waste money.
- Monitor humidity: Refrigeration efficiency is achieved with humidity levels between 40-55%.
- Check for unusual noise or vibration, it may indicate a decrease in the performance of the compressors/motors.

Cooking Equipment Options • Selection • Cooking Methods

- Microwaves are the most energy efficient means to heat or thaw a product.
- Ovens, fryers, steamers are more efficient then range-tops, griddles and broilers.
- Pressure cookers can save up to 66% on energy cost, because they cook at a higher temperature and the cooking is completed faster.
- Convection ovens are 23% more energy efficient then conventional ovens.
- Cooking with lids can save 8%-10% on energy.
- Idle fryers should be lowered or shut down.
- Turn off any other idle or back-up equipment during slow downs. (Example turn off an idle broiler just one hour a day more, can save Rs, 1,5000 annually.)
- Use a steamer whenever possible, it is the most energy efficient.
- Limit pre-heat time on steam tables, grills, and broilers to 10-15 minutes.
- Pre-heat most griddles just 6 minutes and turn off un-used sections. Cook food close together and cover items to reduce heat lose.

Dishwashers

- Low Flow Nozzles
- Booster Heaters
- Chemical Disinfectants
- Maintenance.

Hot Water = 17% of your total energy bill (on average). The good new is, you can drastically reduce this expense by 50% or more with these easy steps.

Solution 1 - Install an inexpensive high velocity - "low-flow" valve into the nozzle of the pre-rinse sprayer. You can save hundreds of rupees per year on your energy bill, as well as cut your water bill in half, by using 50% less hot water. Technology has made some great improvements in recent years on low-flow nozzles that include:

- Greater water pressure (80 lb/psi). That's more power to help get the job done.
- Automatic shut-off value at the hose head. Water is only supplied when needed.

Solution 2 - Install a natural gas heater to your dishwasher. A bigger investment, but it can save 50% or more on your hot water bills and save on costly disinfectant chemicals.

- Most health codes require either rinsing in 180'+ or adding a chemical disinfectant.
- Chemicals can save on energy cost, but have added expenses, require longer drying time and can leave spotting on dishes and glasses.
- A natural heaters is attached to the dishwasher and heats just the required water to the necessary temperature for the Rinse Cycle.
- With the addition of a natural heater, the primary hot water heater can be maintained at a much lower temperature, saving as much as 60% on the cost of heating water and reduce the risk of scalding.
- Natural heaters are low maintenance and have no element to burn out.
- Natural heaters are best suited for larger restaurants that consume lots of hot water to run the dishwasher. Ask about a simple "Cost-Benefit Analysis" to determine if a investment into a booster heater can help you save on your energy bills.
- Turn-off booster heaters at night and when not in use. More **Ways to Save**
- Vent dishwasher heat and humidity out of the kitchen to avoid added burden on air-conditioners.
- Check thermostats for accuracy and program proper water temperatures for each cycle; 140' wash, 160' power rinse, 180' final rinse. Save by not heating water hotter then needed.
- Check water cycles to make sure the water shuts off after the tray goes through.
- Run with full loads only.
- Replace dishwashers older then 10 years with more energy efficient models that require a lot less water and save up-to Rs 1 lakh annually.

HVAC - Hood Systems

- Heating
- Cooling
- Kitchen Ventilation
- Make-up Air
- Air Balancing

Understanding HVAC

HVAC systems consist of; heating, ventilation and air conditioning. The goal is to balance the airflow between these systems to reduce energy consumption. The problem is difficult to manage and understand because you can't see it (except on your energy bills). However, we will try to simplify the issues, as it is very common to find even the most experienced restaurateurs with a ineffective Hood or HVAC System. More importantly, this common problem can cost plenty.

The Three Basics Rules

1. The front-of-house and back-of-house require separate heating and cooling systems, but need to operate together in harmony, not independently.
2. Air that is exhausted through the hood systems and exhaust fans must be replaced with an equal amount of **make-up air** from another source. The goal is to establish the source for make-up air and then manage it. Make-up air should be vented in from the outdoors and tempered when it goes below 40' in the winter
3. A poorly designed or inappropriate HVAC/Hood system will result in higher energy bills, as your profits are literally being sucked out the hood.

Symptoms of an Inefficient Hood System

- Your hoods don't collect all the smoke and steam in your kitchen.
- There is excessive heat in the kitchen and your cooks complain.
- Your dining area has stale, stuffy or unpleasant odors or smells like grease.
- Your exterior doors are difficult to open, a vacuum effect.
- Or outside air rushes in when the front door opens.
- You have excessive or unexplainable utility bills.

Exhaust Fans and Hoods Systems Managing Energy Consumption

Exhaust systems can be your biggest energy hogs. When exhaust fans are not used efficiently they can pull too much conditioned air (heated or cooled) out of the building.

- Exhaust fans need to be started before cooking begins, but also should be turned off at night or when they are not needed.
- Group all heat producing equipment together, under the hood system.
- Hood systems should be 6" longer on each side then the cooking line. Example; 6' cooking line requires a 7" hood.
- Establish a source for "make-up air". You may need to install a system to prevent drawing air from your dining area, that you paid to heat or cool.
- Upgrade to a variable-speed exhaust fan. They're more efficient, useless energy and provide for greater flexibility in managing your exhaust and air flow. Turn-up or down depending on need.
- Rest-room exhaust fans can be connected to light switches, reducing unnecessary loss of conditioned air.
- Dishwashers should have a dedicated exhaust fan and/or hood to remove humidity and heat from the kitchen.

- An easy and cost-effective strategy is to install side panels to an existing canopy hood. This will improve its' performance by minimizing the effects of drafts. Side panels help capture cooking vapours even while reducing the total exhaust rate.
- Designate and train an employee in the kitchen to manage the airflow; to adjust fan speeds as needed, and to turn down or off any idle heat producing equipment.

  CAUTION: Exhaust hoods capture and remove excess heat, smoke, odors, carbon monoxide and grease. It is essential to keep hoods free of grease build-up, the filters clean and the fans operating properly to prevent fires or CO_2 poisoning in gas powered-kitchens.

Heating Systems and Air-conditioning

- Install Energy Star programmable thermostats to automatically control the building's heating and cooling. These should be secure either in a remote location or locked to prevent tampering.
- Small changes in the thermostats result in big changes on the bill. Every additional degree of heating or cooling increase energy use by 4% - 5%. (Cooling a dining area to 73' instead of 76" uses 12% to 15% more energy, during summer months.)
- Turn off or turn back systems (to avoid freezing) when the building is unoccupied. This can save 1/3 of the energy used by these systems.
- Recommended settings for unoccupied buildings: 50% winter and 90% summer.
- Recommended settings for occupied buildings: 68% winter and 74%-76% summer.
- Add a vestibule to your front door; it will drastically reduce the energy for heating and cooling. Notice that most chain restaurants utilize a vestibule to reduce/ manage their energy cost.

HVAC Equipment Maintenance Achieve optimal performance and reduce energy usage with regular maintenance

- Clean or replace air and grease filters regularly.
- Check refrigerant levels regularly.
- Check refrigerant filters/strainers.
- Keep coils free from dirt and dust. This can reduce energy by 25% and prevent early compressor failure. (an expensive repair.)
- Check belts: tighten as needed, replace cracked belts.
- Straighten coil fans with a condenser coil comb.
- Shade outside units from sunlight.

Size Really Matters When Buying a Stainless Steel Sink

Every part of the house is important. Most of the time people are very busy thinking on how they can improve every corner of their house. And kitchen as part of the house, you would like to make it more pleasing to the eye because there are many important chores that you are doing in the kitchen. Of courser you have to keep the kitchen clean because this is the place where you handle and process foods. Of course everybody wants to have the best kitchen and when it comes to the kitchen, kitchen sink will be on the top of the list. There are times that you are stressful in picking the right kitchen sink for your kitchen. Sometimes you prefer to stay for your kitchen sink for as long as you can still use it. But when time comes that your kitchen does not work anymore, well this is the time that you have to switch to the one that will last and easy to maintain. But in choosing the right one you have to consider the right type, the right style and of course the one that is right for your needs. With regards to the kitchen sink you can switch to the stainless steel sink. If you have not tried using a stainless steel sink, well it is time to use it and for sure you will not regret it. It is always good to consider using this sink because it can provide you the things that you want in for your kitchen sink. Whether you buy it on-line or directly to the store what is important is that you have to consider the size of the kitchen that you need. If you have a lot of chore using the sink it is highly recommended that you have to avail a stainless steel sink which has a bigger size that is appropriate with the chore that you are doing. You have to be sure with the size of the stainless steel sink that you are purchasing because if the sink is too big for the space or too small for it you have to do some kitchen remodeling project. This is why it is always important that you have to be specific with the size of the sink that you are buying. It maybe hard for you to find the right size of the sink that you need for your kitchen, but you have to be positive in finding the stainless steel sink that you are looking for. You have to remember that in remodeling your kitchen it I always important that you have to check on the size of kitchen sink that you are going to buy. Of course when it comes to kitchen sink it is better to use the stainless steel sink because it plays a big role for your kitchen and pretty much cost-effective and durable.

Kitchen Wall Clocks

Aside from the accessories and utensils directly related to preparing, and or enjoying food, the wall clock may be the most important piece that you find in a kitchen. Since the purpose of the kitchen is very directly food related, you don't find a lot of unrelated items in the space. However a wall clock is a piece which can be both decorative and functional, and so it is often included in this space any ways.

Decorative Considerations

Wall clocks are hung up high on a wall, and as such are very visible, and tend to dominate the decorative tone of the room. Wall clocks are available in a wide variety of shapes, sizes, colours, and patterns and you can even get custom printed wall clocks to hang in your kitchen. There are also wall clocks available in materials that will match the appliances in your kitchen, such a stainless steel, or brushed copper. Digital wall clocks are sometimes easier to use, but analog clocks are the classic look for this space. You can decide based on the ambiance you are trying to create. The most common colours used in kitchen accessories are warm earth tones including browns, reds, and amber colours. Steal, stone, and brick are some common material colours.

Durability Considerations

Kitchens tend to get very hot. Do not purchase a wall clock for this space which is delicate, or which can warp, distort, or change under high heat pressures. Kitchens are also messy. Make sure that your clock is made from something which is easy to clean such as slate, stainless steal, or glass. You should also be aware as to whether acidic foods such as pasta sauces or juices will cause chemical stains in the clock.

Functional Considerations

Wall clocks are hung in kitchens because they are useful. They help you set the tempo of your work, and keep track of how long things have been cooking. You should purchase a clock which is large enough to easily glance at and get the time. Some wall clocks have alarms, but only purchase these if you plan on hanging the piece somewhere where it will be easy to reach, and turn off. A wall clock can be a wonderful addition to your kitchen, which can provide both useful function, and decorative attraction. Sitting high on the wall, it can cast your choice of effective ambiance over the space. It can also be used with smaller backup alarm clocks or egg timers, which will work in conjunction to give you a more precise measure of several different timeliness.

A GUIDE TO KITCHEN BINS

The kitchen is a busy place and you need a number of practical solutions to help you cope with your kitchen waste efficiently. Kitchen bins play an important role in kitchens, they have to be appealing, stylish and usable as well. Kitchen bins should be made up of the best quality materials and should have a hard covering that should protect it from being spoiled or breaking and that makes it look good which adds in beauty to the kitchen as well. There is a variety available in kitchen bins, push and pedal bins and more. Recycling is made easier with the application of two separate inner bins giving flexibility to make your recycle job easy. Some people just can't help putting their foot in it. However, this waste box is different. Some company bins are very durable The Pedal Bin 30L made up of steel features a double hinge construction and smart closing rim to give a virtually noiseless closure. The pedal bins feature a close fit top for odour prevention and is just designed for easy cleaning with a smooth mechanism. There is also plastic protective rim to prevent damage to the floor. It has made from fire resistant material and matel steel and fitted with the non-sip base. While cooking or cleaning out the mess in the kitchen, one gets sick of getting rid of the trash and walking all the way out to dispose it off. Which is the major reason for people switching over to kitchen Waste Bins inside the kitchen, because it is just perfect and convenient for people to dump the organic waste or the left over's in the bin while working or cleaning up the mess than and there only. Buying a kitchen bin might not be as easy as it sounds as there are a lot of on-line retailers selling who have a wide variety of all types of bins. For that you need to search for the best bin that fits in your budget as well as also is stylish that adds in beauty to your kitchen.

Kitchen equipment

Kitchen equipment can be conveniently grouped into five categories; storage-, preparation-, cooking, accessory and service equipment. Restaurant planners are advised to study all equipment available, manufacturer, source, and compatibility with local standards in force. Storage equipment consists of industrial food-grade shelving. It may be wire or solid. Wire shelving is appropriate for canned goods or boxes, solid shelving is required in refrigerators and freezers. They are easy to clean. All shelving must be arranged appropriately to facilitate adequate air circulation. There are upright, chest, and walk-in freezers. Chest freezers preserve cold air but utilize more floor space, whereas upright freezes use less floor space but allow cold air to escape rapidly each time the door is opened. Walk-in freezers are recommended for operations using considerable amounts of frozen foods. Freezers can be purchased prefabricated, modular, or be custom -made. In every walk-in installation, care should be taken to position the freezer to open into a refrigerator in order to preserve at least part of the cold air, which inevitably escapes each time the door is opened. (Cold air costs three times as much as warm air). There are standard- or blast freezers for quick freezing of vegetables or plated food. Cryogenic freezers use liquid nitrogen or carbon dioxide and freeze fast. They are recommended for hospitals and institutions feeding large numbers of people at set times

Refrigerators

Refrigerators prevent bacterial growth and prolong the shelf life of perishable foods. There are electricity or gas fuelled, reach-in, roll-in, drawer and walk-in refrigerators. Electricity powered refrigerators are the most common.

Reach-in and walk-in refrigerators are readily available in a variety of sizes and configurations. Walk-in refrigerators can be specified modular or custom made. Drawer and roll-in refrigerators are practical and save labour but must be custom manufactured and expensive. All commercial refrigerators must be equipped with thermostats both inside and out. Interiors of all must be easy to reach, clean, and well lit. Walk-in refrigerators must have non-slip floors and equipped to open from inside and outside. All doors must be airtight and equipped with self-closing mechanisms to minimize cold air loss.

A well-designed compressor maintenance programme will help prolong usable life. Wooden storage shelving is not recommended. Tempering refrigerators to re-thermalize plated frozen food is practical in hospital and correctional institutions.

PREPARATION EQUIPMENT

Constitute all equipment employed in food preparation (chopping, dicing, cubing, peeling, slicing, mixing, processing). They speed up all these functions, reduce labour, facilitate quality control and promote consistency. Specify sturdy brands, backed up by a good supply of spare parts, warranties, guarantees and service. Foreign suppliers should be specified only if local manufacturers are inadequate or do not exist.

COOKING EQUIPMENT

All equipment used in cooking fall under this category, and may be fuelled by electricity, propane, natural gas, oil, wood, or steam . The fuel must be selected with due care according to availability and style of cooking being envisaged. Steam generators are available, so are cooking equipment with self steam generating installations. Always specify cooking equipment with the least number of moving parts.

The following cooking equipment is standard:

Ranges:

-Hot top

- Open burners

Deep fryers: electric or gas

Broilers: ceramic brickets

Radiant

Infra-red

Open

Salamanders: (top heat)

Electric

Infra-red

Gas.

STEAM FUELLED EQUIPMENT

Steam jacketed kettles- Floor, counter top, tilting or non-tilting, with or without spout in various sizes are available.

Pressure steamers are suitable for quantity batch cooking. Combi-ovens combine steaming and roasting, and are popular due to their space saving features.

Ovens – A wide range of ovens is available. They can be under ranges, freestanding, electric or gas, steam injected or not. Convection ovens are practical for roasting and rotate hot air speeding up cooking time. Conveyor type ovens are appropriate in high volume pizza operations or in very busy bakeries. Micro wave ovens are used mostly for re-thermalizing.

Griddles – Consist of a stainless steel non-stick surface fuelled either by gas or electricity, equipped with appropriate grooves and grease collectors. They are versatile and very much in demand in short order kitchens and cafeterias.

Tilting Frying Pans- May be gas or electric fuelled. They are practical in large banquet halls or hotel banquet kitchens catering to huge banquets.

Accessories – Electronic thermostats, energy load levellers (reduce peak electricity demand) and automatic shut off switches fall under this category. Service equipment – helps keep prepared foods hot. Steam tables, flambé carts, gueridons, coffee machines, small wares (pots, pans, whips, scoops) self levelling plate dispensers, dishwashers, compactors, filtering devices fall into this category.

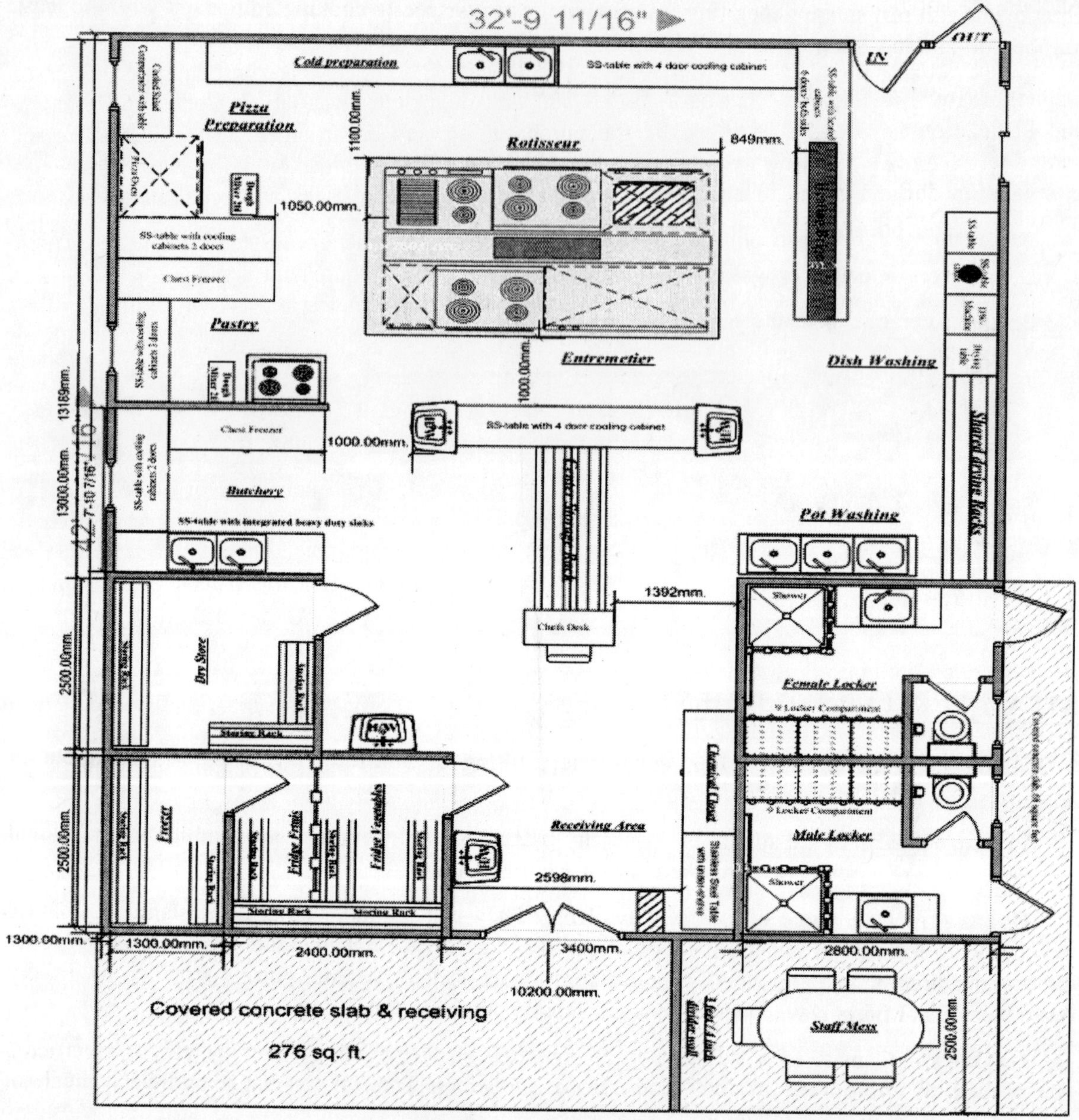

Fig 40.2 Kitchen layout

Once the equipment selection is completed, and the layout determined, the planner must contact utilities and advise them to ensure timely hook up to main supply lines. Floor space dedicated to kettles must be furnished with splash-guards and drainage There is a wide range of manufacturers of kitchen equipment and the planner must carefully specify before making purchase decisions. Equipment is sold by dealers, distributors, jobbers, manufacturer's agents, or directly by the manufacturer pending on the size of the order or the size.

In most cases local or regional restaurant and hotel supply companies are best equipped to serve. Dealers quote F O B (Free On Board) prices and do not include installation. Both transportation and installation have to be arranged by the purchaser or may be arranged by the dealer for an additional charge. If cooking or service equipment is purchased abroad, it is important to check specification and standards to ensure that they comply with local rules and regulations.

Equipment selection and purchasing require due attention to detail, cost and quality. Planners must be knowledgeable, spend time and effort to ensure that all equipment arrives in good order, and is installed to be approved by appropriate government departments and comply with all rules and regulations

LEARNING OUTCOME

Commercial kitchen reflects the nature of the business in which one is involved. Kitchen is planned and designed as per the food offered by restaurants, cafeteria or hotels. Commercial kitchen should be built under the guidance of an architect and great importance should be given to the safety and security of the kitchen. Commercial kitchen should be carefully planed and designed as it is one of the most important parts that have to be perfect in each and every segment or it can leave one on the back foot from the very beginning. The commercial kitchen is a busy place where it has to handle orders of various customers at the peak hours of lunch and dinners, so there should be enough space for the waiters and waitresses to move around and meet the orders of the customers without creating any mess of the kitchen. The efficiency of your kitchen can depend more on how it's laid out than the amount of space you have. When you begin your plan it's a good idea to think about the natural workflows between the primary activity areas: Oven, preparation area and food storage area. Read below to find out the five basic layout shapes that will provide a practical kitchen. Each layout type includes a black line symbolizing the working triangle, which helps to illustrate movement between each of the primary activity areas. To find out more about the working triangle, visit the section on ergonomics. The basic assumption in developing the kitchen layout design tool was that there exists common operational features in the kitchens of same type and same cooking process. To utilise these common features it is necessary to examine and divide these features into smaller parts and form a default data library. The basic menu offerings, serving times, size and number of portions and necessary sections with sufficient space requirements are all characteristics of the kitchen type. The goal is to create smooth traffic patterns and clearly defined workstations that do not overlap. Employees' paths should not cross. To help achieve this fundamental goal, study the layout and use a marker to **trace traffic patterns** of specific kitchen jobs. The kitchen is a busy place and you need a number of practical solutions to help you cope with your kitchen waste efficiently. Kitchen bins play an important role in kitchens, they have to be appealing, stylish and usable as well. Kitchen bins should be made up of the best quality materials and should have a hard covering that should protect it from being spoiled or breaking and that makes it look good which adds in beauty to the kitchen as well. Kitchen equipment can be conveniently grouped into five categories; storage-, preparation-, cooking-, accessory- and service equipment. Restaurant planners are advised to study all equipment available, manufacturer, source, and compatibility with local standards in force.

LESSON END ACTIVITY

- Collect the layout of different commercial kitchen.
- Collect the layout of different commercial kitchen equipments.
- Make a layout of 100 rooms hotels property in which you have to draw a banquet kitchen set (party approx 1000 pax average)

QUESTIONS FOR DISCUSSION

1. Explain the term kitchen designing.
2. Why kitchen designing is important.
3. Explain the different types of kitchen layouts.
4. Explain the computer based Kitchen designing.
5. Explain the different steps in kitchen designing.
6. What are the symptoms of poor kitchen designing.
7. When developing a realistic budget and timeline for your commercial kitchen project make sure you consider which points.
8. Explain the HVAC hood system.
9. Explain the basic rules of HVAC.
10. Explain the procedure of HVAC equipment maintenance.
11. What are the guides to kitchen basin while setup a commercial kitchen.
12. Categorization of kitchen equipment while designing the kitchen and discuss the various standard for different equipments while set up a commercial kitchen.

KEY TERMS

- Cocoa
- Fondant
- Fudge
- Iceings
- Whipped cream
- Dipping.
- Frosting
- Funnels
- Sponge

Chapter 40

Menu Planning and Material Management

After studying this chapter, the student must know

- Introductions
- Types of menus
- Most important aspect of a planning a menu
- Food production control
- Material forecasting
- Culinary skills to minimized wastage
- Recycling used oil
- Material management
- Seven steps to food cost control
- Purchase procedure – perishable and non-perishable
- Receiving and storing of food
- Method of store accounts
- Computerization material management system.

MENU PLANNING

After Food Service the key focal point of restaurant is the menu or bill of fare. It's the number one aspect of food service sales men—A printer communication which can condition the customer to order more building the cheque higher than he probably intended. A Menu is describing as your calling card introducing your product and representing your image.

The main purpose of menu is to present a list of offerings to the customer in an intending manner giving a description of delicacy. A menu should be written in a interesting style which would automatically stimulate sale. Remember your menu is your best advertisement. It's read by 100 of dinners every and value of its obvious.

Type of menus: - Under Three heads

1. **A'la carte.** :—From the card for this menu, every dish is separately price and the price is charged for each course of order. One of the problem of such a menu unless the guest is a gourmet he may well end up ordering a combination of dishes which don't complement each other. Nevertheless an a 'la carte menu generally most profitable. The portion size of this is also larger.
2. **Table'd' hote or table of the host**. It also knows prix-firce (Fixed Priced) Menu because the price is fixed for a complete meal soup /salad main course and dessert.

   A small choice of two or three is offer for three each course. A table d' hote menu provide a restaurant with ample opportunity. Provide a balance meal. The problem are smaller than there a'la carte menu.
3. **Special menu:** These are fixed price menu than straight banquets, formal dinner, wedding parties or any other function. The main difference with prefix menu is that are far more elaborate. The Price varies with a type and number of dishes.

   A gastronomically correct menu is complicated time consuming involve many fundamental and technical aspect and is difficult to compile it's important to :—

   - **Balance Flavour:** Strong Flavour Ingredients are must be balance with more mellow ones, for example, a strongly flavoured meat must be accomplied with a mild sauce.
   - **Vary Texture:-** Other with meal will become monotonous, for example, a meal ladle with cream:- cream soup, cream delicacy or entrée accompanied by a cream sauce and creamy desserts will only be like by the toothless. The menu will not have any thing to buy into chew or crunch.
   - **Colour Contrast:-** To provide visual substitution to serve dish in similar colour in profusion show that the chef has a limited in imaginative capacity, for example, Kasha zhinga put never be served before or all together with murgh labadar because both are dry semi dry predominately tomato base dish.
   - **Provide balance nutrition**:- Carbohydrates most be balance with protein and mineral. A profusion or starches food: potato, rice, corn etc. without an equal number of non carbohydrate food make the menu nutritionally unbalanced.
   - **Provide Variety**: - A menu must not list many dishes of same meat and vegetable even it prepared in a different way.
   - **Vary Garnish**:- Every coarse must a difference garnish, for example, if asparagus has to be served with fish than soup precite should never be cream of asparagus not a soup served without an asparagus with garnish.
   - **Vary Cooking Method:-** Offering dishes cooked by difference method can add a whole new dimension to the menu. A menu which offers only grilled items are only poached item is lightly considered mundane boring.

- **Be seasonal**:- Cold storage and frozen Ingredients are certain to the unappetizing, for example, its will be ridicules' fish in summer. Just as it would be ridicules' ignore cauliflower and peas in summer Again the thick and nourishing soup will be ideal in winter menu. Just as thin or cold soup would be better in summer month.
- **Check out clientele**:- It is important to make a market survey of the area in the of the vicinity of the hotel. This should include the economic and social back ground local taste and competition, for example, an expensive French menu in a middle class area is only recipe for disaster.
- **Take not of your requirement:-** A menu must be compactable with the capability of kitchen equipment, for example, if the menu feature number of grilled items and the grilled in kitchen is very small sizes, it will very difficult to handle a load efficiently, not only the quality but the service as well.

In the case of the table d' hote menu care has to be taken for compiling a menu:

1. Do not being a meal fruity starter, if you want to finish a meal with fruits compote and fruit dessert
2. Don't end the meal with a rich fruit dessert, if the main course itself very heavy.
3. Ones the menu has been complied its ready for printing
4. The quality of printing menu as important as the delicacy on it.

The most important aspects are :

1. **Copy**: All things considerable good copy sale a restaurant. It's important to right clear and comprehensive description of the delicacy it would absorb to be pretense by giving French name to non French dishes. It would be even worse to translate imagine bone funne actually beautifully lady.
2. **Printing**: It is important to choose best paper or folder and then get a menu at a good press. It is best to print a small number of menu. The two major important are :

A) **Can changed frequently**: Any change on price on account of inflation and can be incorporation without loss to establishment. It must be remember that on one hand printing is expensive therefore it is difficult to throw away large number of menu. On the other hand prices corrected with a pan or little strips on paper looks terrible.

B) **Design**: A good layout and artistic but clearly readable typists can help to draw the deacon attention and add much the restaurant reputation.

FOOD PRODUCTION CONTROL

Maintaining control and system at the time of purchasing receiving storing and issuing will not be enough not profitable unless appropriate control is establish on food production in the kitchen. The chef been in charge of the kitchen is responsible for all goods received and should make the best use of them There are various method of keeping control on the production of food and increase the margin of profit the most important are:

1. **Portion control:** - This is one way of maintaining the food cost it mean determines the size whether it volume, weight or otherwise - of each item - one the standard size should be standardized there should be no deviation on it. Any deviation from the standard portion would result either in excess or shortage of food production also it's important that all production and services staff should been familiar with predetermined standard this should be done through training session demonstration of portion sizes and manner of presenting a particular delicacy on plate.
2. **Standard recipes:** - A recipes specifically prepared for use in a particular hotel is called a standard recipe.

   It's prepared to indicate the list of the ingredients and there quantities and method of preparation weight size of a portion and cost per portion. An item prepared for a standard recipes would insure control on the use of Ingredients and at the sometime provide greater consistency in taste on the other hand a basic recipe is one which gives general guidelines on the preparation of an item and is not intended for any particular kitchen.
3. **Quantity approach**: - Another method of production control involves controlling quantity rather than the cost. This is not necessary an adequate measure-because the cost an item depends on the quantity of ingredients uses and price of each ingredients. Therefore, even if correct quantities are used high prices of ingredients may result in high food cost. However in certain circumstance where consumption of food in physical terms is composed with the sale, the application of the quantity at approach would aid in controlling the production For example the sale of tea and coffee can be controlled by comparing it with the total consumption of raw material.
4. **Food Check analysis:** - This method involves a breakdown of issue of food from the kitchen. Its complied from the kitchen order ticket (KOT) receives in exchange of dishes. At the end of the day summary of the dishes serve is prepared. The outlet which is gone for computerization a complete print out give the summary of the dishes sold of the day. The summery complied highlights the most popular item on the menu which could be retained while planning a new menu. The number of portion left unsold plus the items sold should recognized with the plan yield from the quantity of raw material. Use in there preparation If difference is significant there is suitable cause of investigation for ex say 20 chicken has been order from the store for preparation of tandoori chicken. Half a chicken has been set as a portion. If according to the food check analysis the portion sold are 32 than there must be chicken in balance.
5. **Food Cost Analysis**:- This is a widely use method in the hotel in a industry the food items are grouped under different heads for ex meat. Would include mutton or, steak other heads will include poultry, fish, vegetable broccolis etc. Having analysis the total expenditure on food, each group is expressed in terms of % either on total food cost or on total food sales for ex chicken is budget at 14 % of the sales, at the end of the week / month it increases to 16% it would been necessary to find out the reason for 2% increases. This could be the because the combination of the following.

   a. A low selling prices

   b. Poor handling during preparation during cooking

c. Purchase of poor quality, raw material

d. And inflation influences rise in the price of raw material.

6. **Volume forecasting**: - This technique involves correlating the production of food with the anticipated number of covers and gestiminating (estimated by guest) customer preference naturally this kind of estimates is not easy. It proper sales history showing each menu item and the number of portion sold over a fixed period on time is maintained it would help in determining the number of portion of each item to be cooked every day. Volume forecasting should be ensure that near be exact the quantity of food is keeping wastage to the minimum this would also enable the purchase department to order the correct quantity of raw material.

The production process

Before it is sold, food in restaurants goes through following production process;

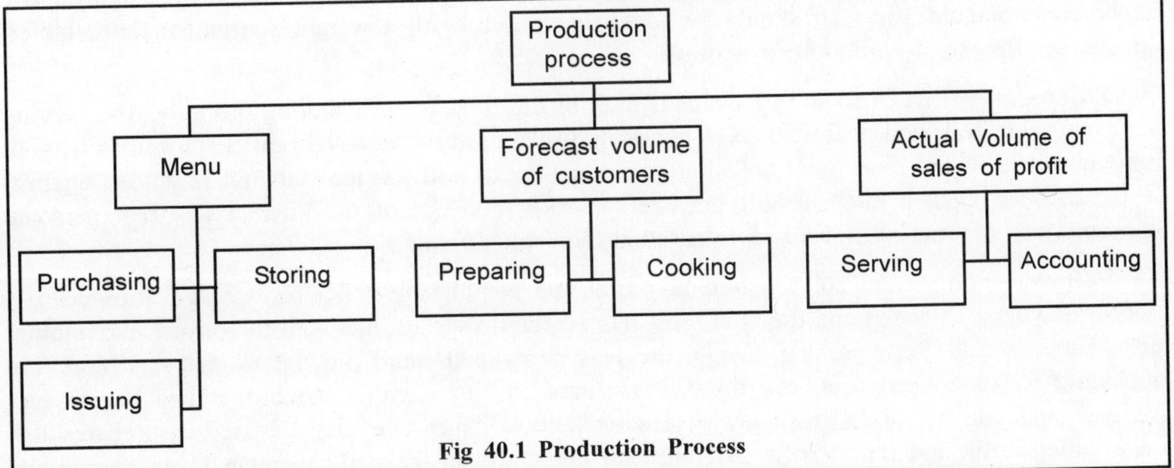

Fig 40.1 Production Process

Each stage of this process requires careful management. The right food must be purchased in the right quality and quantizes. It has been cooked prepared and cooked correctly using the right recipe and method of cooking and it must be right sized portions, presented in the proper way (as shown in figure). Finally we must check that the correctly amount of money has been received for the numbers of portion sold.

Material forecasting: - In order to arrive at the total cost of any one meal it's necessary to analysis the total cost incurred in the production. The total cost consists of three main elements.

1. Material (Food Cost)
2. Labour
3. Overheads.

Its common practice to express each element as the percentage of selling price:

The selling price of a product includes the cost element + the net profit in other words Selling price = food cost + labour + overheads + Net profit. From this equation it follows that

Food Cost = Selling price. – Labour - Overhead - net profit.

To deduces the selling price the cost of the material element in the same total of food production, stock of consume food in the kitchen must be taken into account. The period of accounting may be daily weekly or monthly depending on the size of the hotel the closing stock of one period becomes the opening stock of succeeding one:-

The cost of material is equal to opening stock + Good received - Closing stock.

Culinary Skills: - An item badly cooked burned or over fatted over spiced hard lumpy chewed or over cooked would lead to waste or reduction in yield further a well cooked item. If not slice carved or portion properly would also effect the food cost therefore only a well trained cooked should be allowed to make a dish. The positioning of an item should be done by a skillful and experienced person. The staff should be adequate provide with a weight equipment tools, ladles, spoons scoops etc. To minimized wastage

Pilferage: - Theft of food may occur if pick of the food is not handling properly. The serving staff may obtained food against a KOT check and then collects money from the customer without producing a cash voucher. Such collision between kitchen and service staff not is graded against. It is not done even a kitchen staff may eat or take food out of the kitchen for their personal consumption. A strict vigilances is required to control pilferage.

Leftover food:- Food not consume at buffet and banquet meat not be wastage. Provide it is not to the vogue of degerating the chef must has availability to use his skill to convert into another dish. He may add fresh garnish change the platter make it more piquant or make it more eye appealing for ex-cooked meat can minced and used in pieces cutlet hamburger and kebabs etc- Meat chunks can be mixed fresh gravy or sauces cook fishes can may be used to prepares fish cake cutlet, kofta and for cooking. All this can be future on the daily menu with an appropriate name.

RECYCLING USED OIL FROM THE COMMERCIAL KITCHEN

Oil waste disposal is no longer the problem it once was, thanks to developing energy technologies. It is now possible to convert many used oils into biodiesel fuel—a renewable source of energy derived from vegetable oil. For this reason, "yellow grease" collected from fryers and grease recovery devices have become a valuable commodity.

Many grease collectors, non-profit organizations and biodiesel companies are more than happy to haul away oil waste from grease recovery devices or give restaurants and other food service businesses free bins for depositing their spent fryer oil. These companies do not usually charge fees, and often they will even pay you for the oil waste.

If you have the opportunity to recycle your oil, do so. Here are a few reasons to convert used oil into biodiesel:

- **Earn money.** As fossil fuel costs rise, so does the value of reusable oil waste. Many companies will pay you for your fats, oil and grease (FOG) waste.
- **Minimize waste.** Befouls help the environment by keeping an otherwise wasted commodity out of landfills.
- **Reduce air pollution**. Burning biofuels produces fewer airborne pollutants than burning petroleum-based energy products.
- **Help the economy**. Selling your oil to nearby biofuel producers supports your local economy and decreases your region's dependency on outside sources of fuel.
- **Fill Up and Save Money**
- **To start saving energy**, evaluate your business needs and see what changes you can make to take advantage of the latest developments in energy technology.
- **Use biodiesel fuel in place of petroleum-diesel fuel**. Biodiesel fuel costs less per gallon and can be used without making any modifications to your diesel engines. Various communities around the country are already using locally-produced biodiesel fuels for their public vehicles, such as garbage trucks and buses.

Consider using fryer-oil fuel. Running your vehicles and commercial equipment directly off of used fryer oil has become a viable option with the latest conversion kits. They do require an investment, but the payback period can be surprisingly short

What If My Waste Oil Is Dark Brown?

Oil waste from fryers and automatic grease recovery devices is almost always usable and easy to convert. Low-grade "brown grease" removed from passive grease traps can often be converted, too, although it is more difficult. If you are worried about the usability of your oil waste, look for a company that will haul and convert brown grease.

MATERIAL MANAGEMENTS

Raw material account for 20 to 30% of the cost of food production more and more sophisticated method and techniques are know been develop to manage raw material, efficient material management improves the profitability and rate return of investment considered for example a hotel with a turnover of Rs l0 crore who raw material consumption 4 crore or 40% and net profit is Rs 1 crore or 10%. If the management decide to improve the profitability by 3% or Rs 30 Lakh over a period of time, when two avenues are open to it are.

1. Increase sales by Rs. 42 lakh of which Rs. 12 lakh be the additional raw material component.
2. Reduce the cost of raw material by 3% which would mean the cost of raw material consumption would 3..7 crore or 37%.

Increasing sales required additional marketing and advertising great effort time and expects on the other hand steps. Taken to save on material cost with the existing structure will have to improve profitability without any additional expense, the most appropriate material management system in the hotel industry should be designed to ensure the following.

1. Control over receipts, issue or purchase and stock level.
2. Analysis of consumption
3. Indenting of purchase
4. Re order levels.

If the hotel has gone is computerization follow a on line system which also update all the related repurcussption (reaction) it maintain the over all records of each and every item in the master file and incorporate features like total receipts, issues, reorder levels, physical verification of stock complete blue print for any item from the master file. Current status purchase order. Variance in the item and spoilage which has be written off.

Purchasing:- The successful operation of any business depends to a large extend on the availability of good or raw materials. The right quantity at the right time from right source and at right price.

In todays context purchasing is a much broader concept and include an wide range of activities such as market research, more development vendor rating. Import substitution, follow up, evolving proper system standardization selective control prepurchase value analysis, purchase budget, lean time analysis, price forecasting, indent control, negotiation surplus, disposal, inventory control negotiators. surplus disposal, inventory management, transportation and coordination with other department.

The purchase manager is responsible for the entire purchase of the unit, therefore he must have good knowledge of merchandise source and supply if available description and the items of price, both whole sale and retail.

Seven Steps to Food Cost Control

1. **ORDERING** - The first step is to order right. Having detailed recipes, designing purchasing specifications, doing comparative shopping based on those specifications, and comparing quality, price and service, etc. Oh yes, don't order too early in order to avoid spoilage, wasted storage space and lost interest on your money. Don't order too late, so premium costs and delivery charges accrue. I remember being told standing orders were a bad habit.
2. **RECEIVING** - The fundamentals are obvious: count; weigh; inspect for condition and quality; verify against the purchase order; keep the receiving area clean and uncluttered; limit access to the receiving area; train the person receiving and make him or her responsible. Get credit memos from the delivery driver.
3. **STORING** - Is the method and place of storage for the various items appropriate for the item? Is it secure from pilferage? Are the shelves strong enough for the product, allow air circulation and easy to clean? Are all items stored at a temperature appropriate for that product? Are items dated (with year, in some cases) and priced? Is the storage area orderly and clean? Should shelves be labeled and maybe even stocking quantities noted?
4. **ISSUING** - What is issuing based on? Who has access and or authority to issue or take things from the secured store rooms and walk-ins? Are issues being made in appropriate quantities and at appropriate times? Is there a relationship to volume or reasonable par

stocks? Are issues being accounted for? Is a perpetual inventory or sign out sheet designed specifically for your operation or a particular store room in use?

5. **PREPARATION** - I'm not so clear about the details here any more because it has been a long time since I worked in a kitchen regularly. Phrases that come to mind include: trim properly; use trimmings for stock pots and other recipes. Proper tools, sharp knives, clean and neat working area, enforcing a policy of following recipes, and having photos of finished products available and used regularly are also critical.
6. **COOKING** - Various considerations here, again my readers know more than I. Proper temperatures, proper cooking times, following recipes carefully, using photographs of finished products, correct size, material, and type of utensils and cookware, clean work area.
7. **SERVING** - Serving is not only about portion control, it is also about decisions made regarding portion size and presentation. With a buffet, it is obvious. Proper serving utensils, proper holding/serving equipment, right presentation order, plate sizes, etc. In a bar its easy, too. Jiggers or other measuring and control devices and very strict discipline. I take it back, the discipline isn't easy especially in tight labor markets. Dining room service should be easy to control using good kitchen supervisors, trained cooks, photographs for both cooks and servers, etc. Watch what comes back from bused tables to see if portions are proper. Marketing decisions may drive large portions but if the patrons are not eating it or taking it home, the portion size or the recipe should be reconsidered. Proper china for each item served is important for both presentation and portion control.

PURCHASE PROCEDURE: PERISHABLE AND NON-PERISHABLE

Pershable:- Generally done by inviting tender for an annual date compact this not only help at regular supply at a fixed rate and also enable the management to forecast and calculate the actual food cost on a rational basis for budget purposes. The purchase manager invites vendor and obtain offers sufficiently in advance of commencement of the financial to year. The offer are analysis with a particular references to the availability and the to dependability of the vendor that coated prices, comparison with other vendor etc. the quotation of a short listed vendor are negotiation by the food committee consist of purchase manager Food and beverage manager executive chef, food and beverage control and chief account before the contract is awarded for a duration of the year. Perishable provision which are required for a continuous bases are requisition by the executive chef.

Non-Perishable Purchase:- Like can and bottle provision spices pulses etc are contracted items. Ones the order has been place with the purchase department by the store the purchase manager sent enquiry in this respect to all the well establish manufacture, agents, dealers the sample are obtained and sent to the executive chef and / or food the beverage managers for his/her there approval a final comparitative statement of quotation indicating items brand names, purchase date quantity to be purchases cost and name of supplier to be prepared. The price (as noted from the comparative statement) and quality (as per sample test) are the two factor which decide the choice of factor - non-perishable provision are requisition by the store in charge.

RECEIVING

It's not just expecting off a signing and for goods brought to the hotel it, includes beneficiation of quality and specification. The receiving department therefore required a strong and vigetan staff with a professional background of food and purchasing.

All good handing at the receiving plat form should be accompanied by an invoice is document listing item send to a buyers; stating the price quality and other specification each item in the invoice should be check weighed/ an or counted against the purchase order any unsatisfactory item should be returned the applied immediately and the purchase department to be intimated accordingly. The invoice should then signed dated and stand as received by the receiving clerk. A record should be maintain of the item received and at the end of the day a daily report prepare. This report will should be name of supplier item and quantity. It helps in maintaining control of all the items and provides a base for subsequent verification and accounting. Meat and fish are usually not received in the extract amount, order unless portion control or specially packed. Its necessary that the receiving clerk right the correct way on the invoice and initially it. Its also advisable to received meat fish and poultry in the presence of butchery chef ones approved by him the supply should be weighted and dispatch to the store and deep fridge / walk in or to the butcher shop. All food item should be dated this system established the "FIFO" method for all meat received the meat tag must be used to tag has the printed number Space for the date supplier name the cut, the weight and the price. This aids in issuing as well tagging also helps in discovering the shrinkage. If any at the time of issuing the vendor can be immediately be identified and panelized.

STORING

All food items received should be placed in the stores which may be categorized into three catagories.

Dry stores

For all types of canned and bottles product, cereals and pulse spices and condiments etc. Good circulation of air is necessary for dry storage the food container should be so arranged that they are off the floor and the space in the room to sweep and wash. The store rooms is sprayed against pest (cockroaches and rodents) and kept thoroughly clear with particular attention begin given to dark corner and areas us under the shelf. Personal belonging off the employees should not be kept in the store room which should be locked when authorized person are not managing it-. The recommendation temperature of dry store is between 64° F (18° C) and 70° F (25° C). It should not exceed 97° F (25° C). The higher the temperature lower the shelf life of the Ingredients.

Refrigerated (Deep Frozen store) for vegetable fruits and dairy product ice-cream meats etc.

Temperature are important for correct storage refrigerated and frozen product its important to keep the door or walk in refrigerators and deep freezer shut at all time. Unnecessary opening of doors with cause tempearture variation which is bound to effect the shelf life of perishable. The recommended storage temperature are as follows-

Frozen foods	32° F below/0° C below.
Meat	32° F to 36° F/0 to 2° C
Fruits and vegetable	38 to 45° F/3 to 8° C
Dairy product	33 to 37° F/1 to 3° C.

Perishable should never be stack in front of the blower that circulate air's in the walk in as they would hinder the air circulation and consequently reduce efficiency.

Sundries Stores

For non-food items like paper goods, cleaning supply etc. All goods delivery to the storage and cheek by weighing or by counting and then signed as received and enter into perpetual inventory cardex and fell in to the computer every item is given a code number. The system is adopted will depend on the size of the hotel to depend and the dates to which is expected to provide-

THE MAIN METHOD OF STORE ACCOUNT

Bin Card

Each items received is enter in the bin card showing the description of the commodities, receipts issues and the balance. Its advantage to show the minimum stock in order to facilitate the ordering of further supply's.

Stock books cardex

The alternative is keep the stock book preferably loose leafed card under this system a card is kept for each item shaving the price and the same information that could be recorded on the wing card:-

Issuing

The best way to control over store is to use the requisition system". A requisitions is a formal written order for merchandises and must be signed by an authorized person. No item should be issued from the store room without a proper requisition-While issuing followed the FIFO system. The issue clerk must be rechecked Tag and cannot the merchandises for ex. A requisition mistake 20 chicken of 850 gm each but each chicken may not weigh 850 gm therefore a person must weight a 20 chicken a record a total weight and make a change on all copy of requisition and the requisition are then used by the account department to ascertain the total value of good issued and to determined the food cost of each outlet.

For Perishable

It's usable to price the issue on the bases of actual purchase price or the contract rate price. Where the stock of item consist of several separate lots purchase at different price and an average price should be taken.

For non-perishable

One of several different methods may be adopted where market fluctuates are frequent it's best to work on the basic of an average price. In the case of show moving in frequently purchase item the actual purchase price may be taken as the basics.

Monthly and annual stock taking

A monthly stock taking and inventory of an item should be carried out food and beverage control- On the last day of every month a physical count of every food and beverage item should be carried out in the presence of store personnel- After obtaining a physical count by weighing or counting the detail should be notes. In the mean time store should open new bin card notating a new weight / physical count. The idea of stock taking is to reconsigned the physical consumption with the actual consumption-

The annual or year end inventory should be carried out by an external auditor with the store personnel as well as the food and beverage control in attendance. All the cardax bin card store credit reports and requisition copies should be taken and noted on 3 copies. In the case of Perishable new tags should be made.

While the physical round is being taken random check should be carries out by the auditor to see whether the counting been carried out properly. The details should be taken done on 3 copies and than signed by all 3 parties:- Auditor, store keeper, F and B control. These should be compared with the cardex if there is any discrepancies necessary action shall be taken.

COMPUTERIZATION OF MATERIALMANAGEMENT SYSTEM (MMS)

With the advent of computers the fundamental of the MMS remain same, the entire system from the process of making requisition to placing an order and making receiving report is carried at through computerized software. This makes working easier and the task less cumbersome. The chef or manager creates a requisition on the MMS according to the requirement of the department every product use in the department has a lock which is already fed into the system. In the cost of perishable the ordering is one day is advance taking into consideration the time taken to place the order and the time taken to delivery the items.

The glossary are kept in the store are requisition daily by the chef from the various outlet or kitchen and they carry out the process of ordering the food and beverage items on there computer terminals. The requisition are update in the system and issues from the stores.

FLOW OF COST

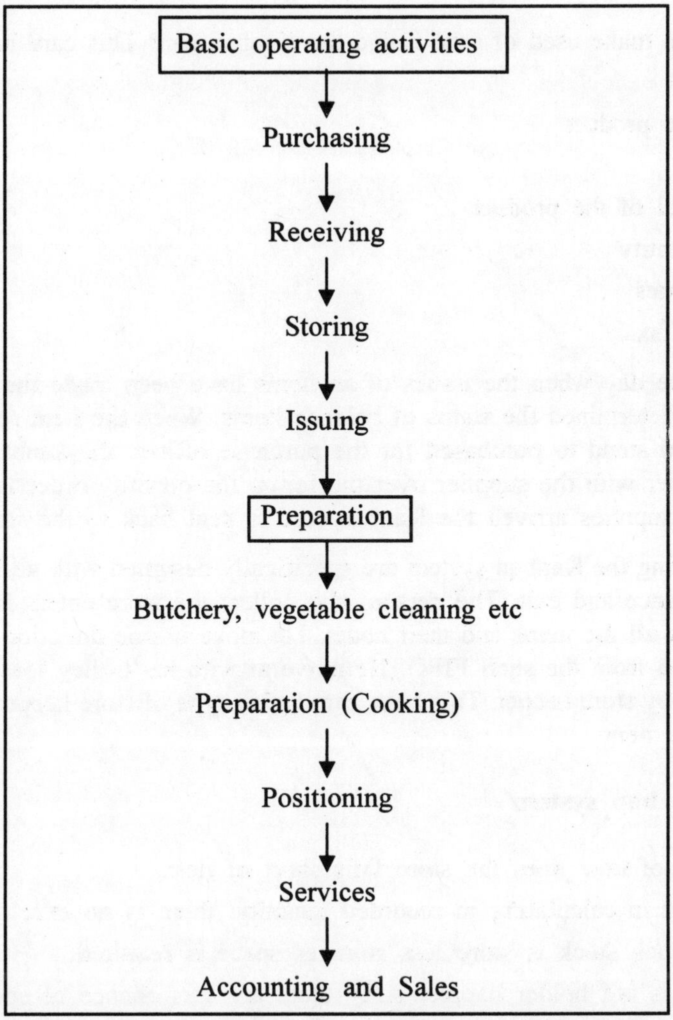

Fig 40.2 Basic operation activities and and there preparation activities

THE KANBAN SYSTEM OF INVENTORY MANAGEMENT

This system is developed on the foundation of the Japanese Principal of Kanban this system is based on the estimated usage of the product. Fine tuning production and supplier system, where inventories are minimize by supplying when needed in production.

In the hotel industry the Kanban system takes into consideration the procurement time span (Generally 2 to 3 days) its applicable in the case of glossary and not on perishable which cannot be stored stocked, its also oversee the par stocked available for the remaining days. It takes a minimum par stock into consideration while placing carrying at a purchase order-

WORKING OF KANBAN SYSTEM

A kanban system make used of card called the Kanban card This card has the following data mention on its:-

1. Name of the product
2. Item code.
3. Reorder level of the product
4. Reorder quantity
5. Supplier names
6. Contact No/fax.

At the end of the day when the issues of an items have been made the store keeper takes a round of stores and determined the status of balance items. When the item reach the reorder level the card is taken and stand to purchased for the purchase officer. the kanban card is a purchase order the item is order with the supplier over the forum the quantity order is the reorder quantity and as soon as she supplies arrived the Kanban card is sent back to the store with the product.

The store following the Kanban system are specifically designed with all item segregated. they have a separate entrance and exit. The person who collect the store enters from one site and has all map of store with all the items and their codes. He move in one direction and keeps collecting all item of requisition from the shall FIFO. He move at with his trolley loaded with items which are physically check by store keeper. This help introducing type of store keeper and the extra labour required to issue the item.

Advantage of Kan ban system

1. At no point of time does the store falls short of item.
2. This is order in calculating in recorded quantity: there is no excess blockage of capital
3. Since not much stock is store less storages space is required.
4. Since stock is not holder happier surly there are less chance of spoilage.
5. The flow of terrific is store is smooth.
6. It involves systematic organization does reducing time of issuing and labour.

Disadvantage of Kan ban system

1. Large unpredictable fluctuation in demand. In the hotel scenario there is a possibility of size in damage which would result in issuing the items kept for three days demands and left with no future supplies.
2. Reorder level of each item has to be changed periodically depending on the use of each item season and time of the year.

3. Often the supplies are not able to meet demands on time the supplies comes well after least time.
4. A physically backup in the form of files is required to be maintained in case of technical failure or loss of card..

LEARNING OUTCOME

The main purpose of menu is to present a list of offerings to the customer in an intensing manner giving a description of delicacy. A menu should be written in a interesting style which would automatically stimulate sale. Remember your menu is your best advertisement. It's read by 100 of dinners every and value of its obvious. Maintaining control and system at the time of purchasing receiving storing and issuing will not be enough not profitable unless appropriate control is establish on food production in the kitchen. The chef been incharge of the kitchen is responsible for all goods received and should make the best use of them. In order to arrive at the total cost of any one meal it's necessary to analysis the total cost incurred in the production. Its common practice to express each element as the % of selling price- The selling price of a product includes the cost element + the net profit in other words selling price= food cost + labour + overheads + Net profit. from this equation it follow that

Food Cost = sellingprice. – labour- overhead- net profit. Oil waste disposal is no longer the problem it once was, thanks to developing energy technologies. It is now possible to convert many used oils into biodiesel fuel—a renewable source of energy derived from vegetable oil. For this reason, "yellow grease" collected from fryers and grease recovery devices has become a valuable commodity. All good handing at the receiving plat form should be accompanied by an invoice is document listing item send to a buyers; stating the price quality and other specification each item in the invoice should be check weighed/ an or counted against the purchase order any unsatisfactory item should be returned the applied immediately and the purchase department to be intimated accordingly. The chef or manager creates a requisition on the MMS according to the requirement of the department every product use in the department has a lock which is already fed into the system.

QUESTIONS FOR DISCUSSION

1. Explain the term menu planning.
2. Explain the types of menu.
3. Explain the term food production control?
4. Explain the production process?
5. Explain the term material forecasting.
6. Explain the process of recycling of used oil.

7. Explain the term material management.
8. Explain the seven steps of food cost control.
9. Explain the procedure of perishable and non perishable.
10. Explain the process of receiving.
11. Explain the procedure of storing.
12. Explain the computerization material management system.
13. Explain the kan ban system of inventory.
14. Explain the working of Kanban system.
15. Explain the advantage and disadvantage of kanban system.

KEY TERMS

* Coordination
* Food control
* Management
* Material
* MMS
* Net profit
* Net profits
* Overheads
* Planning
* Selling price

Chapter 41

Laws Regarding Food

After studying this chapter, the student must know

- Introduction
- Meaning and definition of food
- Food adulteration
- Prevent of food adulteration act 1954
- Prohibition and restriction on some food
- Purchaser food analysis
- Offence and penalties
- Central committee for food standard and central
- Food laboratory
- Food inspectors and its procedure
- Food standards code in India
- Truth menu laws and labeling laws.

GENERAL LAW REGARDING FOODS

Introduction

The earliest food legislation can be traced to England and the Assize of Bread and Ale Act 1266, which regulated the quantity (Not the quality) of supplies. Technology in that area could only measure quantity and unscrupulous operators tended to cheat customers by incorrectly weighting and measuring goods. Customers had to simply rely on their look, touch, feel, smell and taste (Atherton and Atherton, 1998) Since that milestone legislation, there have been many advances in control and regulation of the sale and service of food-not simply in the possessions from quantity to quality, but also in contractual remedies, tortuous liability, consumer protection laws, and criminal liability.

Every country is developing systems to ensure that its citizens must get safe food to eat. But the recent controversies on quality and safety of carbonated soft drinks, liquid explosives, bird flu, food poisoning in mid-day meals, import of fruits and vegetables without pest-risk analysis and many more issues, cases and follow-up actions by various State governments raise the issues of criteria in decision-making process in the country on sensitive and complicated issues related to food safety, food trade and public health. Now, Parliament has passed a new bill on 'Food Safety and Standards'. The purpose is to generate a healthy debate on how to develop a reliable food safety system in the interest of public health in India.

MEANING AND DEFINITION OF FOOD

FOOD means any article used as food or drink for human consumption other than drugs and water.

According to PFA Act 1954, food is any article used as food or drink for human consumption other then drugs and water it includes-

a) Any article which ordinarily enters into or is used in the composition or preparation of food.

b) Any flavouring material or condiments

c) Any other article which the central govt. may having regards to its use, nature, substance or quality declare by notification in the official gazette as food for the purpose of this act.

UNWHOLESOME FOOD

Generally unwholesome means-

- Injurious to physical, mental, or moral health; unhealthy.
- Suggestive of disease or degeneracy: *an unwholesome pallor.*
- Offensive or loathsome.

and unwholesome food means food not fit to be eaten; food which, if eaten, would be injurious.

The article contains any other substance which affects, or if the article is so processed as to affect, injuriously the nature, substance or quality thereof;

The word "unwholesome" and "noxious" when used in relation to an article of food mean respectively that the article is harmful to health or repugnant to human use.

We can say that: Unwholesome foods are foods that are not fresh, whole foods. This includes any "junk foods" and highly processed foods. Untimely dining refers to eating the wrong foods during a particular season of the year.

FOOD ADULTERATION

Adulterated Food : u/s 2 of the PFA Act 1954—

"In general, if anything is added or taken out from the food which adversely affects the quality of the food article, may be treated as adulterated food."

Adulterants are chemical substances which should not be contained within other substances (e.g. food, beverages, fuels or pesticide) for legal or other reasons. Adulterants may be intentionally added to substances to reduce manufacturing costs, or for some deceptive or malicious purpose. Adulterants may also be accidentally or unknowingly introduced into substances.

PREVENTION OF FOOD ADULTERATION ACT, 1954

Food is one of the basic necessities for substance of life. Pure fresh and healthy diet is most essential for the health of the people.

The prevention of food Adulteration (PFA) bill was passed by both the houses of Parliament and received the assent of the president on 19th Sept. 1954 and it came in to force on 1st June 1955 as:

"The prevention of food Adulteration act 1954 37 of 1954"

The above act describe as:

"Adulterated" an article of food shall be deemed to be adulterated.

Objective of PFA Act 1954

Prevention of food adulteration act 1954 extends to the whole of India. The main objectives of the act are-

- To eradicate the antisocial evil and for ensuring purity of food sold to the public.
- To prevent adulteration of food and to protect the health of the citizens.
- The act is a piece of consumer legislation in regulates the consumer supplier relations.
- Adulteration of food is a menace to the public health. The act has been enacted with the aim at eradicating that anti social evil and for ensuring purity in the articles of food.
- The act is intended to protect the consumer against outright frauds.
- PFA Act serves a very important role in securing to the citizen a minimum degree of purity in the articles of food and thereby protecting public health.
- To protect the society against unscrupulous (with out morally cautious) and anti-social dealers.
- The main object of the act and the rules made there under are to ensure the purity of food and maintenance of public health by eradicating the evil of adulteration of food.

Adulteration of food stuffs is a serious matter and it is affecting the whole society to an extent which may well be described almost dangerous.

So the act deals with the regulation of a class of traders with a view to preventing the widespread malpractices and to control them.

All restaurants or food service establishments have to abide by the food laws governed by the prevention of food adulteration act 1954 (FPA) which is a part of the essential commodities act. Govt. of India It is in the interest of the food handlers that they are aware of their obligations to enact the mandatory requirements of FPA.

When An Article Of Food Deemed As "Adulterated Food"

An article of food shall be deemed to be adulterated-

A. If the article sold by a vendor is not of the nature, substance or quality demanded by the purchaser or which it purports to be;

B. If the article contains any substance affecting its quality or of it is so processed as to injuriously affect its nature, substance or quality;

C. If any inferior or cheaper substance has been substituted wholly or partly for the article, or any constituent of the article has been wholly or partly abstracted from it, so as to affecting its quality or of it is so processed as to injuriously affect its nature, substance or quality;

D. If the article had been prepared, packed or kept under insanitary conditions whereby it has become contaminated or injurious to health;

E. If the article consists wholly or in part of any filthy, putrid, disgusting, rotten, decomposed or diseased animal and vegetable substance or being insect- infested, or is otherwise unfit for human consumption;

F. If the article is obtained from a diseased animal;

G. If the article contains any poisonous or other ingredient which is injurious to health;

H. If the container of the article is composed of any poisonous or deleterious substance which renders its contents injurious to health;

I. If the article contain any prohibited colouring.

When an Article of Food Deemed as "Misbranded"

Misbranded food-U/S (2) of the PFA act 1954

In general, misbranding means false claims or something wrong or against the provisions of the PFA act in the labeling of the food article.

1. If it is an imitation of, as is a substitute for or resembles in a manner which is likely to affect, another food article under the name of which is sold.
2. If the article of food is coloured, flavoured or cooked to hide the fact that its damaged and made to appear better or of greater value than it really is.
3. If it is falsely stated to be the product of any other place of country.
4. If it is sold by the name which belongs, to another article of food.
5. If false claim are made for it upon labels or otherwise.

6. If the label bears the name of fictitious name or company.
7. If the name and address of the manufacturer is not given or stated.
8. If false statement regarding the Ingredients are given.
9. If colour and flavour used but not mentioned.
10. If it is not labeled in accordance with requirement of this act.

Preservative: means a substance which when added to food, is capable of inhibiting, retarding or arresting the process of fermentation, acidification or other decomposition of food.

PROHIBITIONS AND RESTRICTIONS

Prohibition On The Manufacture, Sale, Etc. Of Certain Food Articles

No person shall manufacture, store, sell or distribute

(i) Any adulterated food,
(ii) Any misbranded food,
(iii) Food articles to be sold under license without fulfilling the conditions of the license,
(iv) Any food article athe sale of which is prohibited by the Food (Health) Authority in the interest of public health,
(v) Any food article in contravention of any other provision of Act or the Rules, (see 'Conditions for Sale') or
(vi) Any adulterant.

The act of storing an adulterated article of food would be an offence only if storing is for sale. The sale of a part of the stored article constitutes an offence distinct and independent from the offence of storing for sale.

Prohibition on use of certain Expressions While Labelling of Edible Oils and Fats

The package, label or the advertisement of edible oils and fats shall not use the expressions Super-Refined, Micro-Refined, Double-Refined, Ultra-Refined, Anti-Cholesterol Fighter, Soothing to Heart, Cholesterol Friendly, Saturated Fat Free or such other expressions which are exaggerations of the quality of the product.

Prohibition on Sale of Certain Admistures

For example, cream which has not been prepared exclusively from milk, milk which contains any added water, ghee which contains any added matter not exclusively derived from milk fat, a mixture of two or more edible oil as an edible oil and turmeric containing any foreign substances, etc. (Rule 44).

Prohibition on Use of Acetylene Gas (Carbide Gas) In Artificially Ripening of Fruits. (Rule 44AA).

Prohibition on sale of food articles coated with mineral oil, except in accordance with the permitted standards.(Rule 44 AAA and Appendix B).

Restriction on sale of ghee having less than specified Reichert value except under the "AGMARK" seal.

Prohibition on sale of admixutres of ghee or butter or on its use as an ingredient in the preparation of an article of food. (Rule 46).

Any food item resembling honey, but not pure honey, shall not be marked "honey".(Rule 45.

Restriction on sale of kangra tea except only after it is graded and marked in accordance with the provisions of Agricultural Produce (Grading and Marketing) Act, 1937 and the Rules made there under (Rule 44E).

Conditions for sale of flavoured tea only by those manufactueres. Who are registered with Tea Board and the package bearing the laber, 'FLAVOURED TEA' (Common name of permitted flavour, percentage and Registration No.).

Restriction on sale of common salt No person shall, sell or offer or expose for sale or have in his premises for the purpose of sale, common salt for direct human consumption unless the same is iodized. (Rule 44H).

Restriction on use and sale of artificial sweeteners except that saccharin sofium can be added to carbonated water, supar, pan masala and pan flavouring material within the specified maximum limit and appertained may be sold for diabetic use under medical advice. (Rule 47).

Prohibition on sale of permitted food colours, i.e. Synthetic colours, or their mixtures or any preparation of such colours, except under a license.

Prohibition on sale of permitted food additives, except only under the ISI certification marks.

Prohibition on use of coumarin and dihydro cocumarin, tankabean (dipteryl adorat) and b- asarane and cinamylauthracilate, as flavouring agents. Any extraneous addition of flavouring agent should be mentioned on the label attached to any package of food so flavoured, in capital letters in the following manner:

"CONTAINS ADDED FLAVOUR"

Restriction On Use Aof Preservatives, Addition of Class I preservatives i.e. Common Salt, Sugar, Destrose, Glucose (syrup), Spices, Vinegar or acetic acid, honey and edible vegetable oil, in any food is not restricted, provided that the food article to which the preservative has been added conforms to the specifications laid down in Appendix B.

Conditions For Sale Of A Food Article, Every utensil or container, used for manufacturing, preparing or containing any food or Ingredients there, and second hand tin containers for packaging of edible oils and fats, meant for sale, shall be maintained in a clean and sanitary condition, away from impure air or dust, properly covered at all times, and such utensils or containers shall not be used for any other purpose. Use of rusty containers, improperty tinned copper or brass containers, containers of aluminum or plastic not conforming to ISI specifications, etc., in preparation of food, is also prohibited. Besides, certain special conditions for sale of certain articles such as asafetida, salseed fat, lactic acid, edible oils, katha, margarine, milk powder, etc. have also been laid down.

With effect from 22.2.95, on person shall sell powdered spices except in packed form. No person shall sell or serve food in any commercial establishment in plastic articles used in catering and cutlery, unless the plastic material used in catering and cutlery articles, conform to the food grade plastic.

Purchaser May have food Analysed

A purchaser of any article of food, or a recognized consumer association, may also get an article of food analyzed by the public analyst on payment of the prescribed fees, provided that the vendor is informed of this intended action at the time of purchase. Thereafter, the purchaser or the consumer association, have to follow the same procedure as discussed above in the case of Food Inspectors. If the article of food is found to be adulterated, the fees paid by the purchaser or the association shall be refunded.

Offences and Penalties

Import, manufacture, storage, sale or distrinbution of any food article which is adulterated by allowing its quality or purity to fall below the prescribed standard, or is misbranded, or in contravention of any provision of the Act or rules. Penalty is minimum imprisonment of six months that may extend up to 3 years and minimum fine of Rs 1000.

Import, manufacture, storage, sale or distribution of any adulterant not injurious to health. Penalty is minimum imprisonment of six months that may extend up to 3 years and minimum find of Rs 1000.

Preventing a Food Inspector from taking a sample or exercising his powers. Penalty is minimum imprisonment of six months that may extend up to 3 years and minimum fine of Rs 1000.

Giving a false warranty in writing in respect of any food article. Penalty is minimum imprisonment of six months that may extend up to 3 years and minimum fine of Rs 1000.

Import, manufacture, storage, sale or distribution of any food article which is adulterated within the meaning of any of the sub-clauses (e) to (1) of section 2 (ia); or any adulterant which is injurious to health. Penalty is minimum imprisonment of one year that may extend up to 6 years and minimum fine of Rs 2000.

Sale or distribution of any food article containing any poisonous or other ingredient injurious to health, which is likely to cause death or grievous bodily harm. Penalty is minimum imprisonment of three years that may extend up to life and minimum fine of Rs 5000.

CENTRAL COMMITTEE FOR FOOD STANDARDS AND CENTRAL FOOD LABORATORY

The Central Committee for Food Standards. The Central government shall, as soon as may be after the commencement of this Act, constitute a Committee called the Central Committee for Food

Standards to advise the Central Government and the State Government on matters arising out of the administration of this Act and to carry out the other functions assigned to it under this Act.

The Committee shall consist of the following members, namely:

a) The Director-General, Health Services, ex-officio, who shall be the Chairman;
b) The Director of the Central Food Laboratory or, in a case where more than one. Central Food Laboratory is established, the Directors of such Laboratories, ex-officio;]
c) Two experts nominated by the Central Government;
d) One representative each of the Departments of Food and Agriculture in the Central.Ministry of Food and Agreculture and one representative each of the Central Ministries of Commerce, Defense, Industry and Supply and Railways, nominated by the Central government;]
e) One representative each nominated by the Government of each 1***State;
f) Two representatives nominated by the Central Government to represent the 2* [Union Territories]
g) One representative each, nominated by the Central Government to represent the agricultural, commercial and industrial interests;
h) Five representatives nominated by the Central Government to represent the consumers' interest one of whom shall be from the hotel industry;]
i) One representative of the medical profession nominated by the Indian Council of Medical Research;
j) One representative nominated by the Indian Standards Institution referred to in clause (e) of section 2 of the Indian Standards Institution" (Certification of Marks) Act, 1952.] (36 of 1952}.

Central Food Laboratory

The Central Government shall, by notification in the Official Gazette, establish one or more Central Food Laboratory or Laboratories to carry out the functions entrusted to the Central Food laboratory by this Act or any rules made under this Act:

Provided that the Central government may, by notification in the Official Gazette, also specify any laboratory or institute as a Central food Laboratory for the purposes of this Act.

The Central Government may, after constitution with the committee, make rules prescribing-

a) The functions of a Central Food laboratory and the local area or areas within which – such functions may be carried out;
b) The procedure for the submission to the said laboratory of samples of articles of food for analysis or tests, the forms of the Laboratory's reports thereon and the fees payable in respect of such reports;
c) Such other matters as may be necessary or expedient to enable the said Laboratory to carry out its functions.

Analysis of Food

Public Analyses

Public Analyses. The Central Government or the State government may, by notification in the Official Gazette, appoint such persons as it thinks fit, having the prescribed qualifications to be public analysts for such local areas as may be assigned to them by the Central Government or the State Government, as the case may be:

Provided that no person who has any financial interest in the manufacture, import or sale of any article of food shall be appointed to be a public analyst under this section:

Provided further that different public analysts may be appointed for different articles of food.

Food Inspectors

(1) **Food Inspectors.** The Central Government or the State Government may, by notification in the official Gazette, appoint such persona as it thinks fit, having the prescribed qualifications to be food inspectors for such local areas as may be assigned to them by the Central Government or the State Government, as the case may be:

Provided that no person who has any financial interest in the manufacture, import or sale of any article of food shall be appointed to be a food inspector under this section.

(2) Every food inspector shall be deemed to be a public servant within the meaning of section 21 of the Indian.

Penal Code (45 of 1860) and shall be officially subordinate to such authority as the Government appointing him, may specify in this behalf.

Powers of food inspectors

(1) Powers of food inspectors. A food inspector shall have power-

(a) to take samples of any article of food from-

(i) any person selling such article;

(ii) any person who is in the course as conveying, delivering or preparing to deliver such article to a purchaser or consignee;

(iii) consignee after delivery of any such article to him; and

(b) to send such sample for analysis to the public analyst for the local area within which such sample has been taken;

(c) with the previous approval of the Local (Health) Authority having jurisdiction in the local area concerned, or with the previous approval of the food (Health) Authority, to prohibit the sale of any article of food in the interest of public health.

(2) Any food inspector may enter and inspect any place where any article of food is manufactured, or stored for sale, or stored for the manufacture of any other article of food for sale, or

exposed or exhibited for sale or where any adulterant is manufactured or kept, and take samples of such article of food or adulterant for analysis:

Provided that no sample of any article of food, being primary food, shall be taken under this sub-section if it is not intended for sale as such food.

(3) Where any sample is taken under clause (a) of sub-section (1) or sub-section (2), its cost calculated at the rate at which the article is usually sold to the public shall be paid to the person from whom it is taken.

(4) if any article intended for food appears to any food inspector to be adulterated or misbranded, he may seize and carry away or keep in the safe custody of the vendor such article in order that it may be dealt with as hereinafter provided 2 and he shall, in either case, take a sample of such article and submit the same for analysis to a public analyst:

(4a) Where any article of food seized under sub-section (4) is of a perishable nature and the Local (Health') Authority is satisfied that such article of food is so deteriorated that it is unfit for human consumption, the said Authority may, after giving notice in writing to the vendor, cause the same to be destroyed.

(5) The power conferred by this section includes power to break open any package in which any article of food may be contained or to break open the door of any premises where any article of food may be kept for sale.

(6) any adulterant found in the possession of a manufacturer or distributor of, or dealer in, any article of food or in any of the premises occupied by him as such] and for the possession of which he is unable to account to the satisfaction of the food inspector, and any books of account or other documents found in his possession or control and which would be useful for, or relevant to, any investigation or proceeding under this Act, may be seized by the food inspector and a sample of such adulterant submitted for analysis to a public analyst:

(7) Where the food inspector takes any action under clause (a) of sub-section (1), sub-section (2), sub-section (4) or sub-section (6), he shall, call one or more persons to be present at the time when such action is taken and take his or their signatures.

(7B) When any adulterant is seized under sub-section (6) the burden of proving that such adulterant is not meant for purposes of adulteration shall be on the person from whose possession such adulterant was seized.

(8) Any food inspector may exercise the powers of a police officer under section 42 of the Code of Criminal Procedure, 1973 (2 of 1973} for the purpose of ascertaining the true name and residence of the person from whom a sample is taken or an article of food is seized.

(9) Any food inspector exercising powers under this Act or under the rules made there under who

(a) vexatiously and without any reasonable grounds of suspicion seizes any articles of food or adulterant; or

(b) commits any other act to the injury of any person without having reason to believe that such act is necessary for the execution of his duty; shall be guilty of an offence under this Act and shall be punishable for such offence with find which shall not be less than five hundred rupees but which may extend to one thousand rupees.

Procedure to be followed by food inspectors

1. Procedure to be followed by food inspectors When a food inspector takes a sample of food for analysis, he shall-

(a) give notice in writing then and there of his intention to have it so analyzed to the person from whom he has taken the sample and to the person, if any, whose name, address and other particulars have been disclosed under section 14A;

(b) except in special cases provided by rules under this Act, divide the sample then and there into three parts and mark and seal or fasten up each part in such a manner as its nature permits and take the signature or thumb impression of the person from whom the sample has been taken in such place and in such manner as may be prescribed:

Provided that where such person refuses to sign or put his thumb impression the food inspector shall call upon one or more witnesses and take his or their signatures or thumb impressions, as the case may be, in lieu of the signature or thumb impression of such person;

(c) (i) send one of the parts for analysis to the public analyst under intimation to the Local (Health) Authority; and

(ii) Send the remaining two parts to the Local (Health)Authority for the purposes of sub-section (2) of this section and subsections (2A) and 2(E) of section 13.

(2) Where the part of the sample sent to the public analyst under sub-clause (ii) of clause (c) of sub-section (1) is lost or damaged, the Local (Health) Authority shall, on a requisition made to it by the public analyst or the food inspector dispatch one of the parts of the sample sent to it under sub-clause (ii) of said clause (c) to the public analyst for analysis.

(3) When a sample of any article of food or adulterant is taken under sub-section (1) or sub-section (2) of section 12 the food inspector shall, by the immediately succeeding working day, send a sample of the article of food or adulterant or both, as the case may be, in accordance with the rules prescribed for sampling case may be, in accordance with the rules prescribed for sampling to the public analyst for the local area concerned.

(4) An article of food seized under sub-section (4) of section 10, unless destroyed under sub-section (4A) of that section, and any adulterant seized under sub-section (6) of that section shall be produced before a magistrate as soon as possible and in any case not later than seven days after the receipt of the report of the public analyst:

Provided that if an application is made to the magistrate in this behalf by the person from whom any article of food has been seized, the magistrate shall by order in writing direct the food inspector to produce such article before him within such time as may be specified in the order.

(5) If it appears to the magistrate on taking such evidence as he may deem necessary-

(a) that the article of food produced before him under sub-section (4) is adulterated or misbranded, he may order it-

(i) to be forfeited to the Central Government, the State Government or the local authority, as the case may be; or

(ii) to be destroyed at the cost of the owner or the person from whom it was seized so as to prevent itws being used as human food; or

(iii) to be so disposed of as to prevent its being for sale or used for food under its, again exposed deceptive name; or

(iv) to be returned to the owner, on his executing a bond with or without sureties, for being sold under its appropriate name or, where the magistrate is satisfied that the article of food is capable of being made to conform to prescribed standards for human consumption after reprocessing, for being sold after reprocessing under the supervision of such officer as may be specified in the order;

(b) that the adulterant seized under sub-section 6 of section 10 and produced.

Before him is apparently of a kind which may be employed for purposes of adulteration and for the possession of which the manufacturer, distributor or dealer, as the case may be, is unable to account satisfactorily, he may order it to be forfeited to the Central Government, the State Government or the local authority, as the case may be.

(6) If it appears to the magistrate that any such-

(a) article of food is not adulterated: or

(b) Adulterant which is purported to be an adulterant is not an adulterant.

The person from whose possession the article of food or adulterant was taken [shall be entitled to have it restored to him and it shall be in the discretion of the magistrate to award such person from such fund as the State Government may direct in this behalf, such compensation not exceeding the actual loss which he has sustained as the magistrate may think proper.

FOOD STANDARDS CODE IN INDIA

The code is a joint set of food labeling and composition standards developed especially for the Indian food industries. The most important food standards in India are as follows:

A) The Prevention of Food Adulteration Standards

The Prevention of Food Adulteration (PFA) standards were establish in 1955. These lay down the minimum standards for all types of foods and are received periodically to meet the requirement of the manufacturer and the consumer from time to time. If any food not conforming to these standards is said to be adulterated.

B) Fruit Products Order Standards

The Fruit Products Order (FPO) standards were passed in 1946 under the defense of India rules was received under the essential commodities act 1955. The FPO standards are mainly concerned with the standards required for maintaining the quality of fruits, vegetables and any products manufactured from them. The FPO also specified the conditions of hygiene and sanitation required to be maintained by manufacturers of fruit and vegetable products. In addition, the specifications for the labeling and packaging of these products have been laid down. Under the FPO it is necessary for the manufactures to get a license for the manufacture and sale of fruit and vegetable products. The license is only issued if the conditions of manufactures and the quality of the product conform to the standards laid down by the order.

The main objective of the PFA and FPO standards is to determine the minimum level of quality that can be attained, under the farming, manufacturing and retailing conditions in India.

C) The Agmark Standards

These standards are formulated on the physical and chemical charqacteristics of food both the natural as well as those acquired during processing product graded under "AGMARK" include vegetable oils, ghee, cream butter, rice, eggs, potatoes, spices, etc. These standards ensure accurate weights and correct selling practices.

D) Bureau of Indian Standards (BIS)

Bureau of Indian Standards, whose certification mark is "BIS" seen on all products indicating conformity to laid down standards. The BIS is the national organization for Standardization and lays down criteria for standardization of products material, practices and process. These standards cover vegetable and fruit product, spices, meat products, biscuits, sweets, flour, texturised soya products, tea, coffee, or other beverages and so on.

The BIS is the national organization for standardization and lays down criteria for standardized of product, materials practices and possesses. It is also involved with the standardization of items like building materials, safety standards for equipments etc. which the caterer must be aware of when decisions regarding premises and equipment are required to be taken.

Certification marks stamped on packages of foods and food products whether they be BIS, FPO or AGMARK or any internationally recognized seal of quality help the consumer of the products to buy foods with confidence. The above stated marks represent the guarantee of quality. Licenses to manufacturer for the use of the ISI certification mark are granted only if the process of production and the state of the premises in which the food are to be handled meet the requirements laid down. The inspections are carried out by the staff of the Indian standards Institutions, or the Directorate of Inspection in the case of the FPO and AGMARK certification mark.

TRUTH IN MENU LAWS AND LABELLING LAWS

The term LABLE means a display or Written, Printed, Graphic Printed, performed, Stenciled or stamped matter upon the container or crown of any food package.

The law on food labeling and composition is **complex and subject to change.**The information below is not a definitive interpretation to the law as only Courts can provide a definitive interpretation.

Neither is information given regarding guidance on weights and measures law, which also applies to food labels.

The Food Safety Act 1990 makes it an offence to sell food for human consumption which:

- Is injurious to health
- Fails to comply with food safety requirements
- Is falsely described, labeled or advertised for sale.
- Is not of the nature, substance or quality as demanded by the final consumer.

The Trade Descriptions Act 1968 makes it an offence to apply a false trade description to any goods or to offer to supply goods to which a false description is applied.

There are specific regulations enforced under the Food Safety Act 1990 such as:

- The Food labeling Regulations, 1996 (as amended)
- The Food Labelling (Amendment) Regulations 1998 and 1999

As per Rule 30 PFA Act

1. Every package of Food shall carry Label with the name, Trade Mark of the product and description of food contained in the package.
2. The name of Ingredients used in the product in descending order of their composition by weight or volume as the case may be.
3. The name and complete address of the manufacturer, importer and packer.
4. The net weight or measure of volume of content.
5. A distinctive batch No., Lot No., Code No. either in numerical or alphabets or combination.
6. The Month and Year in which the product is manufactured and prepared clearly indicated and the distance between the word and line should not be less than 1.5 mm.

All labels should not contain false or misleading statements.

Labelling is of key importance under the code and requires by Prevention of Food Adulteration Act 1954:

- Name of Food – Food product must be accurately **named and described** on the label.
- Lot identification – **premises where the food is packaged and/ or prepared** and the batch it come from.
- Name and Address – the **suplier's name and business street address** must be displayed.
- **Mandatory warning statements,** advisory statements and declarations for certain Ingredients/ substances-some product require special advisory statements or warnings about the food or Ingredients.
- **Ingredient List-** Ingredients must be listed by their common name, a description or generic name. Ingredients are the substances used in the preparation, manufacture and handling of fod and include food additives, compound Ingredients and added water.

- **Food Additives**— the class name of the additive, followed by its specific name or code number, must be declared. Where an additive is a vitamin or mineral, that name may be used.
- **Date making-** most packaged foods with a shelf life of less than two years must have either a **use by date, a best before date or a baked on date.**
- **Directions for use and storage** - must indicate the period that all food will keep for, indicated by a date mark and the necessary storage requirements.
- **Nutritional Information** - a panel should display a range of information including average quantities or minimum/ maximum quantities.
- **Percentage labeling** - the percentage of characterizing Ingredients, and / or components of most food products must be indicated on the label.
- **Net content** – this is required under the Weight and Measures regulation Act 1976.

BASIC LABELLING REQUIREMENT

Basic information required by law to appear on labels of most pre-packed foods includes the following.

Name of the food

The name should be sufficiently precise to inform the purchaser of the true nature of the food. It may be necessary to add a qualifying statement to clarify the name example "Vegetable Samosa- a spicy vegetable filled pastry parcel."

If there is a name prescribed by law this must be used e.g. "prawns". Reserved names may only be used for foods meeting specific compositional criteria, e.g. coffee, chocolate, and jam. Customary names that have become accepted in the UK without further explanation may also be used example "Cream Crackers" or "Muesli".

List of Ingredients

All the Ingredients of the foods, headed by the word "Ingredients" (or a phrase including that word), must be listed in descending order of weight.. Certain categories of Ingredients such as additives must be identified by category name, e.g. serial number, e.g. " sodium nitrate" or "E250".

Claims – Nutritional Information

Some claims are prohibited, example claims that food can prevent, treat or cure diseases or other "adverse conditions."

Nutritional claims about food such as "reduced energy", "rich in vitamins" etc., can only be made if the food meets set compositional standards. Such claims also require the provision of nutritional information. All nutritional information must be given in the form specified in the regulations.

Truth in menu laws and labelling laws.

Subs by G.S.R. 422(E) 29-04-87 (w.e.f. 29-4-1989)

Every package of food shall carry a label and unless otherwise provided in these rules there shall be specified on every label.

The name trade name or description of food contained in the package.

The name of Ingredients used in the product in descending or der of their composition by weight or value as the case may be.

Rule (Ins. By G.S.R. 380(E) dated 25-6-98 (provide for all non-vegetarian foods)

Whenever any article of food contains whole or part of any arrival including birds and fresh water or marine animals or eggs as an ingredient a declaration to this effect shall be made by a symbol and colour code, so stipulated for this purpose to indicate that the product is non-vegetarian food. The symbol shall consist of a circle with a single chord (straight line) passing through its centre from top left hand side to the right diagonally as indicated below.

The symbol shall be displayed in prominent red colour on the package having contrast background.

Rule Ins by G.S.R. 908(E) 20-6-02 (Provide for all vegetarian foods.

A declaration to this effect shall be made by a symbol or colour code so stipulated for this purpose to indicate that the product is vegetarian food the symbol is

Rule G.S.R. 537(E) dated 13-6-2000 (Best Before Use)

In case of any package containing bread or liquid milk, any package containing dhokla, pizza, khoa, Paneer, any uncanned package of fruits, vegetables, meat, fish, or any other like commodity which has a short shelf life, the date, month, and year in which the commodity is manufactured or prepared for packed shall be mentioned on the lable.

"best before................(Month and Year)"

"best before within.................(Month from the date of packaging/manufacture)"

Other forms of Labels

As per G.S.R. 917(E) dated 17-11-1987 (Coffee-Chicory mixure)

Every package containing a mixture of coffee and chicory shall have affixed to it a label upon which shall be printed following declaration

Coffee blended with chicory
This mixture Contains
Coffee.............%(Percent)
Chicory..............%(Present)

As per rule dated 8.7.1968 (Condensed Milk or Desiccated Dried Milk):-

Every package containing condensed milk or dried milk shall bear a label upon which is printed such one of the following declarations as may be applicable or such other declaration substantially to the likie effect as may be allowed by the state government

Condensed Milk unsweetened
Evaporated Milk
This tin contains the equivalent of
(×————————————————(liter of toned milk)

As per rule (G.S.R. 938 date 26.5.71 (Fluid Milk))

The caps of the milk bottles shall clearly indicate the nature of the milk contained in them indication may be either in full or by abbreviation shown below.

1. **Buffalo Milk** may be denoted by the letter 'B'
2. **Cow Milk** may be denoted by the letter 'C'
3. **Goat Milk** may be denoted by the letter 'G'
4. **Standardized Milk may** be denoted by the letter 'S'
5. **Toned Milk** may be denoted by the letter 'T'

As per rule G.S.R. 55(E) date 31.1.1979 (malted Milk Food)

Every package of mixed masala fried in oil shall bear the following label.

Mixed masala (Fried)
This masal has been fried in
(Name of the edible oil used)

As per rule 55 (E) date 31.1.1979 (Malted Milk Food)

Unless otherwise provided in these rules, every package of malted milk food which contains added natural colouring matter except caramel, shall bear the following label

Malted milk food in the package Contains permitted natural colouring matter

As per G.S.R. 852 (E) date 13-6-1986 (Tobacco)

Every package of chewing tobacco shall bear the following label

CHEWING OF TOBACOD IS INJURIOUS TO HEALTH

As per G.S.R. 641(E) date 9 Aug. 1994 (Irradiated Food)

All packages of irradiated food shall bear the following declaration and logo namely-

Processed by irradi8tion method Date of irradiation License No. Processed by irradiation method date of irradiation

As per G.S.R. 831(E) date 21-10-2003 (Mineral Water)

One time usable plastic bottles of packaged drinking mineral water shall carry the following declaration in capital letters having the size of each letter as proscribed rule 36

A. Natural mineral water

B. Crush the bottle after use

LEARNING OUTCOME

The earliest food legislation can be traced to England and the Assize of Bread and Ale Act 1266, which regulated the quantity (Not the quality) of supplies.

Adulterants are chemical substances which should not be contained within other substances (e.g. food, beverages, fuels or pesticide) for legal or other reasons. Adulterants may be intentionally added to substances to reduce manufacturing costs, or for some deceptive or malicious purpose. Adulterants may also be accidentally or unknowingly introduced into substances. The prevention of food Adulteration (PFA) bill was passed by both the houses of Parliament and received the assent of the president on 19th Sept. 1954 and it came in to force on 1st June 1955 as:

"Central Food Laborator: The Central Government shall, by notification in the Official Gazette, establish one or more Central Food Laboratory or Laboratories to carry out the functions entrusted to the Central Food laboratory by this Act or any rules made under this Act

The term LABLE means a display or Written, Printed, Graphic Printed, performed, Stenciled or stamped matter upon the container or crown of any food package.

The name should be sufficiently precise to inform the purchaser of the true nature of the food. It may be necessary to add a qualifying statement to clarify the name example "Vegetable Samosa- a spicy vegetable filled pastry parcel."

QUESTIONS FOR DISCUSSION

1. Explain the meaning and definitions of food.
2. Explain the PFA act.
3. Explain the PFA act objective.
4. Explain the term food adulteration.
5. When an article says food deemed as "Adulteration food".
6. When an article says food deemed as "un branded".
7. Explain in detail centre food laboratory.
8. Explain the function of food inspector.
9. Explain the power of food inspectors.
10. Explain the procedure to be followed by food inspector.
11. Explain the different food standards code in India.
12. Explain the term truth in labeling.
13. Explain the different laws regarding labelling.
14. As per rule G.S.R. 938 dated 26-5-71 (Fluid Milk) explain that rule.

KEY TERMS

* PFA	* Food inspector	* Adulteration
* Labelling	* Fluid milk	* Code
* CFA	* Laws	* Claims

Chapter 42

Management Standard of Hygiene and Storage

After studying this chapter, the student must know :

- Food hygiene and contamination
- Tips to reduce food poisoning
- Storage of food
- Personal hygiene for handling food
- Premise hygiene
- Guide lines for hygiene standards buffet and catered meals
- Preserving fruits and vegetables

FOOD-HYGIENE AND CONTAMINATION

It is integral that all people working in the food industry practice and possess high standards of hygiene and food handling in the workplace, as bacteria and other organism can infest food and lead to illness or even death.

If hygiene is not maintained, the following situations can arise:

- **Poor product** - Reduced shelf life
- **Quality leading to Increased expenses** Narrowing profit margins, As cost of goods sold increases
- **Customer complaints, which require resolving by personnel**
- **Loss of reputation,** which leads to a loss of customers and therefore less revenue.
- Court proceedings, including **finess, damages or closure of the premises.** This can also lead to loss of profits.
- **Food wastage,** with lower stock turnover and higher stock losses.

Some Important Tips to Reducing the Risk of Food Poisoning

1. Undertaken a food contamination risk assessment and rank foods from a high level of risk to a lower level risk-
   - High risk products include milk, cheese, dairy products, meat, seafood, eggs, soups and desserts.
   - Middle risk products include breads, vegetables, cooked rice and pasta etc.
   - Low risk products include uncooked rice, pasta and dehydrated foods.
2. Commercial Food handlers should observe the following list of practical tips:
   - Raw material should only be purchased from a reputed and approved supplier.
   - Suppliers should chosen their ability to :

   a. Guarantee temperature-controlled transport that ensure the products are fresh and in a usable condition.

   b. Provide frequent delivery times and days, be flexible, and respond on demand and to requirement.
   - Material should be checked on delivery to ensure they are not contaminated or damaged.
   - Food must be delivered within shelf dates and be at the correct temperature on arrival.

Storage

Stock all Ingredients to ensure the stock in restored-first in, first out basis.

Check all shelf-life stickers to ensure the oldest products are at the front to be used first.

Store all foods above the ground to allow for cleaning and ventilation.

Always store food at the correct temperatures:

a. Frozen foods	18° Celsius
b. Perishable and high risk food	05° Celsius
c. Meat and Fish	02° Celsius
d. Fruit	Cool Conditions
e. Dry Goods	Kept Dry

- Keep Food Covered or enclosed in containers, especially food that is ready to eat.
- Dry goods must be kept separate from vegetable or other raw foods
- Raw, Fresh and frozen foods should be kept separately
- Food that is removed from the freezer should not be refrozen.

Cooking

- The ideal cooking temperature is 82° Celsius.

- Water used for processing and preparation needs to be contaminant-free and of a quality fit for human consumption—use of filter water is recommended.
- Ensure that food that is not on display for more than two hours.
- Make sure that food is served as soon as possible after preparation.
- Always keep hot foods Hot and cold food Cold.

Reheating

- Food must be reheated at or above 80 Degree Celsius (for microwave and oven reheating)
- After reheating, food should be eaten as soon as possible.
- Do not reheat food more than once.
- If food is to be kept hot before serving, it must stay above 70 Degree Celsius
- If it is to be refrigerated, it should be cooled quickly and then put in the fridge
- The time between-

  a. Refrigeration and cooking / processing

  b. Cooking and eating

  c. Cooking and refrigeration

  d. Refrigeration and serving must be kept as short as possible.

Handling

- Fooding handling should be minimized, and high-risk food must not be left sitting out at room temperature
- Do not refreeze any frozen goods that have already been thawed
- Use utensils such as tongs, forks, spoons and scoops to handle food, where possible.
- Avoid touching the part of crockery or cutlery that come into contact with food.
- Try and use separate utensils and surfaces e.g. bench space for meat and other fresh food preparation.
- Keep the workspace clean and uncluttered.
- Ensure that dirty dishes are kept separate from clean ones at all times.

Spotting spoilage

- Remove or throw away food with signs of spoilage.
- Signs of spoilage include:

  a. Odour

  b. Sliminess

  c. Discolouration

d. Souring

e. Gas

- If in doubt, throw it out.

Personal hygiene for people handling food

They must—

- Wash their hands before and after handling any food equipment. This should be done with warm water and soap for at least 20 seconds. Wash them at 15 minute intervals to ensure cleanliness.
- Wash their hands immediately after going to the toilet.
- Minimize—

a. Touching their face

b. Licking their fingers

c. Biting their fingernails

d. Sneezing or coughing over food or in open food areas

e. Smoking or when, they must wear another item of clothing over the top of the kitchen uniform

f. Touching their hair, ears and earrings.

- Not prepare or handle any food if they suffered from diarrhea in the previous two or three days
- Cover any cuts or souse on their hands with a bandage and use gloves
- Cover their hairs.
- Keep uniform clean-wash them on a regular basis.
- Remove jewellery as it harbors bacteria, can cause possible injury if caught in machinery, or burns if it comes in contact with heat
- Inform management of sickness or poor health, as you are putting other people at risk.

Selling

Food cannot be sold that is:

- Unfit for human consumption
- Adulterated
- Damaged, deteriorated or perished
- Not to the nature or quality demanded by the consumer
- Not to the standards set by the food standards code.

Packaging

Goods must be in:

- Approved packaging that will not contaminate, harm, or alter the food product.
- Well- sealed and leak-proof packaging
- Packaging that protects the food from damage under normal handling conditions.
- Packaging that is clearly labeled and date coded, with the shelf life date and production date present.

Premises hygiene

- Have a carefully maintained cleaning schedule that ensures that all kitchen items are cleaned efficiently and regularly.
- Pull items out from the walls and clean behind and beneath them regularly.
- Remove dampness in kitchens and storage areas, as rodents and bacteria are drawn to these.
- Launder mops, cleaning cloths, dust cloths and other cleaning equipment frequently.
- Clean underneath bench and stove canopies.
- Clean up food spillage immediately, as they can attract pests and insects.
- Keep all cleaning fluids away from food.
- Store cleaning products in marked containers and follow the manufacture's instructions.
- Ensure that rubbish is removed through out the day to outdoor waste areas. Make sure outdoor waste areas are kept clean and tidy to avoid attracting indesirable rodents or birds.

GUIDELINES FOR HYGIENE STANDARDS BUFFET AND CATERED MEALS

Purchase And Receive

1. Purchase food products and Ingredients from reliable suppliers :
   a. **Temperature**: Ensure that the raw food/Ingredients are received at the propertemperature; eg. chilled food was received in the chilled condition, if applicable.
   b. **Packaging**: Check the packaging. It should be intact. There should be no sign of leakage or damage. The food products also should not have unusual appearance, odour or colour.
   c. **Label and expiry date**: Inspect the label to ensure that the food products have not reached their expiry dates.
3. Store perishable goods like chilled and frozen food items at proper temperature immediately upon delivery.
4. Pay extra attention to high-risk food. What are high-risk food?

High-risk food are those with possible presence of pathogens and may support microbial growth or toxin formation. These include raw seafood like oysters, cooked meat, eggs etc.

Proper temperature control (e.g. chilled food must be kept at or below 40° C, and hot food must be kept at or more than 60°C) of high-risk food is imperative for several reasons: Prevent proliferation of pathogens: High protein food like milk and cooked meat provides favourable condition for microbial growth. Minimise microbial growth in raw, ready-to-eat food as they are not further processed to destroy possible pathogens present. Buffet and catered meals have been receiving great appeal among the Singaporeans. A large variety of food, ranging from raw to cooked food, is usually displayed at the self-service counters or served to the public by caterers and food retail outlets. If adequate measures are not taken during preparation, transport and display, the buffet or catered food may get contaminated or become spoilt, resulting in unpleasant and costly incidents involving food borne illnesses. The set of guidelines presented in this document describes several measures that a catering firm or food retail outlet may implement in order to ensure that the buffet or catered food is wholesome and safe to consume.

STORAGE

Proper storage of food will ensure that the raw food/Ingredients remain wholesome and safe to use.

1. Adopt first-in-first-out principle during storage of food.
2. Ensure that cooked food is stored above raw food in the refrigerator, to avoid contamination.
3. Ensure the food products are kept at an appropriate temperature (e.g. chilled food must be kept at or below 40° C) during storage. Proper temperature control is imperative in preserving the shelf life of food products.
4. High-risk food, which are served raw, should be handled carefully as ready-to-eat food. Since they pose a risk of contamination to other ready-to-eat food as well, they should be stored andhandled separately from such other raw or ready-to-eat food. Reserve a specific storage space and cover properly before storage to prevent cross-contamination.
5. Avoid overloading the refrigerator with warm or hot food, as this will affect the internal cooling effect.
6. Check the temperature display of the refrigerator regularly to ensure that the food are stored at the correct temperature.

PREPARATION OF FOOD

Observe strict personal, food and environmental hygiene practices during preparation of food:

What are these practices?

1. Wash hands frequently with soap and water, especially before preparing and handling food. Not washing hands after going to toilet will put your patrons at a high risk of acquiring food borne illnesses. Your hands may contain microorganisms, which are invisible to naked eye, and may cause gross contamination of food. This may also result in production of toxins on the food.

2. When you have diarrhea, fever or infectious diseases, do not handle or prepare the food.
3. Prevent cross-contamination.
   a. Separate ready-to-eat food and raw food during preparation.
   b. Use separate utensils e.g. knives and chopping boards etc., for handling raw and ready-to-eat food.
4. Where practical, prepare or display food in small batches to avoid prolonged storage of food at room temperature – especially for buffet. Likewise, do not prepare the food too early in advance. Plan carefully beforehand on the amount of food to prepare and the time required for preparation.
5. Thawing of frozen food should be carried out in a chiller or microwave, instead of exposing on a table at room temperature.
6. Cook food thoroughly. Ensure that cooking process or equipment used is capable of cooking the food thoroughly.
7. Pre-chilled Ingredients could be used to prepare cold dishes e.g. salad. This will help to maintain temperature control of these dishes.

DISPLAY AND SERVING

1. Do not display ready-to-eat raw food and cooked food together so as to avoid cross contamination. Isolate them using physically separated compartments. If possible, separate them in different areas.
2. Ensure that the food is kept at appropriate temperature during display. Incidents of food poisoning have been reported when the cooked food was left at room temperature for more than four hours! However, it is best to consume the food at the earliest, owing to factors such as physical condition of the customers, extent of contamination, virulence of the pathogenic microorganisms etc., which may affect the holding time.

What is the danger zone of temperature?

This refers to a temperature zone of 5-60° C, which allows pathogenic microorganisms to multiply rather rapidly.

1. Keep hot food on hot holding equipment and cold food on food grade ice, chiller or refrigerator. Provide lids to cover hot food to maintain temperature of the food.
2. Display food in proper showcase like sneeze guard. Where the food containers are to be kept open during display or serving, ensure that the food is maintained in a hygienic condition.
3. Keep the display time of ready-to-eat food reasonably short (since long display time may lead to food spoilage or formation of bacterial toxins inside the food if the food is contaminated with bacteria/pathogens). Display small portion or small tray of food and replenish them more frequently.

4. Serve condiments in single service packets or containers with lids to prevent cross contamination.
5. Customers may be a source of contamination to the food. Provide serving spoons, tongs, ladles or utensils for customers to pick up the food at the display area.
6. Do not reuse the leftovers that had been served to the customers. Do not re-serve or reuse the ready-to-eat food eg. raw oysters, salmon etc. to be served as cooked dishes.

SERVING

The most important rule to remember with regard to the serving of food is that hot dishes must be served really hot, and cold ones as cold as possible. Always warm the plates and dishes to be used for hot food. Stand them, covered with a cloth, on a rack above the cooker; never attempt to heat them quickly by putting them in the oven. If over-heated they are liable to crack. Salads, grapefruit, etc., should be quite cold when served. If you have no refrigerator, keep them in a cool, dark place, until ready for the table. It is a good plan to set the table well in advance. Water, bread and butter, however, should not be put on the table until shortly before the meal. Dust and flies may settle on them, and they are not at their best condition if exposed to the air.

Always allow the tap to run for a minute or two before filling the water-jug. If filled at once, lukewarm water which may have been standing some time in the pipe will be used.

If you find any difficulty in getting your family to be punctual for meals, sound a warning gong or bell five minutes before dishing up. Nothing is more unappetizing than half-cold food. However busy your family is, it should be able to "down tools" and get ready for the meal should then be on the table, piping hot, at the exact time fixed. Finally, remember the importance of serving dishes which are attractive to the eye. Cutlery, ect., should be carefully washed; scraps of food remaining from a previous meal are most unpleasant.

PRESERVING FRUIT AND VEGETABLES

Drying is a very useful method of preserving fruits and vegetables, as the fruits can be stored in a small space, such as a shelf in a warm, dry cupboard. The drying can be done in any warm place, such as a cooling oven in the kitcheners, or the gas stove after the cooking has been done. Put your fruits in the oven when the gas is out after baking; it will retain its heat for a considerable time. When it becomes too cool, light the gas and turn it very low, then as soon as it is hot enough, turn it out and light it again when necessary. The oven door must always be left ajar to allow a circulation of air and to prevent the fruits being " cooked".

NECESSARY TEMPERATURES FOR DRYING

Apples, pears, peaches, plums, cherries and apricots: 110 to 150 ° C. Small berried fruits: 110 to 140° C. Leaf vegetables, such as spinach: 110 to 145° C. Root vegetables: 110 to 150° C. Peas: 110 to 145° C. do not get the heat above the temperatures given; if it drops it does not matter; the fruits will only take a longer time to dry.

FRUIT FOR DRYING

Apples, pears, peaches, plums, apricots and cherries are excellent dried. Small berries are not so successful; in fact, it does not advise drying them. They are far nicer when bottled. Root vegetables, cut in stgrips and dried, are most useful for soups and stews, especially in the early spring, before the new vegetables come in and the old ones are tough and stringy. All the3 apparatus you need is some drying trays and very thin muslin. Apples, plums, and root vegetables should feel like a piece of leather. Pliable, but not hard enough to break, when they are sufficiently dried. Cut a piece off one end and see if you can press out any moisture; If very moist, they need more drying. Put the vegetables or fruit to be dried on the trays and put them in the oven when the fire is out, or nearly so, and the oven warm, but not hot or fierce, and leave the oven door ajar. They can be left in all night without harm. The drying process is a long one, but it need not be accomplished all at once. If the oven is needed for cooking, the trays can be taken out of the oven and put in again when the cooking is done. In warm weather it is a good plan to put the trays in a sunny window during the heat of the day, but any time when they are out of the oven be very careful to keep them covered with very thin muslin to keep off dust and insects.

PREPARING FRUITS FOR DRYING

Apples and pears should be peeled, cored and cut into rings. These can be dried on the trays or, better still threaded on sticks cut to a size that will lodge on the ridges that hold your oven shelves. Pears may also be cut into slices or halves. To prevent apple-rings discolouring they may be dipped in cold water4 with a good tablespoon of lemon juice to 2 quarts of water. But if this is done they must be well drained and dried in a towel before they are put in the oven.

Plums and similar stone fruit must be washed, if necessary, and each one wiped with a clean cloth. Cut them in half with a silver or plated knife, take out the stones, then place the fruit on the trays the cut side upwards, turning them when that side is dry. Fruit should look quite dry and shriveled when ready to store. Cherries should not be stoned; in the stoning process so much juice and flavour is lost. They should be just ripe, sound and firm.

ROOT VEGETABLES

Artichokes, carrots, parsnips, turnips, etc., must be thoroughly washed and dried, scraped or peeled. They may then be cut into thin strips and dried. Done in this way, they are excellent for julienne soup, etc. They may also be half cooked and then cut in slices and dried.

PEAS

Choose sound, fully grown, but not old peas; shell them, put them on a baking tin lined with butter muslin, and sprinkle over them 1 oz. Of sugar and a dessertspoon of salt for every 2 quarts of peas. Put them in a cool oven in front of a fire, or in the sun, and move them about occasionally until they seem quite dry. Leave them till quite cold, then fill jam jars with them and cover with lid.

MUSHROOMS

Skin them, put them on trays in a cooling oven and leave them until dry and shriveled. Cut one through to test when dry. When ready, put them in paper bags and hang them in a dry place or store in tins. They are excellent for flavouring soups and stews.

BEFORE STORING

When the fruits or vegetables are sufficiently dried, they should be left in a warm room for several days before being stored. Cover them with muslin and stir them about occasionally. They, may be stored in glass jars, tins or wooden boxes, with well-fitting lids.

TO DRY HERBS

All kinds of herbs may be dried. Gather them in full leaf before they begin to flower. Tie them in bunches. Hang them in a warm place in the kitchen or in the sun, protecting them from dust with butter muslin. As soon as they are dry and crisp, put them in paper bags and hang them in a dry place, or pick off the leaves, pound them to powder, store in dry bottles, cork and seal.

TO BOTTLE FRUIT

The thrifty housewife can nowadays bottle sufficient fruit to last the winter through, and so have fruit of all kinds all the year round, for the process is really quite simple. It can be accomplished without any expensive outlay; excellent bottle can be purchased complete with rubber hand and screw tops for six shillings a dozen and they last indefinitely, for there is very little risk of breakages. Both the vacuum and screw-top kinds are equally good. When purchasing, see that the rim of the bottle is perfectly smooth; if there is any flaw or roughness the rubber will not cling, and air will be able to enter. Vacuum bottles have rubber rings and glass or metal tops. Little clips are also supplied with these to keep the tops firmly down while the fruit is being sterilized. Screw bottles have rubber rings, glass covers and metal screw tops.

Any glass bottles or jars can be used for bottling fruit, although, of course, they are generally not so good as patent bottles. The great point is to make them perfectly air-tight. You can do this either by pouring clarified lard or mutton fat an inch deep into the bottles and then covering with parchment or bladder, or by getting corks to fit your bottles, soaking them in cold water overnight and driving them firmly in. A little paraffin wax or pure tallow should then be melted and poured over the bottle tops. Whatever bottles you use, see that they are scrupulously clean. A sterilizer is a good investment, if you bottle yearly for a large family, but it is not a necessity. A sterilizer consists of a kettle of best block tin, with a fixed perforated tray in it, so that the bottles do not stand on the bottom of the pan. There is a place for a thermometer at the side, so that you may read the exact temperature of the water.

Soft fruits should not be washed unless any form of blight is found upon them. Berries need to be very carefully looked over for insects. To wash plums and other hard fruits, put them in a colander and let cold water run well over them, then wipe them with a clean cloth as you put them in the bottles. All stalks must be removed before bottling.

PACKING THE BOTTLES

Pack the fruit in as tightly as possible; the blunt end of a wooden skewer or the handle of a wooden spoon will help considerably in doing this. Shake down into position. Grade the fruit, putting those of equal size together.

TO STERILIZE FRUIT

Having filled the bottles with fruit, pour cold water in gently until it is covered., then let the bottles remain open for a little while to dispense the air bubbles. Dip the rubber rings in cold water, put one on each bottle, being sure that it fits evenly, then put on the top, and, if you are using a vacuum bottle, secure it with a clip. If, however, a screw-top bottle is being used, put on the wet rubber ring, then the glass top, and screw on the metal cover loosely over both. For ordinary bottles just put the corks in lightly. Put a little cold water in the sterilizer, then stand the bottles of fruit in it, adding more cold water if necessary. It should come nearly three parts up the bottles, and must, of course, be high enough to cover the bulb of the thermometer. With a sterilizer the bottles do not need any protection; they will not break even if they touch each other. Put the lid on the sterilizer, place over a low gas ring or at the side of a kitcheners, and let it heat very, very gradually to 160° C. this should take nearly one hour and a half. As soon as the thermometer shows the heat to be 160° C, lower the gas or draw the pan to a cooler part of the stove, and let the heat drop gradually keep that heat for two hours for soft fruits, or three hours for plums, etc., or very large bottles.

Take the bottles out of the sterilizer and stand them on a wooden table. Do not stand them on stone or in a very cold place; they may crack. Leave them for two days, then test if they are air-tight. To do this, remove the clip or metal top, whichever you happen to be using, and see if you can lift the bottles up by the top without any moisture coming out at all. If you can, then your bottling is a success. I have some fruits three years old as good as when I bottled them. Another test is to turn them upside down. If you find the tops will come off or moisture comes out, seek the cause; it will probably be a bottle, lid, or rubber with a flaw. Remedy the trouble and re-sterilize the fruit.

TO BOTTLE FRUIT

Kettle For Boiler

The nearest substitute for a sterilizer is a kettle or boiler. Place the bottles either on the strainer or a wooden stand made of pieces of wood crossed, or else put a piece of cloth at the bottom of the vessel. The idea is to prevent the bottles coming into contact with too great a heat. The bottles should also be bound round with a little hay or cloth. Stand the kettle on an asbestos mat to keep the water under boiling heat. Pack the prepared fruit or vegetables into the bottles and cover the contents with cold water. Fill the kettle with enough cold water to reach the necks of the bottles and place it over very gentle heat until the water begins to simmer. The heat should be so gradual that it will take nearly two hours before it comes to simmering point. Do not let it reach any greater heat than this. Let the bottles remain in this heat for one hour. Screw up or cover while hot.

To Bottle Fruit Without Water

This type of bottling is only suitable for soft juicy fruit, such as currants, raspberries, etc., they retain their flavour and colour better than when water is used. See that the fruit is clean. Fill the bottles as full as possible, shaking them well down. Cover with screw tops, screwing them on very tightly. Put them in the sterilizer or boiler. Fill the boiler with cold water enough to come to be necks of the bottles, and heat very, very slowly. When the juice has flowed and the fruit shrunk, take out the bottles, open them, and fill up some from others. Replace the stoppers. Put the full bottles back in the sterilizer and sterilize for one hour at 155° F. Take them out, screw up tightly, Stand on wood until cold, then store.

To Bottle Fruit In Syrup

Fruits may be bottled in syrup instead of plain water. Use a thin syrup for sweet ripe fruits and a thick syrup for sour fruits. To make the syrup, use 6 lb. of white sugar with 2 quarts of water. For thin syrup, boil together until the sugar has quite dissolved. For thick syrup, boil together until it is slightly thick and sticky. Skim well whilst boiling. When bottling pears or strawberries in syrup, add a dessertspoon of lemon juice to every pint of syrup.

To Bottle Fruit In The Oven

Temperature: gas, ½. Electricity, 275° F.

Make the bottles and covers hot by scalding them with boiling water. Pack them with fruit and put the cover on loosely. Put them in the oven on an asbestos mat. If you are using a gas oven with a back burner, do not put them too far back, as the gas should not be directly under them. Leave them in until they shrink and look cooked.—soft fruits will need about half an hour, hard fruits about one hour. When they are ready, take each one out and fill with boiling water and immediately put on a new rubber ring and the glass top, then screw as tightly as possible. Each one should be done as quickly as possible after it is taken from the oven. To bottle fruit in syrup in the oven, pour boiling syrup on the fruit before putting it in the oven; then put on the rubber rings and covers. Screw on loosely; as you take each one from oven, screw as tightly as possible. After 48 hours remove the screw tops and lift them by the glass lids to see if they are air-tight.

To Bottle Hard Fruits

Peaches, apricots, pears, apples and plums can be very easily bottled in the following manner:-

Make a syrup, allowing 1 lb. of sugar to every quart of water. Bring to the boil, then boil for five minutes. Put the fruit in another pan with plain water and simmer until it is tender but unbroken. Then with a wire or perforated spoon, lift out the fruit and put it in hot bottles. As soon as a bottle is full, cover it quickly with boiling syrup and screw down at once. Turn it upside down to see if there is any leakage; if there is any, unscrew the bottle, add more syrup and screw up again as tightly as you possibly can. The secrets of success with this kind of bottling are:-

Screw-topped bottles and new rubber rings must be used. The bottles must be hot, and both syrup and water must be boiling. Use a hot jug to pour the syrup into the bottles, and work quickly, covering each one as speedily as possible. Bottled fruit will keep good foryears if made absolutely air-tight.

GARNISHING AND SAVING

Bread or toast, cut in small fancy shapes with a vegetable cutter and then fried crisp in a scrap of butter,, make a good garnish for made dishes. So do cooked vegetables-carrots and potato for instance-treated in the same way and arranged in little heaps. A simple but attractive garnish for fish consists of lemon and parsley. The lemon may be just cut in quarters or slices, or Maltese crosses may be formed from the latter by cutting out half the sections. Or decorate with a water-lily design. For this cut the lemon in half across, cut off the end points so that the half lemons will stand;; then cut the rind in petal form. These look pretty among fillets of fish or croquettes. White fish may be decorated in a variety of ways. If it is a freshly-boiled piece of fish, place it whole on the dish, the white skin uppermost. Cut the white of a hard boiled egg in rings and place them down the fish, with a star of beetroot in each. Rub the yold through a sieve and sprinkle in round. Or place tomato slices on the fish alternately with rings of hard boiled egg, and surround with sliced cucumber. If it is left-over fish you want to garnish, divide it in flakes, removing all skin and bone. Pile them in the centre of a dish, cover with mayonnaise, sprinkle with egg yolk or lobster coral, garnish with sliced bananas that have been tossed in mayonnaise, and surround with young lettuce leaves and slices of hardboiled egg. Or on the flaked fish arrange a lattice design with narrow strips of beetroot, and in the spaces formed by the beetroot carefully place little balls of cream cheese. Radishes, too, make a pretty decoration. Out sections round the sides and turn them down to look like the petals of a flower. Place them round a dish of dish with leaves of watercress round. Cucumber is attractive if half the green peel is removed in strips before the cucumber is sliced, giving a striped effect. Make a wall of mashed potato or a vegetable puree of spinach, green peas, lentils or turnips and serve your mince or hash in the centre. Triangles of toast placed round mince is another way of improving its appearance. Scrape of pastry may be used in the same way. Roll them out, cut in crescents or triangles, brush them over with egg or milk and bake a golden brown.

MIXED VEGETABLE GARNISH

A pretty garnish to surround cold meat can be made by mixing together cooked carrot, turnip and celery cut in cubes or shapes and mixed with green peas. Toss them in a thick mayonnaise and use.

LEARNING OUTCOME

It is integral that all people working in the food industry practice and possess high standards of hygiene and food handling in the workplace, as bacteria and other organism can infest food and lead to illness or even death. Fooding handling should be minimized, and high-risk food must not be left sitting out at room temperature.Do not refreeze any frozen goods that have already been thawed. Use utensils such as tongs, forks, spoons and scoops to handle food, where possible. The most important rule to remember with regard to the serving of food is that hot dishes must be served really hot, and cold ones as cold as possible. Always warm the plates and dishes to be used for hot food. Stand them, covered with a cloth, on a rack above the cooker; never attempt to heat them quickly by putting them in the oven. If over-heated they are liable to crack. Salads, grapefruit, etc., should be quite cold when served. Drying is a very useful method of preserving fruits and vegetables, as the fruits can be stored in a small space, such as a shelf in a warm, dry cupboard. The drying can be done in any warm place, such as a cooling oven in the kitcheners, or the gas stove after the cooking has been done. Bread or toast, cut in small fancy shapes with a vegetable cutter and then fried crisp in a scrap of butter,, make a good garnish for made dishes. So do cooked vegetables-carrots and potato for instance-treated in the same way and arranged in little heaps

QUESTIONS FOR DISCUSSION

1. Explain the Some Important Tips to Reducing the Risk of Food Poisoning?
2. Mention the storage temperature of food items.
3. Explain the process of reheating of food.
4. Explain the process of food handling.
5. Explain the guidelines for hygiene standards buffet and catered meals?
6. Explain the process of preserving vegetables and fruits.
7. Explain the process of bottling fruits without water?
8. Explain in details about garnishes and saving.

KEY TERMS

* Buffet
* Food poisoning
* Hygiene
* Preserve
* Contaminate
* Garnsihes
* Meals
* Reheating

Culinary Teams

TERM	EXPLANATION
Aging	A term applies to meat held at a temperature of 34 to 36° F to improve the tenderness.
Agneau	Lamb
A la’	According to the style of a standard in vogue such as; A la’ Francaise Or according to the French way.
A la' Bourgeoise	Family style-plan
A la' broche	Cooked on a skewer. See brochette.
A la' carte	Foods prepare to order, each dish priced separately.
A la' king	Foods served in white cream sauce which contains Mushroom and green peppers and often Pimentoes.
A la' Marengo	Sautéed chicken with mushrooms, tomatoes, olives and olive oil, with deep fried egg on top.
A la' Mode	Usually refers to ice-cream on top of pie but may be other dishes served in a special way. See beef a la' mode.
A la' Provencale	Dishes with garlic and olive oil. See provencale.
A la' Russe	The Russian way.
Alsacienne	Dishes garnished with sauerkraut and spatzeli. Saurkaut, a curled cabbage.
A l’allemande	Garnished with noodles and mashed Potatoes
Allumette Potatoes	Cut like match stick Potatoes and Pomme Poille.
Aldalouse a l’	Consommé and Potage with tomatoes and rice Garnish : Tomatoes, rice eggplant, red peppers Sauce (Mayonnaise will tomatoes and red peppers. Spanish onions, cucumbers tomatoes, egg, oil and vinegar).
Anglaise	In English style

Appareil	Mixture of different elements for preparation for a dish.
Argenteuil	Soups, eggs or garnishes made with asparagus
Aspic	Clear meat or poultry jelly.
Au gratin	Food covered with a sauce sprinkled with cheese, crumbs and baked.
Au'jus	Served with natural juices or gravy.
Au lait	With milk
Au natural	Served in a simple unadorned style.
Aux croutons	Bread cut in fine dices and fried in butter used for soups and canapés
Avocado also avocat	Alligator pear, Brownish or purple berry filled with pulp-like marrow, from Southern California, tropical America and west Indies.
Baba	A yeast raised cake. One famous variety is flavoured and soaked in rum before serving fruit. Cream, whipped cream or Sabayon may be added. Only baba Au Rum is soaked in Rum.
Bain-Marie	Hot or cold water both used to cook food (Double water boiler) to keep food warm (Steam table) or to keep food cold.
Baking	To cook by dry heat, usually in an oven.
Bard	To wrap poultry, game, or dish with thin slices of fat or salted pork.
Baste	To moisten food products with stock, drippings or fat while cooking.
Batter	Mixture of four and liquid of a consistency that can be stirred
Bayleaf	The aromatic leave of the Sweet bay or Laurel Tree, grown in the Mediterranean Countries and in Southern region of USA. Used for seasoning soups fish, sauces, meats (in particularly Beef) etc.
Beansprouts	Mung beans from China. Sprouts are tiny and green when used.
Bearnaise	Mothers Sauce - contains egg yolk, butter, tarragon and seasoning
Bechamel	A rich cream sauce or white sauce.
Béurre	Butter
Bisque	Thick sauce or soup from shellfish or game.
Bisque Ice Cream	High butter fat content ice cream with dried macaroon or sponge cake crumbs
Blanc	White
Blending	Thoroughly maxing two or more Ingredients
Blinis	Russian buckwheat flour pancakes usually served with Caviar.

Boeuf	Beef
Bombe	A frozen dessert made of a combination of two or more frozen mixtures e.g. Ice Cream and Sherbet, Mousse or Spumoni pegged in a round or melon shaped mould and frozen
Borscht	A vegetable soup with the ascent on beefs, some time with duck, Native to Poland or Russia. Often Sour Cream is added.
Bouchee	Small meat patty of pastry shell filled with meat, poultry or lobster.
Bouillabaisse	The much some French Provencal stew made of numerous types of fishes combined with savory spices and olive oil. Served in soup plate with dry toasts (often served with toasted French Garlic Bread).
Bouillon	A clear soup made of one stock which is not as strong as consommé but stronger than broth.
Bouquet Garni	A bouquet of fresh herbs tied together in a cheese cloth bag, to use in soups and stews, removed before dish is served.
Bouquetiere a la	With a variety of vegetables in season.
Brazier	Heavy duty stewing pan with tightly fitting lid cover.
Brine	Liquid of salt and vinegar for pickling.
Brochette	A feathery yeast cake. A favourite breakfast bun in France.
Brunoise	Cutting fine dices.
Buffet	Display of ready to eat foods. Often self servie from a table of assorted foods.
Café noir	Black coffee
Canapes	Small pieces of fried or toasted bread or crackers, topped with a wide variety of appetizers. Eaten with fingers.
Capers	Flower bud of a South European plant which is pickled. Used for flavouring or garnish.
Cardinal Sauce	Bechamel with shrimps or lobster roe and lemon juice.
Caviar	Salted roe or eggs of fish, usually Sturgeon, served as a sandwich spread or in place of appetizers.
Champignons	Mushroom.
Chantilly Cream	Vanilla whipped cream.
Cayenne peper	Hot seasoning; from red pepper.
Celeria	A bulb rooted celery eaten as a vegetable. Only the root is used.

Capes	Species of mushrooms
Champignons	Mushrooms
Chantilly Cream	Vanilla flavoured sweetened whipped cream.
Chantilly Sauce	Hot Hollandaise Sauce with sweetened whipped cream.
Chasseur	Served with tomatoes and mushrooms. Hunter Style.
Chateaubriand	A special cut of meat from the large end of tenderloin, usually broiled. History, Francis August Viscount of Chateubriant (Chate abriant) was born in St. Malo on Sept 14th, 1768 and died on July 4th, 1848. History remembers him as a dogmatice author and Statesman and a brilliant representative of the reactions against the ideas of the French Revolution. When a new dish was invented it was quality, double steak fillet cut, with a pocket stuffed with chopped shallots, bee marrow and spice or herbs of Chef's own choice (in Austgralia they stuff it with snails) moistened with meat glaze. The original recipe has changed to include truffles, mushrooms, and anchovy butter. Today Chateaubriand generally refers to a glazed beef filled, smothered in Maitre D'hotel butter. Most recipe include shallots or small onions and cayenne pepper as seasoning. The steak is often served with Bearnaise Sauce
Chaud	Hot (Temperature-wise).
Chaud-froids	Decorated poultry jelly.
Chef	Chief of Kitchen
Chemise	Potatoes boiled with their skin on.
Cherries Jubilee	Cherries set aflame with Kirshwasser or brandy and liqueurs. Mostly served over Vanilla Ice-cream.
Chervil	An herb resembling parsley, slightly peppery, the leaves of which are used for flavouring or decorations. Used in salads, eggs and poultry dishes, main dishes sauces and many French Dishes
Chicory	A green of the endive family. The leaves are used for salads, the root is used as cooked vegetable or sometimes roasted, ground and used as an adulterant for coffee (war-time in Europe).
Chiffonade	Shredded vegetables or meats used on soups or salads or as garnishing. Also dressing: French dressing with chopped hard-boiled eggs, minced onions, parsley or chervil, olives and pickled beefs added
China Cap	A cone shaped strainer or sieve.
Chives	A variety of greenish onions, delicious in many salads and sauces.

Chow-chow	Chopped vegetables pickles, usually put up with strongly spiced Mustard Sauce.
Choux	Name given to paste because most commonly it is baked in shaped which somewhat resembles cabbage-as cream puff.
Choux	An Indian relish frequently made of fruits, vegetables, spices, vinegar and sugar.
Cisler	To cut, to make an incision in the skin of fish, so it will not crack during cooking.
Cloche, Sous	Under bell, usually glass.
Cobber	A drink with liquor, sugar, sliced fruits and mint. Also a fruit dessert.
Cocotte	Small earthen cooking ware Coddling. Cooking below the boiling point.
Colbert Sauce	A derivative of brown sauce. Brown sauce with shallots, butter and lemon.
Compote	A dish of steved fruits, but usually retaining their natural shapes
Concasser	To chop roughly.
Condiments	Seasonings
Consommé'	A clear soup made from two or more kinds of meats e.g. beef, fowl, or veal, highly seasoned.
Copper	Metal cooking unit, stationery, heated with steam jackets.
Coriander	An Ingredients of Curry Powder. A small aromatic sed used for flavouring.
Cornish Game Hen	Cross between Cornish hen and White Rock, small boned, double breasted, all white meat, ready to cook. Weighs about 1 pound (450 gms)
Court Bouillon	A highly seasoned broth in which fish is cooked.
Cover Charge	Fixed fee for table service independent of the charge for food or drinks.
Crepes	French Pancakes
Crepes Suzette	Thin French pancakes served with rich brandy sauce. Usually flamed.
Cresson	Watercress.
Croissants	Crescent-shaped baked breakfast rolls. Croissants are most favoured by French Customers. Croissants are usually accompanied with Honey.
Croquette	Seasoned Thick white sauce or mashed potatoes base with finely minced meat, fish or vegetables shaped into cones shape or pipes, (may be prepared from rice as well) dipped in beaten eggs and fine bread crumbs and deep fried to golden brown colour before service, accompanied with Tomato Ketchup.

Croutons	Small dices of fried or toasted bread used in Soups or as under liner for all kinds of canapés.
Cuisine	Art of Cookery.
Cumberland Sauce	A sweet sauce made with Port wine, Currant Jelly, orange and lemon juice with orange and lemon peel.
Curry	East Indian dish. Was originally a stew. Now referred to with mixing of pungent curry seasoning.
Danish Pastry	Various shapes of rich yeast dough with puff layers, may have fillings of almonds, cream cheese, fruits or marmalade.
Dauphinoise	Veal or beef roasts or meats garnished with Dauphin Potaoes (mashed potatoes and cream puff dough)
Dejeuner	Lunch
Petite Dejeuner	Break fast
Demi	Half
Demi Tasse	A small or half cup of strong black coffee (French Style)
Diced	Cut into small squares
Dindonneau	Young Turkey
Dragees	Tiny ball-shaped silver or gold candies used as decorations for cakes and pastries.
Drown Butter	Melted butter
Dredging	Coating with drying Ingredients (as flour of sugar powder).
Drippings	The fat and juice which drops from roasting meats.
Dry	A term applied to a beverage (wine) meaning low percentage of sugar.
Dubarry	Any garnish or soup with cauliflower may be called "a lá Dubarry" or Dubarry style.
Duchess Potatoes	Seasoned, mashed or rice potatoes to which beaten egg yolks have been added. Usually squeezed through a pastry bag.
A lá Dugler'	Dishes with onions, shallots and tomatoes.
Dusting	Sprinkling with flour.
Éclair	A Choux-paste puff (cream puff paste) triangular in shape with cream filling, frosted with Chocolate icing. May be served (without icing) is an appetizer, filled with meat, fish, poultry or live stuffing.
Ecossaise	Scottish Style.

Eggplant	Large purple pear shaped brinjals.
Eggs a lá goldenrod	White Sauce with chopped white of eggs poured over toast. Hard cooked yolks pressed through a sieve and sprinkled on top.
Eggs Benedict	Poached eggs served with ham or tongue with Hollandaise Sauce on toasted English Muffins or Toast.
Emince'	Cut fine Referring to something sliced or fan shaped.
Emince' of beef	Thin slices of beef.
En Casseroled	Foods served in the same dish in which they are cooked or baked.
Enchiladas	Mexican tortillas covered with Sauce and grated Cheese, spices etc.
En Chemise	With their skins. Usually potatoes.
En coquille	In the shell
Endive	A curly green salad.
English Pickled Walnuts	A age-old English delicacy made from walnut fruit before the shell harderss and picked in malt vinegar, served with roast meat.
Entrée	Originally referring to accompanying dishes for the first course of a fore meal. A hot Entrée usually precedes the main course and a cold Entrée is served after the main course. In an informal meal. I refers to the main dish of the main course.
Entremet	Usually it refers to the sweet course. Used as a title heading of the dessert section of menu.
Epigromme	Boned breast of lamb.
Escalloped	To cut thin slices sideways.
Escoffier	Trade name for bottled sauces. Also the name of famous French Chef.
Espagnolé	One of the basic sauce made from brown stock, brown roux and mirepoix and strained.
Estamine	Tammy or double thickness of cheesecloth for straining soups and sauces. Also used to pack half limes for fruits accompaniments.
Farce	Stuffing
Farci	Stuffed
Farina	The coarsely ground inner portion of hard wheat.
Farinaceous	Dishes consisting of or made of flour (pasta dishes are farinaceous.
A lá Fermiere	Dishes with slices of carrots, turnips, onions, potatoes, celery and cabbage.

Filet	Strips cut from the underside of the loin of beef, veal, pork or lamb and boned.
Fillets	Boneless fish.
Fine herbs	A combination of chives, chervils and finely chopped parsley used for flavouring soups, sauces and other dishes.
Finnan Hadie	Smoked haddock.
Florentine	With Spinach
Foie Gras	Fatted Goose Liver.
Fondante Potatoes	Oval shaped, partially cooked by boiling, re-shaped in towel, finished in oven.
Fondue	Cheese dish. Usually made with white wine and Swiss Cheese.
Forcemeat	Chopped meats and seasoning used for stuffing.
Frappe'	Partially frozen drinks or desserts.
Frizzling	Cooking in small amount of fat until crisp.
Froid	Cold
Fromage	Cheese
Galantine	Fresh, tender chicken, fish or meat ground and forced through a sieve. The "force' meat it then seasoned, heavy cream and egg white is added to give a spongy consistency. Pack into a muslin cloth to give the sharpe of a bologne and cook in chicken broth or pick into emould (pate) and place to cool in the pan of water and bake in oven. Unmould and decorate before service.
Garbonzo	Chick peas. Spanish national Dish.
Garde Manager	Cold meat department or person in charge of it.
Garnish	To embellish food to decorate.
Garniture	French word for garnish
Gastric	Cooking term for mixture of white wine or vinegar, crushed pepper, shallots and spices.
Gateau	Cake
Gaufres	Wafers
Gaufrettee Potatoes	French Fried potatoes in waffle form
Gefulte Fish	Jewish favorite Stuffed fish. Today usually picked.

Gherkins	Small cucumbers (a few days old) usually pickled in rue and vinegar.
Giblets	Liver, heart and trimmings from poultry
Glace	The proteins (in flour plus liquid) which produces gluten to give bread its framework.
Glaze	A semi-transparent or glossy coating. To cover with same.
Gnocchi	Light dumplings Usually made from farina (cream of wheat).
Goulash	A Hungarian Beef Stew with onions, tomatoes, potatoes and paprika.
Gourmet	Connoisseur of food and drinks, known as epicure. One who eats everything. Overeating.
Au gratin	Sprinkled with grated cheese, cheese sauce, crumbs and baked under the salamander
Grenadine	Pomegranate Syrup used for beverages and desserts.
Gruyere	Swiss type of cheese made in France and Switzerland.
Guava	Tropical fruit. Apple or pear shaped, acidic sweet flavour.
Gumbo	Chicken, onions, okra, green peppers and tomatoes.
Harchi	Hashed, minced.
Hard Sauce	Delicately flavoured sauce made by creaming butter and sugar together with corresponding liquors (Kirsch Brandy and Cordials).
Haricots Verts	Small green string beans.
Hasenpfeffer	German Rabbit stew.
Heifer	A young female cow that I as not had a calf. (A virgin young cow).
Herb Bouquet	Mixed herbs for seasoning
A lá Hongroise	Prepared in Hungarian way, Onions, Sour Cream and Paprika, Garnish: with red and green peppers, cabbage and leeks.
Hors d' oeuvres	Small relishes or appetizers. Served as first course of a mean.
Hush Puppies	Southern deep-fried dish o' corn-meal, baking powder, milk, onion and seasoning.
Hydrogenated Fat	Fat treated with Hydrogen to maintain stable consistency.
Indian Pudding	Slow baked dessert of corn meal, brown sugar, eggs, raisins and seasoning.
Infusion	Liquid obtained from steeping a food.
Irish Stew	National dish of Ireland, made from unbrowned mutton or lamb, potatoes, and cabbage. (white or green) and seasoning with Worcester's Sauce. (Classic, no other Ingredients.)

Italian Minestrone	Vegetable soup with a macaroni product and cheese.
Italians	Veal or chicken dishes garnished with spaghetti or noodles, if Parmesan Cheese is added, it may be called "A LA MILANESE".
Jerked Beef	Sliced beef dried cut in the sun. (Chipped beef, dry beef).
Johnny Cake	Bread from yellow cornmeal, egg and milk
Julienne	Refers to vegetables and meat cuts in fine strips (match stick size) for soups, and salads.
Karo	Corn Syrup, light or dark in colour.
Kasha	Buckwheat gloats.
Kippered herrings	Dried or smoker herrings
Kitchen Bouquet	A mixture of herbs used for flavouring soups and stews etc. It may also be obtained in liquid form which is used to give a brown colour as well as flavour to sauces and gravies.
Khol-Rabi	A variety of cabbage turnip well known in Europe Served sliced with Cream Sauce.
Kosher	Meat sold within 48 hours after butchering in accordance with prescribed Hebrows religious laws. Or, syle of cooking with dietary restrictions.
Kumquats	Gold-orange colour, small oval citrus fruits.
Lait	Milk
Lamb Fries.	Lamb testicles.
Langouste	Crayfish (a shell fish).
Larding	Strips of salted pork inserted into meats.
Lasagne	Very broad flat noodles, for one favorite dish, cooked lasagna is layered with meat, tomato sauce and Mozzaretta Ricotta and Parsean Cheeses and then baked.
Leek	Small onion-like plant.
Legumes	Vegetables. Also refers to such dried food such as beans, peas and lentils.
Lentil	Flat seeds somewhat like peas. Used for soups and garnishes
Lichi Nut	Chinese. Small hard shell dried nuts.
Macedoine	De Fruits means Fruits Salad
Madrilene Soup	Clear Consommé with tomatoes. Highly seasoned, served jellied or hot.
Maggi	Brand name of Swiss liquid seasoning.

Maitre d'Hote	A sauce of softened butter, parsley, lemon juice and seasoning, serve with fish, steak etc.
Maitre d' Hotel	Head of Catering department, head of food service.
Manhattan Clam Chowder	Clam soup with tomatoes.
Maraschino	Italian Cherry cordial. A so refers to Cherries.
Marrow	Soft tissues from inside o cavity of bones
Marsala	Pale golden semi dry Italian Sherry from Sicily.
Marzipan	A paste of sweet Almonds and sugar, may be formed into small fruits or other shapes, diluted with lemon, Kirsch or Cinnamon Water used tor pastry fillings.
Masking	To cover completely (usually with a sauce)
Mate'	South American laraguay Tea.
Matelots	Fish stewed with vine, onions and seasoning.
Meat Tenderizer	Commercial preparation containing enzyme extracted from papaya. Has a tenderizing effect on the connective tissues of meat.
Melba	Vanilla Ice Cream, raspberry sauce or Jelly, whipped cream, served with peach or pear.
Melba Toast	Very Thin slices of white bread, baked in oven until brown
Crème de menthe	Mint cordial
Menu	Bill of fare.
Meringue	Paste made of beaten egg white and sugar.
A lá meuniere	Fish dipped in floor, sautéed in butter, served with brown butter, lemon and sprinkle it with parsley before service.
Mignon	Small tender filet, usually from Beef Tenderloin.
Minced	Chopped fine
Mincing	Chopping in less regular parts, similar to grinding.
Mire Poix	A roughly cuts of vegetables include carrots, onion, leek etc.
Mornay	Thick white sauce with equal amounts of whipped cream, with or without cheese.
Mortadella	Italian Pork and Beef Sausages.
Mousse	Applied to very thick, light dessert, generally prepared with whipped cream, beaten egg whites or gelatin

Mouton	Mutton
Mozzarella	Soft Italian Cheese made of milk, shaped into rounds
Mulligatawny	Famous Indian Soup, rich with meat flavors and spices-curry.
Mushroom Sauce	Brown Sauce, fat flour, stock, mushrooms and seasoning.
Napoleon	French Pastries, sheets spread with frosting, decorated with thin lines of chocolate icing (Tranche Mille-Feuille).
Navarin	Mutton stew with carrots and turnips
Nectarine	Variety of peach, smooth, looks like a cross between peach and plum
Newburg	A cream dish with egg yolk added. Sometimes flavoured with wine or sherry. Most often applied to lobster or shrimps Served or toast.
Noir	Black
Nouilles	(German: Nudlen). Narrow strips of deep fried dough resembling macaroni, used in soups and garnishes.
O'Brian Potatoes	Diced cocked potatoes, sautéed with pimentos and / or green pepper.
Oeufs	Eggs.
Okra	Vegetable pods. Used in soups, gumbos. Also served as a vegetable.
Over-run	Increased volume produced by whipping air, as in ice cream.
Oysters Blue points	Name of oyster from certain Atlantic coast waters. Usually served raw, on the half-shell with tangy sauce
Oysters Rockefellers	Oysters in deep half shells, topped with butter and herb sauce then baked on bed of rock salt in shallow baking pan.
Pain	Bread
Palm Hearts	Hearts of young palms. A canned product.
Panache	Several kinds of mixee birds, fruits vegetables, usually with contrasting colours.
Papaya	Tropical fruit, the juice of which yields an enzyme used as meat tenderizer.
Papillote, Cotelette en	Cutlet cooked in paper.
Paprika	A sweet red pepper of two distinct types. The Hungarian paprika is more pungent and markedly sweet and aromatic Spanish paprika is sweeter and lacking in pungency, but is high in colour.
Parisienne Potatoes	Small round scooppotatoes, specially browned.
Parfait	A mixture containing egg and syrup, whipped cream, frozen without stirring. May be molded but is commonly served in parfait glasses.

Parboiling	Partial boiling
Parmentier, a lá	Soup: Potato soup
Parmesan	Hard, sharp cheese, grated for soups and garnishes.
Parsley	An herb used largely for garnishing
Pasteurized milk	Milk held at 140 degree F. for 30 minutes to check fermentation.
Pastry bag	Cone bag with metal tip at small end. Used to decorate cakes etc.
Pate de Fois Gras	Flaked goose liver and truffles (usually imported from Strasburg).
Pauplette	Stuffed, rolled with slices of meat. Braised.
Peche	Peach
Peppercorn	Whole pepper berry before grinding. White and black come from the same plant but the difference is in maturity.
Petit	Small
Petit fours	Small fancy cakes
Petite Marmite	Strong consommé with beef, chicken and vegetables.
Petites Poise	Small green peas
Picnic ham	Lower end of hog shoulder.
Piece de Resistance	Main dish
Pilaf Rice	A Turkish favourite of rice and onions Also of Patna
Pimiento	Red sweet Spanish Pepper pod
Piquant	Highly seasoned, tangy.
Pistachio nuts	Small, pale green nut from the turpentine tree, used for flavouring ice cream and cakes.
Planks	To cook and serve on a board or plank, usually with an elaborate garnish of vegetables.
Poaching	Cooking in water that bubble slightly.
Poisson	Fish in French
Poivrade (Sauce)	Pepper sauce
Pomme de Terre	Potatoes Literal translation apples of the earth
Popovers	Quick puffed up hot bread of milk and eggs.
Portion control	Control of size and weight of individual portions.

Postum	Cereal Coffee substitute
Potage	Soup, usually thickened.
Pot-au-feu	Meat broth with vegetables.
Potiron	Pumpkin
Potpourri	Mixture.
Poulet Marengo	Cut up chicken sauté in oil with tomatoes, mushrooms, wine, shallots, etc. added.
Poulette sauce	Allemande with sliced mushrooms and chives or parsley.
Praline	Usually a flat sugar candy flavoured with burnt almonds or nuts.
Prefabricated	Refers to meat and associated products trimmed and cut; often to the specification of purchaser.
Processed cheese	Cheese cooked in a steam jacket kettle (double bottom) with emulsifying salts and water added.
Provencale	Served with tomatoes and garlic.
Pullman bread	Sandwich bread.
Puree	Pulp or paste or vegetables or fruit. Thick soup.
Quahog	
Quenelles	Dumpling made in an egg shape
Ragout	Thick savory stew.
Raisins	Dried grapes
Ramekins	Food baked in shallow baking chineware or baking dish itself.
Rasher of bacon	Side portion of back of a pork : 3-4 slices of bacon normally served.
Ratatouille	Vegetable ragout or stew consisting of diced egg plant, zucchinis, tomatoes onions and condiments
Reduce	To reduce volume by cooking or simmering
Rendering	Freeing fat from connective tissues by heat.
Rice, brown	Rice with hulls on before polishing
Rissole'	Browned.
Rissole Potatoes	Potatoes cut into shape of large nut (by scooping) and then browned in the over.
Riz	Rice.

Roasting	Cooking in oven with very little moisture. A method of cooking whereby the foods are cooked in the oven where the foods are cooked with uniform heat from all around the foods.
Robert Sauce	A derivative of brown sauce having onions, flour, stock, lemon juice, French Mustard and white wine.
Roe	Mass of fish eggs.Roe-corn : Single fish egg.
Romaine	Roman Lettuce having long narrow crisp-leaves. Lettuce inner leaves are light green in colour. Also Veal and Beef dishes garnished with Gnocchi Romaine (cream of wheat dumplings)
Roti	Roast
Rouge	Red(specially referred to wines).
Roulade	Rolled meat.
Roux	Equal parts of butter or other fats and flour used in thicken the soups and sauces.
Rusks	Light bread or biscuits, sometimes twice baked.
Russian Dressing	Derivative of Mayonnaise. Mayonnaise with lemon juice, chili sauce, Worcestershire sauce and chopped Pimento's
Sabayon	A dessert made of eggs, served in champagne saucer. Egg yolks, vanilla essence, sugar, sherry and white wine.
Saffron	Seasoning. Genuine saffron is a deep orange, dried part of the purple crocus grown in Kashmir. It is used for colouring and flavouring of Indian Desserts.
Sage	Leaves of an herb, Used for seasoning.
Salamander	A broiler-like stove with heat from above and half below. Open front so that dishes can be put on shelf for glazing.
Salami	Sausage of pork, beef, red wine, highly seasoned.
Salisbury Steak	Chopped or ground raw beef (sometimes mixed with pork). Seasoned, shaped and cooked by broiling, braising, roasting,
Salmagundi	Mixture usually refers to meat, fish, onions and seasoning.
Salsifis	Also called Oyster plant, resembling the Oyster in flavour, a long tapering rock which s white and fleshly. (Asperges de Pauvres).
Saurbraten	Beef (round) marinated in seasoned and white wine a few days before cooking.

Sole	Flat white fish, common an Europe. Also flat fish from the Pacific coast of the United States.
Sommelier	Wine Waiter
Sorbet	Old classical drink made of Rhine Wine or any suitable wine combination to be served between meals or meal courses. Very refreshing. Has low sugar content. Usually served as slush in small pilsner glass (flue, Sekt Glass).
Soubise	A derivative of Béchamel Sauce with chopped onions used for fish, lamb, veal O sweetbreads.Example : Dressed with pastry bag on pre-broiled lamb chops, given the finishing touch under the salamander.
Souffle	Light, fluffed baked custard.
Souffle Potatoes	Potatoes sliced and puffed up like little pillows.
Sous Cloche	Under bell of a glass.
Soya Sauce	A sauce made from Soya Beans which is dark brown in colour. Mostly used for favoring Oriental Dishes (Chinese).
Spanish rice	Rice cooked with tomatoes, onions and green pepper.
Sparkling Burgundy	Bright ruby sparkling wine from Burgundy region of France
Spit	Pointed rod to hold meat or poultry for roasting in front of fire.
Split	A 6 oz. Size bottle.
Springerlis	Popular German-Swiss Cookies, the dough is rolled and pressed with Springer mould, then dried before baking, having raised design on top.
Spumoni	Fancy Italian ice cream containing fruits (Tutti Fruitt)
Squab	Young Chicken.
Sweetbreads	Thymus gland of calf or lamb. The throat sweetbreads are preferred as they are less fibrous.
Swiss Chard	Green tender eaf vegetable prepared like spinach.
Swiss Cheese fondue	A quick delicious Cheese specialty for a real party fun. Made from genuine Switzerland Swiss Cheese, Gruyere-Cheese melted with Swiss Wine. Kirsch. Arrowroot and baking soda Dip your crunchy French Bread in to the Fondue pot having the above mixture and take it on to your plate and eaten as per guest choice Normally accompanies a wine.
Tabasco	A long-padded hot red pepper used mainly in a sauce. A very strong sauce, used in small quantities for flavouring soups. Salads meats etc.

Table d'hote	Fixed priced meal. A meal of definite number of courses, selected by restaurant for price indicated for instance Luncheon or Dinner specials, with no substitutions.
Tamale	Mexican dish most often made of cornmeal, meat, chilli garlie, etc and steaned in corn husks. Can be made of beef, chicken etc.
Tarragon	An aromatic herb, the leaves of which are used both fresh and dried for flavouring vinegar, pickles, sauces etc. An important ingredient for Sauce Bearnaise.
Tartare Steak	Raw hamburger steak mixed with raw egg and heavily seasoned.
Tasse	Cup
Tea black	Indian, Java, Ceylon- leaves are fermented.
Tea, Green	Mostly from Japan, unfermented.
Tea, Oolong	Formosa-semi fermented.
Tea, Orange Pekoe	Pekoe refers to downy appearance of underside and ends of leaf bud.
Terrine	Forcemeat and stuffing molded in earthenware jar. Served cold.
Tete	Head
Thyme	An herb for flavouring.
Timbale	Mixture of meat or vegetables cooked in cup-shaped molds, filled with any of variety of mixture such as Rice Tikbale with Chicken Liver or Rice with fruits or caramel.
Tortilla	A very thin Latin American bread)pancake style) made of corn or maize, baked on stove, eaten alone or used as base of many "South of the Border"dishes (Enchiladas, Tacos etc.)
Tortoni	Italian biscuit made from a frozen mixture containing dried ground macaroons, whipped cream, chapped, blanched, toasted and glazed almonds.
Tripe	The white fatty inner lining of the stomach of food animals, chiefly beef, has a large amount of connective tissue which gelatinize on boiling, making it easy to digest. Tripe a lá Mode de caen Grilled Tripes Swiss style or Neapolitain.
Truffle	A fungus variety of mushrooms which grows beneath the surface of the ground under young trees. It is rooted up by trained dogs and pigs-black considered more choice. *Source*: Italy, specially in Franch (Boulogne, Ordemes) usually comes cinned though fresh ones are now available because of air service-very expensive.Truffles may juttly be described as one of the most curious and least understood articles of food. They

	grow in clusters like potatoes, a few inches under the ground, but without roots or upper parts of any description.The secret of their propagation has never been fully ascertained however, the following theory is, to our knowledge, the only generally accepted. Insects are attracted by the aromatic odor of the truffles which has now permeated the soil. Insects break into the fungus and later unwittingly carry the truffle spores into the leaves of nearby trees. The spores are there developed to some extent and then carried back to the soil as the leaves fall where they sprout downward and commence the formation of new fungi. The truffles show no signs above the ground and are generally located by scent by trained leashed pigs and dogs. The market relies wholly on wild truffles, as attmps to grow them have never proved successful.Different from is counterpart, the well known mushroom, which is cultivated with great success in specially prepared plots, the truffle is only found in the wild.
Try Out	To cook fat until oil is out (as in making lard) Render.
Turkish Coffee	(Café Turque) strong, sweet coffee, made of equal amount of pulverized coffee and sugar.
Turtle Soup, Green	Acknowledged by epicure as the king of soups. This world famous soup is made from giant deep-sea Caribbean Turtles. Seasoned and blended with Sherry Wine.
Tutti Fruity	Referring to a mixture of all fruits candied, as Tutti Fruity Ice-cream.
Vanilla Beans	Dried beans of a climbing vine of orchid family (Plan folia) packed in a glass tube or jar to conserve the aroma.
Veal Birds	Thin slice of veal rolled around seasoned stuffing. May be stewed or cooked in covered casserole.
Vermicelli	Long, thin threads of pasta. Like spaghetti.
Vert	Green
Viande	Meat
Wan Tan	Stuffed noodle paste, with Chinese soup. Stuffing can be of chicken, pork or vegetables.
Washington Pie	Cake with cherries (often raspberry or loganberry jam) between layers.
Waterless Cooker	Cooking utensil of heavy metal in which foods are cooked in their own juices.
Welsh Rarebit or Rabbit	Cooked Cheese, butter, beer, eggs flavoured with Worcestershire Sauce and spices. Usually served on crisp crackers or toast. (French-fondue a lá Angles)

Westphalia Ham	Famous for centuries throughout Europe, it is cured by a special process NOT COOKED, but slowly smoked and dry cured. Sliced ham served with potatoes. Salad or as an hors d'oeuvre on German rye or pumpernickel bread
Wheat Pilaf	Is a new, modern version of burger wheat, a favorite food in the Mediterranean near East. There it has been served for centuries as staple food which has helped to keep the people strong and healthy, (a kind of mills, known in the Hawaiian Island as Al).
Whey	The liquid remaining after the removal of fat and casein from the milk. Has considerable food value as well as a refreshing quality.
Whipping	Rapid beating to increase the volume of mixing air.
Wild rice	The Northern Regions of Minnesota in USA is dotted with innumerable blue, at allow sweet-water lakes. Wild rice grows on almost al of these lakes. In the late summer it is harvested by Indians who go over the lakes in canoes. Two in a canoe, one poodles while the other gathers the "Wild rice" by shaking the franches of rice tops. The rice falls into the bottom of the canoe as it flides slowly over the water. It is ironically called rice but is really a water grass seeds. Served with poultry and game. Extremely expensive.
Worcestershire Sauce	A pungent, dark coloured sauce, varying widely in composition but usually, containing soya, vinegar, onion juice, lime juice, garlic, chili and spices.
Steaming	Cooking in steam
Scaloppine	Thin small pieces of meat (mostly, ilk-fed veal) sautéed brown and then braised till cooked. May have Marsala wine, mushrooms, tomato sauce and cheese.
Searing	Browning surface by intense heat
Sec	French term used for wines which means DRY. Wines having high content of a alcohol.
Semolina	High gluten flour from durum wheat.
Serviette	Napkin which is used by guests.
Shad	Fish of Herring family.
Shallots	Vegetable of onion family with a stronger but more mellow flavour than come on variety such as Bermuda Onions etc.
Shaslik of lamb	(Brochette of Lamb) Seasoned lamb broiled on a skewer.
Sherbet	Made from one kind of fruit juice, may have milk, cream, egg white or gelatin added.

Shirred Eggs	Eggs baked in a casserole with butter.
Shish-Kebab	Skewered lamb
Shoestring Potatoes	Like French Fries but cut very thin.
Simmering	Slow cooking at just below boiling point.
Sizzling Steak	Steak served on an sizzler platter which has been heated so that the steak and juices sizzle.
Skewer	A long pin of wood or metal to hold meat or other foods in shape while cooking.
Smorgasbord	Swedish tidbits or appetizers including fish, salads, cheeses, relished and pickles. The word in USA often used for buffet having fish dominance and Scandinavians Specialties.
Smother	To cooked in covered kettle until tender. To cover with (such as smothered in onions).
Soiree	Evening Party.
Steeping	To soak in liquid below boiling point to extract flavour or colour.
Steer	A young castrated beef animal
Sterilizing	Destroying bacteria and microorganisms by boiling in water, heat or steam.
Stew	Cooking in water on top of the stove.
Stirring	Mixing foods in circular motion.
Stock	The liquid in which meat, poultry, fish or vegetables have been simmered for at least 12-14 hours so that the extract or the foods are drawn in the liquid
Sub-gum	Base of many Chinese dishes. Bamboo shoots, water chestnuts, French mushrooms
Suet	Hard fat in beef veal, mutton and lamb.
A lá Suissi	Swiss style
Sukiyaki	Popular jananese dish consisting of thin slices of sautéed lean
Yams	Much like sweet potatoes. From the Southern United States and West Indies.
Yorkshire Pudding	An English dish usually served with roast bear. A proper like mixture which may be baked with the meat or separately with some of the drippings from the roast.
Zucchini	Italian Squash
Zwieback	A hard crispy German bread or biscuit. Twice baked. Used largely for feeding small children or people with a delicate stomach.

Bibliography

- Aidells, Bruce and Denis Kelly, Illustrated (2001), Mary, Houghton Mifflin Cookbooks.
- Allen, Lucy Grace (1941), A Book of Hors D'oeuvre, Bramhall House, London.
- Arora, K.L Theory of cookery Press Frank Brothers
- Bacus, Jim, "Utilization of Microorganisms in Meat Processing – a handbook for meat plant operators", Research Studies Press.
- Baltzer, Lynne E. (2002), Food Preparation Study Course, Blackwell Publishing
- Baltzer, Lynne E. (2002), Food Preparation Study Course,Blackwell Publishing.
- Barham, Peter (2001), The Science of Cooking, Springer.
- Barker, Alex, Cooks Potato Book, Lorenz Books / Anness Publishing Inc.
- Bashline, Sylvia G. (2000), Fixin' Fish: The Complete Guide to Cleaning and Cooking, Creative Publishing International
- Berolzheimer, Ruth (1988), Culinary Arts Institute Encyclopedic Cookbook, Perigee.
- Binns, Brigit Legere (2001), Hors D'oeuvre, Simon and Schuster Publishers, London.
- Brown, Douglas Robert (2003), The Restaurant Manager's Handbook, Atlantic Publishing Company.
- Burgtorf, Xenia, 2004, Sandwiches, Silverback Books.
- Campbell-Platt, G and Cook, P. (Eds) (1995) "Fermented Meats", Blackie Academic and Professional, Glasgow.
- Chan, W., Robert Alexander and McCance (1995), Meat, Poultry and Game, Royal Society of Chemistry.
- Child, Julia, Louisette Bertholle, Simone Beck (2001), Mastering the Art of French Cooking, Knopf Publishing Group.
- Conforti, Frank D. (1997), Food Selection and Preparation: A Laboratory Manual, Blackwell Publishing.

- Cookbook, Hearst Books. Robin Nelson (2003), Fruits, Lerner Publications.
- Cottrell, Edyth Young (2004), The Oats, Peas, Beans and Barley Cookbook, TEACH Services, Inc.
- David, A.V. Dendy (2001), Cereals and Cereal Products, Springer.
- David, Elizabeth (1999), French Provincial Cooking, Penguin Classics, London.
- David, J., Textbook of Hotel Management, Anmol Publication (P) Ltd.
- Dunnington, Rose (2006), Super Sandwiches, Lark Books.
- Escoffier, Auguste (1979), The Complete Guide to the Art of Modern Cookery, Heinemann.
- Farrell, K.T. (1998), Spices, Condiments and Seasonings,Springer.
- Groves, Tony *et al.* (1996), Food Preparation and Cooking, Nelson Thornes.
- Hallam, Eleanor (2005), Food Technology, Nelson Thornes.
- Heath, Henry B. (1981), Source Book of Flavors, Springer.
- Hirasa, Kenji and Mitsuo Takemasa (1998), Spice Science and Technology, CRC Press
- Hutchinson, Raymond Charles (1966), Food Storage in the Home, Edward Arnold.
- International Food Information Service 2005, Dictionary of Food Science and Technology, Blackwell Publishing.
- James, Kenneth (2006), Escoffier: The King of Chefs, Continuum International Publishing Group.
- James, Peterson (1998), Sauces, John Wiley and Sons.
- Johansson, Thomas B. and Laurie Burnham (1993), Renewable Energy: Sources for Fuels and Electricity, Island Press.
- Joseph, A. Kurmann, *et al* (1992), Encyclopedia of Fermented Fresh Milk Products, Springer.
- King, Shirley, Illustrated by Glenn Wolff (1999), Fish: An Illustrated Guide to Selecting and Cooking Fresh Seafood, Houghton Mifflin Cookbooks
- Knowles, Tim (2002), Food Safety in the Hospitality Industry, Butterworth-Heinemann.
- Larkcom, Joy (2007), Oriental Vegetables, Frances Lincoln Ltd.Susan Westmoreland (2004), The Good Housekeeping
- Leffmann, Henry (2007), Analysis of Milk and Milk Products, Read Books.
- Martino, Maestro, (2005), The Art of Cooking: The First Modern Cookery Book, University of California Press.
- Martino, Maestro, Luigi Ballerini, Jeremy Parzen, Stefania Barzini
- McGee, Harold (1984), On Food and Cooking, Macmillan.
- McGee, Harold (1990), The Curious Cook, Macmillan

- Nelson, Robin (2003), Vegetables, Lerner Publications.
- Olney, Richard (1979), Soups, Time-Life Books, London.
- Peter, K.V. (2004), Handbook of Herbs and Spices, Woodhead Publishing.
- Philip, Thangam, Modern Cookery volume I and II
- Raina, Usha (2005), Basic Food Preparation: A Complete Manual, Orient Longman Limited.
- Rombauer and Becker (2000), The Joy of Cooking, Running Press Book Publishers.
- Rosengarten, Frederic Jr., Frederic Rosengarten (2004), The Book of Edible Nuts, Courier Dover Publications.
- Ruffin, Frances E. (2005), Kitchen Smarts: Food Safety and Kitchen Equipment, The Rosen Publishing Group.
- Seranne, Ann (1983), The Complete Book of Egg Cookery, Collier Macmillan
- Ser-Vo-Tel Institute (1974), Food Care and Food Storage, Cahners Books
- Smith, Delia (2006), Soups, Dorling Kindersley, London.
- Sokolov, Raymond (1976), The Saucier's Apprentice, Knopf.
- Souhami, Jessica (2006), Sausages, Frances Lincoln Ltd.
- Steele, Louise (1989), The Book of Sandwiches, HPBooks.
- Swatland, H. J. (2004), Meat Cuts and Muscle Foods: An International Glossary, Nottingham University Press
- Tamime, A.Y. and R.K.Robinson (1999), Yoghurt: Science and Technology, Woodhead Publishing.
- Tull, Anita (1996), Food and Nutrition, Oxford University Press.
- www.asiarecipe.com/
- www.chinesefood-. com
- www.cuisinenet.com/
- www.iaqnow.com
- www.ihj.com.
- www.importfood.com/
- www.kitchen designsite.com
- www.kitchenbin.com
- www.rapidswholesale.com

Index

J

L

M

O

P

□□□